PERCEPTION
of
PRINT

Reading Research in
Experimental Psychology

PERCEPTION
of
PRINT
Reading Research in
Experimental Psychology

Edited by

Ovid J. L. Tzeng
Harry Singer
University of California, Riverside

LEA LAWRENCE ERLBAUM ASSOCIATES, PUBLISHERS
1981   HILLSDALE, NEW JERSEY

Copyright © 1981 by Lawrence Erlbaum Associates, Inc.
   All rights reserved. No part of this book may be reproduced in
   any form, by photostat, microform, retrieval system, or any other
   means, without the prior permission of the publisher.

Lawrence Erlbaum Associates, Inc., Publishers
365 Broadway
Hillsdale, New Jersey 07642

Library of Congress Cataloging in Publication Data

Main entry under title:

Perception of print.

   Bibliography: p.
   Includes indexes.
   1. Reading, Psychology of.   I. Tzeng, Ovid J. L.
II. Singer, Harry.
BF456.R2P4   153.6   81-1102
ISBN 0-89859-154-6   AACR2
Printed in the United States of America

Contents

Preface

In recent years, reading research has become a true interdisciplinary endeavor with flavors of anthropology, artificial intelligence, cognitive psychology, educational psychology, linguistics, neuroscience, and instructional technology. The integration of knowledge generated from various fields of research on the one hand and knowledge of what is needed for the practitioners of reading instruction on the other is necessary at every level of schooling. Without such interaction, research merely for the sake of research can go on within the framework of each discipline and easily become so esoteric that in reality no reading instructor can benefit from the outcome of such effort. But given appropriate integration, results from these diverse perspectives can enhance our understanding of reading behavior tremendously, both in its acquisition and in its skilled functioning. Thus, the enthusiasm for such interdisciplinary interaction has been quite intense for some time. In the last several years, the National Reading Conference has been doing everything possible to accelerate this interaction. The chapters in this book are the fruits of that effort.

Experimental psychologists' interest in how the printed materials are processed has a history as long as the discipline itself. However, the focus was never really on reading problems (Venezky, 1980). Rather, from the very beginning, the work on word perception had as its purpose the discovery of the basic mental units in the structure of the mind. Also, in those earlier days (the late 1800s), investigators' own elitism often blinded them to other problems in reading acquisition. The situation is very different today. Ever since cries of "Why can't Johnny read?" have been heard everywhere from PTA to Congress and the issue of reading disability has become national in scope, experimental psychologists—with their renewed interest in reading—have played a key role in working to alleviate such a concern. The research now focuses on specifying skills in identifying alphabetical elements and the rules that govern their combination, on constructing models that characterize the recognition of individual words and the interpretation of texts, and on discovering what factors are responsible for blocking the normal acquisition process in many children. Chapters 2 through 12 of this book reflect these changing foci. They are nevertheless sandwiched by two chapters that deal with the historical background and future outlook of reading instruction. The implications of such an arrangement should be clear. Although the interaction between experimentalists and practitioners should go in both directions, the experimental investigation must be constrained by the pragmatic considerations of reading instruction if experimental psychologists are to help in resolving the problems of reading disability.

Undoubtedly, the reading research in experimental psychology represented in this book reflects the continuation of Wundtian traditions. At the same time, it also shows the new outlook of cognitive science. We hope such an interdisciplinary integration under the rubric of reading research will continue to be an important mission of cognitive scientists.

On behalf of the contributors to this book, we wish to express our gratitude to our publisher, Larry Erlbaum, whose patience, understanding, and most of all, whose zeal for promoting psychological research makes this book a reality. Thanks are also due to Susan Stone who contributed invaluable editorial assistance and to Katie Malley for her sharp eyes in detecting many errors in the original manuscripts.

Ovid J. L. Tzeng and Harry Singer

PERCEPTION
of
PRINT

Reading Research in
Experimental Psychology

Overview: Relevancy of Experimental Psychology to Reading Instruction

Ovid J. L. Tzeng
University of California, Riverside

Experimental psychology just marked its one hundred year anniversary. In celebration, the 23rd International Congress of Psychology was held at Leipzig, Germany, where the first experimental laboratory was established in 1879. The theme was, of course, to honor Wilhelm Wundt, credited as the founder of experimental psychology. Also, a special series of symposiums and addresses was held at the 1979 meeting of the American Psychological Association in New York City. Many leading psychologists were invited to these meetings to present historical reviews and critical assessments of their own subfields of psychology. From the comments made in these centennial papers, the common view is that psychological knowledge gained over the first century in each subfield has been noncumulative and incohesive and that the discipline of psychology has become increasingly fragmented rather than unified (Leary, 1980). Despite these negative conclusions, there was also a positive excitement about the future of a new cognitive science. The renaissance of cognitive research in experimental psychology has been brought about by the new developments in psycholinguistics, artificial intelligence (computer technology and cybernetics), and information processing approaches to learning and memory. In retrospect, experimental psychology started at Leipzig with laboratory study of the elements and dimensions of consciousness, then progressed outward to the investigation of environmental-behavioral relations (under the rubric of Behaviorism), and finally, returned to the concern for the construction of Mind (albeit with graphic charts and a proliferation of boxes and arrows). It seems as though experimental psychology, after one hundred years of striving to be scientific and objective in its methodology, has finally rediscovered itself in its origin.

The current cognitive reorientation can be characterized as having four distinctive movements. First, a willingness to accept rationalistic arguments has led many investigators to change their subject matter from behavior to cognitive (i.e., from the surface structure to the deep structure of subject matter, see Leary, 1980). The impact of Chomskian linguistics in the 60's is particulary relevant to this movement. Second, the rejection of small-scale models resulting from task-specific experiments has led many investigators to argue for a more global theory of comprehension. This preference for applying a general global theory to answer the timeless questions of *meaning* reflects the strong influence on psychology of research in artificial intelligence. Third, the broadening of perspectives as well as interactions with other fields of science has made the new cognitive research a truly interdisciplinary endeavor. Many research topics, such as attention, memory, decision processes, communication, etc. which were once exclusive to experimental psychologists, are shared by researchers in biology, neuro-science, anthropology, biochemistry and many other disciplines. Fourth and finally, the new cognitive science shows a tremendous sensitivity to socio-cultural contexts of behavior and thus, an increasing emphasis on the ecological validity and real-life applications of research findings.

The shaping of a new cognitive science with these four major orientations can best exemplified in the experimental psychologists' renewed interest in and current approach to reading research. Historically, the systematic study of the processes involved in reading can be traced back to Wundt's laboratory where sensation, perception and reaction time experiments became some of the foremost concerns of a newly founded laboratory. In fact, shortly after the establishment of the laboratory, James McKeen Cattell, Wundt's first American student, wrote his dissertation on the topic of reading. In those early years, basic reading research was considered to be one of the major tools of analyzing the contents of mind. In Edmund Huey's words:

> And so to completely analyze what we do when we read would almost be the acme of a psychologist's achievement, for it would be to describe very many of the most intricate workings of the human mind, as well as to unravel the tangled story of the most remarkable specific performance that civilization has learned in all its history."
> (1908/1968) [p. 6]

Judging from this quotation, it is no wonder that reading research soon moved to the center of the stage in experimental psychology at the end of the 19th century. A great deal of knowledge about reading processes was cumulated during these golden years (Venezky, 1977). In Paris, Javal (1878) discovered *saccadic* eye movements which were characterized as discontinuous, erratic and sometimes long jumps that were contrary to the reader's phenomenological experience. At the University of Halle, Erdmann and Dodge (1898) computed the speed of an eye movement from one fixation to the next and provided evidence showing that no perception could take place during those rapid movements. In other studies, Erdmann and Dodge demonstrated that words could be perceived at a distance at which isolated letters could not be identified. This later finding was consistent with Cattell's (1886) observation that the perceptual span for letters in meaningful words was considerably greater than that for letters in random strings. These results were further corroborated by Pillsbury's (1897) work in America on the "creativity" of the apperceptive faculty. In his experiment, subjects were asked to identify distorted words (words in which a letter was blurred with an overlapping "x" or replaced by another letter or words with missing letters) that were presented very briefly. The results showed that subjects typically reported seeing the stimulus words as normal and in some cases insisted that a replaced letter was clearly seen. Pillsbury took these results to support the Wundtian theory of apperception and concluded that the apperceptive process had apparently made a correction or had filled in the missing letters.

Another important figure in those early days of reading research was J. O. Quantz (1897), the first investigator to discover that the eye's position on the written line usually precedes that of the voice by a few words. He further found that such an *eye-voice span* has a maxium of seven words with an average span of five. This estimation was consistent with Wundt's conclusion that the limit on the scope of apperception is six or seven items. But the most impressive aspect of Quantz' work is his attempt to formulate stage-by-stage reading models, anticipating the information processing approach of modern days. In fact, his descriptions of "after-images" and "primary memory images" in the stage-analysis of word recognition resemble in many ways the "iconic storage" and "short-term storage" of the present information processing models.

In 1908, Edmund Burke Huey, a graduate from Clark University who later worked with Javal at Paris and with Erdmann in Germany, published his classic book, *The Psychology of Reading and Pedagogy,* in which most of the reading research of this early period was carefully and scholarly summarized. Oddly enough, soon after the publication of this book, the proliferation of basic research in reading suddenly came to an end and experimental psychologists' interests in mental processes gave way to the analysis and specification of the functional relationship between *stimulus* and *response* in behavioral act. Furthermore, verbal learning experiments in the Ebbinghaus tradition became the focus of research on the analysis of verbal behaviors. Even within the education circle, investigators were preoccupied with a concern for assessment and as Kolers commented in his introduction to the 1968 reprinting of Huey's book, "remarkably little empirical information has been added to what Huey knew" (Huey, 1908/1968, p. xiv).

The return of interest in basic reading research was brought by several important forces. First, the renaissance of the Cartesian idea of "innateness" led by Chomskian transformational linguists shifted researchers' attention from descriptions of surface structure toward analyses of deeper structures in natural languages. Second, advances in computer technology in both hardware and software created a new research technique, namely computer simulations of the higher mental processes such as problem-solving, thinking, and comprehension. Comparisons of such "artificial intelligence" on the one hand and "natural cognitive behaviors" on the other have continued to generate insights into our understanding of understanding. Third, the psychochronometric procedure (i.e., reaction time experiments), abandoned after condemnation of Donder's subtraction method, has developed to a level of sophistication such that its reliability can be established independent of the stochastical processes involved (Sternberg, 1970; Posner, 1978). Such procedures have been proved to be useful for experiments of word recognition, lexical decision, sentence verification, and inferential processes in comprehending texts. Furthermore, reaction time experiments are usually accompanied by complicated models of information processing which attempt to specify basic internal stages as well as their interactions during reading. Fourth, a great deal of knowledge concerning different levels of speech signals has been accumulated in the experimental analysis of speech perception and production. Such knowledge enables investigators to more precisely specify the script/speech relationship embedded in various writing systems and to examine the role of speech in processing printed materials (Liberman, Liberman, Mattingly, & Shankweiler, 1980). Fifth, and possibly most important, Rudolf Flesch published a book in 1955 called *Why Johnny Can't Read.* This book had an enormous impact on the public and the issue of reading problems soon became a national concern. Consequently, federal funding for basic research related to the improvement of education was appropriated by Congress, with the goals of strengthening the scientific and technological foundation of education (Venezky, 1977). Undoubtedly, the availability of financial support plus the cognitive reorientation within experimental psychology will sustain a vigorous pace in basic reading research, hopefully with many fruitful results.

While the experimental research in reading is gaining its momentum, important questions should be raised: What kind of impact is basic research going to have on the improvement of education in general and reading instruction in particular? Will the current excitement about the experimental research justify more funding? Questions such as these are hard to answer. A look at the history of experimental psychology, however, leads one to say that there has been a very close relationship between basic reading research and reading instruction. Admittedly, early reading research was almost synonymous with studies of attention and had little to do with reading acquisition and instruction. However, the separation was largely due to Wundt's antipathy to the whole field of education and to his insistence that pedagogical and scientific interests are two very different matters. Worst of all, Wundt believed that good teachers are usually born that way and what they may gain in scientific sophistication usually results in a loss in their ability to understand and interact with children (Leary, 1980). Regardless of the presumably purified pursuit of scientific knowledge, findings of early experimental research had an unintentional profound effect on reading instruction. For example, Cattell's (1885) demonstration that skilled readers could read from three to four unconnected letters or two unconnected words at a very brief exposure time was suggested as the basis for the whole-word approach to reading instruction. On the other hand, Goldscheider and Muller's (1893) finding of "dominating letters" in the identification of briefly exposed words was taken as an argument for the "part" or "synthetic" approach to reading instruction. Furthermore, in Huey's book we can clearly see his effort in trying to relate basic research findings to pedagogy, especially in the visual domain, e.g., appropriate lengths of printed lines, appropriate type sizes, etc. As Buchner (1909) cogently commented on the virtue of Huey's work: "probably its most striking feature is the tempered, yet progressive mixture of science and practice." (p. 149).

Even after Huey, when reading research lost the intensity and excitement of its earlier period, theories and findings of experimental psychologists (e.g., Thorndike, Skinner), especially those having to do with basic "learning" processes, continued to play major roles in the directions of reading instruction programs. However, it soon became apparent that successful application was still a remote possibility. The lack of ecological validity of the laboratory tasks made it difficult, if not impossible, to apply those "learning principles" generated from highly contrived laboratory situations to real life classroom settings. Some educators (e.g., Ausubel, 1968) even consider such blind applications harmful to children's meaningful learning experiences.

The gap between experimental psychologists and the practitioners of reading instruction becomes wider and wider and the reluctance to communicate with each other grows stronger and stronger. Two examples will suffice to illustrate such a devastating state of affairs. Between the 1940's and 50's, there was a persistent belief that irregular spellings in English are one of the major factors which seriously retard acquisition of literacy and many educators, as well as reading instructors, in both England and the United States were actively campaigning for the simplification of English spelling. Yet experimental psychologists paid no attention to such a claim in their research on word recognition until the late 1950's (Venezky, 1980). Similarly, since the mid-60's, experimental evidence strongly favors a phonics-drill approach, yet reading instructors tend to ignore such evidence and resist any componential analysis of reading behavior (Williams, 1979). Unless the situation can be improved, the promised impact of experimental research is far from clear.

There are justifiable reasons for the reluctance of practitioners to accept the results and conclusions of experimental psychologists. First, experimental psychologists usually focus on adults rather than children. Thus, the resulting reading models better describe an accomplished reader than a beginning reader. Second, experimental psychologists rarely appreciate the complexities of curricular design and classroom practice. Hence, most of their studies are irrelevant to the practitioner's concerns for the "what" and "how" of instruction. If the new cognitive orientation in experimental psychology is to lead to fundamental understandings about reading and reading failure, then investigators should commit themselves to these concerns.

Thus, this volume is intended to serve an important function. It attempts to foster communication between reading instructors and experimental psychologists. Thirteen chapters are included. The first and last chapters were written by Harry Singer who, for many years, has been involved in questions concerning the application of reading instruction. Sandwiched between these two chapters are eleven papers describing various concerns of experimental psychologists on reading processes. Both Johnson's and Johnston's papers deal with the issue of word recognition process. The former presents the up-dated version of his pattern-unit model and the latter provides a latest account of the so-called "word superiority effect." The next two chapters discuss the nature of the "context" effect in word recognition experiments. Gough, Alford, and Holley-Wilcox distinguish the transient local context from the more stable global context and show that they have differential effects on word recognition. Spoehr and Schuberth discuss their new experimental paradigm and compare the context effect obtained in such continuous recognition to that obtained in the isolated word recognition paradigm. Following the four chapters on word recognition process, Jackson and McClelland's paper attempts to specify individual differences in reading ability by componential analysis. The next two chapters deal with the issue of speech recoding in reading. Banks, Oka, and Shugarman critically re-examine evidence for and against the concept of recoding and show that further evidence is needed to end this debate. Fowler, representing the orientation of Haskins Laboratories, also discusses the issue of speech recoding but the concern is more with beginning readers than adult readers. Orthography has not been carefully studied in experimental psychology. Adams' paper asks: What good is orthographic redundancy ? Wang's paper asks: What is an optimal orthography? Tzeng and Hung raise a further question: What are the behavioral consequences of being literate in different orthographies? Finally, Nickerson discusses the relationships between listening and reading comprehension from the perspective of an *interactive* model of information processing.

The implication should be clear: experimental research in reading must be constrained within the framework of reading instruction if we, experimental psychologists who are interested in *reading* research, are to help in solving the severe reading problems now confronted by many children of this country.

REFERENCES

Ausubel, D. P. *Educational psychology: A cognitive view*. New York: Holt, Rinehart and Winston, 1968.

Buchner, E. F. Review of The psychology and pedagogy of reading by E. B. Huey. *Psychological Bulletin*, 1909, 6, 147–150.

Cattell, J. M. Ueber die zeit der erkennung und benennung von schriftzeichen, bildern und farben. *Philosophische Studien*, 1885, *2*, 635-650.

Cattell, J. M. The time it takes to see and name objects. *Mind*, 1886, *11*, 63-65.

Erdmann, B., & Dodge, R. *Psychologische unter schungen uber das lesen auf experimentellen Grundlage*. Halle, Germany: Niemeyer, 1898.

Flesch, R. P. *Why Johnny can't read and what you can do about it*. New York: Harper, 1955.

Goldscheider, A., & Muller, R. Zur physiologie und pathologie des lesens. *Zeitschrift fur Klinische Medicin*, 1893, *23*, 131-167.

Huey, E. B. *The psychology and pedagogy of reading*. New York: Macmillan, 1908. Reprinted by M.I.T. Press, 1968.

Javal, L. E. Essai sur la physiologie de la lecture. *Annales d'Oculistique*, 1878, *82*, 243-253.

Leary, D. E. One hundred years of experimental psychology: An American perspective. *Psychological Research*, 1980, *42*, 175-189.

Liberman, I. Y., Liberman, A. M., Mattingly, I. G., & Shankweiler, D. Orthography and the beginning reader. In J. F. Kavanagh & R. L. Venezky (Eds.), *Orthography, reading and dyslexia*, University Park, Maryland: University Park Press, 1980.

Pillsbury, W. B. A study in apperception. *American Journal of Psychology*, 1897, *8*, 315-393.

Posner, M. I. *Chronometric exploration of mind*. Hillsdale, N.J.: Erlbaum, 1978.

Quantz, J. O. Problems in the psychology of reading. *Psychological Monographs*, 1897, 2 (1,whole No.5).

Sternberg, S. Memory scanning: Mental processes revealed by reaction time experiments. In J. S. Antrobus (Ed.), *Cognition and affect*. Boston: Little and Brown, 1970.

Venezky, R. L. Research in reading processes: A historical perspective. *American Psychologists*, 1977, May, 339-345.

Venezky, R. L. Overview: From Sumer to Leipzig to Bethesda. In J. F. Kavanagh and R. L. Venezky (Eds.), *Orthography, reading and dyslexia*. Baltimore, Maryland: University Park Press, 1980.

Williams, J. Reading instruction today. *American Psychologists*, 1979, *34*, 917-922.

1 Teaching the Acquisition Phase of Reading Development: An Historical Perspective

Harry Singer
University of California, Riverside

Reading development consists of two interrelated phases: (1) an acquisition phase in which students are taught how to read and (2) a learning-from-text phase in which students mainly apply their reading ability to comprehending or interacting with printed materials (Anderson, Spiro, & Montague, 1977; Singer, 1977a; Singer & Donlan, 1980). Although the two phases of reading instruction overlap, the major emphasis in the primary grades is on acquisition. During this stage of development, most students tend to reach a level of performance where they can automatically respond to commonly occurring words and integrate these responses with their oral language abilities (Singer, 1977a). They can then shift most of their attention in reading to comprehending the text (LaBerge & Samuels, 1974). This level of development can probably be attained during the elementary grades by most students in the normal range of development, which is about IQ 65 and above, provided that the students receive instruction over these grades that is continuous, cumulative, and coherent (Bloom, 1971; Carroll, 1963; Singer, 1977b). This kind of instruction can be exemplary in not only teaching students how to read, but also in accommodating to individual differences in rate of learning to read (Singer, 1977b).

The second phase of reading development, learning from text, continues to develop throughout a person's lifetime. As a person's experience, lexicon, concepts, and knowledge of the world increase (Anderson et al., 1977; Winograd, 1972), his or her ability to learn from text can concomitantly improve.

In Chapter 13, I explain in greater detail this second phase of reading development, which is more popularly known among teachers as reading comprehension or among reading specialists or researchers as interaction between the reader and the text (Adams & Collins, 1977). But in this chapter, I focus on the

9

initial stage of reading development because the emphasis throughout this book and in teaching students how to read is on perception of print or word recognition. Consequently, I emphasize methods of teaching word recognition as the changes that have occurred in American reading instruction are summarized.

AMERICAN READING INSTRUCTION:
THEN AND NOW

Over its 250-year history, the reading instruction that dominated particular periods changed. The changes were not abrupt or uniform (Smith, 1965), but they occurred in a surprisingly systematic way. During the colonial period, children were introduced to reading through the smallest unit of text, the letter (alphabet method). In the 1800s, they used a larger unit, the word (whole-word method) or word parts (phonics method). In the early 1900s, teachers used the sentence for the initial level of instruction (sentence method). Finally, during the 1920s, reading instruction began with the largest unit of text, the story (experience-chart method, which is more commonly known today as the language-experience approach). Smith (1965) noted that over this period the rate of change had accelerated: As much change took place in the last 50 years as had occurred in all the preceding 200 years.

Changes in reading instruction have been influenced by many factors. Among them are the innovation and modification of methods by experimentally minded teachers and the adoption of innovative practices that have proven successful in school settings (Russell & Fea, 1963). Some proponents of how and when reading should be taught have also influenced American reading instruction. For example, Horace Mann, who innovated public-school education in the United States in 1854, succeeded in switching the emphasis in American reading instruction to the whole-word method after he had visited Europe and had seen Froebel demonstrate its success. Another influential figure was Carleton Washburne, Superintendent of the Winnetka, Illinois public-school system. On the strength of a study that Morphett and he (1931) had conducted and his popularity as a speaker at national conferences, he persuaded school districts to adopt a mental age of 6½ years as the criterion for reading readiness. One reason Morphett and Washburn's reading-readiness criterion was so widely accepted was because their research findings agreed with the conventional wisdom of the day (Chall, 1967), which had a maturational bias (Durkin, 1968).

A most prevalent influence throughout American reading instruction has been the availability of published materials. The material adopted for instructional use had contents that were consistent with changes that have occurred in the prevailing mores of society (Russell & Fea, 1963). Smith (1965) found that changes in emphasis in reading instruction were indeed related to changes in the mores of the country and perceived the changes as occurring in eight time periods. In summarizing her work, we can follow her division of American reading instruction into these eight periods.

Emphasis on Religion

During the colonial period, teachers predominantly used *The New England Primer*. First published in 1690, it was the main textbook for the next 100 years. It was called a primer not because of its priority in reading instruction but because of its basic religious content. Indeed, the motive for learning to read during the colonial period was religion. Protestantism held that each individual was directly responsible to God for salvation and therefore must read the word of God and reach his or her own conclusion without any intermediary. The Primer not only served as a religious manual and catechism, but also as a speller and reader. Although other books, such as the Hornbook and the ABC book, were also used during this period, *The New England Primer* was the standard textbook for teaching reading throughout the colonies. It used the alphabet method for initiating reading instruction. First, students learned the alphabet perfectly, backwards and forwards, and then randomly. Next, they read each letter followed by an illustration of a key word in a couplet whose initial consonant was the particular letter being learned. For example, the letter *G* was illustrated by an hourglass, followed by this couplet: "As runs the Glass, Man's life doth pass." Next, the students were taught to combine and read the letters in a syllabary that contained two-letter, consonant–vowel syllables, as shown in Table 1.1.

Following this, the students progressed rapidly to reading words of five syllables. Then they spelled the words from the Primer until they knew at least the shortest words at sight. Finally, the students read sentences from the Bible arranged in alphabetical order and memorized the Lord's Prayer, the Creed, and

TABLE 1.1
The New England Primer's Easy Syllables
for Children

Ab	eb	ib	ob	ub
ac	ec	ic	oc	uc
ad	ed	id	od	ud
af	ef	if	of	uf
.	.	.	.	.
.	.	.	.	.
.	.	.	.	.
az	ez	iz	oz	uz

[1]This table is a modified version of a table in N. B. Smith, *History of American Reading Instruction*. Newark, Delaware: International Reading Association, 1965. It is reproduced here with permission.

other verses. After this reading acquisition phase, the students went on to the learning-from-text phase using the Bible as their text.

This second phase of instruction does not differ very much from current methods of teaching students to learn from text, except that students today have various ways of identifying words. The teacher aroused curiosity for the story by telling students a little about it. Then, using spelling as the only technique in their repertoire for identifying unknown words, they read the chapter, got practice in reading orally, and afterwards answered easy comprehension questions posed by the teacher. At home, oral reading of the scriptures in the evening and on the Sabbath was a customary practice that provided students with a motive for learning to read aloud.

A method of teaching reading in use today that comes closest to the alphabet method is the letter-to-story sequence. This sequence begins with instruction in contrastive letter features, such as matching the letter *b* when given the easy choices of *b, m, o,* and *u,* and eventually getting to the more difficult choices of *p, d, b, q,* then progressing to letter-sound relationships and blending the letter-sound sequences, resulting in identification of whole words (Gibson, 1965; Samuels, 1976a, b). For example, the letter *m* is identified, then *a* and *n*. Then instead of trying to blend all three letters at the same time students are directed to combine the first two letters together to obtain *ma* and next add *-n* to form the word *man* (Resnick & Beck, 1976). With the acquisition of a few more letter-sound correspondences, enough words can be formed to make sentences. Readers can be taught to expect letter-sound relationships, syntactically determine words, select semantically acceptable meanings in sentences, and test their expectations (Pearson, 1976; Samuels, Dahl, & Archwamety, 1974). Gradually, they learn to read stories. This process of reading, which starts with letters and builds up to the comprehension of a story, is known as a "bottom–up" process.

The period of religious emphasis changed after the American Revolution and the formation of the United States. The new emphasis was on the establishment of an American identity and consciousness. Smith called this the period of nationalistic-moralistic emphasis.

Emphasis on Nationalism-Moralism

After the revolution, control over education shifted to the state. The goal of education changed to the development of national loyalty, knowledge of national traditions and institutions, inculcation of ideals of moral behavior consistent with good citizenship, and purification of the American language. These goals were exemplified in Noah Webster's *The American Spelling Book,* more popularly known as the Blue-back Speller because its wooden covers were encased in pale blue paper. In Webster's book, religious catechism was replaced by a moral and federal catechism. The book contained patriotic speeches, literary selections from American authors, and historical and geographical information about the

United States. For teaching reading, it started with the alphabet, then syllables, and lists of words; it laid great stress upon rules and exercises for correct pronunciation for the purpose of overcoming dialect variation and for unifying the American language.

The impact of *The American Spelling Book* can be inferred from its distribution. From its inception in 1790 and for some 30 to 40 years thereafter, it was the dominant book in American education. During this time, some 24,000,000 copies were distributed. Then it was replaced by the *McGuffey Readers,* which appeared between 1836 and 1844 and became the dominant book during the era of education for intelligent citizenship.

Emphasis on Education for Intelligent Citizenship

The dominant instructional method during this period was the whole-word method. Mann, the most influential American educator of this time, had visited Prussia where he saw the Pestalozzian whole-word method of teaching reading in operation. He described this method to the Massachusetts Board of Education: The teacher drew a picture of a house on a board; under the picture, he wrote the word *house* in script and also printed it. Then, he traced the word with his pointer, and children imitated him, writing with their fingers in the air. Next, the children copied the word *house* in script and in print. Then came letter-sound correspondence instruction and the spelling of the word according to its sounds, not the names of its letters. After repeating this instruction for several words, the teacher pointed in succession to words that together formed a familiar sentence. Mann favored the whole-word method over the alphabet method, which he denounced for its slowness and lack of intellectual stimulation.

During this period, children were divided for the first time according to age and achievement, with a single teacher for each group. Graded series of readers were developed for this graded school system. The most popular series was the *McGuffey Eclectic Readers.*

McGuffey is credited with developing the first carefully graded series of readers, with one reader for each grade. The first reader contained about 150 pictures. It started with the alphabet, but lesson one showed the whole-word emphasis. It consisted of an illustration of an ox, under which there were two-letter words. These words combined to form a sentence: *Is it an ox?* Next, there were these words and sentence: *It is an ox. It is my ox.* Altogether, 11 words were introduced on this page, as shown in Table 1.2. Note the repetition of the 11 words that are introduced in the first lesson. This repetition is still characteristic of basal readers today, but spelling instruction is completely separated from today's basal readers, whereas the method of word instruction has not changed in any significant way. To learn a new word, the student sees the word, hears it pronounced, has its meaning illustrated or used in a sentence, and later learns to analyze the word into its constituent sounds and name its letters or spell

TABLE 1.2[1]
McGuffey Reader: Lesson 1

Spelling	Reading
is it an ox	Is it an ox?
it is an ox	It is an ox.
it is my ox	It is my ox.
do we go	Do we go?
do we go up	Do we go up?
we do go up	We do go up.
am I in	Am I in?
am I in it	Am I in it?
I am in it	I am in it.
so is he in it	So is he in it.

[1]This table is from N. B. Smith, *History of American Reading Instruction*. Newark, Delaware: International Reading Association, 1965. It is reproduced here with permission.

the word. After the new word is introduced, it is used cumulatively and repeatedly to provide necessary repetition for learning and maintaining a correct response to the word.

The McGuffey Readers showed the further decline in religious-moralistic emphasis. The first Reader had only one page of religious material and five pages of moralistic content. Instead, the content consisted of sentences about children and animals. Accompanying these sentences were drills on phonetic elements and review of previously taught words. This feature of starting with whole words and later introducing phonics is also characteristic of basal readers in use today.

After the acquisition stage, the content of McGuffey's Readers continued the earlier tradition of moralistic, patriotic, religious, and geographical materials. But his more advanced readers were of a high literary standard and they also stressed elocution. Through his Reader, McGuffey played a leading role in influencing the American temperament (Mosier, 1947). By 1880, the nation had matured to a stage of tranquility and security, and it had the leisure time for cultural pursuits. In response, reading materials ushered in the next period of emphasis, which stressed development of a permanent interest in literature as a cultural asset.

Emphasis on Reading as a Cultural Asset

As usual, in forming a dominant emphasis, teachers were admonished by speeches and by courses of study to teach students not only how to read, but also to apply this ability to reading good literature. Indeed, during this period, there arose an argument for literary emphasis that is still heard today: Instead of using basal readers to teach reading, use selections from good literature.

During this period, there was a reaction against the whole-word method. Stress was placed on phonetics, including the use of a contrived "scientific alphabet" and phonetic system with diacritical marks, which was thought to make it easier for children to learn how to read. A typical sentence with this alphabet is the following: Rip Van Win-kl slept twen 'ti yirz, and hwen hî wōk up, hi wez an ōld man with gre hār and bîrd.

The scientific alphabet that first appeared in 1902 was revived with some modifications in 1960. It was then known as the "Augmented Roman Alphabet," also as the "Initial Teaching Alphabet" (ita), with all lower-case letters. However, the scientific alphabet was not widely used, but ita was, particularly in England. It has 44 symbols to go with 44 phonemes. To use it, teachers and students had to learn to write and spell a novel alphabet and then make a transition back to traditional orthography in grades two and three. Its distribution of achievement was somewhat comparable to traditional orthography (Bond & Dykstra, 1967). After several years it died out.

A widely used phonetic method was Pollard's synthetic method, published in 1889. She stipulated that instead of teaching a word as a whole and later analyzing it phonetically, start with the sounds of letters and use them to build up families of whole words. There must be no reference to pictures, no guesswork, and no waiting for a story to develop thought. After a child sounds out the words, the child's own words will enable the child to understand what was read. Pollard also innovated use of children's interest in her stress on phonetics. For example, she used the *puff-puff* of a steamboat for teaching the initial consonant, *p*.

Today, phonics is taught in most basal readers after students have learned some sight words. It is sometimes taught deductively by stating a generalization such as: "A vowel in a closed syllable, a syllable which ends in a consonant, usually has a short sound, for example, *bat, set, kit, cot, tub.*" Students then practice applications of this generalization in identifying other closed monosyllabic words.

Phonics is also taught inductively (Heilman, 1977). The inductive phonic method can be used for teaching any aspect of word recognition such as: initial and final consonants, digraphs (*ch, th,* etc.), consonant blends (*fry, sled,* etc.), vowels (long and short), phonograms (*make, lake,* or *right, light,* etc.), syllabication, or word meaning constituents such as prefixes, roots, and suffixes. The teacher starts by listing at least three familiar words on the board, shown in Table 1.3.

The teacher makes sure students know these words by pointing to each word and saying it aloud. The students repeat this process. After all the students in the group have had a turn, the teacher points to the letters at the top of the column and identifies them by name, big *C* and little *c*. Then, the teacher draws attention to the beginning letter of each word and has students identify its name. After all

TABLE 1.3
Listing of Words for Teaching a Symbol-
Sound Correspondence for an Initial
Consonant

$C\ c$	
cat	cat
cow	cow
cup	cup

three have been identified, the teacher asks for the generalization that all three start with the same letter. Having established this generalization, the teacher goes on to teach the generalization for the initial sound of each word, first by having the students listen to the sound they hear at the beginning of each word. Although the sound of the initial consonant cannot be said in isolation without adding a syllable and saying "uh," the sound of the initial consonant that spreads across the entire word (Liberman, Shankweiler, Liberman, Fowler, & Fischer, 1977) can nevertheless be *mentally* abstracted (Gleitman & Rozin, 1977). The teacher then asks the students to listen to the initial sound of all three words and to think of another word that starts with this sound. The words that students volunteer are written in a column under the three words already on the board. Thus, the teacher has the students form a symbol-sound generalization and tests the validity of their generalization by having the students transfer their generalization to a new word. If children volunteer words that begin with *k,* such as *kit, kite,* and *kick,* the teacher can put these words in another column, teach them that day, and thus create the generalization that the same sound is given to these two letters, which Levin and Watson (1963) referred to as a "set for diversity." Alternatively, the teacher can inform students that they will learn this letter on another day and subsequently develop a set for diversity. After the students have learned the symbol-sound generalization, the teacher can have them apply this knowledge by consciously signaling with a tap of a finger whenever they respond to this initial consonant as they read their next story. Through this follow-up, students not only can apply their generalization, but also integrate it into their mental repertoire of word-recognition skills that they must mobilize in an ever-changing sequence as they identify words while reading. In an analogy to an automobile's transmission with all its gears that must mesh synchronously for the car to accelerate and progress in a harmonious way, Holmes (1953) referred to this process of mobilizing responses to printed symbols in the correct sequence and at the appropriate time as *psychosynchromeshing.*

But in the 1900s, phonics such as Pollard's synthetic method was taught without immediate transfer to meaningful materials. After Pollard's method was in use for awhile, teachers reacted against its meaningless phonics (Russell & Fea, 1963). They switched back to the whole-word method of the previous period and expanded it into the sentence method. For example, some materials used during this period were *The Sentence Method* and *The Story Hour Readers.*

The essential steps of the method were the following: After the teacher told a story or a nursery rhyme, the children would memorize and dramatize it. Then, they would analyze the story into its separate phrases and words, and the words into their separate sounds. Then, they would read the same material from the book. Also during this time, graded literature was introduced, which consisted of folk tales, including the famous story of the *Little Red Hen.* Later readers contained Greek myths and literature from American authors, such as *Rip Van Winkle* and *Hiawatha.*

The beginnings of research in reading emerged in this period with the eye-movement studies of Javal (1879) in France and the influence of Wundt in Germany upon his American students such as Cattell (1886), who returned to the United States and conducted studies in visual perception. From 1884 to 1910, a total of 14 studies were published, which heralded the period of emphasis on scientific investigation.

Emphasis on Scientific Investigation

Research in reading was part of the scientific movement in education. This movement was associated with the publication of Thorndike's handwriting scales in 1910, Courtis' arithmetic tests, Buckingham's Spelling Scale, and Gray's Standardized Oral Reading Paragraphs. Giving impetus to research in reading was the startling finding that many American soldiers in World War I could not read well enough to follow printed instructions. Consequently, during the period, remedial reading techniques were developed, particularly by Gray (1922) and Gates (1927), and reading clinics were established, the first by Fernald at the University of California, Los Angeles, in 1921. Also, a transition was made from oral to silent reading, aided by Huey's (1908) discussion of meaning in reading, Thorndike's (1917) definition of reading as reasoning, Buswell's (1920, 1922) research on eye-movement behavior, and Judd and Buswell's (1922) research, which demonstrated the superiority of silent reading over oral reading in both speed and comprehension. Between 1915 and 1918, a number of silent reading tests were published, including those by Monroe and Courtis. When administrators started using these tests, teachers began to emphasize silent reading. Soon, publishers developed seatwork materials for silent reading that stressed such responses as drawing, construction work, multiple-choice statements, and completion statements.

The materials in readers with titles such as *The Silent Reading Hour* and *The Silent Readers* emphasized factual material and exercises to check on comprehension after each selection, much as some current "laboratory" kits do. A frequently used method of teaching silent reading was to print sentences on the board that required an action response such as: "Come here." The teacher would communicate the intended meaning, not by saying the words and having students repeat them orally, but by using pantomime and getting children to respond with the actions called for by the printed sentence. Seatwork followed up these action sentences and words. Even though oral reading was also taught, it did not have the dominant emphasis it had previously enjoyed.

Oral reading does not have any greater emphasis today. Teachers use oral reading for initial instruction but switch to silent reading as soon as they can. They then employ oral reading for diagnosis and for reading to an audience.

In the 1920s, a further development occurred with the invention of the experience-chart method. The method consisted of discussing an incidentally planned experience the class had. Then the children dictated sentences about this experience to the teacher who wrote them on the board, and the children read these sentences. This method is widely used today, but it has come to be known as the "language-experience approach," and integrates reading, writing, and spelling because the method now quickly progresses to children writing their own stories.

The experience-chart method can be illustrated in greater detail. It does not differ much today from the original method: Students have a common experience, such as watching a goldfish bowl, listening to the teacher talk about it, and then feeding the goldfish. Subsequently, the teacher has the students recall their experience and write their responses on the board or a chart. Usually the teacher prompts the students with questions:

Teacher:	What did we see?
Debbie:	We saw a goldfish bowl.
Teacher:	What was in the bowl?
Robert:	Goldfish were in the bowl.
Teacher:	What were the goldfish doing?
Ann:	They were swimming.
Teacher:	What did we give them?
Abe:	We gave them food.
Teacher:	What did they do with the food?
Kimberly:	They ate the food.
Teacher:	Did you like feeding the goldfish?
Julie:	We liked feeding the goldfish.

Teacher: What shall we call our story?
Tom: "Feeding the Goldfish."
The result is the following story:

Feeding the Goldfish

We saw a goldfish bowl.
Goldfish were in the bowl.
They were swimming.
We gave them food.
They ate the food.
We liked feeding the goldfish.

The teacher next has the children read their lines. Then other children volunteer to read lines they did not give. Eventually, some children can read the entire story.

In another lesson, the teacher might review the story and teach students to use their semantic and syntactic abilities for anticipating words or ideas in sentences. The teacher can do so, for instance, by covering up a word and having children read the sentence and fill in the missing word or idea: We saw a goldfish (*bowl*), (*swim*), (*eat*), etc. After teaching students to use their language expectancies, the teacher asks students to point to particular words: Which word says *goldfish*? Is there another word that also says *goldfish*? Which word says *we*? Is there another *we* in the story? And another *we*? This procedure might continue until the students become adept at identifying individual words. Then the teacher may scramble up the words in a sentence and have the class rearrange them to the original sentence. Eventually, all the words in the story can be scrambled and put back into the original order. Finally, the class can use the words to make up new sentences.

When the class has developed a repertoire of sight words, the teacher can test to determine if the children can orally segment words into their constituent sounds. If so, the teacher then teaches cues within words, including cues to letters.[1] The goldfish story lends itself to teaching cues for the letter and sound of *w*. The teacher writes *w* on the board and explains the features of the letter *w* in *we* and *were* by pointing out the sequence of slanted lines. Then the teacher has the children listen for the sound made by *w* as he or she pronounces and points to *w* in the words *we* and *were*. The next step is to have the class look at additional words and listen for the sounds at the beginning of the words to determine whether they start with the letter *w* and have the sound of *w*. Subsequently, the teacher has the class use the *w* cues for letter and sound in additional experience-chart stories.

Thus, the teacher can take a class from the story to sentences, then words, and finally letters and letter-sound correspondences, and repeat the process for another experience chart. This sequence is currently called a "top–down" process (Adams, Anderson, & Durkin, 1978). In this process of reading, the readers form expectancies for words because of their knowledge of language, including its semantic and syntactic determinants (Goodman, 1965b; Weber, 1970). Children also know the sounds of their language because they have been using them for some years in their daily speech. What then do students have to learn to become readers? They have to learn: (1) to use their language expectancies when reading and (2) to relate print to sounds.

Although the range of reading methods had now been developed, more changes in instruction were still to come, as we see in the next period of em-

---

[1]Some advocates of the use of natural language and the language-experience approach in teaching reading would not emphasize development of sight words and symbol-sound correspondences.

phasis, which was a continuation and application of research begun in the 1920s. Consequently, Smith referred to the period between about 1925 to 1935 as the first period of intensive research and application.

The First Period of Intensive Research and Application

During this period, a split occurred that is still apparent today. Some educators believed in using experience charts to introduce reading and to lead into basal readers with emphasis on systematic skill development supplemented with recreational reading. Other educators believed in the activity theory, which abandoned basal readers and substituted reference books and self-selected stories. In addition, the Washburne plan of individual instruction (Morphett & Washburne, 1931) using graded instructional steps that had been devised in Winnetka, Illinois, was continued, but with decreasing interest. In general, this period's objectives for teaching reading expanded into all content areas and toward satisfying individual differences in children's interests.

The activity movement in education led to the use of the project or unit method. Students would define an activity they were interested in, such as Indians, and they would formulate their own questions, select books to read for answers to their questions, and report to the class without systematic reading instruction from the teacher.

Thus, with a split emphasis in reading instruction, the country entered its next period, which was dominated by international conflict.

Period of International Conflict

In the 1940s, World War II again revealed inadequacies in reading ability. Also, efforts were made to improve the reading ability of officers. The Army established reading improvement programs on college campuses, which continued after the war as reading improvement centers for college students.

In reaction to the activity movement, educators again stressed systematic reading instruction and extended it to "developmental reading" (Bond & Bond, 1941) for grades 1 through 12 and in each content area under the slogan: "Every teacher is a teacher of reading." Although elementary teachers accepted this slogan, secondary teachers preferred another slogan: "Every secondary teacher teaches students to learn from text" (Singer, 1979; Singer & Donlan, 1980).

Toward the end of the 1940s, basal readers such as the *Ginn Basic Readers* (1948) used a vertical (through the grades) and horizontal (across a grade) development of skills, interrelated the basal reader with language arts instruction, and correlated its stories and informational content with social studies instruction at each grade level. Also, context clues for anticipating new words from the preceding semantic and syntactic context and structural analysis and the division of words into their constituent syllabic or word-meaning parts appeared as word-recognition techniques. Although phonics was also used, it was not emphasized until the end of first grade.

Basal readers continued to be used throughout the 1950s and the early 1960s, which Smith referred to as the period of expanding knowledge and technological revolution.

Expanding Knowledge and Technological Revolution

The national concern for defending democracy against totalitarianism accelerated the knowledge expansion and rapidity of the technological revolution. President Truman declared a national emergency in 1950 as North Korea attacked South Korea, and soon the United States was embroiled in the Korean conflict, which President Eisenhower brought to a conclusion. About this time, *What Ivan Knows that Johnny Doesn't* (Tracey, 1951) was published. The book explained that Ivan gets a larger vocabulary in his reading materials than Johnny gets in his basal reader. However, defenders of the American system were quick to point out that Johnny gets supplementary readers and reading materials in content areas that actually give him a vocabulary superior to Ivan's. Indeed, Johnny begins to accelerate his reading ability and, at successive grade levels, he knows an increasing number of words than those taught by his basal reader (Gates, 1962). Nevertheless, in subsequent basal readers, their density increased. While Eisenhower was still in office, criticism of the whole-word method began to be heard as part of the attack on public education. Under the title *Why Johnny Can't Read and What You Can Do About It* (Flesch, 1955) (He isn't learning phonics; teach him phonics), pressure was brought on the schools to shift to using phonics for initiating reading. But, before any real shift could occur, Russia beat the United States into outer space when it launched Sputnik in 1957.

The United States quickly reacted. Among other measures to compete more effectively with the Russians, the United States passed a National Defense Emergency Act and, under the general welfare provision of the constitution, began an era of increasing federal influence in education. Funds were made available for developing science curricula; for training mathematicians, physicists, and engineers; for establishing classes for gifted students; and for in-service training of teachers, including reading teachers.

Reading instruction was also influenced by the changes occurring within the nation. Consistent with winning the technological competition against Russia, America began to favor development of readers at an earlier age by starting instruction prior to first grade. Moore, a Yale sociologist, using Skinnerian learning theory and an electric typewriter, taught his 3-year-old daughter how to read. Many experiments were also conducted in kindergarten to demonstrate that reading instruction could begin at an early age. Durkin (1968) discovered that 1% of students could read at about grade-level equivalent 2.3 when they entered school. Many children had been taught by their parents or by an older sibling who was learning to read in school and practiced "playing school" by teaching the preschooler how to read. She observed that this shift to early reading instruction represented a change in conventional wisdom from a maturational bias—which proposed waiting until the child reaches a mental age of 6½ years before starting reading instruction—to an environmental emphasis—stimulating the reading development of the child (they can learn to read at an earlier age).

In the 1960s, the nation also became concerned with civil rights. President Johnson declared a war on poverty and joblessness in 1963. Schools began to carry out the 1954 Supreme Court mandate of desegregation. Teachers were made aware of dialect differences in reading; dialect was said to be a barrier to comprehension (Goodman, 1965a). However, efforts to develop basal readers that used black English in attempting to match the language of the basal to the dialect of black children were aborted by negative reactions from the black community. Linguists became quite involved in reading and advocated a wide range of programs that were consistent with linguistic principles. These programs ranged in emphasis from teaching symbol-sound correspondence through minimal contrasting pairs, such as *pen* and *pin* (Fries, 1966), to an adaptation of transformational-generative grammar for teaching oral reading. For example, children transformed active sentences, such as *I see daddy coming,* to their negative and passive forms and also used intonation in various ways to express increasing excitement as *daddy* got closer (Martin, 1966).

The explanation that dialect was a barrier to reading comprehension was retracted (Goodman & Buck, 1973). Researchers began to discover that children could adapt to the dialect differences found in reading materials. Indeed, insofar as basal readers had a dialect of their own characterized by repetitious language, all students who used these readers had to adapt to different dialects. Nevertheless, teachers learned to adapt to dialect differences by presenting new words in context and by using meaning as a criterion for determining whether students had made an accurate response to printed words (Lucas & Singer, 1975).

Related areas of reading instruction also benefited from the nation's concern. Federal funds became available for all aspects of reading instruction. Some funds were earmarked for establishing elementary school libraries in 70% of the schools without them and for providing textbooks to meet the demands of the knowledge explosion and the rapid revision of the curriculum. Throughout the country, reading came into the limelight as churches, social groups, and service clubs organized free reading instruction for adults and youths.

Not only did the country invest in instruction, but also in research. Holmes (1953) published the first theoretical model of reading, and Singer (1962) explained how it could be used for teaching reading. Other theories and models of reading, based on psycholinguistics (Goodman, 1966), information processing (Gough, 1972), and transformational-generative grammar (Ruddell, 1976) were constructed and reported (Singer & Ruddell, 1976). The increase in theoretical models and the trend to more basic research in reading was seen as the beginning of a spurt of creative activity in the field (Holmes & Singer, 1964).

During this period, basal readers remained the dominant materials for teaching reading. In fact, 90% of first-grade teachers were using them (Barton & Wilder, 1962). But other instructional materials for teaching beginning reading had become available. Inasmuch as these materials significantly differed in method of teaching, the United States Office of Education decided to undertake a large-scale investigation known as the Cooperative Research Program in First Grade Reading Instruction in order to determine whether the variations made any significant difference in comprehension at the end of the first grade. Comparisons were made of six instructional materials:

1. The basal reader with its emphasis on word-frequency control over vocabulary and gradual introduction of phonics and other word-recognition skills, such as context clues and structural analysis.

2. An Initial Teaching Alphabet which uses 44 symbols and purports to have one symbol for each sound or phoneme.

3. A linguistic emphasis in which children are taught through sequencing of word patterns; these patterns enable them to discover symbol-sound correspondences by a method of minimal contrastive pairs of words, e.g., *pin* and *pen*. Each has three phonemes, but they differ or contrast in only one in *NBC announcer English*.

4. A purely synthetic phonics program that starts with one symbol-sound correspondence, then teaches another, and combines the two to make a whole word. Gradually, this approach leads to the reading of sentences and finally stories.

5. A language-experience approach in which students dictate stories about their experiences to the teacher, who writes them on the board so that students can read their own stories. Subsequently, they write and read their own and each other's stories.

6. A basal reader supplemented with phonics materials.

The results indicated that variation in instructional materials did not result in significant differences in comprehension at the end of the first grade. Even though the nonbasal programs—which emphasized instruction in symbol-sound correspondence, faster pace in introducing new words, the writing of symbols, and systematic instruction in word study—resulted initially in more rapid development or word-recognition skills, this initial spurt was not maintained and did not result in superior comprehension (Bond & Dykstra, 1967).

However, within any one method, there was great variation among teachers—more so than among methods. But teachers misinterpreted the variation among teachers to mean that "it's the teacher, not the method that makes the difference." Using this slogan as license and abetted by federal funds that favored "innovation" in education, teachers began to adopt their own methods and materials for teaching reading. The result was that in some schools a student would change methods and materials at each grade level, much like a highly mobile student who moved from one school district to another each year.

In the 1970s, a reaction occurred to the rapid changes of the 1960s. This next period, which we are currently in, might be known as emphasis on retrenchment and reaction.

Emphasis on Retrenchment and Reaction

Although Americans were elated that they had beaten the Russians in the space race by landing astronauts on the moon in 1969, the mood of the country soon shifted. In the aftermath of withdrawal from Viet Nam and the resignation of President Nixon when confronted by impeachment proceedings, the nation began to realize that its power and resources were limited. One reaction was to require that. schools and teachers be held accountable for the education of students, particularly for achievement of basic skills. The National Assessment of Educational Progress was initiated, and states began to adopt state testing programs for assessing achievement of basic skills. States also mandated minimal competency or proficiency tests on reading, writing, and arithmetic (Law, 1979). Students had to pass these tests by the 12th grade in order to receive a high school diploma. The implementation of these requirements has brought about civil rights suits because the functional or real-life skills assessed by these tests—such as ability to read a menu, a recipe, or a road map—are not part of the regular curriculum and consequently are not directly taught in the classroom (McClung, 1979). Indeed, a prominent feature of education in the 1970s has been the passage of laws affecting education and educational issues being resolved in the courts.

Societal pressures for accountability also affected teachers. Instead of selecting their own reading programs, they served on committees to construct or adopt a reading curriculum for their schools. They learned to write objectives for skills-based reading programs and to administer criterion-objective referenced tests. These tests were devised by teachers, adopted from commercial sources, or from the federally funded Research and Development Center's Wisconsin Design of Reading Skill Development (Otto, Rude, & Spiegel, 1979). The Wisconsin Design is basically a management system for organizing, recording, and sequencing instruction, using objective-referenced tests that are indexed to a multitude of reading materials, including various basal readers. Thus, through criterion-referenced tests and skills-based instruction, teachers demonstrated that they were meeting the demands for accountability.

Critics of the skills-based program, led by Goodman (1976), objected to the fractionation of the flow of printed language into a series of discrete skills. They felt that children should learn to read printed language in the same natural way they learned oral language. Although Goodman (1965b) adduced some evidence to support his theory by demonstrating that children could identify words in context that they could not identify in isolation, he did not specify how to teach children to identify printed words.

However, some critics accepted the language-experience approach as a lead-in to reading children's literature in an individualized program. But the natural language advocates offered no evidence that their approach was superior to a skills-based program.

Those who favored the skills-based approach—such as Samuels (1976a), Resnick and Beck (1976), and Williams (1976)—argued that a skills-based program in which children are systematically taught and learn such aspects of word identification as sound-symbol correspondence, blending word parts, and the use of semantics and syntax for anticipating words in sentences enables students to learn and transfer these skills to identification of novel words. However, the advocates of a skills-based reading instruction could adduce no evidence for a particular sequence of skills (Samuels, 1976b). Apparently, students can successfully follow various skills-based routes to the goal of learning to read.

An innovation in reading instruction that might be equally acceptable to the natural-language or the skills-based approach is the method of "repeated reading" (Chomsky, 1976; Samuels, 1979). In this method, low-achieving readers in the intermediate grades read and listen to a tape-recorded version of a passage. Then they continue this dual input until they can "automatically" identify the printed words in the passage. When they can, they read the printed passage alone. On this reading, they can allocate most of their attentional processes to comprehending the text. Thus, they gain the kind of experience in text comprehension that good readers do on their own when they first learn to read. They read and reread their favorite stories and, through repeated reading, progress through various levels of processing print—from word identification to comprehension of the story—each time with greater ease and enhanced enjoyment. However, care must be taken in using the method to insure that students have their own tape recordings of the passage so that they can control the audio rate to match their reading rate.

Nevertheless, the debate between a natural-language approach versus a skills-based approach is still continuing. But there is no debate over the change in basal readers. Acting on the issues favored by the civil rights movement, basal readers have shifted from the theme of a middle-class family living in a little white house on a hill to stories with multicultural and multiracial characters from various socioeconomic strata. In addition, women and men have begun to be portrayed in nonsexist roles. However, as the 1970s came to a close, states such as California began to debate whether bilingual programs that had been initiated to meet the needs of little- or non-English speaking students were really necessary.

Although we cannot see into the future, we are nevertheless inclined to think that the rate of change in reading instruction will continue. For example, we anticipate that basal readers will incorporate functional and real-life skills and will apply recent research that will include methods of teaching based on an interaction concept of reading (Adams & Collins, 1977). This concept draws upon schema theory (Anderson et al., 1977), scripts (Schank & Abelson, 1977), world knowledge (Winograd, 1972), and differentiation between reproductive and reconstructive memory (Spiro, 1979). We are also likely to have declining funds for supporting education.

As we come to the end of our story, we can look back on the history of reading instruction. We then realize that we have accumulated a host of methods, materials, and motives for teaching the acquisition phase of reading development.

REFERENCES

Adams, M. J., Anderson, R. C., & Durkin, D. Beginning reading: Theory and practice. *Language Arts,* 1978, *5,* 19-25.

Adams, M. J., & Collins, A. *A schema-theoretic view of reading* (Tech. Rep. No. 32). Champaign, Ill.: University of Illinois, Center for the Study of Reading, 1977.

Anderson, R. C., Spiro, R. J., & Montague, W. *Schooling and the acquisition of knowledge.* Hillsdale, N.J.: Lawrence Erlbaum Associates, 1977.

Barr, R. C. Instructional pace differences and their effect on reading acquisition. *Reading Research Quarterly,* 1973-74, *9,* 526-554.

Barton, A., & Wilder, D. Columbia-Carnegie study of reading research and its communication. *Proceedings of the International Reading Association.* New York: Scholastic Magazine, 1962.

Bloom, B. S. Mastery learning and its implications for curriculum development. In E. W. Eisner (Ed.), *Confronting curriculum reform.* Boston: Little, Brown, 1971.

Bond, G. L., & Bond, E. *Developmental reading in high school.* New York: Macmillan, 1941.

Bond, G. L., & Dykstra, R. The cooperative research program in first-grade reading instruction. *Reading Research Quarterly,* 1967, *2,* 5-142.

Buswell, G. T. An experimental study of eye-voice span in reading. *Supplementary Educational Monographs* (No. 17). Chicago: University of Chicago Press, 1920.

Buswell, G. T. Fundamental reading habits: *A study of their development. Supplementary Educational Monographs* (No. 21). Chicago: University of Chicago Press, 1922.

Carroll, J. B. A model of school learning. *Teachers College Record,* 1963, *64,* 723-733.

Cattell, J. McK. The time it takes to see and name objects. *Mind,* 1886, *2,* 63-65.

Chall, J. *Learning to read: The great debate.* New York: McGraw-Hill, 1967.

Chomsky, C. After decoding: What? *Language Arts,* 1976, *53,* 288-297.

Durkin, D. When should children begin to read? In H. M. Robinson (Ed.), *Innovation and change in reading instruction.* Chicago: University of Chicago Press, 1968.

Flesch, R. P. *Why Johnny can't read and what you can do about it.* New York: Harper and Row, 1955.

Fries, C. C. *Merrill linguistic readers.* Columbus, Oh.: Merrill, 1966.

Gates, A. I. *The improvement of reading.* New York: Macmillan, 1927.

Gates, A. I. The word recognition ability and reading vocabulary of second and third grade children. *Reading Teacher,* 1962, *15,* 443-448.

Gibson, E. J. Learning to read. *Science,* 1965, *148,* 1066-1072.

Gleitman, L. R., & Rozin, P. The structure and acquisition of reading, I: Orthographies and the structure of language. In A. S. Reber & D. Scarborough (Eds.), *Toward a psychology of reading.* Hillsdale, N.J.: Lawrence Erlbaum Associates, 1977.

Goodman, K. S. Dialect barriers to reading comprehension. *Elementary English,* 1965, *42,* 853–860. (a)

Goodman, K. S. A linguistic study of cues and miscues in reading. *Elementary English,* 1965, 42, 639–643. (b)

Goodman, K. S. A psycholinguistic view of reading comprehension. In G. B. Schick & M. M. May (Eds.), *New frontiers in college-adult reading.* Fifteenth Yearbook of the National Reading Conference. Milwaukee, Wisconsin: The National Reading Conference, 1966.

Goodman, K. S. Reading: A psycholinguistic guessing game. In H. Singer & R. Ruddell (Eds.), *Theoretical models and processes of reading* (2nd ed.). Newark, Del.: International Reading Association, 1976.

Goodman, K. S., & Buck, C. Dialect barriers to reading comprehension revisited. *The Reading Teacher,* 1973, *27,* 6–12.

Gough, P. B. One second of reading. In J. F. Kavanagh & I. G. Mattingly (Eds.), *Language by ear and by eye.* Cambridge, Mass.: MIT Press, 1972.

Gray, W. S. *Remedial cases in reading: Their diagnosis and correction.* Supplementary Educational Monographs 22, Chicago: University of Chicago Press, 1922

Guthrie, J. Models of reading disability. *Journal of Educational Psychology,* 1973, *65,* 9–18.

Heilman, A. *Principles and practices of teaching reading* (4th ed.). Columbus, Oh.: Merrill, 1977.

Holmes, J. A. *The substrata factor theory of reading.* Berkeley, Cal.: California Book Company, 1953 (Multilith—out of print).

Holmes, J. A., & Singer, H. Theoretical models and trends toward more basic research in reading. *Review of Educational Research,* 1964, *34,* 127–155.

Huey, E. B. *The psychology and pedagogy of reading.* New York: Macmillan, 1908. (Reprinted by MIT Press, Cambridge, Mass., 1968)

Javal, E. Essai sur la physiologie de la lecture. *Annales d'Oculistique,* 1879, *82,* 242–253.

Judd, C. H., & Buswell, G. T. Silent reading: A study of the various types. *Supplementary educational monographs* (No. 23). Chicago: University of Chicago Press, 1922.

LaBerge, D., & Samuels, S. J. Toward a theory of automatic information processing in reading. *Cognitive Psychology,* 1974, *6,* 293–323.

Law, A. I. CAP—Statewide testing comes of age. *California School Boards,* Sept. 1979, 16–22.

Levin, H., & Watson, J. The learning of variable grapheme-to-phoneme relationships. *A basic research program on reading.* Ithaca, N.Y.: Cornell University Cooperative Research Project, No. 639, 1963.

Liberman, I. Y., Shankweiler, D., Liberman, A. M., Fowler, C., & Fischer, F. N. Phonetic segmentation and recoding in the beginning reader. In A. S. Reber & D. Scarborough (Eds.), *Toward a psychology of reading.* Hillsdale, N.J.: Lawrence Erlbaum Associates, 1977.

Lucas, M. & Singer, H. Dialect in relation to oral reading achievement: Recoding, encoding, or merely a code? *Journal of Reading Behavior,* 1975, *7,* 138–148.

McClung, M. S. Legal implications of intelligence and competency testing. Cambridge, Mass.: Harvard University: Center for Law and Education, (Summary) 1979.

Martin, B., Jr. *Sounds of home.* New York: Holt, Rinehart & Winston, 1966.

Morphett, M., & Washburne, C. When should children begin to read? *Elementary School Journal,* 1931, *31,* 495–503.

Mosier, R. D. *Making the American mind.* New York: King's Crown Press, 1947.

Otto, W., Rude, R., & Spiegel, D. L. *How to teach reading.* Reading, Mass.: Addison-Wesley, 1979.

Pearson, P. A psycholinguistic model of reading. *Language Arts,* 1976, *53,* 309–319.

Resnick, L. B., & Beck, I. L. Designing instruction in reading. In J. T. Guthrie (Ed.), *Aspects of reading acquisition.* Baltimore, Md.: Johns Hopkins University Press, 1976.

Ruddell, R. B. *A longitudinal study of four programs of reading instruction varying in emphasis on regularity of grapheme-phoneme correspondences and language structure on reading achieve-*

ment in grades two and three (Final Rep., Project Nos. 3099 & 78085). Berkeley, Cal.: University of California, 1968.

Ruddell, R. B. Psycholinguistic implications for a systems of communication model. In H. Singer & R. B. Ruddell (Eds.), *Theoretical models and processes of reading* (2nd ed.). Newark, Del.: International Reading Association, 1976.

Russell, D. H., & Fea, H. Research on teaching reading. In N. Gage (Ed.), *Handbook of research on teaching.* Chicago: Rand McNally, 1963.

Samuels, S. J. Hierarchical subskills in the reading acquisition process. In J. T. Guthrie (Ed.), *Aspects of reading acquisition.* Baltimore, Md.: Johns Hopkins University Press, 1976. (a)

Samuels, S. J. Modes of word recognition. In H. Singer & R. B. Ruddell (Eds.), *Theoretical models and processes of reading* (2nd ed.). Newark, Del.: International Reading Association, 1976. (b)

Samuels, S. J. The method of repeated reading. *The Reading Teacher,* 1979, *32,* 403-408.

Samuels, S. J., Dahl, P., & Archwamety, T. Effect of hypothesis/test training on reading skill. *Journal of Educational Psychology,* 1974, *66,* 835-844.

Schank, R. C., & Abelson, R. P. *Scripts, plans, goals, and understanding.* Hillsdale, N.J.: Lawrence Erlbaum Associates, 1977.

Singer, H. Substrata-factor theory of reading: Theoretical design for teaching reading. In J. A. Figurel (Ed.), *Challenge and experiment in reading.* Proceedings of the Seventh Annual Convention of the International Reading Association, Vol. 7. New York: Scholastic Magazines, 1962, 226-232.

Singer, H. IQ is and is not related to reading. In S. Wanat (Ed.), *Issues in evaluating reading.* Arlington, Va.: Center for Applied Linguistics, 1977. (a)

Singer, H. Resolving curricular conflicts in the 1970's: Modifying the hypothsis, "It's the teacher who makes the differences in reading achievement." *Language Arts,* 1977, *54,* 158-163. (b)

Singer, H. Research in reading that should make a difference in classroom instruction. In S. J. Samuels (Ed.), *What research has to say about reading instruction.* Newark, Del.: International Reading Association, 1978.

Singer, H. Attitudes toward reading and learning from text. In M. L. Kamil & A. J. Moe (Eds.), *Reading research: Studies and applications.* Twenty-Eighth Yearbook of the National Reading Conference. Clemson, S. C.: The National Reading Conference, 1979.

Singer, H., & Donlan, D. *Reading and learning from text.* Boston: Little, Brown, 1980.

Singer, H. & Ruddell, R. B. (Eds.) *Theoretical models and processes of reading.* Newark, Del. International Reding Association, 1976

Smith, N. B. *American reading instruction.* Newark, Del.: International Reading Association, 1965.

Spiro, R. J. Etiology of reading comprehension style. In M. L. Kamil & A. J. Moe (Eds.), *Reading research: Studies and applications.* Twenty-Eighth Yearbook of the National Reading Conference. Clemson, S. C.: The National Reading Conference, 1979.

Thorndike, E. Reading as reason: A study of mistakes in paragraph reading. *Journal of Educational Psychology,* 1917, *8,* 323-332.

Tracey, A. S. *What Ivan knows that Johnny doesn't.* New York: Random House, 1951.

Weber, R.-M. First-graders' use of grammatical context in reading. In H. Levin & J. Williams (Eds.), *Basic studies on reading.* New York: Basic Books, 1970.

Williams, J. Reaction to modes of word recognition. In H. Singer & R. B. Ruddell (Eds.), *Theoretical models and processes of reading* (2nd ed.). Newark, Del.: International Reading Association, 1976.

Winograd, T. Understanding natural language. *Cognitive Psychology,* 1972, *3* (Whole issue).

2 Integration Processes in Word Recognition

Neal F. Johnson
The Ohio State University
Columbus, Ohio

During the past decade experimental psychologists have shown a growing interest in the reading process. To a certain extent, this increased attention has occurred because investigators in both psycholinguistics and visual-information processing have found the reading task to be a natural laboratory for examining issues in cognitive processing. However, as with any phenomenon subjected to the scrutiny of the scientific community, the issue of reading has emerged as a multifaceted problem, with critical components of the task varying all the way from noncognitive aspects of preperceptual processing (e.g., Jackson & McClelland, 1975) to the operation of the complex cognitive mechanisms involved in the utilization of scripts (e.g., Bower, Black, & Turner, 1979) and the construction of inferences (Clark, 1977). In addition, given the large number of psychological phenomena that appear to be part of the overall task, it seems clear that if there is such a thing as a psychological moment of reading, it will surely reveal itself as being both temporally extended and entailing a constellation of subskills and phenomena.

The focus of this chapter is on just one of the component phenomena in reading, namely the integration or unitization process, and through the medium of that issue the intent is to examine the way in which the perceptual-mental representation of a word may change through time. In particular, the concern of the chapter is on both the unit of representation at each point in processing (i.e., what is integrated) and the extent to which that representation is subject to cognitive control. In addition, although there are some relatively complex integration and unitization effects evident in the later stages of comprehension (e.g., Bransford & Franks, 1971), the present concern is somewhat more limited and centered on the nature of these effects in word perception.

29

MODELS OF WORD PERCEPTION

As a beginning, it may be worthwhile to consider a few of the issues that have emerged within the context of models of word perception. Although only a very few models have dealt specifically with unitization phenomena in any direct manner, most of them have considered the question of part–whole relationships in word perception, and in that context they seem to have rather clear implications regarding both the location and the nature of unitization in word perception. Given that is the case, the following discussion focuses primarily on this aspect of the various models.

Letter-Integration Models

We can start by noting that one of the historical distinctions between the various models of word perception has involved the question of whether words are assumed to be perceived as wholes or as a collection of parts with perceptual processing occurring on a letter-by-letter basis (e.g., Adams, 1979; Huey, 1968). One of these positions, the letter-by-letter or letter-integration view, adopts the assumption that word identification must be preceded by some analogous but preliminary stages of feature and letter identification, whereas the other group of theories views word perception as being holistic and not involving the prior identification of component information. The critical distinction between these positions, then, seems to be in the role played by component information in the identification and formation of word-level encodings, and the issue of unitization can be viewed as questions concerning the nature and extent of component-level integration prior to the availability of a word-level encoding.

Although the major assumption underlying the letter-integration models does appear to be quite clear and unambiguous, it is also the case that there are several different ways one can view the relationship between parts and wholes within this general framework. That is, even though the various theories all subscribe to the position that processing involves a hierarchy of stages, with an attendant variation in units and levels of representation, they differ in terms of both the specific levels that are assumed to appear within the hierarchies and the relationshps among the levels.

Units and Levels of Representation

For example, Gough's (1972) model assumes an iconic representation of letters that is transferred into short-term memory on a letter-by-letter basis, with the short-term memory representation then being assigned a set of systematic phonemes (Chomsky & Halle, 1968). McClelland (1976), on the other hand, assumes a hierarchy of analyzers that are used to encode features, letters, and words, with the output at each level being an identification of the input, and Massaro (1975) and Massaro and Klitzke (1977) have adopted a similar position.

Somewhat more complicated hierarchies are assumed by models such as LaBerge and Samuels (1974), Gibson (1971), and Spoehr and Smith (1973) in that they have emphasized the importance of intermediate-level representations such as letter clusters, spelling patterns, syllables, and vocalic center groups. However, regardless of the specific levels included within these models, it does seem clear that each model assumes that word-level representations are preceded by some preliminary component-level identification.

Relationships Among Levels

In terms of the relationships among the levels, there is also a great deal of diversity. For example, models such as those of Gough (1972) and McClelland (1976) assume that processing occurs in a relatively strict hierarchy from the lowest level to the highest, with the output at each level being the input to the next higher level. The Massaro–Klitzke (1977) and LaBerge–Samuels (1974) models also include a hierarchy of levels, but they assume that certain levels can be bypassed in the process of word identification. In the case of the LaBerge–Samuels model, it is assumed that there are times when features and letters can feed directly into word-level encodings, whereas in other situations those components would be an input to another, although somewhat higher, component level. The Massaro–Klitzke model includes a similar assumption, but it goes further and assumes that under some circumstances word decisions might even be made on the basis of feature information alone, without any higher-level recoding.

A much more complicated view of the relationships among levels or stages is represented by the interacting-levels approach. The major difference between this view and those just discussed is that the interacting-levels theories make no strict assumptions regarding the order in which the various levels or stages must perform their function. For example, Rumelhart's (1977) model assumes that processing can go on at all levels at the same time, and that subjects can use information obtained at one level as a source of hypotheses regarding confirming information that could be sought at other levels. Krueger (1975) also has an interacting-levels model, but he assumes that information represented at higher levels can be fed back to clarify or sharpen lower-level perceptual representations. However, even with such a flexible processing structure, it is clear that both these models also assume a hierarchy of levels of representation.

One final point is that these models also differ in the extent to which they assume that the stages can overlap. For example, whereas the Gough (1972) model appears to assume that each stage of analysis is completed before the next begins, the McClelland (1976), Massaro–Klitzke (1977), and LaBerge–Samuels (1974) models all assume that the stages can overlap to a certain extent, with the only restriction being that the onset of lower-level stages has to precede the onset of higher-level stages. In the case of the Rumelhart (1977) and Krueger (1975) positions, however, it is not clear that even this latter assumption need be made, although a bottom-to-top ordering does occur during the initial stages of processing.

Summary

Although this review of a few of the issues involved in letter-integration models falls considerably short of being complete, it does highlight some of the common aspects of these theories. In particular, they all seem to share the assumption that word perception involves a hierarchy of encoding levels, with the output at each of the levels being an identified or identifiable representation of the components at that level. Given that is the case, not only should there be unitization at each of these levels, but the unitized representation should be available prior to any word-level encoding of the same information, and as is subsequently noted, it is this latter point that has been the major focus of the empirical work on this issue.

Whole-Word Models

The view that word perception is holistic has been a popular position ever since the empirical work on reading first began (e.g., see Cattell, 1886; Huey, 1968), and to a certain extent this popularity has been fostered by our own intuitions regarding what happens when we see a word during reading. That is, when we see a word it seems to be an integrated perceptual pattern, and the individual letters do not appear to maintain separate identities within the pattern. The impact of this impression also can be noted in terms of the specifics of much of the early research. For example, the general notion of holistic processing was supported by Cattell's (1886) work indicating that words can be perceived as fast as single letters, and the fact that letters lose their individual identities was illustrated by Pillsbury's (1897) early demonstration that when word perception is complete, subjects may not know what specific letters they perceived.

However, as was the case with the letter-integration theories, the basic assumption underlying the whole-word theories has been realized in different ways within specific theories. For example, several of the early theories (e.g., circa 1900) seemed simply to stipulate that word perception was holistic, whereas more contemporary views have tried to come to terms with the fact that there is a need for some type of initial perceptual registration along with an interfacing mechanism between that representation and the ultimate word-level encoding. In fact, this point has led LaBerge (1976) to suggest that rather than talking about a letter-by-letter versus whole-word distinction, it may be more appropriate to distinguish between two-level theories and theories that assume a hierarchy of intervening stages and levels.

The Issue of Direct Access

The primary way the various whole-word or two-level theories have differed is in terms of whether they assume any attendant component-level processing, and, if so, what is its nature and in what form is the information available to the perceiver. A secondary issue has concerned whether it is possible for word-level decisions to be made on the basis of anything but word-level representations, but this point has emerged in the context of only a limited number of models (e.g., Chambers & Forster, 1975).

In terms of whether component processing and encoding occurs at all, some models do not include that option. For example, Theois and Muise (1977) assume that iconic representations of words activate long-term memory word-level files directly, with any component information subsequently being derived from the files. Similarly, Frank Smith's (1971) model explicitly denies the possibility of any component processing during word perception, with features directly activating word-level encodings. Chambers and Forster (1975), on the other hand, assumes that words are processed at all levels simultaneously, and Morton's logogen model (1969) also would allow for that possibility, although it is not an explicit part of his theory. However, given the rather extreme diversity on this issue, it seems clear that although the possibility of ancillary component processing and encoding may be a theoretical issue within the group of two-level theories, it cannot be an issue that distinguishes these views from the previously described letter-integration or multilevel theories.

Component Processing

The other issue concerns the nature of the component processing and the extent to which that information is available at the time of word perception. Again, the models seem to take rather widely divergent positions. For example, Chambers and Forster (1975) assume that processing occurs simultaneously at all levels of representation, with all the information being available when processing is complete. In fact, they assume word identification can take place on the basis of whatever level completes its processing first. The Morton (1969) logogen model also allows for the possibility of activating long-term memory codes for components, but that model would be somewhat more conservative in assuming that word-level decisions could be made only on the basis of word-level representations (i.e., logogens).

The other extreme on the issue of component availability would be represented by Smith's (1971) model, which assumes that subjects can process a word's feature array at either the component level (e.g., letters) or at the word level, but this model rules out the possibility of analyzing or encoding such an array at more than one level simultaneously. That is, perceivers would have the option of encoding the array as either a letter set or as a word, but they could not encode it both ways. Given that is the case, component information should not be available at the time a word-level encoding is accessed.

Finally, what might be viewed as an intermediate position can be illustrated by the Theois and Muise (1977) model. Their model seems to allow for only one type of processing, which results in the subjects accessing a set of word-level files for the item. However, although the file for the name code is assumed to be the one most immediately available, it also is assumed that component information would be represented in the set of files as well, and once the entire set had been accessed those component files also would be available. Given that construction of the process, this view would seem to imply that iconic arrays are not in any sense *analyzed for* component information, but rather that information is assumed to be *derived from* the word-level representation (i.e., the set of files).

Summary

Although this discussion of the two-level theories has been rather limited, it does point out that about the only feature they have in common is the assumption that the word-level representation can be derived directly from the initial perceptual registration of the information. Almost any view of secondary component processing and encoding seems to be consistent with these theories, and there seems to be an equal variety of options regarding the subsequent availability of the component information.

In addition, however, it does seem clear that all the various theories assume an initial uninterpreted perceptual registration of the information along with the word-level encoding, but none of them go into much detail regarding how that perceptual representation was established. In these terms, about the only thing that seems to be denied is that word perception must be mediated by a stage of letter or letter-cluster identification, although there could be a variety of preliminary stages involved in establishing the perceptual registration that leads to the word-level encoding.

Furthermore, the fact that these are two-level theories in terms of the nature of the psychological representation does not necessarily imply that they are one-stage theories in terms of the process of transforming the information from one form of representation into the other. That is, the only thing that is assumed is that there are two levels of representation, but there could be several steps or stages involved in going from one of them to the other.

Finally, in terms of the unitization issue, the only consistent point is that all the theories seem to have few if any implications regarding unitization at the perceptual level, although unitization is assumed to be more or less complete at the time the word-level representation is accessed. The ambiguity regarding the perceptual representation is highlighted by the fact that some models deal with it in terms of features, whereas others view it as being iconic, in which case the data would indicate letters to be the minimum level of unitization. Regardless of that problem, however, it is clear that there would be no units of representation involved in word perception between the letter and the word, and no identified units of any type below the level of the word, and this seems to be quite different from the implications of the multilevel theories described earlier.

THE PATTERN-UNIT MODEL

The pattern-unit model (Johnson, 1975, 1977) is an attempt to provide a rough outline of the processing events that occur between the retina and the final pattern-level encoding when a small visual pattern is presented, although it is intended to be a somewhat more general model than those previously considered. That is, not only is it designed to handle word perception, but it also should provide an account of the way subjects process other readily integratable visual arrays like good forms (Palmer, 1977) and intact pictures of common scenes (Biederman, 1972), as well as unintegratable arrays like consonant strings and scrambled pictures. However, this increased generality notwithstanding, it also is the case that the model can be evaluated in terms of the foregoing considerations.

Outline of the Model

To begin, the basic structure of the model consists of a perceptual component that deals with precognitive processing, a cognitive-memorial component that describes the way word-level representations are handled, and an interfacing mechanism that accounts for the way information is transferred from one system to the other. Given such a structure, the model clearly falls within the group of whole-word or two-level theories, but both the details of the perceptual processing and the specifics of the interfacing mechanism are a bit more complex than those involved in some of the models previously described.

Background Issues

In part, this increased complexity has stemmed from a growing appreciation for some of the issues that led LaBerge (1976) to reconstrue the whole-word theories as involving two levels of representation. For example, as has been noted elsewhere (Johnson, 1979), when one begins with a two-level theory it is tempting to assume that features, letters, and the various types of letter clusters are simply irrelevant to the process of word identification. However, it also has been noted that subjects have no trouble making discriminations between items such as *send* and *lend* or *SHOW* and *SNOW*. The fact that subjects can make the first discrimination indicates that they must have letter information available in some form, and for the other pair of items, the nature of the feature in the middle of the second letter is the only differentiating item, which would indicate that that information must be available, as well. Clearly, if this analysis is correct, it must be the case that some form of feature and letter information is available and used in word perception, and one of the problems encountered by two-level theories is accounting for that fact within the context of their basic assumption regarding the two levels of representation.

The solution to this problem adopted by the pattern-unit model has been to distinguish between the issue of whether information is available for use and the issue of the form in which it is available. Obviously, as the foregoing examples illustrate, no model of word perception can deny the availability of feature and letter information to the perceiver, but it may be possible to suggest that the form in which that information is available differs substantially from the form of availability for the word-level code. In particular, the word-level code is assumed to be an interpreted or interpretable cognitive representation of the information that can be used for selecting responses and making decisions, whereas the feature and letter information is assumed to be encoded only as uninterpreted units within the perceptual system, and not in a form that could be used for response selection. Therefore, the distinction is not in terms of whether there is some type of precognitive unitized representation of feature and letter information, but rather whether that unitized representation is subject to cognitive control.

The Perceptual System

These points can be illustrated by the schematic representation of the model provided in Fig. 2.1. The top line of the figure represents the perceptual component, and it is assumed that perceptual processing begins with some type of receptor activity. That receptor activity is then immediately recoded into a neural signal, which is transmitted through the peripheral system via the optic pathways to a set of central-processing mechanisms. In addition, the model assumes that very little in the way of complicated encoding of the signal occurs during this period of time, but once the signal reaches the central-processing mechanisms it is assumed that a process of feature detection and encoding begins. Given that is the case, what is passed on from the point at which central processing begins would be an encoding of the original signal, rather than the signal itself. More specifically, the model assumes that both peripheral and central processing are temporally extended, with the latter involving the detection and encoding of feature information. The result of that process is the construction of a perceptual representation that the perceiver can use for contacting traces within memory such that decisions can be made.

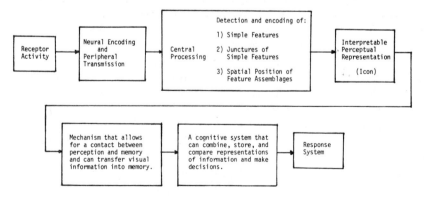

FIG. 2.1.   Outline of the pattern-unit model.

Peripheral Processing.   In terms of peripheral processing, the model assumes that the main function of that system is simply to relay the signal from the receptors to the central-processing mechanisms and, at the same time, prepare the signal such that it is in a form that is compatible with the central-processing mechanisms. To this extent, the model would assume that the signal is still relatively undifferentiated when it reaches the central-processing mechanisms and could be interpreted by the cognitive system only after central processing produced a highly differentiated representation.

Central Processing.   In terms of the specifics of feature detection and encoding, it is assumed that although the central mechanisms immediately begin the process of detection for all the potential features within an array, the process is not instantaneous, and it involves some period of time to be completed. In addition, it seems likely that the amount of time needed to detect and encode a feature will vary from feature to feature, such that the perceptual representation of some features might emerge before that of others.

Within the model, the features themselves are divided into three classes. The first class consists of simple features such as curves, diagonal lines, and horizontal and vertical lines, while the second class consists of the junctures of these features. For example, an upper-case A would have two diagonal lines and a horizontal line as simple features, but it also would have three juncture features that represent the intersections of the three simple features. In addition, it also is assumed that the juncture features act as a mechanism for fusing the simple features into the higher-order feature assemblages or units that correspond to letters, and these are assumed to be the highest-order unit of representation within the perceptual system.

The third class of features is assumed to represent the positional information within an array. Also, it is assumed that this positional information is an attribute of a feature assemblage, rather than an attribute of the features themselves. That is, it would be assumed that simple features would be positioned relative to other simple features in the same assemblage by the juncture features that fuse that particular assemblage into a unit, but there also would need to be some way in which that particular assemblage as a unit could be positioned with respect to other assemblages in the same array such that subjects would be able to draw distinctions between items like *saw* and *was*. It should be noted, however, that although these features would properly position the letters, they would not unitize them in any way in terms of a word-level representation.

The Transfer of Information and the Cognitive System

Once the process of feature detection and encoding has resulted in an interpretable perceptual representation, the next step is to transfer the information to memory such that cognitive operations and mechanisms can be applied to the information. The next stage in processing, then, is the transfer mechanism, and although the specifics of this procedure are not included within the schematic representation of the model in Fig. 2.1, it is the point at which word-level unitization is assumed to occur, and the details are provided later.

The final component of the model involves the cognitive system where various types of interpretive events takes place. For example, the subject's job during the course of reading normally would be either to compare an item with some representation already existing in memory or to take a particular perceptual representation and seek out its appropriate lexical entry. It is assumed that these steps would have to take place within the cognitive system.

The Perceptual System and Its Supporting Evidence

The first issue to be examined in some detail is the process of encoding and unitizing the visual information within the perceptual system. As the preceding discussion would indicate, the model begins with the assumption that there is an initial peripheral representation, and inasmuch as it is assumed that there is little or no recoding of information within the peripheral system, it would be expected that this information would be represented within the signal in a more or less undifferentiated manner. However, once central processing begins and specific features within the signal are detected and encoded, one would assume that the form of the representation would become increasingly differentiated. That is, the model would assume that all the necessary information regarding the visual characteristics of a word would be carried within the peripheral representation, but that representation would be relatively undifferentiated, and in order for the information to be used it would be necessary to detect and encode it in a somewhat more specific form.

The Masking Paradigm and the Temporal Characteristics of Processing

The particular experimental paradigm that has been used most frequently to examine the issue of feature detection and encoding is called masking. The basic idea underlying this technique is that if visual information processing is temporally extended, then the phenomenal experience of "seeing" a word may not coincide exactly with the period of time that the word is stimulating the eye. For example, we have found that if a single word is presented to subjects for a duration of approximately 15 to 20 msec they seem to have little or no trouble identifying the word. In fact, with such a display followed by a dark visual field, subjects will almost always identify the word and report it correctly.

Now, however, assume that the brief display is followed immediately by a brightly lighted complex visual pattern rather than the dark field. A common pattern used in such experiments is constructed by simply typing an array of either alternating or overlapping X's and O's, such as:

XOXOXOX   ⊗⊗⊗⊗⊗⊗⊗
OXOXOXO or   ⊗⊗⊗⊗⊗⊗⊗
XOXOXOX   ⊗⊗⊗⊗⊗⊗⊗

If such a display immediately follows a 20 msec presentation of a word, not only are the subjects unable to report which word was presented, but they frequently are uncertain as to whether any word at all preceded the masking stimulus.

In terms of the model, the important point illustrated by this experimental outcome is that we have completely determined whether a word would or would not be seen on the basis of something that occurred after the display of the word terminated. If that is the case, then it is clear that the "seeing" of the word must have occurred after the termination of the display, and not while it was stimulating the eye.

A second interesting outcome from masking experiments such as these is the fact that the likelihood of correctly reporting the presented word increases if a delay is introduced between when the word display disappears and the masking stimulus is first presented. If one assumes that this masking effect occurs because the interfering stimulus (i.e., the mask) demands and obtains the attention of the processing mechanisms still needed by the target word (Kolers, 1968; Turvey, 1973), then this result would indicate that the longer subjects are allowed to continue processing the target word before the mask is presented, the more information they will have about the word, and therefore, the greater will be their accuracy. In general, the results of a variety of experiments (Seery, 1978; Turvey, 1973) have supported this point and have suggested that if the delay is as long as 150 to 200 msec the subjects' report accuracy starts approximating that which is obtained when no mask is presented at all.

Peripheral Processing

Although these results would indicate that perceptual processing is temporally extended, it also is necessary to demonstrate a distinction between the early stages of processing that involve the peripheral system and the more complex encoding events that occur later during central processing. In terms of peripheral processing, the major points of the model are that the end product of this stage should be a relatively undifferentiated representation of the signal, and, inasmuch as it is assumed that little recoding occurs during this stage, the characteristics of the signal should match those of the originating stimulus very closely.

Regarding this latter point, one implication is that the energy level of the originating stimulus should be an important determiner of the peripheral representation, although that information might not be maintained after the onset of the type of complex recoding that is characteristic of central processing, and Turvey (1973) has reported a series of experiments demonstrating that to be the case. That is, Dustman and Beck (1965) reported that the first evidence of cortical activity related to a visual stimulus occurs somewhat less than 100 msec after the onset of the target, and Turvey's (1973) experiments showed that within that same time range the relative energy levels of a target and mask are critical determiners of the masking effect. On the other hand, if a peripheral interaction between the target and mask is precluded by setting the time between the onset of the target and mask greater than 100 msec, or by presenting the two stimuli to different eyes, then the relative energy levels of the target and mask seems to have little or no influence on the masking effect. Clearly, these results indicate that the energy level of a target stimulus does have an important influence on the characteristics of the peripheral signal, but that attribute of the representation appears to be lost once central processing begins.

Concerning the extent to which the peripheral signal is a differentiated representation of the target, the data also seem to be in accord with the model. For example, if the signal is undifferentiated there would be no basis for any type of specific similarity relationship between a target item and a masking stimulus, and, if that is the case, it would be expected that any masking effect obtained during peripheral processing would not be influenced by target-to-mask similarity.

In line with this point, not only do the figural characteristics of the mask seem to be irrelevant when the masking is peripheral (Turvey, 1973), but it appears that there may be no need for any figural characteristics at all. This point is illustrated in a study by Spencer (1969), which demonstrated that even an elevation in brightness can act as an effective mask if that masking stimulus is allowed to interact with the target before any central processing of the target begins. Furthermore, the effectiveness of that type of stimulus as a mask seems to be an increasing function of its energy level, and together these points would suggest that not only is energy a relevant attribute of a peripheral representation, but it may be the only relevant attribute of a peripheral representation.

Central Processing

The absence of any figural effect in peripheral masking is highlighted by the fact that the situation is quite different if a 100-msec delay is introduced between the onsets of the target and mask, or if they are presented to different eyes. Under those circumstances, it is reasonable to assume that the two stimuli would interact centrally, and the available evidence would indicate that in this situation a stimulus will act as a mask only if it consists of the types of features included in the target (Kahneman, 1968; Spencer, 1969; Turvey, 1973). In addition, once central processing of the target begins, its energy characteristics—relative to those of the mask—become irrelevant, and that would seem to suggest that subjects are dealing with a recoded version of the peripheral signal rather than the signal itself (Turvey, 1973). Clearly, then, there is a difference in the necessary physical characteristics of a mask that depends on the interstimulus interval, including its figural characteristics, and that difference has been taken to suggest that central masking is a disruption of a recoded version of the original signal, which may require a greater target-to-mask similarity.

Feature Detection and Encoding: The Basic Effect.   As previously noted, a rather well-documented explanation for central masking is that the second stimulus (i.e., the mask) demands and obtains the use of feature detectors and encoders that are still required and being used by the target. Within these terms, masking is explained as resulting from the fact that certain features would be absent from the perceptual representation of a target if a mask was presented, and, in the general case, the more features that were missing, the poorer should be the perceiver's report performance. Therefore, it would seem to follow that not only should a mask have figural characteristics in order to be effective, but the degree of masking should be an increasing function of the degree of feature overlap (i.e., similarity) between the two stimuli. This phenomenon does seem to occur, and it has been used to examine the process of feature detection and encoding.

In addition, as might be supposed, with increasing spatial distance between the retinal locations of a target and mask, there is a decrease in the magnitude of the masking effect, and that seems to be true regardless of whether the time interval between the two stimuli indicates the interaction to be peripheral or central (Averbach & Coriell, 1961). This point has been taken to suggest that we may not operate on the basis of just one set of feature detectors, but rather we may have many sets of feature detectors that are tied to specific retinal locations, with their distribution across the retina being roughly proportional to the distribution of receptors (Bjork & Murray, 1977; Estes, 1977).

Therefore, given all these considerations, it might be expected that if two stimuli are presented simultaneously and spatially close together, there would be a masking effect, and that does seem to occur. It is referred to as lateral masking (e.g., Townsend, Taylor, & Brown, 1971), and it has been used to explain why the letters at the ends of words can be perceived more readily than those in the middle. However, if part of this interference effect can be attributed to the fact that the adjacent items are competing for the same feature detectors, as suggested by the foregoing considerations, then the magnitude of the effect should be related to featural overlap between the letters.

Bjork and Murray (1977) examined this issue in a particularly effective way. Subjects were shown a small four-by-four target display that contained either one or two letters, with the other 14 or 15 cells of the display being filled with the symbol #. Each display contained at least one B or one R, but there was never more than one letter in any one column. After that display was terminated, a new posttarget display appeared that consisted of a four-by-four array of dollar signs ($), with an arrow pointing to one of the four columns, and the subject then was to report whether a B or an R had appeared in that particular column of the previous target display.

In some cases the target letter was the only letter in the target display, although one additional letter appeared in the other target displays, and that additional letter was either another instance of the target letter, the alternative target letter, or an unrelated letter. In addition, when a second letter appeared, it could be either adjacent to the target letter or separated by some distance.

In terms of the foregoing account of visual information processing, the perceptual processes involved in the detection of a target in a task such as this should be slowed if a nearby pattern would compete for the same feature detectors. The interesting aspect of this experiment is the fact that the pattern that would be expected to cause the greatest interference and reduction in rate of perceptual processing would be a second instance of the same letter (i.e., an item that could not give rise to any cognitive interference). The results of the study were in accord with expectations. If the target display contained two letters, performance was lower than if there was only one letter, and if two letters did appear in the target display, the most disrupting case was when the nontarget item was the same letter as the target. In addition, this disruption decreased in terms of both errors and speed of responding if the two letters were separated rather than adjacent.

These results seem to offer support for the perceptual component of the model. That is, the interference effect appears to be quite consistent with the idea that a process of feature detection is involved at some point in the formation of a perceptual representation of an orthographic array. In addition, the fact that the interference decreased when spatial separation increased would support the hypothesis that there may be spatially distributed perceptual channels (Bjork & Murray, 1977; Estes, 1972, 1977). In general, then, these data combined with those described earlier would suggest that the development of a differentiated representation is characteristic of later stages of perceptual processing, and it results from the detection and encoding of physical features in the display by a set of spatially distributed processing mechanisms.

Feature Detection and Encoding: Temporal Extension.   Regarding feature detection and encoding, the other issue is the extent to which it is temporally extended. In terms of the masking paradigm, a temporally extended process would imply that not only should masking be a function of the target-to-mask similarity, but this relationship should change systematically with increasing degrees of target-stimulus processing before the mask is presented.

This issue can be illustrated with a recent experiment by Seery (1978). In this study the subjects were presented with two rows of five consonants, and their job was to report as many of the ten letters as they could in their correct position. The displays came on for a period of approximately 30 msec, and that was followed either 0, 50, 150, or 400 msec later by a masking stimulus that was composed of either all X's or all O's, such as:

```
X X X X X       0 0 0 0 0
  X X X X   or     0 0 0 0
X X X X X       0 0 0 0 0
```

Within each target display there was one critical letter that was composed of curves (e.g., *Q, C, G,* or *O*), one that had diagonal lines (e.g., *A, N, V,* or *X*), and one that had straight lines (e.g., *H, E, F,* or *T*). The other seven letters were selected randomly and functioned as fillers.

The major concern of the experiment was whether the effect of target-to-mask similarity might change as a function of the interval between the onsets of the two stimuli (i.e., increasing degrees of target processing). If the peripheral representation of the target is in the form of a relatively undifferentiated signal, as suggested by the prior data, then the X-mask and the 0-mask should be equally effective on all three types of critical target-letter, provided the target and mask are presented close together in time (i.e., the onset-to-onset interval is less than 50 msec). On the other hand, if the central processing of the target is allowed to begin before the mask is presented, then some degree of target-to-mask similarity should be necessary in order for a masking effect to be obtained. That is, if the perceptual disruption from central masking occurs because the masking stimulus demands and obtains the attention of feature detectors and encoders still being used by the target, then a masking effect can be obtained only if the target and mask share features (i.e., demand the same detectors and encoders). Furthermore, if central processing is temporally extended, as the subject is allowed to process the target stimulus for an increasing amount of time before the mask is presented, there would be an increasing need for target-to-mask similarity in order to be certain that the masking stimulus would demand one of the feature detectors-encoders still being used by the target. In general, then, not only would one expect an effect of target-to-mask similarity during central processing, but the similarity should become increasingly important as the interval between the target and mask increases.

The general trend of Seery's (1978) results was very much in accord with expectations. First, in agreement with the previous studies, when there was no interstimulus interval, and the masking effect would be assumed to reflect peripheral processing, the figural characteristics of the mask were irrelevant. Not only was there a substantial disruption from the masks under those conditions, but the X-mask and 0-mask seemed to be equally effective on all letters.

However, with a 50-msec interval between the two stimuli, when there would be reason to suppose that some central processing of the target might have begun, the figural characteristics of the mask did appear to show the beginning of an effect. With that interval, there was more disruption of the subjects' ability to report the target letters that were similar to the mask than those that were dissimilar, and with a 150-msec interval that similarity effect was even larger.

One potential problem with the Seery (1978) data is that the pretarget fixation display consisted of the masking stimulus, which could mean that at least part of the effect she obtained might have been the result of fatiguing feature detectors. Nevertheless, even if that were the explanation, the same general points regarding feature detection and encoding would hold, and the overall conclusion would be unchanged. More to the point, however, Hellige, Walsh, Lawrence, and Prasse (1979) have reported the same type of effect as obtained by Seery (1978), and they used a blank pretarget fixation field that would eliminate the problem of fatigued feature detectors. Therefore, the details of the expected change in the similarity effect as a function of interstimulus interval do seem to have been supported by both these studies.

In terms of the time span over which central processing occurs, the Seery (1978) data would indicate it to be surprisingly long. For the case in which the target and mask were dissimilar, the data indicated that the subject's performance increased rapidly with an increasing interstimulus interval out to a maximum of 150 msec, and by that point the mask appeared to have lost its effectiveness completely. For the case in which the target and mask were very similar, however, the situation was quite different. The rise in performance with increasing interstimulus interval was very gradual, and even with a 400 msec interval there was evidence of some perceptual disruption. This could be interpreted as suggesting that at least some feature detection and encoding were still in progress that long after the target had been presented.

Seery (1978) obtained one additional interesting result with the straight letters. If subjects are asked to make similarity judgments among the letters used in this experiment, they generally view diagonal letters and straight letters as being somewhat more similar to one another than either of those classes are to curved letters (Gibson & Levin, 1975). That might result in predicting that the X-mask would be more effective in disrupting the perception of straight letters than would the 0-mask, but the results that Seery obtained indicated that this was not the case. That is, the two masks were equally effective on the straight letters, and the masking function looked much more like that obtained when the target and mask were dissimilar than when they were similar.

This result might be taken to suggest that the feature detection and encoding process is very specific and that detectors and encoders respond only to the specific information to which they are sensitive. To that extent, then, the Seery data can be taken to indicate that not only is feature detection temporally extended, but these selective masking effects would indicate that the feature detectors and encoders are quite independent of one another. In addition, the fact that there is some degree of similarity in the cognitive or interpreted encodings of two features does not mean that there must be an analogous similarity in their precognitive perceptual representations.

The Unitization of Features.   Given that our perceiver has, over some temporal interval, detected and encoded the simple features that make up a letter, the next issue concerns the way in which the simple features are fused into the higher-order feature assemblages that constitute single letters. At least three possibilities seem to exist.

The first is that once the simple features have been detected, they are transferred individually from the perceptual representation into memory, and the fusion of these features into the appropriate higher-order letters is the result of some kind of active memorial processing. A second possibility is that each perceptually encoded simple feature tends to activate a memory code for any letter that contains it, and the whole feature set is encoded into memory as the letter that receives the greatest activation. This would be similar to Morton's (1969) logogen model, but it would be assumed that a memorial encoding of each feature also would be activated.

The third possibility, and the one characterized by the pattern-unit model, is that juncture features also are detected and encoded within the perceptual system and that they act as a device that fuses the features into a higher-order perceptual pattern, with the fused pattern then being the basis of memorial contact. This particular view would suggest that the simple features that share a common juncture feature (i.e., those simple features that are physically contiguous) are fused into a higher-order perceptual unit or pattern while the information is still in the perceptual system and before any cognitive processing begins.

Under the conditions specified by this third alternative, only the pattern, and not the features from which it is composed, would be immediately available to cognitive-processing mechanisms, although if a feature were presented in isolation (i.e., it did not share a juncture with any other feature) it would be immediately available to cognitive-processing mechanisms. For example, if a V was presented, this view would suggest that there would be a cognitive representation of the V, but there could be no separate cognitive representations of the two diagonals. On the other hand, if the two diagonals of the V were separated by a small gap, which would preclude their sharing a juncture feature, they would have separate cognitive encodings. The other two views, on the other hand, would assume a memorial or cognitive encoding of the individual features, along with such an encoding for the pattern, regardless of whether the features touched. If that is the case, the featural information in a display always should be immediately available to the perceiver. The issue, then, resolves to the question of whether features that are physically contiguous to other features are as immediately available to cognitive-processing mechanisms as are features that appear in isolation.

The experimental paradigm that was used to examine this issue is one in which subjects are presented with a target item, and their job is to determine whether a subsequent display either contains the target item or is the target item. Within this general paradigm two different procedures have been used, depending on whether one is interested in the type of encoding and comparison processes that occur within the perceptual system or those that occur within the memorial system (Turvey, 1978). In the discussion that follows, this type of experimental task is termed the *standard* paradigm, with a specification of whether it involves perceptual or cognitive processing.

The task one uses when examining the nature of perceptual encoding and comparisons is to present both the target item and the to-be-searched display at the same time. For example, one might present an item on one line of a small display and another item on a second line and then ask the subjects either to determine if the second line is the same as the first or determine whether the second line contains the item on the first line as a component. What makes the perceptual comparison possible in this case is the fact that the target item and the item to which it is to be compared are represented within the perceptual system at the same time.

The alternative task used for examining memorial or cognitive encoding and comparisons is essentially the same, with the single exception being that a time delay is introduced between when the subject is informed of the target and the time when the to-be-searched display is presented. It would be assumed that under these circumstances the subject would have to process the target item into memory in order to mediate the delay, and when the subsequent display was presented it would be necessary to process it into memory as well before the comparison could be made.

The first of these two procedures was used in this experiment, and the displays presented to the subjects consisted of a single feature such as a diagonal or a curve (i.e., a semicircle) being presented on one line. On the line immediately below it were two features that were two instances of the same feature type (i.e., either two diagonals or two curves). Each feature was one quarter of an inch high, and the viewing distance was about 30 inches (e.g., the visual angle was about one half of the height of your thumb nail with your arm fully extended). When the features did not touch, the gaps between the closest points were either 8.5 mm or 4.0 mm. The subjects' task was to determine whether the second line contained the feature that was presented on the first line, and the issue was the extent to which that comparison would be delayed if the two features on the second line touched. For example, if the top line was a diagonal line, it would be assumed that if the second line contained either a V or an X the time needed to respond would be considerably longer than if the two converging diagonal features on the second line did not touch.

The results of the experiment were quite striking. If the features did not touch, the results were about the same regardless of whether the gap was 8.5 mm or only 4.0 mm, and, if the features did touch, the time to respond to a V or an X was about the same, but it took the subjects about 130 msec longer to indicate that a V or an X contained a diagonal as a component than it did to make the same response if the two features on the second line of the display did not touch or intersect. That difference represented an increase of about 20%, and it occurred even when the target and the to-be-searched display were not presented at the same time. In addition, subsequent work has suggested that it cannot be explained simply in terms of lateral inhibition. The most reasonable explanation would appear to be that by the end of perceptual processing any features that are physically contiguous to one another have been fused into a higher-order perceptual pattern and that the features themselves are no longer immediately available to the perceiver as separate entities.

The Perceptual Code

To this point, the data, as well as the theory, provide a story of perceptual processing that includes the relay of an initial but rather undifferentiated representation of a visual stimulus through the peripheral system to central-processing mechanisms. These mechanisms then detect and encode the feature information from the signal, and that stage is followed by a fusion of contiguous features into higher-order perceptual patterns or feature assemblages. The final question regarding perceptual processing, then, concerns the nature of these feature assemblages and the form in which the information is represented at that point.

Although the details of the work on this issue have been described elsewhere (Johnson, 1977), it can be noted that it is based on a technique in which subjects are cued to make a direct access of an item in a perceptual array (Sperling, 1960). The cue itself is a specific attribute of the target item (e.g., its color, its position in the display, its being a digit versus a consonant, etc.), and if the subject is able to find the target item in the perceptual array, and report it correctly, it must be the case that the target item was coded for that attribute while it was still in the perceptual system. Without its having been coded that way, the subject would never have been able to find it.

The results of these experiments have indicated that the feature assemblages seem to be coded only for the physical characteristics of the display (e.g., color, position, shape, etc.), and any attribute that would involve cognitive processing or an interpretation (e.g., what it sounds like, or whether it is a consonant or digit) does not seem to be available (D'Avello, 1976; von Wright, 1968, 1970). In general, then, although the features seemed to be encoded and then fused into the higher-order feature assemblages, the assemblages themselves do not seem to have been subject to any type of interpretive processing. In addition, as will be detailed later, there is no evidence to suggest the possibility that two or more assemblages might be integrated into any type of higher-order unit at this point.

The Transfer Mechanism and Cognitive Processing: Supporting Data

Once perceptual processing has been completed, the next step is to transform the information from that type of precognitive representation, involving unitized but uninterpreted letter assemblages, into word-level encodings that can be subjected to various types of cognitive-processing mechanisms. A more detailed schematic representation of the model is presented in Fig. 2.2 with: (1) the perceptual system being everything up through the icon; (2) the transfer mechanism consisting of the feature assigner, tester, and parser; and (3) the rest of the cognitive system being permanent and working memory, the comparator, and the response system. Although this aspect of the model has been described in more detail elsewhere (Johnson, 1977), the following summarizes its main points.

As can be noted, the icon can feed directly into the comparator, and that allows a perceiver to make comparative judgments regarding two items that are available simultaneously within the perceptual system. However, if one of the to-be-compared items is presented before the other, it already would be registered in working memory when the second item appeared. Consequently, it would be necessary to move the second item into working memory as well,

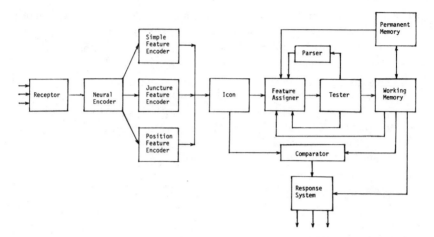

FIG. 2.2.   Detailed flow representation of the pattern-unit model. (From Johnson, 1977.)

because only in that way would the two items be encoded in the same form such that a comparison could be made. Therefore, as was noted earlier, through the simple expedient of presenting the two items either simultaneously or with a time delay we can examine how comparisons are made either immediately before or immediately after information has been transferred from the perceptual system into memory. From that comparison it is possible to gain an understanding of the way the transfer mechanism works.

In terms of the specifics of the assignment process, it is assumed that the memorial representation used for cognitive processing is a pattern-level feature set, with the features being memorial or cognitive features rather than perceptual features. Furthermore, it is assumed that the number of features is fixed, and the same number is used to encode all small displays, regardless of their size or complexity, provided that the display can be represented by a single feature set.

The major implication of this latter point is that just as the magnitude and complexity of a peripheral representation (i.e., energy characteristics) become irrelevant once central processing recodes and integrates the information into feature-level units, and the feature-level magnitude and complexity become irrelevant once they are recoded or unitized into feature assemblages, it is assumed that the magnitude and complexity of the assemblage-level representation also should become irrelevant once the information is recoded into word-level units. Quite simply, that should mean that the number of letters or syllables in a word should not influence either the process of memorial-feature assignment or the subsequent cognitive processing of that encoding, given that the display was not degraded in any way.

In addition, if one assumes that there is no particular quantitative relationship between a code and the specific characteristics of the information to be represented by that code, it seems clear that the component information cannot be available to the perceiver while it is in the coded form. That is, codes should be opaque (Johnson, 1970). If a word were to be presented, the first encoded representation available to cognitive-processing mechanisms would be the word-level code, and, if the subject's task was to identify a component letter, it would be necessary to decode that word-level code in order to determine if the array contained the specific target letter. The subject could not just return to the perceptual representation, because at that level the feature assemblages are not interpreted, and any attempts at interpretation or cognitive encoding would just result in another word-level representation. Therefore, the only source of component information would be the word-level code, and it is clear that some sort of unpacking or decoding of that representation would have to occur to make that information available.

The transfer process itself is assumed to involve: (1) the assignment of a single word-level encoding: (2) the testing of that encoding for its adequacy; and (3) the registration of that encoding within working memory. In this framework, the most basic assumption of the model is that the initial attempt to assign a cognitive encoding to a perceptual array *always* involves a single unitary and integrated representation for all of the information in the display, and any fractionation of the display into components would occur only after these initial attempts to unitize it had failed.

For example, it is likely that subjects would have available an encoding to unitize a display such as *word,* but it is unlikely that a subject would have available a unitary encoding that could be used for a display such as *sbjf.* Nevertheless, it would be assumed that in both cases the initial attempts to move the information into memory would involve trying some type of unitary encoding, with those attempts failing for a display like *sbjf.* In that situation, the subject then would have to fractionate the display and move it into memory on a letter-by-letter basis.

Once the feature assigner has provided an encoding of some type, the next step is to test that encoding to determine whether it is adequate to achieve the task presented to the subject. If a word is presented, a unitary encoding should be immediately available to the subject, and it should be adequate for almost any type of task presented to the subject. In that case, the tester should pass the item on to working memory.

On the other hand, if the array consisted of an unfamiliar string of consonants like *sbjf,* it is unlikely that there would be any useful unitary encoding available, and the tester should reject whatever encoding had been assigned. In that case, the tester would signal the feature assigner to try again, and that process would be repeated until either an adequate unitary encoding had been assigned or there had been some fixed number of failures to do so.

In the latter event, it is assumed that the tester then would shunt the perceptual representation to the parser, which would fractionate the display and feed the elements to the feature assigner in a serial element-by-element manner. Given the display is a consonant string, it would be assumed that the elements would be individual letters, and there would be every reason to suppose that an adequate unitary encoding could be assigned to each one of them. In that situation, the display would be processed into memory in a serial letter-by-letter manner, rather than as a single unit.

The third component of the model is working memory and the comparator, and the function of working memory is just to hold encoded information in a state of immediate availability, if that is required by a task. The comparator, on the other hand, is the mechanism that makes comparisons, and it is assumed that information that shares a common form of encoding is always compared if the items are either in close spatial or temporal proximity. Finally, the result of the comparison (i.e., same or different) can be relayed to the response system, but only if that is required by the task.

The Transfer Process

The model predicts that the visual information representing a word should be recoded from a set of integrated but uninterpreted feature assemblages into a word-level encoding in one step. In addition, once that has occurred, the individual letter information should not be available to the perceiver unless he or she were to decode the word-level representation into its components.

Part–Whole Relationships.   The issue of component availability has been examined in an experiment (Johnson, 1975) that used the successive-comparison (memory) paradigm described earlier. The subjects were presented with single words as displays, and in one condition they were to indicate whether the displayed word conformed to a predesignated target word (word-search task), whereas in a second condition their task was to determine whether the display contained a predesignated target letter (letter-search task). The display durations were sufficient for the subjects to see the item clearly, and the issue was the speed with which they could make their yes/no decision.

If words are perceived holistically, as the model suggests, and component information can become available only by subsequently decoding the word-level code, then subjects should be able to indicate that a display conforms to a target word faster than they can indicate that it contains a particular target letter, and the data indicate this to be the case (Johnson, 1975). Furthermore, the effect holds even when the target letter in the letter-search task always appears only in the first letter position in the word (Johnson & Marmurek, 1978), as well as when targets and foils in the word-search task differ by only one letter (Johnson, Turner-Lyga, & Pettegrew, 1979; Sloboda, 1976, 1977). For example, in this latter situation a target might be *n* or *nest,* depending on the task, and the subsequent display would be either *nest* or *best,* depending on whether it was a "yes" or "no" (foil) item. Clearly, regardless of whether the task involved letter search or word search, the subject would have to use exactly the same stimulus information to make a decision (i.e., the presence or absence of the *n*), with the result being that there would be no way of explaining the word advantage in terms of differences in stimulus information.

Although these results would indicate that the cognitive representation of a word is in terms of a single unitary encoding, if the display was an unfamiliar consonant sequence there would be no way of assigning a unitary encoding. According to the model, a display of that type would have to be moved into memory on a letter-by-letter basis, and the representation most immediately available to cognitive-processing mechanisms should be encodings of the individual letters. Given that is the case, the only way a subject could determine whether the display conformed to a target sequence would be through a set of letter-by-letter comparisons.

An experiment that examined that issue followed the standard successive-comparison paradigm (Johnson, Turner-Lyga, & Pettegrew, 1979). The displays consisted of consonant sequences that contained either three or four letters, and in one condition the subjects were to determine if it conformed to a predesignated target sequence, whereas in another they were to determine if the sequence started with a predesignated target letter. The results indicated that, contrary to what was obtained with words, the subjects were faster in the letter-search task, and when they had to respond to the whole sequence their reaction time was influenced by the length of the sequence. It does appear, then, that although the cognitive representation of a word is unitary, such is not the case for the cognitive encoding of a consonant sequence.

The next issue concerns when the word-level unitization occurs, and the model predicts that the transfer process does the unitization. If that is the case, then the feature assemblages should not be unitized into a higher-order unit at the end of perceptual processing, but such a unitization should have occurred by the time the information is first registered and available within the cognitive system in working memory. Although the foregoing experiments indicate the latter to be the case, the issue of higher-order unitization within the perceptual system remains to be considered.

If the unitization does occur at the interface between the two systems, then the unit of representation for a word should be at the letter level in the perceptual system and at the word level in the cognitive system. In this regard, an experiment by Marmurek (1977) is particularly interesting. He used the standard experimental paradigm described earlier and compared performance in the word-search task to that in the letter-search task using both a simultaneous (perceptual comparison) and a successive (memory comparison) presentation of the target and display.

Again, the displays were single words, and the predesignated target item was either the first letter of the word or the word itself. In addition, the subjects were instructed that they were to look at the top line of a display and determine whether the bottom line either was the same as the top line or contained the letter that was on the top line. In the latter case, the letter on the top line always appeared immediately above the first letter of the word on the second line (i.e., immediately above the letter to which it was to be compared). In addition, the subjects were told that for half of the experimental session the two lines would appear simultaneously, whereas for the other half of the session the first line would appear and then go off for a 3 sec delay before the bottom line appeared.

If letters are the unit of representation within the perceptual system, then a condition involving a simultaneous presentation of the target item and to-be-searched display (i.e., a perceptual-comparison condition) should show faster reactions in the letter-search task than in the word-search task. That is, the word-level decision could be made only after all the corresponding letters on the two lines had been compared to one another, whereas only a single comparison would be needed in the letter-search task. Just the reverse should be obtained if a successive-comparison task is used. That comparison could occur only after the display information had been moved into working memory, and at that point it would have been unitized into a word-level representation. Therefore, subjects should be able to make unitary word-level comparisons immediately, but a component-level decision could be made only after the word-level code had been decoded.

Marmurek's (1977) results were quite unambiguous. If the presentation of the target and display was successive, the subjects were able to make word-level decisions faster than component-level decisions, but that effect was completely reversed if the two items were presented simultaneously. In addition, if the subjects were processing the words in a letter-by-letter manner in the simultaneous comparison, in the event of a foil or "no" item the reaction time should be an increasing function of the number of overlapping letters, and that effect was obtained. However, what highlights that point is the fact that once the feature assemblages that correspond to the letters have been recoded at the word level there no longer would be any basis for that type of point-to-point similarity, and Marmurek's data indicate that the similarity effect was severely reduced when the task involved a successive comparison (albeit, not eliminated). In general, then, the data seem quite consistent with the idea that words are represented as sets of integrated feature assemblages within the perceptual system, with the assemblage being the unit of comparison, whereas at the postperceptual cognitive level the word is the unit of comparison, with the assemblage or letter encodings no longer being immediately available.

Length-Difficulty Relationship.   Another approach to this same issue has been to examine the effect of word length on performance in the word-search task of the basic experimental paradigm. If the word-level representation does not reflect the quantitative characteristics of the information it represents, which is the most basic assumption underlying the entire concept of unitization, then there would be no reason to expect any relationship between a word's length and reaction time. The results of a variety of experiments have supported this prediction. Even when the difference in length is as great as three letters versus eight letters, there appears to be no effect of word length on either the time to identify a target or the time to reject a foil display (Johnson, 1977).

Terry, LaBerge, and Samuels (1976) also found no effect of word length on cognitive processing, but they used a slightly different task. In their experiment the subjects were given a word class as the target (e.g., animal names), and their task was to determine whether each displayed word was a member of the class. They included a rather large variation in length (i.e., from three to twelve letters), but it had no effect on the time needed to make the semantic decision.

This point can be carried a step further by noting that any small pattern that can be assigned a single unitary encoding should be treated no differently than any other such pattern. This would imply, for example, that a single letter and a word should be processed equally fast, and a number of experiments, beginning with Cattell's (1886) early work, have demonstrated that to be the case (Johnson, 1975; Marmurek, 1977)[1]

The fact that subjects seem able to respond to letters in isolation with the same facility as they respond to words would indicate that the very slow response when the target is a letter within a word stems from the word context, and is not just because letters might be processed more slowly than words. In addition, however, it also has been noted that any context of other letters slows the response, even when they do not constitute a word (Sloboda, 1976), but that is as it should be. The model would predict that the initial attempts to encode any multiletter array into memory would be by assigning a single unitary code, and only after several unsuccessful attempts would there be any parsing or fractionation of the display. Those initial unsuccessful attempts to assign a unitary encoding to a consonant sequence would delay the subsequent encoding of any individual letter, as compared to encoding that same letter when it was presented in isolation.

A possible question that might be raised regarding these experiments concerns the extent to which the technique is sufficiently sensitive to detect any length effects. One way this issue has been examined was by comparing the impact of word length on reaction time in the standard paradigm to the effect of length when the displays consist of a sequence of consonants. In the latter case it would be assumed that there would be no unitary encoding available, and the only way

---

[1]Massaro and Klitzke (1977) have recently reported that the reaction to words in a situation like this can be slowed if the targets and foils are made very similar to one another, but it is difficult to interpret the experiment because they did not include any directly comparable variation in the similarity of single letters.

the sequence could be moved into memory would be on a letter-by-letter basis. Given that is the case, it would be expected that there would be a length effect for that type of display.

The results of the experiment (Johnson, Turner-Lyga, & Pettegrew, 1979) again indicated no length effect on reaction time if the display was pronounceable, regardless of whether it was a meaningful word, but if the display was an unpronounceable string of consonants there was a reaction-time difference, even when the length difference was as small as one letter (i.e., three versus four). Clearly, the failure to obtain a length effect with words cannot be attributed simply to some limitation of the experimental paradigm.

As with the issue of part–whole relationships in word perception, the question of whether the decision is based on a perceptual or a memorial comparison also is an important consideration with regard to the effect of length. As has been noted, once the perceptual array has been integrated into a cognitive representation within working memory, the specific nature and magnitude of the component information should be irrelevant, and the foregoing data obtained using the successive-comparison task indicate that to be the case. However, if the perceptual representation is in terms of a set of feature assemblages conforming to the individual letters, then a simultaneous-comparison (perceptual) task should show a length effect because the word-level decision can be made only by matching the corresponding letters in the two items.

Eichelman (1970) did use such a task, and he found that indeed there was a length effect for words under those circumstances. In addition, Marmurek (1977) demonstrated that although words and single letters in isolation could be compared with their respective targets with equal speed in a successive-comparison (memorial) task, in a simultaneous-comparison (perceptual) task there was a marked advantage for the single letters. Again, the data seem to indicate that the perceptual representations of the letters in a word are not integrated into higher-order word units, whereas that integration has occurred once the information has been transferred into working memory.

Although these comparisons between the outcomes of experiments using the simultaneous-comparison and the successive-comparison tasks suggest that the unitization of the word does occur during the transfer process, a study described by Allport (1977) suggests that the specific point of unitization may be when the information is read from the perceptual system, rather than when it is registered in the cognitive-memorial system. In an earlier study that employed a masking paradigm, Sperling (1963) demonstrated that if a visual array consists of a string of consonants, the longer the interval between the target and mask the more consonants the subjects seem able to report. In particular, the subjects were able to report one additional letter with each increase of about 10 to 20 msec in the interval.

Allport (1977) conducted a very similar experiment, only the display "items" were short words rather than consonants, and his data indicated that one new word was reported with each increase of 10 to 20 msec in the interval. This would seem to indicate that the information was read from the perceptual representation in word-level units and that the unitization occurred during that readout process. It also would seem to imply that the readout mechanism itself was sensitive to orthographic regularity, although that might not be the case. For example, the readout mechanism could be sensitive to meaning, which would mean that orthographically regular nonwords would be processed on a letter-by-letter basis.

The Decoding of Word-Level Representation.   The next source of information regarding the nature of word-level units and the unitization process involves a set of experiments in which subjects were asked to respond to components of a visual display. The issues at stake are both whether such information is immediately available to a perceiver and, if it is not immediately available, what are the steps that must be taken to make it available, and what is the form of the information when it then becomes available?

In terms of the model, the prediction is that if a display can be unitized into a word-level representation, then the components are not immediately available to cognitive processors, whereas if the display could not be unitized the components would be immediately available. Previously described data support both those points. However, if word-level representations need to be decoded in order to obtain component-level information, the next question would concern the rule or system whereby the decoding took place.

One possibility is that words are always decoded into letter elements, and if subjects were to identify a syllable within a word, they would then have to integrate the obtained letter codes within memory. An alternative view would be that in decoding a word subjects could cycle down through a hierarchy of units until they obtained the needed component. Both of these views would predict that subjects would be faster in a word-search task than in one involving components, but the first view would predict that subjects could find a target letter within a word faster than a target syllable, whereas the other view would predict the reverse.

A third position would be that once the word is encoded into working memory the subjects are flexible, and cognitive mechanisms can decode it immediately into whatever elements or components the task requires. Within this view, finding a component should take longer than finding the whole word, but whether the component was a letter or a syllable should not make any difference.

Turner (1978) has reported a study that examined this issue. Her displays consisted of compound words (e.g., *cupcake* or *lipstick*), and depending on the condition, the predesignated target for which subjects were to search was either the compound word, the first syllable of the compound word (which was always a three- or four-letter word), or the first letter of the compound word. Her results indicated that searching for a component was slower than searching for the compound word, but whether the component was a letter or a syllable seemed to make little difference. The results would suggest, then, that subjects have some flexibility regarding the components into which they decode a word-level code.

Once a word-level code has been decoded it would be assumed that all the component information would be immediately available to the subject. If a display consisted of *cake* it would be assumed that there would be encodings of *c, a, k,* and *e* available in working memory immediately after the decoding was complete, and if subjects were to search for a target letter they would simply scan the available letter set. Therefore, every letter would be immediately available in working memory before the decision was made, and not only should the target item influence subjects' behavior, but every other letter could do so as well.

This issue was first examined in an experiment by Johnson and Marmurek (1978) in which subjects were to determine whether a displayed word began with a predesignated target letter. In the event the display did not start with the target letter (i.e., the appropriate response was "no"), the major question in the experiment was whether the reaction time would be slowed if the target letter did appear in some other position within the word. That confusion effect should occur if all the letters are immediately available in working memory before subjects make their comparisons and decisions.

The results of the experiment indicated that the subjects were slower in responding "no" when the target letter appeared in a noninitial position than when it did not, but which noninitial position was unimportant. If the target was *b,* they could reject *come* faster than *comb* or *able,* but they were equally slow on the latter two. In addition, the effect was not attributable to a general strategy to go slow when there was a chance of being confused because it only occurred on the specific items that contained the target in noninitial positions. Therefore, it did appear that when subjects were in a position to make a decision regarding a component letter within a word all of the letters were immediately available to them in working memory.

An interesting implication of both the model and this experimental outcome is that when subjects look for a component letter within a word they do not do so by going back to the stimulus information in the environment and directly encoding the letters. According to the model, if they went back to the stimulus, or the perceptual representation of the stimulus, and started to reprocess it, all that would happen is that once again it would be encoded at the word level. That would just begin an endless cycle, and the subjects would never get to the component information. Therefore, the model would assume that if subjects are to determine whether *cake* contains a *c* the only source of information they have for making the decision is an encoding created during the process of decoding *cake* within memory, and there never would be any direct encoding of the environmental stimulus information with which it was correlated.

Although the Johnson and Marmurek (1978) data are quite consistent with that view, those data can be highlighted by noting that the prediction would be very different if the display consisted of a string of consonants such as *cfjq*. If that were the case, no unitary encoding could be assigned, and the parsing mechanism would fractionate the array into letter components. The letters then would be encoded into working memory individually in a serial manner, and if the subjects' task was to determine whether the display contained a *c* in the first position, the decision could be made the moment the first letter reached working memory. However, that also would mean that the decision would be made before the cognitive encoding of any other letter had been established, and under those circumstances the presence of the target letter in a noninitial position could have no influence on the subject. Therefore, if the subjects were to determine if a target letter *b* appeared in the first position of an array, it would take them longer to reject *comb* than *come,* but *cgmb* and *cgme* should be rejected equally fast, and the results of a recently completed experiment indicate that to be the case.

As a set, these experiments seem to indicate that once a word-level code has been established, subjects have the option of decoding it into any relevant component. However, once it is decoded, all the elements are immediately and simultaneously available in working memory. On the other hand, if the visual array does not constitute a word, then the components would be moved into working memory letter-by-letter, and no decoding of higher-order codes would be necessary. In addition, there would be times when some but not all of the letters would be available in working memory. Finally, and what may be the most interesting point, the data suggest that subjects may not be able to "see" the letters directly within a word if the word can be encoded into memory in a unitary manner. That is, what we experience when we note the letters within a word may be the product of an inference-like process that results from the decoding of the word-level code, rather than the direct encoding of stimulus information in the environment. The Theois and Muise (1977) model implies a similar type of indirect access to component information.

Semantic Processing During Reading

The last issue to be considered is the extent to which the word-level encodings examined in the foregoing experiments have any semantic component. Obviously, at some point in processing, the word code must have a semantic interpretation, but whether that information is available before component information is available may be open to question.

One of the unstated assumptions underlying this work is that the type of reflexive or automatic processing described by LaBerge (1973) and LaBerge and Samuels (1974) is characteristic of everything up through the word-level representation, with the added point that none of the products of the automatic preword-level processing steps would be immediately available to the perceiver. The data have been rather consistent with this view, but the question now being asked is whether that automatic processing also includes the access to a semantic representation.

The procedure in these experiments (Johnson, 1979) involved asking subjects to read short stories of about 70 words, and they were to search for either a word that began with a particular letter (i.e., letter-search condition) or for a word that belonged to a particular semantic category (e.g., an animal name). The target items could appear either toward the beginning, middle, or end of the stories, and in the letter-search condition the target item was the only instance of that letter within the story. The subjects were told to read the story for comprehension, but when they found the target they were to say "yes," state the word, and then finish reading the story. After reading 24 such stories, 12 involving each type of target, they were given a comprehension test that consisted of specific questions regarding the content of all the stories.

The results indicated that the type of target for which the subjects were searching (i.e., letter or semantic category) had no effect on either the error rate during search or the comprehension score, but the subjects were much slower in their reading when the target was the first letter of a word than when it was a semantic category. This was true for the time needed to find the target and the time needed to finish reading the story, as well as the time needed to determine that the target had not appeared in the story in the case of a foil item.

The fact that subjects can ascertain the meaning of a word faster than they can determine its first letter again suggests that component information becomes available only very late in processing and that there does not seem to be any specific cognitive encoding of the component information prior to accessing the meaning of a word. However, this does not necessarily mean that the meaning is accessed before the subject begins to access the component information. It could be the case that processing is automatic only up to some nonsemantic word-level (i.e., lexical) encoding, but the time needed to decode the word code into components is greater than the time needed to access a semantic interpretation. On the other hand, if processing is automatic up through a semantic encoding, then semantic information should be as available as any other word-level information. This would mean that subjects should be as fast as determining that a displayed word conforms to a predesignated semantic class as they are at determining that it matches a specific predesignated word, provided, of course, that the semantic specification was completely unambiguous.

That issue also was examined by using the story task just described, and the subjects were to search for either a specific word or a word that was an instance of a prespecified semantic category. The results indicated no effect of target type on either errors or reading time, and it appeared that the subjects could make the two word-level decisions with equal ease. When that effect is coupled with the slow reading time obtained when subjects search for a target letter, the data seem to suggest that word processing is more or less reflexive or automatic up through a representation of the word that includes at least some semantic specification.

SUMMARY AND CONCLUSIONS

The story presented in this chapter has concerned the encoding and unitization of visual information during the process of word perception, and the script that it has followed was provided by the pattern-unit model. In addition, the focus or theme of the presentation has involved questions centering on the nature of the perceptual elements, the locus and nature of the various unitization processes, and the availability of the component information once the components have been integrated or unitized into higher-level units. Finally, the conclusion of the story was not only a description of the processing and unitization events that occur during word perception, but a note was made that it may be necessary to reinterpret some of the traditional distinctions between theories of word perception.

Documentations of the Model

In terms of details, the story begins with an undifferentiated visual signal being relayed from the retina to central-processing mechanisms by way of the optic pathways. The data taken to support the idea that the signal is undifferentiated involve the fact that a second or masking stimulus will interfere with a peripheral encoding of a target stimulus, regardless of the physical similarity between the target and mask. That is, the specific figural characteristics of the interfering mask appear to be irrelevant.

The next step is the central processing of the perceptual representation, and it is assumed to begin with a temporally extended process of feature detection and encoding. In terms of the empirical support for this point, the results of masking studies also can be used here. That is, as a masking stimulus is delayed longer and longer after the target stimulus has been presented, there is an increase in the subjects' accuracy in reporting the target, and the importance of having featural overlap or similarity between the target and mask seems to increase. If the two stimuli are presented close together in time, the second stimulus will mask the first, even if they are quite dissimilar, but if the presentations of the two stimuli are separated in time, there must be a great deal of physical similarity in order to obtain any masking effect.

Simple features (i.e., diagonals, curves, and straight lines) are assumed to be unitized as the result of juncture features (i.e., encodings of the contiguities and intersections of simple features). The juncture features are assumed to fuse any touching or intersecting simple features into higher-order patterns or feature assemblages, and the supporting data for that point are the fact that subjects can react more rapidly to the presence of a feature, when two are presented, if there is a small gap between them than when the two features are touching or intersecting. In the latter case they would share a juncture feature, and that would fuse them into a higher-order perceptual pattern, with the features themselves no longer being immediately available for processing.

At this point in processing, the representation of a word would be in terms of a set of feature assemblages conforming to the letters within the word, but they would be neither interpreted nor integrated into any higher-order letter-cluster or word-level unit. This latter unitization would occur only when the perceptual representations of the feature assemblages were recoded into a cognitive encoding, and at that point the result would be a word-level representation, without any intervening subword letter-cluster units.

The data supporting this part of the model came from experiments that allowed us to examine encoding and comparison processes that occur only within the perceptual system and compare them to those analogous processes that occur only after information has been moved into the cognitive-memorial system. The fact that features are integrated into assemblages within the perceptual system is supported by the foregoing data, and the fact that the assemblages are uninterpreted at this point in processing is indicated by the fact that subjects cannot make even very gross cognitive distinctions such as between letters and digits. In addition, the individual letter assemblages seem to be more immediately available for comparison purposes than is a word, and the time needed to make word comparisons is an increasing function of the number of letters in the display. This latter point would suggest that the word-level decision in this situation might be made by way of a serial comparison of the individual assemblages.

If the experimental task allows a comparison only within the cognitive-memorial system, the situation is somewhat different. For example, the fact that there can be acoustic and associative confusions between letters indicates that they must be interpreted, at least along those two dimensions. In addition, subjects can compare two words much more rapidly than they can compare a letter to a letter within a word, and the word-to-word comparisons seem to be completely uninfluenced by the number of letters within the words. Finally, subjects seem able to compare a word to a semantic specification of a word with the same ease as they make the word-to-word comparison. Clearly, then, the data indicate that in a perceptual encoding and comparison task the uninterpreted letter assemblages are the most immediately available units for processing, whereas an interpreted representation at the word level seems to be the most immediately available unit in a cognitive-memorial task, and that is quite consistent with the description provided by the pattern-unit model.

Conclusion

This story of ever-increasing detail and unitization during word perception adds further support to the idea that we must reinterpret the traditional distinction between letter-by-letter models and whole-word models of word perception. A logical consideration of the type of discriminations that average readers make as they are reading, as well as the foregoing data, indicates that feature and letter information must be available to them in some form. Given that is the case, it would seem that a more meaningful way to categorize a theoretical position would be to evaluate the form in which it expects the information to be encoded at the different levels of representation and the extent to which those encodings are assumed to be immediately available to the perceiver.

Viewing the issue in these terms, the discussion provided in this chapter would suggest that under normal conditions of word processing (i.e., the displays are not degraded in any way), the encoding cycles within the perceptual system are completely automatic, and the products of those encodings are neither interpreted nor in a form that is usable for making cognitive-level decisions. Furthermore, the encoding of the perceptual array into a cognitive word-level representation also appears to be automatic, but the data indicate that the product of that encoding step is both interpreted, including a semantic representation, and available for making cognitive decisions. Clearly, the transition from the uninterpreted perceptual encoding to the next higher encoding at the word level involves a qualitative change in terms of the form of the representation, and almost any model that fits into the traditional category of letter-by-letter processing would have some difficulty in dealing with that phenomenon.

ACKNOWLEDGMENTS

In part, the work reported in this paper was supported by a grant from the Graduate School of The Ohio State University. In addition, part of this work was done while the author was a Visiting Professor at the University of California at Berkeley.

REFERENCES

Adams, M. J. Models of word recognition. *Cognitive Psychology,* 1979, *11,* 133–176.

Allport, D. A. On knowing the meaning of words we are unable to report: The effects of visual masking. In S. Dornic (Ed.), *Attention and performance VI.* Hillsdale, N.J.: Lawrence Erlbaum Associates, 1977.

Averbach, E., & Coriell, A. S. Short-term memory in vision. *Bell System Technical Journal,* 1961, *40,* 308–328.

Biederman, I. Perceiving real-world scenes. *Science,* 1972, *177,* 77–80.

Bjork, E. L., & Murray, J. T. On the nature of input channels in visual processing. *Psychological Review,* 1977, *84,* 472–484.

Bower, G. H., Black, J. B., & Turner, T. J. Scripts in memory for text. *Cognitive Psychology,* 1979, *11,* 177–220.

Bransford, J. D., & Franks, J. J. The abstraction of linguistic ideas. *Cognitive Psychology,* 1971, *2,* 331–350.

Cattell, J. M. The time taken up by cerebral operations. *Mind,* 1886, *11,* 377–392.

Chambers, S. M., & Forster, K. I. Evidence for lexical access in a simultaneous matching task. *Memory & Cognition,* 1975, *3,* 549–559.

Chomsky, N., & Halle, M. *The sound pattern of English.* New York: Harper & Row, 1968.

Clark, H. H. Inferences in comprehension. In D. LaBerge & S. J. Samuels (Eds.), *Basic processes in reading: Perception and comprehension.* Hillsdale, N.J.: Lawrence Erlbaum Associates, 1977.

D'Avello, D. *Letter feature selection from iconic memory.* Unpublished Master's thesis, The Ohio State University, 1976.

Dustman, R. E., & Beck, E. C. Phase of alpha brain waves, reaction time and visually evoked potentials. *Electroencephalographic Clinical Neurophysiology,* 1965, *18,* 433–440.

Eichelman, W. H. Familiarity effects in the simultaneous matching task. *Journal of Experimental Psychology,* 1970, *86,* 275–282.

Estes, W. K. Interactions of signals and background variables in visual processing. *Perception & Psychophysics,* 1972, *12,* 278–286.

Estes, W. K. On the interaction of perception and memory in reading. In D. LaBerge & S. Samuels (Eds.), *Basic processes in reading: Perception and comprehension.* Hillsdale, N.J.: Lawrence Erlbaum Associates, 1977.

Gibson, E. J. Perceptual learning and the theory of word perception. *Cognitive Psychology,* 1971, *2,* 351–368.

Gibson, E. J., & Levin, H. *The psychology of reading.* Cambridge, Mass.: MIT Press, 1975.

Gough, P. B. One second of reading. In J. F. Kavanagh & I. G. Mattingly (Eds.), *Language by ear and by eye.* Cambridge, Mass.: MIT Press, 1972.

Hellige, J. B., Walsh, D. A., Lawrence, V. W., & Prasse, M. Figural relationship effects and mechanisms of visual masking. *Journal of Experimental Psychology: Human Perception and Performance,* 1979, *5,* 88–100.

Huey, E. B. *The psychology and pedagogy of reading.* Cambridge, Mass.: MIT Press, 1968.

Jackson, M. D., & McClelland, J. L. Sensory and cognitive determinants of reading speed. *Journal of Verbal Learning and Verbal Behavior,* 1975, *14,* 565–574.

Johnson, N. F. The role of chunking and organization in the process of recall. In G. Bower (Ed.), *The psychology of learning and motivation* (Vol. 4). New York: Academic Press, 1970.

Johnson, N. F. On the function of letters in word identification: Some data and a preliminary model. *Journal of Verbal Learning and Verbal Behavior,* 1975, *14,* 17–29.

Johnson, N. F. A pattern-unit model of word identification. In D. LaBerge & S. J. Samuels (Eds.), *Basic processes in reading: Perception and comprehension.* Hillsdale, N.J.: Lawrence Erlbaum Associates, 1977.

Johnson, N. F. The role of letters in word identification: A test of the pattern-unit model. *Memory & Cognition,* 1979, *7,* 496–504.

Johnson, N. F., & Marmurek, H. H. C. Identification of words and letters within words. *American Journal of Psychology,* 1978, *91,* 401–415.

Johnson, N. F., Turner-Lyga, M., & Pettegrew, B. S. *Part–whole relationships in the processing of small visual arrays.* Unpublished manuscript, The Ohio State University, 1979.

Kahneman, D. Method, findings, and theory in studies of visual masking. *Psychological Bulletin,* 1968, *70,* 404–426.

Kolers, P. Some psychological aspects of pattern recognition. In P. Kohlers & M. Eden (Eds.), *Recognizing patterns.* Cambridge, Mass.: MIT Press, 1968.

Krueger, L. E. Familiarity effects in visual information processing. *Psychological Bulletin,* 1975, *82,* 949–974.

LaBerge, D. Attention and the measurement of perceptual learning. *Memory & Cognition,* 1973, *1,* 268–276.

LaBerge, D. Perceptual learning and attention. In W. K. Estes (Ed.), *Handbook of learning and cognitive processes* (Vol. 4). Hillsdale, N.J.: Lawrence Erlbaum Associates, 1976.

LaBerge, D., & Samuels, S. J. Toward a theory of automatic information processing in reading. *Cognitive Psychology,* 1974, *6,* 293–323.

Marmurek, H. H. C. Processing letters in words at different levels. *Memory & Cognition,* 1977, *5,* 67–72.

Massaro, D. W. Primary and secondary recognition in reading. In D. W. Massaro (Ed.), *Understanding language: An information processing analysis of speech perception, reading, and psycholinguistics.* New York: Academic Press, 1975.

Massaro, D. W., & Klitzke, D. Letters are functional in word identification. *Memory & Cognition,* 1977, *5,* 292-298.

McClelland, J. L. Preliminary letter identification in the perception of words and nonwords. *Journal of Experimental Psychology: Human Perception and Performance,* 1976, *2,* 80-91.

Morton, J. Interaction of information in word recognition. *Psychological Review,* 1969, *76,* 165-178.

Palmer, S. E. Hierarchical structure in perceptual representation. *Cognitive Psychology,* 1977, *9,* 441-474.

Pillsbury, W. B. A study in apperception. *American Journal of Psychology,* 1897, *8,* 315-393.

Rumelhart, D. E. Toward an interactive model of reading. In S. Dornic (Ed.), *Attention and performance VI.* Hillsdale, N.J.: Lawrence Erlbaum Associates, 1977.

Seery, A. K. *The role of interstimulus interval on similarity effects in backward masking.* Unpublished Master's thesis, The Ohio State University, 1978.

Sloboda, J. A. Decision times for word and letter search: A wholistic word identification model examined. *Journal of Verbal Learning and Verbal Behavior,* 1976, *15,* 93-101.

Sloboda, J. A. The locus of the word-priority effect in a target-detection task. *Memory & Cognition,* 1977, *5,* 371-376.

Smith, F. *Understanding reading.* New York: Holt, Rinehart & Winston, 1971.

Spencer, T. Some effects of different masking stimuli on iconic storage. *Journal of Experimental Psychology,* 1969, *81,* 132-140.

Sperling, G. The information available in brief visual presentations. *Psychological Monographs,* 1960, *74*(Whole No. 498).

Sperling, G. A model for visual memory tasks. *Human Factors,* 1963, *5,* 19-31.

Spoehr, K. T., & Smith, E. E. The role of syllables in perceptual processing. *Cognitive Psychology,* 1973, *5,* 71-89.

Terry, P., Samuels, S. J., & LaBerge, D. The effects of letter degradation and letter spacing on word recognition. *Journal of Verbal Learning and Verbal Behavior,* 1976, *15,* 577-585.

Theois, J., & Muise, J. G. The word identification process in reading. In N. Castellan & D. Pisoni (Eds.), *Cognitive theory* (Vol. 2). Hillsdale, N.J.: Lawrence Erlbaum Associates, 1977.

Townsend, J. T., Taylor, S. G., & Brown, D. R. Lateral masking for letters with unlimited viewing time. *Perception & Psychophysics,* 1971, *10,* 375-378.

Turner, M. *On the process of letter and word identification within whole word presentation.* Unpublished Master's thesis, The Ohio State University, 1978.

Turvey, M. T. On peripheral and central processes in vision: Inferences from an information-processing analysis of masking with patterned stimuli. *Psychological Review,* 1973, *80,* 1-53.

Turvey, M. T. Visual processing in short-term memory. In W. K. Estes (Ed.), *Handbook of learning and cognitive processes* (Vol. 5). Hillsdale, N.J.: Lawrence Erlbaum Associates, 1978.

von Wright, J. M. Selection in immediate memory. *Quarterly Journal of Experimental Psychology,* 1968, *20,* 62-68.

von Wright, J. M. On selection in visual immediate memory. *Acta Psychologica,* 1970, *33,* 280-292.

3 Understanding Word Perception: Clues from Studying the Word-Superiority Effect

James C. Johnston
Bell Laboratories
Murray Hill, New Jersey

Almost 100 years ago, Cattell (1886) discovered that letters are perceived more accurately when they appear in words than when they appear in other contexts. This word-superiority effect (WSE) has been actively investigated, with only a few lapses in interest, ever since. The WSE has thus been studied for about as long as psychology has been a distinct discipline. It is reasonable to ask why, at this late date, so many researchers, including myself, still find this phenomenon so intriguing. The answer is that the WSE has continued to defy explanation by any theory of how word perception works. The more we know about the WSE, the less adequate any simple explanation seems to be. Study of the WSE thus continues to lead us to more complex and, we hope, more revealing theories of how people perceive printed words.

This chapter is divided into seven sections that attempt to: (1) describe the WSE and how it is measured; (2) divide up the universe of theories about the WSE into three types; (3) present evidence against Type 1 (more features) theories; (4) present evidence against Type 2 (redundancy) theories; (5) discuss the major problem faced by Type 3 (retention) theories; (6) present a new retention theory, which avoids this problem; and (7) present some experimental evidence that supports the new retention theory. Several recent reviews of the voluminous WSE literature are available (Baron, 1978; Krueger, 1975; Smith & Spoehr, 1974), and I do not attempt to provide another here. This chapter advocates a particular theoretical point of view, and the discussion leans heavily on evidence that has been influential in the development of that point of view (much of it from my own experiments and those of my close colleagues).

MEASURING THE WORD-SUPERIORITY EFFECT

The label word-superiority effect (WSE) has been applied to various demonstrations showing that when a letter appears in a word it is perceived better, but "better than what?" is a vexing question. Perception of a letter in a word needs to be compared to perception of a letter in some nonword context, yet it is virtually impossible to prove that any particular nonword context provides a truly "neutral" baseline for comparison. Fortunately, the WSE has been found using a variety of control conditions: a letter in a string of unrelated letters, a letter alone, and a letter in a string of "dummy" nonletter characters. As we see later, the ease of explaining the WSE depends somewhat on which kind of context is being compared to a word context.[1]

A further choice confronts the experimenter in deciding how to measure the "goodness of perception" of letters. Perhaps the most fundamental choice is whether to measure the time to process a letter (in which case a WSE means faster perception of a letter in a word) or the accuracy of processing a letter (in which case a WSE means more accurate perception of a letter in a word). The measurement problems, as well as the results, with each type of method differ. I choose, somewhat arbitrarily, to deal here solely with the WSE based on accuracy measurement. Even with this restriction, there are more than enough complexities left to occupy us.

Three basic methods for measuring perceptual accuracy have been used to obtain a WSE. These are: (1) whole report of all letters displayed; (2) partial report, usually of only one of the displayed letters; and (3) forced choice between two alternative letters, one of which appeared in the display.

The latter two methods present the experimenter with the option of specifying the critical letter position and/or the alternative choice letters either before exposure of the target string or after. Considerable evidence has accumulated showing that when choice alternatives or a critical letter position are specified before target exposure, the WSE is weak or nonexistent (e.g., Bjork & Estes, 1973; Holender, 1979; Johnston, in press; Johnston & McClelland, 1974; Thompson & Massaro, 1973; however, see also Purcell, Stanovich, & Spector, 1978). Later I attempt a theoretically motivated explanation of why advance information undermines the WSE. For now, we restrict our attention to methods that do not involve advance information and that produce a healthy WSE. With this important proviso, there is good reason to believe that the remaining dif-

---

[1]In addition to "neutral" nonword contexts, other nonword contexts have been studied, which are not intended to be neutral. Of particular interest are pseudoword contexts designed to mimic the orthographic structure/pronounceability of real-word contexts. Study of perceptual performance with pseudowords is useful in attempting to determine what portion of the WSE depends on orthographic string properties rather than lexical string properties. The section entitled "A New Type 3 (Retention) Theory" discusses how pseudoword performance can be treated in a manner compatible with the present theoretical approach.

TABLE 3.1
Results from a Typical Demonstration of the Word-Superiority Effect[a]

	Sample Target	Mask	Sample Choices		Proportion Correct Forced Choices
Word	COIN	⊠ ⊠ ⊠ ⊠	COIN	JOIN	.845
Unrelated letters	CPDT	⊠ ⊠ ⊠ ⊠	CPDT	JPDT	.686
Single letter	C	⊠ ⊠ ⊠ ⊠	C___	J___	.710

[a] From Johnston (1978).

ferences among measurement techniques are less important. For instance, McClelland and Johnston (1977) and Johnston (1978) have compared whole-report performance with forced-choice performance within the same experiments and found that, corrected for guessing, performance levels were nearly the same.

Before leaving the question of how to measure the WSE, a more concrete account of a representative WSE experiment (Johnston, 1978) should be useful to the reader not already familiar with the area. What we want to do is compare the perceptibility of a letter in a word, a letter in a string of unrelated letters, and a letter alone (see Table 3.1). So we present subjects on different trials (blocked according to type) with the same critical letters in different contexts (e.g., a C in COIN, in CPDT, and alone in the first-letter position). In each case we present the target letter or letters for a very short duration (usually about 30 msec), followed by a patterned mask to obliterate any afterimage. In order to test how well the target letter C was seen, we then present subjects with a choice between two alternatives—what they saw and another alternative in which the C is replaced with, for instance, a J. Note that the alternative letter always makes another word in the word context (e.g., JOIN), so there is no way to do better than chance without having processed the C itself. The right-hand column in Table 3.1 shows that people are quite a bit better at perceiving a letter in a word than at perceiving a letter in a string of unrelated letters, or even a letter alone. This result is found in spite of the fact that accurate performance on single-letter trials requires processing only one letter, whereas accurate performance on word trials requires processing all four letters (position of the letter to be tested is unknown until after display termination).

THEORIES OF THE
WORD-SUPERIORITY EFFECT

In this section, a way of classifying major types of theories of the WSE is presented. The classification scheme is designed to group together theories whose fate depends on the same lines of evidence. The basic division of theories into types (following Johnston, 1978) is shown in Fig. 3.1.

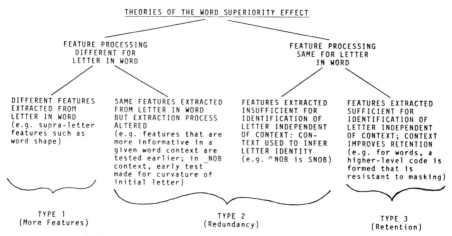

FIG. 3.1.   Major types of theories of the word-superiority effect.

At the top of the diagram, we first divide the set of all theories of the WSE according to whether or not the WSE is attributed to different processing of visual features of a letter when the letter is in a word. Where visual feature processing in words is hypothesized to be different (on the major left branch) this difference can be further subdivided into the extraction of different features (e.g., word-shape features) or an altered extraction process for the same features. An example of a theory supposing an altered extraction process is Wheeler's (1970) proposal that word context is used to rearrange the sequence of testing for letter features; tests that will decide between contextually permitted letters are performed earlier. For instance, if the last three letters in a four-letter word are *NOB* we need only test the first letter to see if it is curved—if so, the letter is *S* (in *SNOB*), if not it is *K* (in *KNOB*).

Theories assuming that feature processing is not affected when a letter is in a word lie on the right branch of Fig. 3.1. These theories can be subdivided depending on whether or not it is assumed that enough feature information is extracted from each letter to identify it independently of context. If not, then we have the class of theories for which word context supplies additional information to help identify a letter (e.g., if it is only known that the initial letter has a curve at the top, knowing that the context is _*NOB* allows the inference that the first letter is *S*). The final (and, in a sense, residual) class of theories supposes that letter features are extracted independently of word context and that enough features are extracted to identify a letter independently of context. When errors are made, they must, therefore, be due to a failure to *retain* adequately the feature information extracted, and the WSE must be attributed to *better retention* of feature information from a letter in a word. For example, the WSE could be due to better retention of word codes than of letter codes. This classification of WSE theories is intended to be exhaustive (every theory should belong to at least one class), but the classes are not mutually exclusive (a theory can rely on multiple sources of superiority for a letter in a word; see Johnston, 1978).

Before moving on to deal with evidence that bears on the theories, it is useful to collapse the middle two of the four classes of theories displayed from left to right in Fig. 3.1. For both of the middle two classes, letter identification is accomplished by pooling two sources of information about the identity of a letter: extracted feature information and contextual information. The second class uses context to *alter* feature extraction, whereas the third class uses context to *supplement* feature extraction. Both classes of theories rely on the fact that, given a word context, a letter is partially redundant because we know something about what letters are possible or probable. (The example given for both the second class and the third class relies on the fact that, given the _NOB context, only S and K are possible as initial letters.) Because both classes of theories rely on redundancy, they stand or fall on the same kinds of evidence.

After collapsing the middle two of the four classes of theories, we arrive at a three-way typology of WSE theories, which is used in the remainder of this paper: Type 1(more features), Type 2 (redundancy), and Type 3 (retention).

EVIDENCE AGAINST TYPE 1
(MORE FEATURES) THEORIES

Type 1 theories of the WSE suppose that people identify letters in words at least partly on the basis of visual features not used to identify individual letters. These features might be properties of entire words (e.g., outline or word shape), or they might be properties of smaller groups of letters that commonly occur together. Wheeler (1970) has made the interesting suggestion that the shape of spaces between adjacent letters might be a useful feature.

Several lines of evidence reduce the attractiveness of Type 1 theories of the WSE. First, the WSE is quite strong when target words are printed entirely in upper-case letters (as in most recent WSE experiments, including the one presented in Table 3.1). This reduces the likelihood that word-shape clues are heavily used because word shape depends largely on patterns of ascenders and descenders. Another important piece of evidence is that a sizable WSE is found using words and unrelated letter strings presented in mixed (alternating) upper and lower case (McClelland, 1976; see also Adams, 1979). For instance, words presented looked like *rEaD* and *GrAb*. Performance was better when a letter appeared in a mixed-case word than when in a mixed-case unrelated letter string. Subjects had presumably never seen words printed in this way before. It hardly seems plausible that they could have learned to extract features from units larger than a letter without having seen these units previously. One possible problem in interpreting these results is that many letters are highly similar in their upper- and lower-case forms, and therefore familiar multiletter units should sometimes have occurred in nominally mixed-case words. McClelland (1976), however, found similar results when he analyzed data separately for words composed with letters that are especially different in upper-case and lower-case versions (A/a, D/d, E/e, G/g, R/r). McClelland (1976) did report that the WSE was somewhat smaller for mixed-case targets than for same-case targets, a finding that may indicate a small residual role for multiletter features. However, in a closely related experiment, Adams (1979) failed to find any reduction at all in the WSE when radically different type fonts were mixed.

I have recently been investigating a different kind of distortion, with results that seem to me to present further difficulties for Type 1 theories. I presented words and unrelated letter strings with large gaps between some adjacent letters (see Table 3.2). The gaps distort the shape of whole words and also distort many other spatial properties of units larger than single letters. The data, however, show a remarkably small effect of irregular spacing (a 12.0% WSE with irregular spacing vs. a 15.3% WSE with regular packed spacing). Meyer and Gutschera have also found, in a recent unpublished study, that people can identify a short word very rapidly even when an asterisk is inserted somewhere in it (e.g., *BA*RK*). The presence of an asterisk should severely distort any multiletter features present. If people rely heavily on multiletter features to identify words, surely an embedded asterisk would undermine performance severely.

Another line of evidence bears unfavorably on the use of features for familiar pairs of adjacent letters (e.g., Wheeler's gap-shape features). If people learn to extract features for bigrams, one would expect them to learn to do so better for bigrams that occur more frequently. In tachistoscopic perception experiments, one would therefore expect higher performance on more frequently occurring bigrams. A number of recent studies have found that, within the class of ortho-graphically regular/pronounceable letter strings, bigram frequency has virtually no effect on performance (Gibson, Shurcliff, & Yonas, 1970; Manelis, 1974; McClelland & Johnston, 1977; Spoehr & Smith, 1975). Even when relatively large differences in bigram familiarity have been compared (McClelland & Johnston, 1977), no such effect has been found. Johnston (1978) has also reported finding no effect of bigram frequency on the perceptibility of letters in words.

Overall, I think the evidence is persuasive that Type 1 (more features) theories cannot explain more than a small part of the WSE.

TABLE 3.2
Word-Superiority Effect with Different Spacing Configurations
of Target-Letter Strings

Configuration	Size of Word-Superiority Effect
Regular, packed spacing (READ)	15.3%
Regular, wide spacing (R E A D)	7.7%
Irregular spacing (RE AD, R EAD, REA D, RE A D, R EA D, R E AD)	12.0%

EVIDENCE AGAINST TYPE 2
(REDUNDANCY) THEORIES

Let us now move on to consider Type 2 theories. These attribute the WSE to reliance on redundancy within words. In principle we should not need as much feature information to identify any given letter if we know something about the other context letters in a word. Earlier the instructive example in which a four-letter word has been analyzed sufficiently to know that the last three letters are *NOB* was discussed. Given this information, one only needs to know whether the initial letter is curved or not to know its identity because from context it has to be *K* or *S*.

If redundancy theories are valid, performance should be better where context more strictly constrains letter possibilities. For many years, this prediction was tested only across different types of letter strings. Advocates of redundancy theories (e.g., Miller, Bruner & Postman, 1954; Morton, 1969; Smith, 1971) were apparently satisfied to know that, *on the average,* letters in words (and in pronounceable nonwords) are constrained by context, and that this is matched *on the average* with better performance for letters in these types of letter strings than for letters in unrelated letter strings. Unfortunately, performance differences across types of letter strings might just as well be due to other correlated factors (such as pronounceability and familiarity). A more exacting test for redundancy theories is to see if they can predict performance differences between words. Does performance on a letter in a word depend on how severely the identity of that letter is constrained by the rest of the word?

Johnston (1974, 1978) compared matched pairs of items with the same critical letters in the same position (such as *DATE—GATE* and *DRIP—GRIP;* see Table 3.3). Contextual constraint was relatively low in one pair and relatively high in the other. That is, one context permitted many letters (nine for ——*ATE*), and one permitted only a few (three for ——*RIP*). High constraint and low constraint items were matched for word frequency and bigram frequency. Table 3.4 shows the surprising results. There was virtually no difference in performance at all, and indeed on the forced-choice measure performance was several percentage points higher when constraint was low—where many letters were possible.

TABLE 3.3
Design for Testing Redundancy Theories of the Word-
Superiority Effect[a]

Low-Constraint Sample Item	*High-Constraint Sample Item*
target: DATE	target: DRIP
choices: DATE GATE	choices: DRIP GRIP
(context permits nine letters)	(context permits three letters)

[a] From Johnston (1978).

TABLE 3.4
Results of Testing Redundancy Theories of
the Word-Superiority Effect[a]

Dependent Variable	Degree of Contextual Constraint	
	Low	High
Free report		
All four letters correct	.310	.308
Free report		
Critical letters correct	.544	.545
Forced choice		
(two alternatives)	.795	.768

[a] From Johnston (1978).

Fig. 3.2 shows a scatterplot of performance for items with differing degrees of contextual constraint (indexed by number of letters permitted by the word context). The low positive correlation found indicates that, if anything, performance had a slight trend toward higher accuracy where context allows *more* letters. Type 2 (redundancy) theories predict higher accuracy where context allows fewer letters. Number of letters allowed is, however, only one of many possible indices of contextual constraint. Several of other plausible measures were therefore tested against the data to see if they fared better. One alternative measure, instead

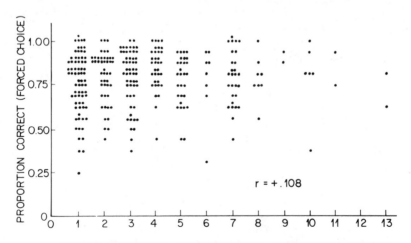

DEGREE OF CONTEXTUAL CONSTRAINT OF THE CRITICAL LETTER
(Number of letters which make a word with context letters)

FIG. 3.2. Scattergram of forced-choice accuracy for different degrees of contextual constraint (from Johnston, 1978). Constraint decreases from left to right as more letters make a word when combined with context letters.

of simply counting the number of letters that would make words, weighted letter possibilities according to the relative frequencies of words formed. At the other extreme, another alternative measure was tried that ignored lexical considerations entirely and considered only the constraint on letter possibilities imposed by orthographic rules. Still another measure considered only "local constraint"— the predictability of a letter given only the adjacent letters, rather than all letters in a word. No significant trend toward better performance with higher degrees of contextual constraint was found using any of these measures of constraint.

Although these results conflict with many theorists' expectations, there are several other recent findings in a similar vein. Estes (1975) found only small effects of contextual constraint in a related tachistoscopic task, and Coltheart, Davelaar, Jonasson, and Besner (1977) reported that lexical decision time is affected very little by constraint on letters in words.

THE PROBLEM WITH TYPE 3
(RETENTION) THEORIES

We have found compelling reasons to doubt that Type 1 and Type 2 theories can adequately account for the WSE. By elimination, we are left with Type 3 theories. According to these, the WSE occurs because information about a letter is *retained* better when the letter occurs in a word.

For many decades after the WSE was discovered, retention theories were very popular. The single-letter control had not yet been investigated under appropriate conditions, so all that needed to be explained was why performance was better for a letter in a word than for a letter in an equally long string of unrelated letters. It was not hard to believe that people could retain a mental code for one word better than they could retain many separate mental codes for each unrelated letter. In fact, Baddeley (1964) convincingly showed that people *do* have trouble retaining the letters in an unrelated letter string even when we know they have identified them.

About a decade ago, Reicher (1969) found that a letter in a word was actually perceived better than a single letter alone. The existence of this new variant of the WSE (sometimes referred to as the "word-letter phenomenon"; Johnston & McClelland, 1973) appeared to be impossible for retention theories to explain. Why should a word code be any easier to remember than *one* letter code? In fact, why should people ever forget one letter at all when they have nothing else to do in the task? This objection has appeared to many researchers (including myself) to be a decisive objection against Type 3 (retention) theories of the WSE.[2]

---

[2]As discussed later, a perceptual advantage for a letter in a word over a single letter alone is only obtained using patterned masking. Without patterned masking, a small advantage for a letter in a word over a letter in an unrelated letter string still occurs (e.g., Juola, Leavitt, & Choe, 1974). Difficulties in retaining codes for multiple letters remain a viable explanation for the residual WSE obtained under no-mask conditions.

A NEW TYPE 3 (RETENTION) THEORY

We have now compiled impressive cases against all three types of theories of the WSE. Nevertheless, the WSE still exists. Such an impasse requires us to reconsider one or more of the three types of theories. I believe that the most attractive alternative is to reconsider Type 3 (retention) theories.

The apparently decisive argument against retention theories is that one identified letter should not present any retention problems. Upon reflection, this argument appears to assume that an identified letter is represented in short-term memory or something akin to it. It is possible, however, that an identified letter (or word) is first represented in some more peripheral form of storage, from which even one item can be "forgotten." McClelland and I have proposed a theory of this kind, which we believe can successfully explain the WSE (Johnston & McClelland, 1979). In this section, I briefly sketch this theory of word identification (which we call the hierarchical theory) and show how it explains the WSE.

The main component of the theory is a hierarchy of detectors for visual features, letters and words (see Fig. 3.3 for an illustrative fragment of such a

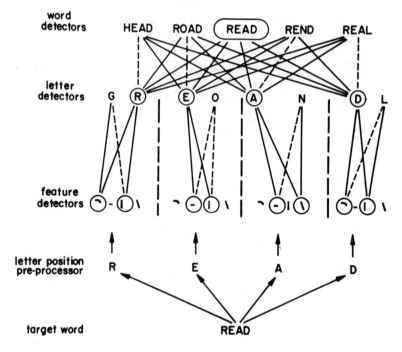

FIG. 3.3. Schematic diagram of a fragment of proposed hierarchical theory of word identification (from Johnston & McClelland, 1979). Diagram shows hypothetical activation state of the detector network after presentation of the target word *READ*.

hypothetical detector network). Detectors in this hierarchical network are hypothesized to function outside of conscious awareness. Activity in detectors can be reported (or used to guide other overt responses) only if central attentional processes monitor the network and retrieve information from it.[3] Thus, the fact that a letter or word is briefly able to activate an appropriate detector does not ensure that it can be reported or can guide responses to a forced-choice test. The fate of information in the detector network depends on how long detectors remain active and whether central processes can access them before these detectors return to inactivity.

Let me describe what happens when a target word, such as *READ*, is briefly displayed. The word must first be separated into component letters, each of which is then sent to a bank of feature detectors—a different bank of feature detectors for each letter position. We postulate that detectors for features that are present in a letter are activated, and detectors for features that are not present are deactivated. For instance, for the second letter (*E*) detectors for "horizontal segment" and "vertical segment," among others, might be activated (shown by circling). Detectors for "curve at top," "diagonal," and others would not be activated. Active feature detectors send signals to banks of letter detectors (a separate bank of letter detectors for each letter position).

The rules for connecting feature detectors to letter detectors are simple:

1. Only active detectors send any signal out.
2. If an active feature is *consistent* with a letter, *excitation* is transmitted to the detector for that letter. (For instance, Fig. 3.3 shows horizontal and vertical detectors in the second position exciting the detector for the letter *E;* excitation is marked by a solid connecting line.)
3. If an active feature is *inconsistent* with a letter, *inhibition* is transmitted to the detector for that letter. (For instance, the horizontal and vertical detectors in the second position are shown inhibiting the letter *O;* inhibition is marked by a dashed connecting line.)

The rule for combining multiple inputs to a detector need not be specified precisely, but it should give decisive weight to any inhibition.[4] Thus, letter detectors should typically be activated only if they receive excitation but no inhibition. This should normally result in only one letter detector being activated in each letter position—the detector for the letter actually presented. Some feature or another of the letter presented should be inconsistent with all other letters.

The analogous rules apply to connections from letters to words. Only active letter detectors send a signal. Active detectors for letters consistent with a word

[3]A possible exception is that with highly overlearned stimulus–response sequences, detectors might be able to exert control over responses without mediation by central attentional processes.

[4]This provision is analogous to the Rumelhart and Siple (1974) provision that only letters consistent with all extracted feature information are considered as viable alternatives.

send excitation to the detector for that word, but detectors for letters inconsistent with a word send inhibition. Any inhibition is normally sufficient to keep a word detector from being activated. In the example shown in Fig. 3.3, the detector for the word presented, *READ,* should be activated and no others. Note that letters are considered to be inconsistent with a word unless they occur in the correct position. Thus, *R* in the first position will inhibit the detector for *DEAR* (not shown), and the system will not confuse *DEAR* with *READ.*

The result is that shortly after a brief glimpse of the target word *READ,* it is represented simultaneously at the feature, letter, and word levels of the detector network. After a brief glimpse of the letter *E* alone, it would be represented at the feature and letter levels, but, of course, not at the word level.

So how does this theory predict the WSE? The critical fact needed is that the WSE depends on the use of a patterned mask following target exposure (Johnston & McClelland, 1974).[5] For our purposes the critical property of a good patterned mask is that it contains many letter features. Moreover, some of its features should be inconsistent with each letter in the alphabet. One frequently used patterned mask consists of O's, overprinted with X's.

Let us now consider (see Fig. 3.4) what happens to the detector network when the target word *READ* is followed by an X—O mask. At the feature level, detectors for the features of *READ* are deactivated, and detectors for the mask features are activated. Detectors for the features "curve at top" and "diagonal" are among the hypothetical feature detectors that might be activated (again shown by circling). At the letter level, detectors for all letters should receive inhibitory input and be deactivated because some detectors for features inconsistent with each letter have been activated. At the word level, detectors will receive no new input because letter detectors are all silent. The previously activated detector for the word *READ* will therefore not receive any inhibitory input and thus will not be turned off. Instead the detector for *READ* should remain active for some time until it passively decays, which we postulate to be a much slower process than being deactivated by inhibition. Thus, when a target is followed by a feature mask, a word detector activated by the target will remain active longer than letter detectors activated by the target. We assume that an increase in the time during which a detector remains active leads to an increase in the probability that central attentional processes will find the active detector. We thus arrive at the conclusion that activated word detectors are more likely to be found than activated letter detectors. This, in a nutshell, is the main source of the WSE according to our theory of word perception.

The hierarchical theory just presented provides a useful theoretical framework for two phenomena closely related to the WSE. First, as noted earlier, the WSE

---

[5]More precisely, Johnston and McClelland (1973) showed that obtaining the WSE with a single-letter control condition requires a patterned mask. A small WSE can be obtained without a patterned mask using an unrelated letter string control condition (e.g., Juola, Leavitt, & Choe, 1974; Rumelhart & Siple, 1974). The more traditional retention problem of forgetting letters from short-term memory can account for this finding without resort to any novel retention explanations.

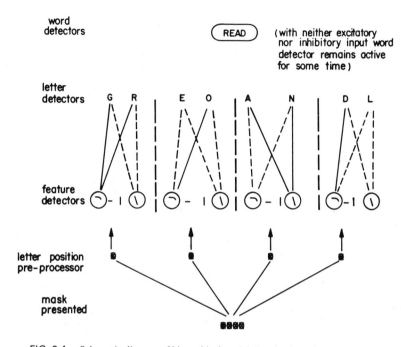

FIG. 3.4.   Schematic diagram of hierarchical model showing hypothetical activation state of the detector network after presentation of a patterned mask, following previous presentation of target word *READ*.

is typically found to be either weak or nonexistent when measured with methods that involve precuing a particular letter position and/or alternative choice letters. From the perspective of the hierarchical theory, this phenomenon can readily be interpreted as due to a change in the behavior of central attentional processes. It is quite plausible that precuing leads to a restricted search of the detector network, limited to those detectors that appear to be especially relevant to the task demands. Depending on what is precued, attention may be directed only at detectors in one particular letter position, at detectors for several specific letter identities, or possibly at detectors for features that most readily differentiate between two letter alternatives (cf. Smith, Haviland, Reder, Brownell, & Adams, 1976). In any case, attention can be expected to be diverted away from word detectors, leading to a reduction in WSE.

Second, the WSE depends only partly on lexical properties of words. "Pseudowords"—nonwords that have Englishlike orthographic structure and are pronounceable—are perceived more accurately than entirely unrelated strings of letters (see McClelland & Johnston, 1977, for a review), and a letter in a properly constructed pseudoword can be identified better than a letter alone (McClelland & Johnston, 1977). Because the hierarchical theory relies on word detectors to explain the WSE, a further explanation is required to account for pseudoword performance. McClelland & Johnston (1977) have argued that there are no preexisting detectors for novel pseudowords and that hence the perception of pseudowords must involve the construction of new representations rather than merely the activation of previously established detectors. The nature of the representations constructed (orthographic, phonological, or abstract) is not important, for present purposes, as long as the construction is based on letter identities supplied by letter detectors in the hierarchical network. If so, pseudowords should be shielded from the effects of patterned masking for the same reason that word detectors are shielded. The hierarchical theory assumes that patterned masks do not activate any letter detectors. Thus, any representation that receives input from letter detectors will not, as a result of patterned masking, receive any new inhibitory input of letter identities contradicting the target-letter identities. Thus, pseudoword representations—like active word detectors—should tend to remain active even after letter detectors have been deactivated by patterned masking. Therefore we have explained why, with patterned masking, a letter is perceived more accurately in a pseudoword than in an unrelated letter string or alone.[6]

SOME EVIDENCE FOR THE NEW THEORY

The line of reasoning by which the hierarchical theory accounts for the WSE leads to an elegant prediction. Suppose targets were followed by a mask made up of letters rather than the traditional mask, which contains letter features but not letters (except for overstruck letters, which act like nonletters according to the theory). Shortly after a letter mask is presented, detectors for the mask letters should be activated. These detectors should now provide inhibitory input to the detector for a previously presented target word, leading to its rapid deactivation. (It is assumed that the mask letters have been chosen to be different from the target letters.) Thus, with a letter mask, detectors for target words as well as target letters should be rapidly deactivated, and the WSE should be greatly reduced. McClelland and I tried this experiment, and it worked as predicted (Johnston & McClelland, 1980). We compared the size of the WSE with letter masks and with feature masks (made up of nonletters closely matched in feature properties to letters). Results (see Fig. 3.5) showed a 20.6% WSE with the feature masks, but only a 7.5% WSE with the letter masks; the interaction of

---

[6]One possible objection to this account of pseudoword performance is that it may seem unparsimonious to attribute word performance to the activation of word detectors inside a detector network, while explaining pseudoword performance on the basis of representations constructed outside of the detector network. However, Carr, Davidson, and Hawkins (1978) have recently provided evidence that pseudoword performance is more responsive to strategic factors than is word performance. Such a difference is in the direction one would expect if the detector network functions more automatically (with less need for central attention) than constructive processes operating outside the network.

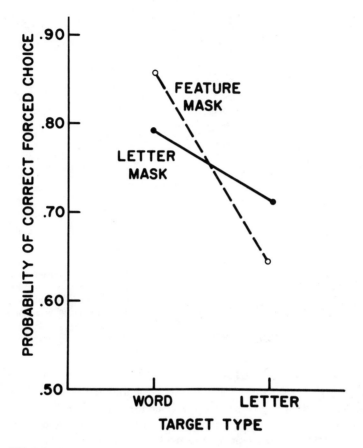

FIG. 3.5. Word-superiority effect results from comparison of feature masks and letter masks (from Johnston & McClelland, 1980). Target exposure durations were 10 msec longer for letter masks than for feature masks.

letter versus feature masks with letter versus word targets was highly significant. (Note: Exposure durations used were 10 msec longer for letter masks than for feature masks in order to center performance around the 75% level for each mask type.)

A related prediction from the new theory is that if a mask contains letters, masking effectiveness does not depend on whether these letters spell a word or not. Because inhibition works only in an upward direction, deactivation of target letters depends on the presence of letter features in a mask, and deactivation of target words depends on the presence of letters in a mask. The presence of a word in a mask has no further consequences at all for performance. Johnston and McClelland (1980) have found that word masks and letter masks do produce virtually identical results (see Fig. 3.6).

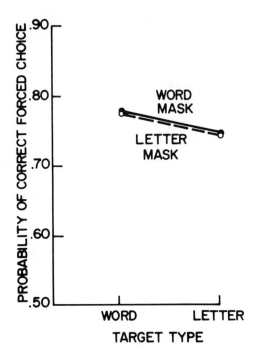

FIG. 3.6. Word-superiority effect results for comparison of letter masks and word masks (from Johnston & McClelland, 1980). Target exposure durations were equally long for letter masks and word masks.

Experimental corroboration of these predictions strengthens our confidence in the new theory, especially because these predictions run counter to the usual expectation that masking is more severe when mask and target are more similar (e.g., Mayzner & Tresselt, 1970; Smith et al., 1976). According to this rule, one would expect letter masks to provide particularly severe masking for target letters (not words), leading to an increase in the measured WSE (rather than the decrease found). Furthermore, one would expect that making mask letters spell a word would hurt performance on target words, whereas (in accordance with our theory) it made no difference at all.

One problem remains. Although masks having letters do, as predicted, greatly reduce the size of the WSE, there is a small but real residual WSE. On the basis of our discussion so far, it would seem that the WSE should disappear entirely. After all, the new theory predicts that with a letter mask there is no reason to expect detectors for target words to remain active any longer than detectors for target letters. Both types of detectors should be briefly activated—just a quick blip—before being deactivated by the mask. One must, however, also consider the likelihood that central processes will encounter a relevant detector blip and represent that fact in a response buffer, before the blips are gone. It is reasonable to expect that if there are additional blips that have a chance of being noticed, the probability of noticing *at least one* blip should be higher. If an *E* is presented alone, only detectors for its features or for the letter itself will be available. If, however *E* is presented in the word *READ,* the detector for this word will be active in *addition* to feature and letter detectors. An *extra* encoding opportunity should help performance even if this opportunity is by itself no better than the other opportunities.

Our theory thus provides both a minor and major explanation of the WSE. The minor explanation is that having an *additional* detector active—a word detector—provides another opportunity to encode stimulus information. The major explanation—which explains the bulk of the WSE obtained with the usual patterned mask—is that activity in word detectors persists longer after the onset of a patterned mask.

CONCLUSION

I would like to close by noting that our new variant of retention theory suggests that people frequently can come away from a perceptual episode with a high-level abstract code, but no remaining representation of the lower-level properties that mediated formation of the high-level code. There is considerable support for this aspect of the model. It has been shown that people frequently know what letter or word has been presented but do not know whether it was upper or lower case (McClelland, 1976).

I have come across another indication of this loss of visual properties in my previously mentioned experiments altering the spacing of letters. The left-hand pair of curves in Fig. 3.7 shows WSE data using a traditional forced-choice test between two alternatives that differ only in the identity of one critical letter. On the right-hand panel of the figure is an example of a different kind of test also used—a forced choice of whether a space was small or large (e.g., the middle space in *R EAD* vs. *R E AD*). It might seem that such a choice would be easy. A variety of different cues (overall length, character density, etc.) could mediate a correct response. Results show, however, that performance was barely above the 50% chance level on this test,[7] whereas at the same exposure durations performance on the traditional letter test was at about the 75% level. Even when subjects were instructed to attend to the spacing configuration at the expense of attending to what letters were presented, performance was still only about 55%. In keeping with the spirit of the new retention explanation of the WSE, it seems that people can retain high-level character and word codes in circumstances where they cannot retain the spatial layout of the display.

The present revival of retention theory is consistent with a more general conclusion about the human mind that I believe now has widespread support.

---

[7]Further experimentation is being directed at the question of whether the small 3% advantage for word targets on the spacing test is reliable.

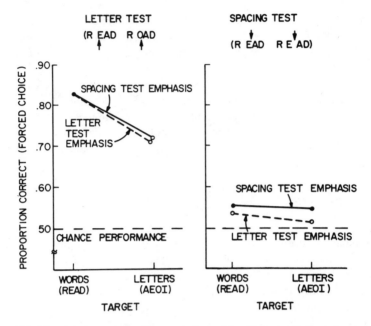

FIG. 3.7.   Word superiority effect results for traditional letter test (left panel) and for spacing test (right panel). In spacing test the two choice alternatives contain the same strings of letters but differ in the size of a space between two adjacent letters.

This conclusion is that people go through many intermediate processing levels before reaching the deepest levels, even though on superficial analysis it may appear that the deepest levels have, mysteriously, been reached directly. Like a pocket calculator, the mind tends to make available to conscious awareness only the final products of its processing. The intermediate steps are usually hidden. Not only are they usually hidden from the conscious awareness of the person doing the processing, they are usually also hidden from the view of psychologists looking straightforwardly at consciously controlled responses. All of our ingenuity as scientists is required to reveal the hidden intermediate processing steps through indirect clues. That is why we doggedly pursue laboratory curiosities like the WSE. So far, there is reason to hope that the clues we are accumulating are in fact also leading us to a better understanding of how the mind perceives printed words outside of the laboratory.

ACKNOWLEDGMENTS

I would like to thank T. K. Landauer for his helpful comments on an earlier version of this manuscript.

REFERENCES

Adams, M. J. Models of word recognition. *Cognitive Psychology*, 1979, *11*, 133–176.

Baddeley, A. D. Immediate memory and the "perception" of letter sequences. *Quarterly Journal of Experimental Psychology*, 1964, *16*, 364–367.

Baron, J. The word-superiority effect: Perceptual learning from reading. In W. K. Estes (Ed.), *Handbook of learning and cognitive processes* (Vol. 6), Hillsdale, N.J.: Lawrence Erlbaum Associates, 1978.

Bjork, E. L., & Estes, W. K. Letter identification in relation to linguistic context and masking conditions. *Memory & Cognition*, 1973, *1*, 217–223.

Carr, T. H., Davidson, B. J., & Hawkins, H. L. Perceptual flexibility in word recognition: Strategies affect orthographic computation but not lexical access. *Journal of Experimental Psychology: Human Perception and Performance*, 1978, *4*, 674–690.

Cattell, J. M. The time taken up by cerebral operations. *Mind*, 1886, *11*, 220–242.

Coltheart, M., Davelaar, E., Jonasson, J. R., & Besner, D. Access to the internal lexicon. In S. Dornic (Ed.), *Attention & Performance, VI.* Hillsdale, N.J.: Lawrence Erlbaum Associates, 1977.

Estes, W. K. The locus of inferential and perceptual processes in letter recognition. *Journal of Experimental Psychology: General*, 1975, *104*, 122–145.

Gibson, E. J., Shurcliff, A., & Yonas, A. Utilization of spelling patterns by deaf and hearing subjects. In H. Levin & J. P. Williams (Eds.), *Basic studies in reading.* New York: Basic Books, 1970.

Holender, D. Identification of letters in words and of single letters with pre- and postknowledge vs. postknowledge of the alternatives. *Perception & Psychophysics*, 1979, *25*, 313–318.

Johnston, J. C. *The role of contextual constraint in the perception of letters in words.* Unpublished doctoral dissertation, University of Pennsylvania, 1974.

Johnston, J. C. A test of the sophisticated guessing theory of word perception. *Cognitive Psychology*, 1978, *10*, 123–153.

Johnston, J. C. The effects of advance precuing of alternatives on the perception of letters alone and in words. *Journal of Experimental Psychology: Human Perception and Performance*, in press.

Johnston, J. C., & McClelland, J. L. Visual factors in word perception. *Perception & Psychophysics*, 1973, *14*, 365–370.

Johnston, J. C., & McClelland, J. L. Perception of letters in words: Seek not and ye shall find. *Science*, 1974, *184*, 1192–1194.

Johnston, J. C., & McClelland, J. Experimental tests of a hierarchical model of word identification. *Journal of Verbal Learning and Verbal Behavior*, 1980, *19*, 503–524.

Juola, J. F., Leavitt, D. D., & Choe, C. S. Letter identification in word, nonword, and single letter displays. *Bulletin of the Psychonomic Society*, 1974, *4*, 278–280.

Kreuger, L. E. Familiarity effects in visual information processing. *Psychological Bulletin*, 1975, *82*, 949–974.

Manelis, L. The effect of meaningfulness in tachistoscopic word perception. *Perception & Psychophysics*, 1974, *16*, 182–192.

Mayzner, M. S., & Tresselt, M. E. Visual information with sequential inputs: A general model for sequential blanking, displacement, and overprinting phenomena. *Annals of the New York Academy of Sciences*, 1970, *169*, 599–618.

McClelland, J. L. Preliminary letter identification in the perception of words and non-words. *Journal of Experimental Psychology: Human Perception and Performance*, 1976, *2*, 80–91.

McClelland, J. L., & Johnston, J. C. The role of familiar units in perception of words and nonwords. *Perception & Psychophysics*, 1977, *22*, 249–261.

Miller, G., Bruner, J. S., & Postman, L. Familiarity of letter sequences and tachistoscopic identification. *Journal of General Psychology*, 1954, *50*, 129–139.

Morton, J. Interaction of information in word recognition. *Psychological Review*, 1969, *76*, 165--178.

Purcell, D. G., Stanovich, K. E., & Spector, A. Visual angle and the word superiority effect. *Memory & Cognition*, 1978, *6*, 3-8.

Reicher, G. M. Perceptual recognition as a function of meaningfulness of stimulus material. *Journal of Experimental Psychology*, 1969, *81*, 275-280.

Rumelhart, D. E., & Siple, P. Process of recognizing tachistoscopically presented words. *Psychological Review*, 1974, *81*, 99-118.

Smith, E. E., & Haviland, S. E. Why words are perceived more accurately than nonwords: Inference versus unitization. *Journal of Experimental Psychology*, 1972, *92*, 59-64.

Smith, E. E., Haviland, S. E., Reder, L. M., Brownell, H., & Adams, N. When perception fails: Disruptive effects of prior information on perceptual recognition. *Journal of Experimental Psychology: Human Perception and Performance*, 1976, *2*, 151-161.

Smith, E. E., & Spoehr, K. T. The perception of printed English: A theoretical perspective. In B. H. Kantowitz (Ed.), *Human information processing: Tutorials in performance and cognition*. Hillsdale, N.J.: Lawrence Erlbaum Associates, 1974.

Smith, F. *Understanding reading*. New York: Holt, Rinehart & Winston, 1971.

Spoehr, K. J., & Smith, E. E. The role of orthographic and phonotactic rules in perceiving letter patterns. *Journal of Experimental Psychology: Human Perception and Performance*, 1975, *104*, 21-34.

Thompson, M. C., & Massaro, D. W. Visual information and redundancy in reading. *Journal of Experimental Psychology*, 1973, *98*, 49-54.

Wheeler, D. Processes in word recognition. *Cognitive Psychology*, 1970, *1*, 59-85.

4
Words and Contexts

Philip B. Gough, Jack A. Alford, Jr., Pamela Holley-Wilcox
University of Texas at Austin

Students of reading disagree about many things. They disagree about the role of letters, about the role of phonological form, and even about the role of the printed word itself. But most are agreed that context is an important determinant of word recognition. In one form or another, "contextualism" is embraced by nearly every student of reading.

The forms of contextualism vary considerably. There is a kind of methodological contextualism like that espoused by Haber (1978), who, in a recent review of reading research, refused to consider any studies of the recognition of isolated words or letters on the grounds that they have nothing to do with reading. At another extreme, there is the kind of radical contextualism offered by theorists like Goodman (1976) and Smith (1971), who seem to hold that context is everything in reading, that the only role of the individual word is to confirm the expectations of the reader. But whatever the precise form of their obeisance, virtually all students of reading honor the role of context in word recognition.

There is certainly good reason for this respect. Context determines the referent of pronouns and other deictic terms. Context determines the form class of uninflected words (like *sleep* and *shovel*); it selects the appropriate reading for homographs (like *letter* and *table*). Context lowers the recognition threshold of appropriate words and raises that of inappropriate ones. Context can not only facilitate the correct recognition of a word, it can even produce a word's misrecognition, as Goodman (1970), Kolers (1970), and Weber (1970) have observed.

Context clearly has profound effects on word recognition, and these effects are recognized by nearly everyone who has theorized about reading. But despite this all but universal respect, we know very little about *how* context influences word recognition. In fact, we would argue that it is just because of this harmony that we know so little; disagreement is a powerful incentive to research, and if there is nothing to doubt, there is nothing to challenge.

It is in this context, then, that we want to offer some observations on the role of context in word recognition. We believe that the role of context in reading has been misunderstood, and we hope to promote our understanding of context by calling into question the received views on the matter.

CONTEXT AND CONTEXT

We would like to begin by observing that context is not just context. There are several, if not many, different kinds of context, ranging from the reader's physiological condition to the syntactic category of the immediately prior word. We have little to say about this enormous range of possibilities; it certainly seems reasonable that any or all of them might have some effect on the recognition of some words (cf. studies of food deprivation and the recognition of food-related words; Brozek, Franklin, Guetzkow, & Keys, 1946). But we do think it important to draw at least one basic distinction among the many forms of context: the distinction between global and local context.

By *global* context, we mean the text in which the target word is embedded— the book, chapter, or passage in which the reader finds the word. By *local* context, we mean the immediately surrounding phrase or sentence.

Both of these classes of context can be shown to affect the recognition of a word. For example, readers of a biology text seldom interpret the word *cell* to mean part of a jail. And you, the reader, are not likely to take *mean* to signify surly in the preceding sentence.

But the effects of global and local context must be very different in one important respect. The effect of global context must be semantic and not syntactic. That is, global context must facilitate the recognition of words in certain semantic categories, but, in doing so, it must ignore the syntactic categories of those words. A book on surgery, for example, will provide a global context that will presumably facilitate the recognition of words like *trephine, scalpel,* and *surgical,* but it must promote the recognition of these words without regard to their form class; it must be essentially indifferent to syntax. The effect of local context, in contrast, must have an important syntactic component. If a sentence begins, *After removing her tumor, the . . . ,* words of two or three syntactic categories are permissible, but most are excluded. Thus, local context may also facilitate the recognition of words in a particular semantic category, but it must pay attention to their syntactic status as well.

Because of this difference, the effects of local and global context must have very different time courses. The effect of global context must be stable. It must hold across phrases and sentences—if not paragraphs and pages—to sustain semantically appropriate words. The effect of local context, on the other hand, must be transitory. If local context correctly predicts that the next word is an article, its prediction for the word after that must be different.

We are led, then, to seek distinct mechanisms to explain the effects of global context on the one hand, and local context on the other. Let us look first at global context.

GLOBAL CONTEXT

We have observed that the effect of global context must be semantic. Accordingly, we seek a mechanism by which a given context can facilitate words in a particular semantic category. We know of only two ideas that have been offered to account for such an effect. One is the idea of *spreading activation,* and the other has been called *location shifting.*

The idea of spreading activation is by far the more popular. It has provided the basis for a popular theory of semantic memory (Collins & Loftus, 1975); it has also been used to explain the effects of semantic relatedness in a variety of tasks, ranging from sentence verification to lexical decision (in which subjects decide if strings of letters are words or not).

The basic idea is that the mental representation of words and the concepts that underlie them are arranged in a kind of network, and the activation of a concept node in the network when a word is recognized spreads to other, semantically related concepts. Thus, if a reader has just seen the word *doctor,* activation will spread to concepts like nurse, facilitating the subsequent recognition of the word *nurse.*

We do not share others' enthusiasm for this idea. As we see it, an explanatory model should tell us the parts that underlie a phenomenon, how they fit together, and what they do. In short, it should specify a mechanism. The notion of spreading activation does not; it says only that the activation of a given word will spread and facilitate the recognition of related words. It might as well be called spreading facilitation, for it seems to us to provide only a circular explanation of the effect of semantic relatedness on recognition.

But the notion of spreading activation is taken seriously by many of our colleagues, and we might well ask whether such a thing could account for the effect of semantic context in reading.

A paradigm for the study of such effects has been offered by Meyer, Schvaneveldt, and Ruddy (1972). They asked subjects to decide whether strings of letters formed words and measured the latencies of their decisions. They found that the time it took to decide whether a given string of letters formed a word was reduced if that word was immediately preceded by a semantically related word. (Thus, subjects' decisions that *nurse* is a word were faster when that string followed *doctor* than when it followed an unrelated word like *carrot.*) This effect has been taken to be an exemplary instance of spreading activation, and we might well wonder whether the facilitation observed in this task underlies the effect of semantic context in ordinary reading.

The problem with this idea is that semantically related words rarely occur next to one another, at least so it seems to Forster (1979) and us. Thus, a demonstration that the occurrence of a related word immediately before a target word facilitates recognition of the latter is of questionable relevance to ordinary reading.

If the effect of global context is to be mediated by spreading activation from semantically related words, that activation must reach across—or persist through—a number of intervening words. On the face of it, spreading activation seems unlikely to do this. For one thing, Neely (1977) has recently provided evidence that the effect of semantic relatedness in the lexical decision task decays very rapidly unless it is sustained by a conscious strategy which could scarcely figure in ordinary reading. But Meyer et al. (1972) have shown that the effect of semantic relatedness persists over one intervening word. Moreover, Scarborough, Cortese, and Scarborough (1977) have shown that the effect of *repeating* an item in the lexical decision task is undiminished by as many as 32 intervening items. (That is, a subject's decision that *nurse* is a word is faster if *nurse* has previously occurred in the list, even if the earlier occurrence was 32 items back.) If we took word identity to be the very extreme of semantic relatedness in the lexical decision task, then we might expect to see a persistent effect of semantic relatedness. And if we were to see such a persistent effect, then we might be able to maintain the view that the effect of global context in normal reading is due to spreading activation. Accordingly, we conducted the following experiment.

Experiment 1

We asked each of 16 graduate students and faculty members to make lexical decisions about each of 300 letter strings. On each trial, a three- to six-letter string appeared on a cathode ray tube (CRT) controlled by a DEC PDP 8/I computer; the letters were all capitals, and the string subtended a maximum visual angle of 1.5 degrees. The subject indicated his or her decision by pressing the appropriate button, and the computer recorded each response time in milliseconds.

Half of the strings formed words; half formed pronounceable nonsense syllables. Eighty of the 150 words were considered target words; paired with each target word was a closely related priming word. Each of the target words was preceded by its priming word at one of seven lags: 0, 1, 2, 4, 8, 16, or 32 intervening items; for 10 of the items, the priming word was omitted from the list (yielding, in effect, an indefinitely long lag).

Words were rotated through conditions across subjects such that each subject saw 10 different words in each of the eight conditions, and each of the words occurred equally often at each lag. Median response latency was computed for each condition for each subject, and means of those medians are presented in Fig. 4.1.

As one would expect, the occurrence of a related word just prior to the target (0-lag) facilitated the recognition of that target, reducing the time it takes sophisticated subjects to decide that it is a word by 20 msec. But the intervention of a single item virtually eliminated that facilitation, and beyond a one-word lag there is no evidence in our data that the prior occurrence of a semantically related word has any effect at all on lexical decision latency.

These results provide no encouragement for the view that spreading activation might explain the effect of semantic context on word recognition. We expect that an advocate of spreading activation might argue that our results are not relevant to ordinary reading, in that ordinary reading matter does not interpose lists of up to 32 randomly selected words and nonsense syllables between a pair of related words. We must agree, but we would add that ordinary reading matter almost never juxtaposes semantically related words either. Hence, if we discount the present results on this basis, we must also discount those many studies of semantic context in the lexical decision task, which like Meyer et al. (1972) have used adjacent pairs of semantically related words. In any event, we would argue that there is simply no evidence that spreading activation could account for the effect of semantic context on word recognition in ordinary reading.

We are inclined toward the location-shifting view. According to this idea, the reader's mental lexicon is organized, like Roget's original thesaurus (Roget, 1852), along semantic lines. Thus, each word is grouped with related words into semantic regions, which, like the pages in a small computer's memory, are

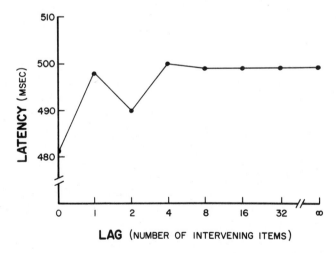

FIG. 4.1.   Lexical decision latency as a function of number of intervening items (lag).

functionally distinct. So words closely related to a given word are nearby in the same region, whereas unrelated words are located in remote locations. As in the computer, we assume that words in the current region can be directly accessed, whereas words in other regions require either indirect addressing or a shift in location. Thus, related words can be easily accessed, but unrelated words cannot.

The location-shifting view was rejected by Meyer et al. (1972) on the basis of a single result: In a triple lexical decision task, the third lexical decision is facilitated if the first word is related to the third even if the second is not (e.g., *doctor-shovel-nurse*). Meyer et al. argued that, according to the location-shifting view, recognition of the unrelated second word (*shovel*) must require shifting location from the semantic region of the first (and third) word and so should eliminate any facilitation between these words. But facilitation was observed, so Meyer et al. decided against location shifting.

We believe their rejection of this hypothesis was premature. For one thing, all we need assume to defend the hypothesis against the Meyer result is that the reader can keep more than one page at a time in working memory. But more importantly, we doubt that the reader's location in semantic memory—the current page—is determined by single words. Rather, we suppose that it is determined by the substance of the text he or she is reading, and we suspect that it would seldom be changed by a single unrelated word.

We believe that location shifting holds more promise than spreading activation. But we have no evidence for the location-shifting view, and as yet, it is little more than a metaphor. We would conclude that if this is the best idea we have about how semantic context effects word recognition, we do not understand how global context works.

LOCAL CONTEXT

There is abundant evidence in the psycholinguistic and reading literatures to show that sentential context can dramatically facilitate word recognition. For example, Tulving and Gold (1963) demonstrated that the presence of a sentential context like *Far too many people today confuse communism with* in the preexposure field of a tachistoscope can reduce the duration threshold of an appropriate word like *socialism* by as much as a third. But there is little evidence as to why this should be so. In fact, precious few ideas have been offered to show how the sentence might have this effect.

Probably the most prevalent idea is that sentential context enables the reader to predict what is coming and that this prediction somehow facilitates the processing of the predicted material.

The idea that context increases predictability feels right. It is consistent with the observation that the readability of text is closely related to its predictability (Rubenstein & Aborn, 1958), and the reading process certainly seems to be disrupted by the occurrence of an unexpected and inappropriate word. But that the idea feels good should not be sufficient for us to accept it. We should demand more of a theory than we do of a warm bath. As Gibson and Levin (1975) have pointed out, any theory which holds that the reader proceeds by forming hypotheses and testing them cannot be evaluated until we are told *what* is predicted. This is an important point, and it cannot be emphasized too strongly because in the absence of this specification an hypothesis theory runs a serious risk of being circular. One can always say that material facilitated was expected, material misread unexpected. If we are to entertain the idea seriously that word recognition is facilitated by the reader's expectations, guesses, hypotheses, or predictions, we must specify just what is expected, guessed, hypothesized, or predicted.

Unhappily, hypothesis theorists like Goodman (1976) and Smith (1971) are frustratingly vague on this score. We expect that they might deny that the reader formulates hypotheses about specific words. Instead, they would probably argue that the reader's expectations concern the gist—the substance—of the reading matter (not any particular words). This may well be, but if the first n words of a sentence are to influence the recognition of the $n + 1st,$ then the reader's hypothesis must have some bearing on that word. Thus, we are led to ask what prediction the reader might make about the $n + 1st$ word, and what effect such a prediction might have.

At one extreme, sentential context might lead the reader to predict a specific word. This possibility has some appeal to us: The next word sometimes feels inevitable to the reader, and knowledge that a certain word is under fixation clearly enhances its recognition.

Thus, a hypothesis theory claiming that the reader hypothesizes specific words would seem to have real explanatory power. But the problem it faces is that specific word predictions are seldom correct.

The reader may not realize just how difficult it is to predict the exact word in running text. To demonstrate this point, we asked a colleague to guess—one at a time—the first 100 words of each of 10 ordinary reading selections. Before we began each selection, we gave our subject its author, title, and subject matter. He then began to guess. After each guess, we read the correct word, and then repeated (at our subject's request) the entire text up to and including that word. Thus, he had available, at every point, the entire preceding context to assist him. His results are presented in Table 4.1.

As the table shows, our intelligent, well-educated reader, given unlimited time to select a word, predicted only about one word in four, with the exception of one book which appeared to be highly redundant for him. We would submit that this must be near the upper bound of predictability, and the accuracy that could be achieved in real time by the average reader must be far, far less. Still we can ask whether performance like this would, in fact, enhance word recognition if it were achieved. It seems fair to assume that the reader's correct predictions

TABLE 4.1
Proportion of Correct Guesses of the First 100 Words of 10 Books by
Subject DJF, Ph.D.

Author	Title	Proportion
Cash, W. J.	The mind of the south	.20
Fischer, B.	Bobby Fischer teaches chess	.21
Foss, D. J., & Hakes, D. T.	Psycholinguistics	.74
Gardner, J.	October light	.21
Gould, S. J.	Ever since Darwin	.39
Guevara, C.	The diary of Che Guevara	.23
Malinowski, B.	Magic, science, and religion	.20
Stillman, I. M., & Baker, S. S.	The doctor's quick weight loss diet	.32
Wooden, J.	They call me coach	.25

would facilitate the recognition of the predicted words. But what about the false predictions, which outnumber the true by at least three to one? To answer this question, we ran a simple experiment.

Experiment 2

We asked 12 of our friends (faculty and graduate students) to recognize and name aloud each of 75 words as quickly as possible without making mistakes. The words were presented one at a time on a CRT, and prior to each word, we gave the subject a vocal warning signal. On one third of the trials the warning signal was the word that would subsequently appear; on one third it was another, unrelated word; and on one third it was the word *ready*. Presentation of the target word started a timer, the onset of the subject's response triggered a voice-key that stopped the timer, and our computer recorded each latency.

Mean naming latencies for the three types of trials are presented in Table 4.2. As the table reveals, a correct prediction did facilitate the recognition and naming of the word by about 30 msec. But a false prediction had the opposite effect, retarding recognition by about 12 msec. If these estimates are anywhere near the true values, it is clear that the net effect of prediction at the level of the single word cannot be to facilitate word recognition: The cumulative effect of the more

TABLE 4.2
Mean Naming Latency as a Function
of Type of Forewarning

Type	Latency (msec)
Ready signal	442
Target word	413
Unrelated word	454

frequent false predictions would be to swamp the advantage of the occasional correct one. Thus, we are led to conclude that readers cannot be picking their way through text, anticipating it word by word. We must look for another idea.

The hypothesis that the reader expects or anticipates particular words is the limiting case of a more general hypothesis that local context facilitates word recognition by reducing the number of alternatives. It is generally accepted that the time it takes to make a choice is well approximated by a linear function on the logarithm of the number of alternatives. In other words, every time you double the number of alternatives, you increase choice reaction time by a constant amount. By the same token, decreasing the number of alternatives has the opposite effect, so that if context reduces the number of available alternatives, this might be expected to reduce the time it takes to recognize the target word.

At first glance, this is an appealing hypothesis because of its parsimony. As Garner (1972) puts it in discussing Tulving and Gold's results: "... it is likely that the context improves recognition accuracy by a mechanism which is not at all unique to the use of words as stimuli. Most likely, the context provides a smaller message set for the observer, and thus improves accuracy of recognition [p. 278]." In one or another version, this view has been widely accepted by students of reading, prominently including Smith and Holmes (1971). But closer inspection raises a disturbing question.

Although choice reaction time is known to vary linearly with the logarithm of the number of alternatives over a wide range of stimuli and responses, the slope of that function varies inversely with stimulus–response compatibility and with practice (Fitts & Posner, 1967). In naming Arabic numerals, for example, Mowbray (1960) found no effect of number of alternatives whatsoever. Given that word recognition involves highly practiced, highly compatible stimulus–response pairs, there is a serious question as to whether reducing the number of alternative words could be expected to have any effect at all on their speed of recognition.

We are aware of four attempts to resolve this issue experimentally. Unfortunately, though, these four experiments have produced conflicting results. For example, in an experiment reported by Frick (1953), subjects named words that were presented individually on a screen. Each experimental word was preceded by a list of from 4 to 1024 words, one of which was the subsequently presented target word. Frick reported that naming latency increased linearly with number of alternatives. But, unfortunately, the details of this study were not reported, so we cannot be sure just how the experiment was conducted or how large the effect was. A similar study reported by Pollack (1963) collected data from five subjects over a period of 4 months and also found that naming time increased with number of alternatives, at a rate of about 13 msec per log unit. But here again, evaluation of the experiment is difficult because Pollack tells us that he was reporting data left behind by his predecessors and admits knowing very little about the procedures of the experiment. Thus, even though these experiments seem to support the idea that reducing the number of alternatives facilitates word recognition, we must evaluate their findings with some caution.

The other two experiments reached somewhat different conclusions. Pierce and Karlin (1957) asked subjects to read aloud lists of 256 words drawn from vocabularies ranging from 2 to 256 words. As expected, they found that reading time for the list increased monotonically with vocabulary size, but the function was markedly negatively accelerated; although there was a dramatic effect as vocabulary increased from two to four items, there was little effect beyond that. Approaching from the other direction, what this means is that reducing the number of alternative words had virtually no effect until the reader was constrained to fewer than four. These data offer little support for the idea that the facilitative effect of context on word recognition is mediated by a reduction in the number of alternatives, for, as Shannon (1951) has shown, the average uncertainty of a word in English text is about eight bits. Inasmuch as 2^8 equals 256, what this means is that, on the average, sentential context reduces the number of alternatives to 256 words. The Pierce and Karlin results clearly indicate that such a reduction would have absolutely no effect on speed of recognition.

In the most recent experiment to be reported, Theios and Muise (1977) obtained pronunciation latency data for single words drawn from vocabularies ranging in size from 2 to 24. Their results showed little or no effect of vocabulary size on pronunciation latency, again supporting the conclusion that number of alternatives has no effect on reading time.

We cannot easily account for the divergence of findings in these four experiments, largely because some of them were not reported in enough detail to allow for meaningful comparisons. So we attempted to obtain our own evidence by conducting still another experiment that manipulated the number of alternatives and measured their effect on the latency of recognizing individual words.

Experiment 3

We once again prevailed on our friends to name single words, presented one at a time on a CRT, and measured the naming latency for each word. Prior to each word, a subject was handed a three-by-five card on which were typed all (and only) the words that might be presented on that trial. The card contained from 1 to 32 alternatives, which subjects were asked to read aloud; when finished, they pressed a button to present the target word and named it as quickly as possibly.

The results for five highly practiced subjects are shown in Fig. 4.2. There was a large increase in naming latency from one alternative to two, reflecting the difference between simple and choice reaction time, but for all larger numbers of alternatives, there were no significant differences, according to a Newman-Keuls test. A linear-trend analysis over all numbers of alternatives greater than one failed to show evidence of a linear relationship between the log (base 2) of

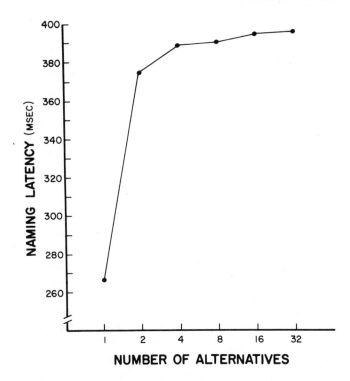

FIG. 4.2. Naming latency as a function of number of alternatives.

the number of alternatives and naming latency F $(1,4) = 3.67$, $p > .10$. Inasmuch as even a minimal sentential context appears to reduce naming latency, it is tempting to conclude that the effect of syntactic context cannot be mediated by a reduction in the number of alternatives.

For the present, we dare not draw this conclusion because our study has two shortcomings. First, as we did not include conditions beyond 32 alternatives, we cannot be sure that the full effect of reduction in the number of alternatives might not be enough to account for the contextual effect. Second, the set of alternatives from which our words were drawn were totally arbitrary, quite unlike the sets that context might provide. Until these weaknesses are remedied, we cannot be positive that the effect of context could not be mediated by a reduction in the number of alternatives. But neither our results nor those of the other two well-documented experiments reported earlier provide any support for the almost universally accepted assumption that it is. Hence, we do think it is fair to conclude that there is little evidence that the reader's expectations, guesses, hypotheses, or predictions mediate the influence of sentential context on word recognition.

FORM AND CONTEXT

In the end, global and local, semantic and syntactic context converge on the word under fixation. At that point, contextual information must combine with the visual information arising from the printed page to determine the recognition of a word. The question of how these two sources of information combine is crucial to theories of reading.

There are only two answers to this question. One is that context and visual form provide independent sources of information in determining the word; the other is that they interact in some way.

The latter view is certainly the more popular. Most theorists (e.g., Gibson & Levin, 1975; Goodman, 1976; Smith 1971), if we interpret them correctly, hold that context and form interact, such that context influences the extraction of visual information from the word. But the issue cannot be decided by election; it must be settled in the laboratory.

Some 15 years ago, Tulving, Mandler, and Baumal (1964) apparently settled this matter in favor of interaction. Their argument went as follows: Suppose one knew the probability of recognizing a word given only a certain amount of information about its form (and nothing about its context); call this f. Suppose one also knew the probability of recognizing the same word given only a certain amount of context (and nothing about its form); call this c. Finally, suppose one knew the probability of recognizing the word given *both* form and context; call this p. If form and context are independent, then these probabilities must combine according to:

$$p = f + c - fc$$

If they do not, form and context cannot be independent, and they must be interacting.

Tulving et al. (1964) proceeded to measure the probability with which subjects recognized tachistoscopically presented words given various amounts of context and form. The target words were the final words of nine-word sentences. Context was varied by presenting 0, 2, 4, or all 8 of the preceding words of the sentence in the preexposure field. Form information was varied by exposing the target words for eight different durations, ranging from 0 to 140 msec in 20-msec steps.

Estimates of f at each of the eight exposure durations were obtained from the 0 context conditions, and estimates of c at each of the four levels of context were obtained under the 0 exposure duration condition. The remaining seven levels of form combined with three degrees of context then yielded 21 separate opportunities to test the independence hypothesis. In every instance, the probability of recognition given both form and context exceeded that predicted by the independence hypothesis. Tulving et al. naturally rejected that hypothesis and concluded that context and form must interact in word recognition.

The logic of the argument made by Tulving et al. (1964) seems irrefutable. If the estimates of f and c are valid, and if these are independent, then they must combine according to Equation 4.1. Observed performance clearly exceeded predicted values, so apparently we are forced to conclude that the two information sources are not independent.

There is, however, a weak link in the chain of argument. The argument clearly depends on the validity of the estimates of f and c. If these estimates are too low, then we must underestimate performance when form and context are combined, not because form and context interact, but simply because we have underestimated their independent contribution. It occurred to us that Tulving et al. might have done this by allowing each subject only one response on each trial. A brief tachistoscopic exposure, or a few words of context, seldom narrows the list of possible alternatives to one word. If subjects under these conditions are limited to a single response, they may be forced to choose among several possibilities, which the form, or context, suggests. If subjects choose anything but the target word, the probability of either form or context having brought the target word to mind will be underestimated.

An analogy may make this point clearer. Suppose 100 subjects were asked to name a floor covering and assume that 50 of them said *rug*. Now suppose another 100 subjects were given the form *r———g* and asked to complete the word, and again assume that 50 said *rug*. We take the first proportion to estimate c and the second to estimate f. We assume these probabilities to be independent, and we predict that the probability of saying *rug* given both clues will be .50 + .50 − (.5)(.5) = .75. But we observe that the performance of a third group given both clues is very close to perfect. We cannot conclude from this finding, however, that contextual and visual information interacted because the apparent interaction is nothing but a failure to estimate the amount of information provided by the two clues accurately. For example, given *r———g*, although only half the subjects gave *rug* as their first response, even those who thought *rag* or *rig* most likely also thought of *rug*.

In this example, it is clear that what we should do to estimate f or c accurately is allow our subjects to give more than one response and set f and c equal to the proportion who include *rug* among their responses in each case.

In similar fashion, we reasoned that Tulving et al. may have underestimated the amount of information their subjects extracted from tachistoscopically presented words by limiting them to a single response and that a better estimate would be obtained by permitting the subject to make multiple responses. So we decided to replicate the experiment and do just this.

Experiment 4

After substituting new sentences for a few of the Canadianisms used by Tulving et al., we used a projection tachistoscope to present words to 20 friends. Each stimulus word was presented for 20, 40, 60, or 80 msec and was both preceded and followed by a pattern mask. Prior to the presentation of each item, the subjects read zero, four, or eight words of context. After each word was presented, subjects were asked to write down as many guesses as they liked. On the average, our subjects wrote down less than three. We then obtained our estimates of f by counting the proportion of subjects who included the correct word among their responses.

We did not try to obtain estimates of c in the same manner because we feared that even allowing multiple responses could not result in a valid estimate. The problem is that partial contexts, especially when they are not sentence initial, provide so little constraint that large numbers of words are congruous with such contexts. Thus, the number of guesses a subject might give in the absence of form would be limited only by the subject's endurance and enthusiasm for the task. An ambitious subject might maximize performance (i.e., c) by listing every word in the language; to stop a subject anywhere short of that would be arbitrary. For this reason, we felt that we could not obtain a valid estimate of c directly, so we decided instead to finesse the problem.

We observed that the independence formula can be rewritten as:

$$p = c + (1 - c)f$$

In this form, it is clear that the assumption of independence predicts that the probability of a correct response given both form and context should be a linear function of the probability given form alone, with intercept c and slope $(1 - c)$. Thus, if we were to combine a given level of context with various amounts of form and plotted the obtained results against those obtained with form alone, they should lie on a straight line whose slope is equal to one minus its intercept.

Our results are presented in Fig. 4.3, along with straight lines fitted by least squares. The data fall very close to those straight lines, which is to say that the probability of word recognition given both form and context conforms very closely to the values one would obtain if the contributions of form and context were totally independent.

We take these results to show that, at least in the tachistoscopic situation, context and form do not interact. This conclusion directly contradicts that recently drawn by Meyer, Schvaneveldt, and Ruddy (1975) and Becker and Killion (1977) from results they obtained in the lexical decision task.

Both groups of investigators found that the prior occurrence of a semantically related word facilitated the recognition of a target word more as the visual quality of the target was reduced (by degradation in one case, by reduction in brightness in the other). Thus, the effect of context varied inversely with the effect of form, and form and context were not independent in this task.

As noted earlier, we do not think that adjacent related words in the lexical decision task are representative of context in ordinary reading. Given this reservation, we were led to wonder how sentential context would combine with form to determine word-recognition latency. So we conducted a final experiment.

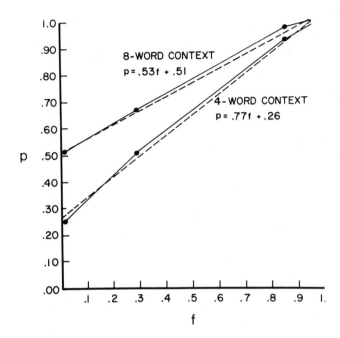

FIG. 4.3. Probability of correct recognition given both form and context as a function of probability correct given form aloen (f).

Experiment 5

We asked 16 faculty members and graduate students to name words varying in both intensity and context. Each subject named 100 words—half in isolation, half preceded by four words of sentence-related context, at each of two levels of intensity. The latencies of their responses were recorded, and their means are presented in Fig. 4.4.

Words presented at high intensity were recognized 23 msec faster than low-intensity words ($min\ F = 31.97$, $p < .001$). The effect of context was also significant, with words preceded by sentence context being recognized 19 msec faster than words preceded by neutral context ($min\ F = 22.07$, $p < .001$). But the interaction of context and intensity effects is not significant ($min\ F = 1.27$, $p < .10$).

These results are not consistent with those obtained by Becker and Killion: Both context and brightness have significant effects on naming latency, but the contextual effect is not greater on the lesser form; if anything the effect goes in the opposite direction.

These results surely suggest that the effect of sentential context (i.e., the kind of context normally encountered in reading) is independent of the effect of form. In the terms of information processing, they suggest that context influences a separate (and presumably later) stage than that in which form is processed. These

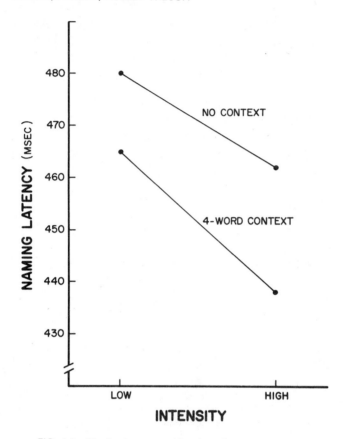

FIG. 4.4.   Naming latency as a function of target-word intensity.

results are even consistent with the extreme view that context has nothing to do with word recognition until visual processing of the word is complete. One could interpret this to mean that we must seek a theory of reading that could get the reader from print to meaning without benefit of hypotheses, expectations, or even psycholinguistic guessing.

SUMMARY

First, we have observed that the effects of local and global context on word recognition must depend on different mechanisms because local context must involve a syntactic component lacking in global context. Inasmuch as the former changes every moment, the effect of local context must be transitory. But the effect of global context must be stable.

Second, the effect of global context cannot be mediated by the spreading activation between semantically related words commonly assumed to operate in the lexical decision task, for that is not stable. It does not persist across intervening items, and semantically related words rarely occur in adjacent positions.

Third, the effect of local context cannot be mediated by the reader's expectations, guesses, hypotheses, or predictions because, if they are precise enough to help, they are wrong too often to do so.

Fourth, however the effects of normal syntactic and semantic context are mediated, they do not seem to interact with the effects of form; form and context are processed independently.

We began with the observation that students of reading have disagreed about virtually everything except context. We hope we have shown that there is also room to disagree about context.

REFERENCES

Becker, C. A., & Killion, T. H. Interaction of visual and cognitive effects in word recognition. *Journal of Experimental Psychology: Human Perception and Performance*, 1977, *3*, 389–401.

Brozek, J., Franklin, J. D., Guetzkow, H., & Keys, A. Human behavior in prolonged semi-starvation. *American Psychologist*, 1946, *1*, 269–270.

Collins, A. M., & Loftus, E. F. A spreading-activation theory of semantic processing. *Psychological Review*, 1975, *82*, 407–428.

Fitts, P., & Posner, M. I. *Human performance*. Monterey, Cal.: Brooks/Cole, 1967.

Forster, K. I. Levels of processing and the structure of the language processor. In W. E. Cooper & E. Walker (Eds.), *Sentence processing: Psycholinguistic studies presented to Merrill Garrett*. Cambridge, Mass.: MIT Press, 1979. 27–86.

Frick, F. C. Some perceptual problems from the point of view of information theory. In B. MacMillan (Ed.), *Current trends in information theory*. Pittsburgh, Pa.: University of Pittsburgh Press, 1953.

Garner, W. R. Information integration and form of encoding. In A. W. Melton & E. Martin (Eds.), *Coding processes in human memory*. Washington, D.C.: Winston, 1972.

Gibson, E. J., & Levin, H. *The psychology of reading*. Cambridge, Mass.: MIT Press, 1975.

Goodman, K. S. Reading: A psycholinguistic guessing game. In H. Singer & R. B. Ruddell (Eds.), *Theoretical models and processes of reading* (2nd ed.). Newark, Del.: International Reading Association, 1976.

Haber, R. M. Visual perception. In M. R. Rosensweig & L. W. Porter (Eds.), *Annual review of psychology* (29). Palo Alto, Cal.: Annual Reviews, 1978.

Kolers, P. Three stages of reading. In H. Levin & J. P. Williams (Eds.), *Basic studies on reading*. New York: Basic Books, 1970.

Meyer, D. E., Schvaneveldt, R. W., & Ruddy, M. G. *Activation of lexical memory*. Paper presented at the meeting of the Psychonomic Society, St. Louis, Mo., November 1972.

Meyer, D. E., Schvaneveldt, R. W., & Ruddy, M. G. Loci of contextual effects on visual word recognition. In P. Rabbit & S. Dornic (Eds.), *Attention and performance V*. New York: Academic Press, 1975.

Mowbray, G. H. Choice reaction time for skilled responses. *Quarterly Journal of Experimental Psychology*, 1960, *12*, 192–202.

Neely, J. H. Semantic priming and retrieval from lexical memory: Roles of inhibitionless spreading activation and limited-capacity attention. *Journal of Experimental Psychology: General*, 1977, *106*, 226–254.

Pierce, J. R., & Karlin, J. E. Reading rates and the information rate of a human channel. *Bell System Technical Journal*, 1957, *36*, 497–516.

Pollack, I. Verbal reaction time to briefly presented words. *Perceptual & Motor Skills,* 1963, *17,* 137–138.

Roget, P. M. *Thesaurus of English words and phrases, classified and arranged so as to facilitate the expression of ideas and assist in literary composition.* London: Longman, Brown, Green & Longmans, 1852.

Rubenstein, H., & Aborn, J. Learning, prediction, and readability. *Journal of Applied Psychology,* 1958, *42,* 28–32.

Scarborough, D. L., Cortese, C., & Scarborough, H. S. Frequency and repetition effects in lexical memory. *Journal of Experimental Psychology: Human Perception and Performance,* 1977, *3,* 1–17.

Shannon, C. E. Prediction and entropy in printed English. *Bell System Technical Journal,* 1951, *30,* 50–64.

Smith, F. *Understanding reading.* New York: Holt, Rinehart & Winston, 1971.

Smith, F., & Holmes, D. L. The independence of letter, word, and meaning identification in reading. *Reading Research Quarterly,* 1971, *6,* 394–415.

Sternberg, S. The discovery of processing stages: Extensions of Donders' method. In W. G. Koster (Ed.), *Attention and performance II.* Amsterdam: North Holland Publishing Co., 1969.

Theios, J., & Muise, J. G. The word identification process in reading. In J. Castellan, D. Pisoni, & G. Potts (Eds.), *Cognitive theory* (Vol. 2). Hillsdale, N.J.: Lawrence Erlbaum Associates, 1977.

Tulving, E., & Gold, C. Stimulus information and contextual information as determinants of tachistoscopic recognition of words. *Journal of Experimental Psychology,* 1963, *66,* 319–327.

Tulving, E., Mandler, G., & Baumal, R. Interaction of two sources of information in word recognition. *Canadian Journal of Psychology,* 1964, *18,* 62–71.

Weber, R. First graders' use of grammatical context in reading. In H. Levin & J. P. Williams (Eds.), *Basic studies on reading.* New York: Basic Books, 1970.

5 Processing Words in Context

Kathryn T. Spoehr
Brown University

Richard E. Schuberth
Rice University

How do skilled readers identify words? Research directed at answering this question has been carried out for nearly 100 years by investigators in both education and experimental psychology (Cattel, 1885; Huey, 1908). Although the process of recognizing a single word would seem to be relatively simple in comparison to the complex linguistic and memory processes necessary to comprehend written discourse, an understanding of how word recognition takes place has remained relatively elusive. One reason why it has been difficult to build appropriate models of word recognition is that the process combines the operation of some mechanisms usually designated as strictly perceptual with those generally considered to be linguistic.

A brief review of the factors that seem to affect the word-recognition process will highlight the diversity of mechanisms responsible for its operation. At a strictly visual level, it is clear that factors affecting the visual quality of a word to be recognized will influence the speed and/or accuracy with which this is done. Such factors include the intensity of the stimulus material (e.g., Becker, 1976), the presence or absence of visual noice (e.g., Meyer, Schvaneveldt, & Ruddy, 1975), and the duration of the presentation (e.g., Tulving & Gold, 1963). Such variables presumably affect the usefulness of the visual information extracted from the stimulus. Also affecting word recognition at the visual level are featural characteristics such as type font (e.g., McClelland, 1977) and word and letter shape (e.g., Bouma, 1971). That letters within strings influence each other is shown by the fact that statistical redundancies between letter positions facilitate word recognition (e.g., Thompson & Massaro, 1973). However, there are a host of linguistic phenomena that appear to influence word recognition at least as much as the preceding visual factors. These include pronounciability (Gibson,

Pick, Osser, & Hammond, 1962), the presence of spelling regularities (Massaro, Venezky, & Taylor, 1979), and frequency of the stimulus string (Broadbent, 1967) and of its component letters and substrings (Mason, 1975).

Despite the considerable amount of information that has accrued over the years on how words are recognized in isolation, systematic study of how that process operates in connected text has been undertaken only relatively recently. Inasmuch as one of the goals of understanding word recognition is to understand an important component of reading, it seems particularly important to know whether the information gained from studying the recognition of isolated words is applicable to understanding normal reading. The differences between these two related processes make the generalization of single-word results nontrivial.

The differences between isolated word recognition experiments and reading are both many and obvious. First, in reading the visual input is rarely degraded visually, nor is the reader's processing time restricted externally, either by limited presentation duration or time pressures for rapid responses. In practice, of course, skilled reading does contain elements of quick presentation and the masklike qualities of successive visual inputs due to rapid eye movements. However, there is a qualitative difference in having these limits imposed by an experimenter—as they are in word-recognition studies—as opposed to controlling them oneself in reading.

A second obvious difference between reading and word-recognition experiments is that reading requires the extraction of meaning through the integration of previous semantic and syntactic information with new visual input. Isolated word recognition, on the other hand, depends not at all on syntax and very little, if at all, on semantics. This dependence in reading on syntax and semantics brings us to a third difference between reading and word recognition. It is very rarely the case in natural reading that subjects can devote their entire processing resources to the task of identifying a single word. However, in isolated word recognition, the analysis of the visual input takes place in the absence of demands on memory or the preattentional pattern-recognition mechanisms that separate relevant visual input from extraneous sources of stimulation.

Given these differences between isolated word recognition experiments and normal reading it is reasonable to ask how the word-recognition process operates in situations more closely resembling natural reading. There are two related reasons for pursuing this type of research. One is to determine how semantic and syntactic context do influence the word-recognition process so that the resulting theoretical accounts are more directly applicable to natural reading. It is clear from the early work of Tulving and Gold (1963) that contextual cues provided by a sentence do influence the word-recognition process. The basic result of interest is illustrated in Fig. 5.1 and was obtained in a tachistoscopic task in which the dependent measure was the exposure duration at which the subjects could accurately report the final word of the sentence. Prior presentation of semantic and syntactic context, as provided by a sentence frame, improves a subject's ability to reconize a word that completes that frame sensibly. However, prior presenta-

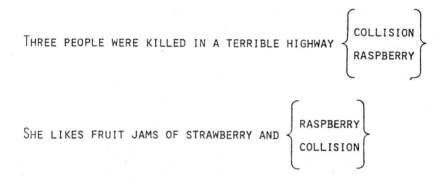

FIG. 5.1. Examples of sentence frames and targets from Tulving and Gold (1963).

tion of the same sentence will impede a subject's ability to report a word that is an unlikely completion for the frame. This is the basic congruity effect: A context facilitates recognition for congruous words and inhibits word recognition for incongruous words.

The second reason for examining how words are processed in context is to determine the extent to which our already considerable knowledge of how word recognition takes place in isolation can be applied to the process of natural reading. In order to facilitate this comparison, we examine data from context studies that use many of the same experimental paradigms used in studies of isolated words. The two most common tasks that we discuss are the naming and the lexical decision tasks. In the former, the stimulus of interest is presented to the subject under various contextual conditions, and the amount of time taken by the subject to pronounce or read the stimulus aloud is measured. In the lexical decision task, stimuli are either words or nonsense strings, and the subject's task is to decide as quickly as possible whether the stimulus is an English word. As in the naming task, we measure the latency of the response under various contextual conditions.

In the following sections we summarize a large body of research in which the naming and lexical decision tasks are used to examine the influence of context on word recognition. Along with these empirical findings, we present and evaluate several theoretical accounts of word processing in context and present some of our own research that sheds light on how context influences word recognition.

EFFECTS OF SINGLE-WORD CONTEXTS

The simplest case under which contextual effects can be studied is one in which the recognition of some particular word is influenced by a single other word. Meyer and his associates (Meyer & Schvaneveldt, 1971; Meyer et al., 1975) have used this procedure extensively to determine what processes operate during word recognition and how context influences them. In the initial study, Meyer and Schvaneveldt (1971) presented subjects with two letter strings, one printed above the other. The subjects were required to respond "yes" if both strings were English words and "no" otherwise. Meyer and Schvaneveldt varied the degree of semantic association between the two items presented on a single trial and found that subjects were faster in responding "yes" when the two words were semantically associated than when they were semantically unassociated. The facilitation presumably arises because processing or accessing the first item in memory allows more rapid processing of other words associated to it. This may happen because similar words require similar recognition processes, which can proceed more efficiently the second time they are used within a short period of time. Alternatively, facilitation may occur because activation spreads to semantically related memory locations as a result of recognition of the top member of the stimulus pair (Collins & Loftus, 1975).

Meyer et al. (1975) built upon the earlier results by employing an additive factors analysis of similar reaction-time data. The logic of their experiments is based upon the assumption that word recognition involves three general stages of processing. First, the stimulus letter string is encoded into an internal representation. This encoding may be purely visual (graphemic), or it may have phonemic or semantic information included as well. A lexical retrieval stage then matches this stimulus encoding to stored representations until a match is found, and a third response generation stage produces a response based on the results of lexical retrieval.

Using Sternberg's (1969) additive factors reasoning, it is possible to determine at which of these three stages context has its effect. Meyer el al. (1975) successively presented letter strings in pairs, and subjects made lexical decisions to each member of the pair. Context was manipulated on trials in which both strings were words by presenting words that were either associated or unassociated in meaning. An orthogonal variation in stimulus quality was introduced for the second word of each pair. On some trials the second item was clearly visible (intact), whereas on other trials it was degraded by the superimposition of a grid of dots. Sternberg's (1969) results had indicated that visual quality affected stimulus encoding operations. Thus, Meyer et al. reasoned that if contextual congruity (association) was additive with visual quality, the two factors must influence different stages of processing, whereas if they interacted it could be assumed that they both influenced stimulus encoding. The results of the lexical decision task show that contextual congruity reliably interacts with stimulus quality.

The conclusion that context and quality must therefore both affect stimulus encoding and not lexical retrieval is reinforced by similar results from a naming latency task. Meyer et al. point out that naming aloud does not necessarily require lexical access because pronunciations can be constructed using spelling-to-sound rules to convert graphemic input to a phonemic form. Moreover, they also counted those responses that were allowable pronunciations for stimuli but that did not correspond to the correct word pronunciations (e.g., pronouncing *pint* with a "short" *i*). Inasmuch as subjects did not have to locate entries in lexical memory to perform this task, the interaction between quality and congruity must have arisen from the earlier stage of processing.

Another factor that clearly affects lexical decision time is word frequency. Rubenstein, Garfield, and Millikan (1970) showed that verification times were faster for frequent words than for infrequent words. The likely locus of this type of effect in the Meyer et al. (1975) framework is in the lexical retrieval stage where it is assumed that more frequent words are easier to locate than less frequent words. Thus, the additive factors logic would dictate that frequency should be additive with both stimulus quality and contextual congruity. Stanners, Jastrzembski, and Westbrook (1975) factorially manipulated stimulus quality and frequency of words in a lexical decision task and obtained the expected additivity of the two factors. Becker (1976) and Becker and Killion (1977) have replicated many of these results using stimulus intensity, rather than dot degradation, as an index of stimulus quality. Again it was found that contextual congruity, as measured by semantic association between the first and second words in a stimulus pair, reliably affected the lexical decision time for the second item and that congruity interacted with quality. Furthermore, frequency was found to be additive with quality as it was in the Stanners et al. study.

Although the serial-stage model of Meyer et al. (1975) seems capable of handling all of the single-word context data up to this point, it fails to explain two important recent findings. Neely (1976) used three single-word priming conditions in a lexical decision task: a condition in which the prime and the target word were semantically related, one in which they were unrelated, and one in which a neutral prime consisting of a row of X's was used. Neely found that the prior presentation of a related prime facilitated decisions relative to the neutral prime condition and that an unrelated prime lengthened decision latencies relative to the neutral condition. This pattern of facilitation and inhibition relative to a neutral condition has been replicated by Neely (1977) and Becker (1978). Although the facilitative process suggested by Meyer et al. can accommodate facilitation effects for related primes, it provides no mechanism for the inhibitory effects of unrelated contexts. The second result that cannot be accommodated by the serial-stage model has been reported by Becker (1979). In this experiment the relatedness of the prime to the target and the frequency of the target were manipulated. Becker found a significant interaction between these two factors. The serial-stage model could predict this result only if frequency and congruity affected the same stage of processing. As this clearly cannot be the case because of the additivity of frequency and quality and the interaction of quality and congruity, the serial-stage model must be abandoned or modified.

The interaction of stimulus and contextual information has been accounted for in an entirely different fashion by Morton (1969, 1970). Under Morton's system each lexical item is represented in memory by a counting mechanism called a "logogen." As the visual feature analysis system identifies features from the input string, those logogens that represent lexical items containing the features extracted increment their counters; the more visual information that is consistent with a particular word, the more its logogen will be incremented. A response is made by the system when some logogen exceeds a threshold value, at which point the corresponding response code is sent to the response buffer. The inhibitory effects of stimulus degradation—either by lowered intensity or by visual noise—can be accounted for by the Logogen Model by assuming that the rate of feature extraction is slowed by degradation, thereby increasing the amount of time before some logogen exceeds threshold.

Morton incorporates the effects of context and frequency by making some additional assumptions. First, it is assumed that high-frequency words have lower response thresholds than low-frequency words. This has the effect of making logogens for high-frequency words exceed threshold sooner and thus be recognized more quickly. In addition, the logogen system is assumed to receive input information from a "context system." That is, previous semantic and syntactic input will serve to increment the counters of words that are related to or belong in the stimulus context. Thus, context will cause the logogens of congruous words to exceed threshold more rapidly than those of incongruous words, and the former will be identified more rapidly.

Although the logogen approach provides mechanisms that correctly predict the main effects of stimulus quality, frequency, and congruity, it does not adequately account for all of the observed patterns of interaction when two or more of these variables are manipulated factorially. Detailed derivations of the predictions have been published elsewhere (Becker & Killion, 1977; Schuberth & Eimas, 1977), but a brief summary here can make the strengths and weaknesses of the model clear. First, the logogen approach accurately accounts for the quality by congruity interaction. This is because the effects of semantic context are necessarily larger for degraded than undegraded stimuli (see Becker & Killion, 1977). However, the model predicts that frequency and contextual congruity must be additive because they both affect the relative difference between the count on a particular logogen and the threshold at which it will fire. As Becker (1979) has demonstrated, these factors interact rather than add. Finally, the Logogen Model fails to account for the additive effects of stimulus frequency and quality observed by Stanners et al. (1975) and Becker and Killion (1977). Instead, the model suggests that they should be interactive under the same logic applied to the interaction of quality and contextual congruity.

In order to account for the single-word data, Becker (Becker, 1976, 1979; Becker & Killion, 1977) has suggested a Verification Model, which recognizes lexical items using an analysis-by-synthesis approach. The Verification Model views visual encoding as a process of visual feature extraction during which stimulus information is matched to a detector system at the level of the entire word. Any given stimulus is likely to trigger several detectors of words that are visually similar to it, and these items are assumed to constitute a visually defined set of elements upon which a later verification process operates. This verification process retrieves memory representations of the words in the visually defined set and compares each retrieved representation to the stimulus information until a successful match is found. In cases where semantic and/or syntactic context is provided, the contents of the visually defined set may be bypassed altogether. Context is assumed to activate word detectors for congruous words, which then make up a semantically defined set of items upon which the verification process operates. The representations of these semantically defined items are then compared to the visual representation of the stimulus by the verification process until a match is found. If none of the semantically defined items match the input, the verification process may then go on and test the contents of the visually defined set.

The congruity effect is explained because congruous elements will be part of the semantically defined set and will be recognized more quickly than the incongruous items that are verified later from the visually defined set. Of course, if no context is provided, verification operates immediately upon the contents of the visually defined set, and no facilitation or inhibitory effects occur. The interaction of context (congruity) with stimulus quality is accounted for by assuming that lower intensity or stimulus degradation leaves the rate of verification unchanged but slows the rate of feature extraction. The formation of the visually defined set is therefore delayed, and this delay influences decisions only for incongruous items that would be in the visually defined set. Congruous targets could be classified quickly from the semantically defined set regardless of how long it takes to form the extraneous visual set. The additive effects of frequency and stimulus quality are explained by the fact that frequency influences the verification process, whereas stimulus quality influences the independent process of feature extraction. Finally, the interaction of frequency and congruity follows from the assumption that frequency influences the verification process for the visually defined set but not for the semantically defined set. That is, recognition of a word presented after an incongruous or unrelated context results from sampling from the visually defined set. Sampling from this set is determined by the frequencies of the items in it. The semantically defined set, on the other hand, is sampled according to the strength of relationship with the context and not according to frequency. Therefore, words presented in a related or congruous context are recognized by verification from a semantic set in which frequency plays no role. The Verification Model thus successfully accounts for the pattern of relationships found between the factors of stimulus quality, congruity, and frequency with single-word contexts.

EFFECTS OF SENTENCE CONTEXT

As we noted earlier, it is a well-established finding that the provision of a sentence context affects the recognition of a subsequently presented word stimulus (e.g., Morton, 1964; Tulving & Gold, 1963; Tulving, Mandler, & Baumal, 1964). Several studies have been undertaken recently to examine further the nature of such contextual effects. For example, Schuberth and Eimas (1977) required subjects to make lexical decisions about word and nonword completions to incomplete sentence contexts. The word stimuli were either high- or low-frequency items and either semantically congruous or incongruous with respect to the sentence contexts. Contextual effects were assessed by comparing decision latencies for the stimuli when context was presented and when it was not. The presentation of context decreased decision latencies for congruous words and increased decision latencies for incongruous words. In addition, the frequency of a word and its congruity in context had independent and additive effects on decision latency.

Fischler and Bloom (1979) have more recently employed the lexical decision priming paradigm in an attempt to delineate those conditions under which the facilitative and inhibitory effects of context occur. These investigators found that the presentation of sentence context decreased decision latencies for highly probable words, had no effect on decision latencies for congruous but unlikely words, and increased decision latencies for incongruous words. Increasing the interval of time during which the context was presented did not alter this pattern of effects, and subjects could not eliminate the facilitative and inhibitory effects of context when they were instructed to ignore the implication of each context. However, the inhibitory effects of context were eliminated in a condition in which all of the test words were incongruous with respect to the sentence context.

Fischler and Bloom's finding—that context did not decrease decision latencies for the set of congruous words as a whole—contrasts with the results of Schuberth and Eimas (1977). The most likely reason for these contrasting results is that the distribution of Cloze probabilities for the word stimuli was wider and better balanced in the Fischler and Bloom study. These authors argue that the presence of high-probability word stimuli may have prompted subjects to allocate attention primarily to those word candidates that provided highly dominant completions to the context of each trial. Thus, as a result of this strategy, context decreased decision latencies only for a small subset of the words that meaningfully completed the context.

The demonstration of facilitative and inhibitory effects of sentence-context priming on word recognition parallels the findings of Neely (1976) who employed single-word primes in a lexical decision task. Although this parallel in results would seem to suggest that the two types of context influence word recognition in a similar fashion, there is a growing body of evidence suggesting that single-word and sentence contexts affect word recognition differently. For example, the effect of the semantic relatedness of the stimulus and a single-word context on lexical decision latency has been found to interact with the effects of the frequency (Becker, 1979), visual quality (Meyer et al., 1975), and intensity of the stimulus (Becker & Killion, 1977). In contrast, the effect of an incomplete sentence context on lexical decision latency combines additively with the effects of the frequency (Schuberth & Eimas, 1977; Schuberth, Spoehr & Lane, in press) and the visual quality (Schuberth, Spoehr & Lane, in press) of the stimulus. Additional evidence for the additivity of sentence context and stimulus quality effects has been obtained by Stanovich and West (1979a) who employed a pronunciation task and by Mitchell (1979) who employed a self-paced reading task (Mitchell & Green, 1978).

Schuberth et al. (in press) have recently proposed two mechanisms within the framework of the Verification Model to account for the differential effects of single-word and sentence-context priming on the lexical decision process. One possible basis for these differential effects is that the semantic sets generated by single-word contexts may be much smaller than those generated by low-constraint (i.e., eliciting a large number of different responses) sentence contexts. Such a mechanism permits an interpretation of the observed differences in the combined effect of the frequency of a word and its congruity in context on decision latency.

Consider the finding that the frequency of a congruous-word stimulus and its predictability in a sentence context have independent and additive effects on decision latency (cf. Schuberth et al., in press). Two additional assumptions are required in the Verification Model to accommodate this result. First, when semantic set items become available for verification, there is an initial assignment of set members to a high- or to a low-probability group. High-probability set members are sampled for verification before low-probability set members. Second, within the high- and the low-probability groups, high-frequency items are sampled before low-frequency items. With low-constraint sentence contexts, the high- and the low-probability semantic set groups are likely to contain several items, yielding substantial frequency effects. When single words are used as context, the order in which semantic set items are sampled should conform to the assumptions previously outlined. However, if the semantic set consists of only a few items that are strongly associated with the context word, then the effect of frequency should be negligible. Becker (1979) reported a frequency effect of 53 msec across levels of strength of association to the context. To accommodate this finding, he has suggested that as the strength of the relationship between the context and the stimulus decreases, the probability that the stimulus word will be included in the semantic set also decreases. Thus, according to this argument, the decision latencies for related words obtained by Becker (1979) may reflect a mixture of decision latencies for words treated as related and decision latencies for words treated as unrelated. This explanation is consistent with the notion that when single words provide the context, the semantic set may consist of the few associates that are strongly related to the context.

The observed difference in the combined effect of word frequency and congruity in context follows logically from the proposed mechanism. In Experiment 2 reported by Schuberth et al. (in press), transition probabilities of congruous word stimuli were equated. Word frequency should therefore have been the sole factor governing the order of sampling from both the semantic set and the sensory set. The obtained additivity of frequency and congruity suggests that a comparable number of verification cycles preceded the recognition of semantic set and sensory set items at the same level of frequency. When a single word provides the context, the frequency effect for semantically related words is smaller than the frequency effect for semantically unrelated words (cf. Becker, 1979) because the sensory set is likely to contain more items. Thus, in the larger sensory set, a greater difference should exist between the average number of verification cycles needed to recognize high-frequency items and low-frequency items.

The second mechanism through which single-word and sentence contexts may differentially affect the lexical decision process is rooted in the speed with which semantic set members become available for verification. As Fischler and Bloom (1979) have pointed out, the processing demands of a sentence context far outweigh those of a single-word context. For example, there may be "configurative" aspects of the sentence that cannot be obtained from the meaning of individual words (cf. Foss & Harwood, 1975). In addition, sentence contexts contain no single word that is strongly related to the stimulus. It seems reasonable to assume, then, that given a limited amount of time to process each type of context, semantic associates of a single-word context should be activated more rapidly than words providing congruous completions to a sentence context. Consistent with this notion are the results of Fischler and Goodman (1978) and Cosky and Gough (1973). The former investigators have shown that priming effects can be obtained when a single-word context precedes the test stimulus by as little as 40 msec. In contrast, Cosky and Gough reported that a sentence context must be displayed for a considerably longer period of time to affect word recognition.

The idea that sentence contexts generate semantic set items more slowly than single-word contexts provides a basis for interpreting the observed difference in the combined effect of the congruity and visual quality of the stimulus on lexical decision latency. In Experiment 2 reported by Schuberth et al. (in press) and in the study by Meyer et al. (1975), degrading the stimuli with a random-dot pattern produced a substantial increase in decision latencies both for congruous words and incongruous words. In the Verification Model, the increase in decision latencies for congruous words would presumably arise during the verification of semantic set items because context has functioned to bypass the feature analyzer component of the model. However, because Becker and Killion (1977) conceptualize the verification process as serial and self-terminating in nature, word frequency and visual quality should most likely interact in their combined effect on decision latency (cf. Sternberg, 1969). That is, if one assumes that stimulus degradation increases the time needed to complete each cycle of the verification process, then the effect of stimulus degradation should be less pronounced for high-frequency words than for low-frequency words. This prediction follows logically from the assumption that fewer cycles of the verification process are required to recognize high-frequency words than low-frequency words. The additivity of word-frequency and stimulus-quality effects reported by Schuberth et al. (in press) and by Stanners et al. (1975) fail to confirm this prediction.

Additional modifications of the Verification Model are therefore necessary to accommodate the effects of reductions in the visual quality of the stimulus via random-dot degradation. Stimulus degradation may be assumed to initiate a preprocessing operation that functions to reduce the visual noise superimposed on the stimulus percept (cf. Neisser, 1967; Sternberg, 1967). Upon completion of preprocessing, visual features are extracted from the stimulus representation and are sent to the system of lexical detectors. One effect of the postulated preprocessing operation is thus to delay the formation of the sensory set. Another, indirect effect of stimulus preprocessing may occur when context is presented. As soon as the semantic set is established, set members are compared against the contents of the visual store. If the verification of semantic set items begins prior to the completion of stimulus preprocessing, then an increment in time will be added to each verification cycle that is completed while visual noise remains superimposed on the stimulus percept. When the preprocessing operation is complete, the rate at which semantic set items are verified approximates the rate of verification when the test stimulus is of normal visual quality.

A second proposed mechanism for explaining the differential effects of single-word and sentence contexts—the generation of semantic set items following the presentation of a sentence context—is assumed to be a slow process. It is possible that when the test stimuli are degraded, the preprocessing operation is nearing completion when semantic set items become available for verification. An increase in decision latencies for congruous word stimuli will occur, and the extent of this increase will depend on the number of verification cycles that are completed before the stimulus representation is fully preprocessed. When the test stimulus is a degraded incongruous word, the exhaustive sampling of semantic set items is assumed to extend beyond the time needed to complete stimulus preprocessing and to form the sensory set. Immediately after the semantic set has been exhaustively sampled, the verification of sensory set items proceeds at a normal rate until a match with the stimulus representation is obtained. Thus, when sentence contexts are employed, the effect of stimulus degradation for both congruous and incongruous words reflects the increase in time needed to verify semantic set items. The additivity of visual quality and congruity effects reported by Schuberth et al. (in press) is consistent with this analysis.

The generation of semantic set items following the presentation of a single-word context is assumed to occur rapidly. When the stimulus is degraded, the verification of semantic set items will be slowed because this process begins when the visual quality of the stimulus representation is still poor. Thus, decision latencies for stimuli that are related to the context will increase. Because the semantic set is thought to contain only a few items, an exhaustive sampling of set members is assumed to be completed prior to the formation of the sensory set, which is delayed substantially by stimulus preprocessing. Therefore, when the stimulus is a degraded incongruous word, the obtained increase in decision latency reflects the longer delay associated with stimulus preprocessing. The significant visual quality-x-congruity interaction effect reported by Meyer et al. (1975) is consistent with this analysis.

To summarize, two mechanisms have been proposed within the framework of the Verification Model by which single-word and sentence contexts may differentially affect the lexical decision process. The proposed mechanisms together provide a reasonable explanation of several sets of results. Moreover, because the verification framework is compatible with top–down approaches to reading comprehension (cf. Rumelhart, 1977), it appears to be a promising approach to the study of word recognition.

CONTEXT USAGE AND READING SKILL

The acquisition of proficient reading skills is believed to be mediated, to a large extent, by an increasing ability to utilize the semantic and syntactic cues inherent in contextual information (cf. Gibson & Levin, 1975). In this light, it is interesting to note that there have been relatively few attempts to examine the changes that occur in contextual effects as a function of age and reading skill. Although readers of all ages and skill levels seem able to make use of context, investigators have generally failed to find that the facilitative effect of context on word recognition increases with age and reading skill (e.g., Biemiller, 1977–1978; Doehring, 1976; Perfetti, Bell, Hogaboam, & Goldman, 1977; Samuels, Begy, & Chen, 1975–1976; Schvaneveldt, Ackerman & Semlear, 1977; West & Stanovich, 1978).

Evidence obtained in recent investigations suggests that younger and poorer readers benefit more from contextual information than do older, better readers. For example, in a study by Schvaneveldt et al. (1977), second- and fourth-grade children made lexical decisions about word stimuli that were either semantically related or unrelated to a context word. For both age groups, decision latencies were shorter for related words than for unrelated words. However, the contextual effect was greater for the second graders than for the fourth graders, and correlations between the size of the contextual effect and standardized reading test scores were negative for both age groups. Similar results were obtained by Samuels et al. (1975–1976) who employed a tachistoscopic recognition task. These investigators reported that the magnitude of the effect of a single-word context on task performance was inversely related to reading level in a group of fourth-grade children.

West and Stanovich (1978) attempted to assess both the facilitative and inhibitory effects of context on naming latencies at three different age levels. Fourth graders, sixth graders, and college students rapidly pronounced word stimuli that were either preceded by a sentence context or by the word *the*. The word stimuli were either congruous or incongruous with respect to the sentence contexts. The naming time data failed to reveal any increase in contextual effects with age. That is, the extent to which context decreased naming times for congruous words did not differ across age groups, and context slowed the responses of fourth and sixth graders to incongruous words, but not the responses of college students. In addition, correlations between reading achievement scores and the size of contextual effects suggested that poorer readers made greater use of context.

The developmental findings with regard to contextual effects have been explained in terms of age changes in the relative speeds of automatic word recognition and contextual mechanisms (cf. West & Stanovich, 1978). The word-recognition speed of younger and poorer readers is slow relative to the speed of contextual mechanisms. Context, therefore, has a substantial effect on the word-recognition process for these individuals. In contrast, the word-recognition speed of older and better readers has become so rapid that the influence of contextual mechanisms is greatly reduced. This mode of theorizing is consistent with the notion that single-word decoding skills rather than the utilization of contextual information is the primary factor differentiating good from poor readers (cf. Biemiller, 1977–1978; Perfetti et al., 1977; Perfetti & Hogaboam, 1975; Stanovich & West, 1979b; West & Stanovich, 1978). Stanovich and West (1979b) have suggested that the differences between good and poor readers might fruitfully be examined in terms of compensatory models of reading subskill organization. In this framework, higher-level processes (e.g., mechanisms mediating semantic and syntactic redundancy) compensate for deficiencies in lower-level processes. Thus, one way the poorer reader may compensate for deficiencies in word processing is to rely *more* on contextual information (e.g., Samuels et al., 1975–1976; Schvaneveldt et al., 1977; West & Stanovich, 1978).

Frederiksen (1978) has presented a slightly different view of how context use fits within the larger constellation of reading subskills, reporting evidence that the differences in the use of contextual information by good and poor adult readers are qualitative rather than simply quantitative. High-school subjects pronounced letter strings that were either preceded by an incomplete sentence or presented without a context. Low-skilled readers showed a clear ability to use contextual information to facilitate task performance only when the context was semantically constraining and the target word was high in frequency. In contrast, highly skilled readers benefited from the presentation of context even when it was of the type that provided only subtle cues for identifying the target. In addition, the facilitating effect of context was the same for high- and low-frequency target words. These results have led Frederiksen to hypothesize the existence of a hierarchy of context usage skills, only parts of which can be used by individuals at lower levels of reading proficiency.

The research on reading skill and use of context in word recognition appears to be more suggestive than definitive. Clearly, contextual factors interact differently with other determinants of word recognition for individuals of varying experience and skill. How these reading subskills are organized and used at different levels of reading proficiency and under different experimental conditions remains to be studied systematically.

EXPERIMENTS INVESTIGATING
WORD PROCESSING IN SENTENCE CONTEXTS

The word-recognition experiments reviewed thus far address both visual and memory processes in contextual word recognition. However, these tasks have relatively little to say about how processing changes as contextual cues create more and more constraint. It seems clear that semantic and syntactic context can be useful to subjects only insofar as they can integrate meaning across several words—either phrases or entire sentences. Such integration means maintaining information in working memory and using it to place constraints on each successive word to be processed. Using a somewhat different experimental technique it is possible to make observations about how contextual information exerts its cumulative effect.

The technique is a variant of the rapid serial visual presentation method developed by Forster (1970) called the continuous lexical decision task (CLD) (Fig. 5.2). Instead of presenting a sentence frame and gathering reaction-time data on only the final completion element, the subject makes lexical decisions on each of the words in the sentence. However, so that not all of the responses are positive "word" responses, we mix in nonword strings throughout the sentence in a random fashion. Thus, on any given trial the subject does not know whether to expect the next stimulus in the series to be a word from the current sentence or a nonword element. In order to insure that we are observing word-recognition processes as they change with increasing amounts of contextual constraint, we require the subject to remember the words as they appear so that by the time the last response is made he or she has integrated information from the entire sentence. At the end of the CLD procedure for each sentence series the subject must write down the sentence before proceeding to the next series.

A computer-controlled system displays each stimulus immediately after the response to the previous one and records both decision times and errors. From the subject's point of view it is very much like a standard lexical decision task for single-letter strings, except that contextual constraints are being built up as each sentence element appears. We have not yet begun to examine the effects of all the parameters of interest, such as frequency and transition probability, but we do have data on such basic variables as sentence length and amount of context preceding each decision. The stimulus materials were generated from sentence lengths of five, six, seven, and eight words with either five, six, seven, or eight nonwords mixed in. This yielded stimulus series in the range of 10 to 16 deci-

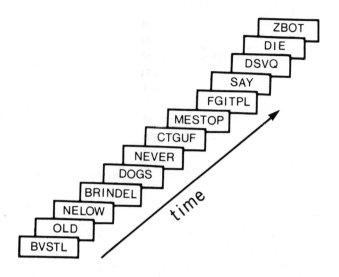

```
          AMOUNT OF CONSTRAINT (NUMBER OF WORDS)

          0        1        2        3        4        5
         ___      ___      ___      ___      ___      ___

WORDS     OLD     DOGS    NEVER     SAY      DIE      --


                 NELOW
PNW       --     BRINDEL    --     MESTOP    --       --


                                   CTGUF
NPN      BVSTL     --       --     FGITPL   DSVQ     ZBOT
```

FIG. 5.2. Example of the continuous lexical decision (CLD) task.

sions before sentence recall, though contextual constraint as measured by memory load varied only from zero to eight items.

The lexical decision times are broken down according to whether the string was a word, pronounceable nonword, or unpronounceable nonword, and further within each of these categories according to both the sentence length from which it came and the number of words providing contextual constraint when the decision was made. In the examples shown in Fig. 5.2 we have a sentence of L = 5 with eight nonwords mixed in. The breakdown at the bottom of the figure shows which stimuli from this series contribute reaction times for each amount of contextual constraint. Although not all sentences contributed observations for each type of stimulus item at each amount of contextual constraint, there are observations in all of the cells across the 50 sentences used in the experiment.

The results for the lexical decision task are shown in Fig. 5.3 for each of the sentence lengths. First, note the significant main effects of the type of material,

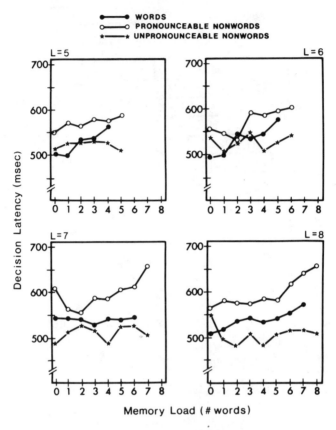

LEXICAL DECISION TASK

●——● WORDS
○——○ PRONOUNCEABLE NONWORDS
★——★ UNPRONOUNCEABLE NONWORDS

FIG. 5.3. Lexical decision latencies from the CLD task for sentences of five, six, seven, and eight words as a function of amount of contextual constraint.

with unpronounceable nonwords showing significantly faster classification times than words, which in turn are faster than pronounceable nonwords: $F(2, 10) = 7.10$, $p < .025$; $F(2, 10) = 17.12$, $p < .01$; $F(2, 10) = 7.21$, $p < .025$; and $F(2, 10) = 14.27$, $p < .001$ for L = 5, 6, 7, and 8 respectively. Second, although there are only marginal main effects of amount of contextual constraint ($.05 < p < .10$), constraint seems to operate on words and pronounceable nonwords only, and not on the unpronounceable nonwords. The interactions of item type with amount of constraint were significant for three of the four sentence lengths and just missed significance for the other: $F(8, 40) = 2.60$, $p < .05$; $F(10, 50) = 2.09$, $p < .05$; $F(12, 60) = 1.78$, $.05 < p < .10$; $F(14, 70) = 2.11$, $p < .05$ for L = 5, 6, 7, and 8 respectively.

Figure 5.4 shows that the results from a variant of this task, in which subjects must decide whether each stimulus string is pronounceable or not, are quite different. First there is a main effect of stimulus type, which is caused largely by the fact that unpronounceable nonwords are classified much more quickly than either words or pronounceable nonwords: $F(2, 10) = 7.89$, $p < .01$; $F(2, 10) = 9.33$, $p < .01$; $F(2, 10) = 8.16$, $p < .01$; and $F(2, 10) = 8.77$, $p < .01$ for L = 5, 6, 7, and 8 respectively. This is particularly striking because in the stimulus set (the same one used in the lexical decision task) pronounceable stimuli outnumbered unpronounceable stimuli by two to one. Therefore, it appears that in this task, as well as in the previous one, subjects can execute a fast negative response to the unpronounceable nonwords based on orthography rather than

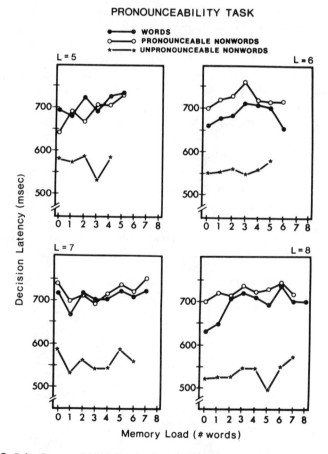

FIG. 5.4. Pronounciability decision latencies for sentences of five, six, seven, and eight words as a function of amount of contextual constraint.

lexical access. Such a decision is sufficient for the pronounciability task but is not adequate for lexical decisions where further processing, influenced by contextual constraint, is required to distinguish pronounceable nonwords from actual words. Thus, we observe significant differences between words and pronounceable nonwords in the lexical decision variant but not in the pronounciability variant. Inasmuch as it appears that processing beyond a check for orthographic regularity is unnecessary to execute the pronounciability decision, it is not surprising that we find neither a main effect of amount of contextual constraint, nor an interaction between constraint and stimulus type. In the pronounciability task, the operations that are influenced by context are not executed.

The data from the CLD task indicate that accessing lexical memory involves the contents or facilities of active, working memory. If it were merely the case that increasing memory load impedes performance, we ought to have observed increasing reaction times for all stimuli in both tasks instead of only for words and pronounceable nonwords in the CLD. Of course, one way to support the assumption that the latency effects for words and pronounceable nonwords are caused by contextual constraint rather than memory load is to employ the CLD with stimulus series where the words from the sentence are scrambled or are generally unrelated, yet still impose the memory requirement. Figure 5.5 shows the results from such a task contrasted with the results of the CLD task in which the sentences were syntactically correct. The three panels show the results for words, pronounceable nonwords, and unpronounceable nonwords, and the data have been collapsed over sentence lengths. As the presence versus absence of syntactic cues was a between-subjects factor in these data, the obvious difference

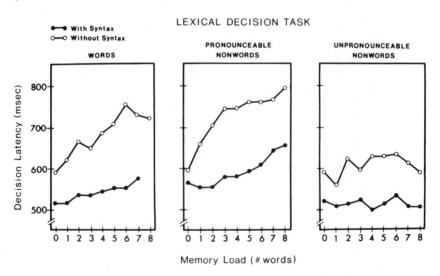

FIG. 5.5.   Lexical decision latencies from the CLD task, contrasting performance with and without syntactic cues.

between performance with and without syntax may be as much a function of differences between the two groups of subjects as it is a function of differences in the difficulty of the two tasks. What is more revealing, however, is the interaction between amount of constraint and type of syntactic cue. We see that although decision latencies for words and pronounceable nonwords increase as a function of amount of constraint even with syntactic cues present, the increase is not nearly as large as it is when syntactic cues are absent: $F(8, 96) = 5.88$, $p < .01$. Thus, syntactic constraint creates a steady increase in savings with respect to the load imposed on short-term memory by having to remember preceding items. In line with our previous argument, it appears that short-term memory is not involved with decisions made on unpronounceable nonwords, either when syntax is present or when it is absent.

The CLD task data have some important implications for both the Verification Model and a general understanding of how context affects word processing. First, it is clear that word recognition with or without the benefit of context need not operate at the level of full word recognition. That is, the visual processing system must be sensitive to orthographic regularity at some point before recognition of the entire word. This means that the visually defined set upon which a verification process operates may be the result of several types of featural extraction processes (e.g., LaBerge & Samuels, 1974; Spoehr, 1978). Second, the effects of context clearly interact with active memory. This may mean either that the semantically defined set derived from contextual cues must reside in active, working memory and can therefore be interfered with by increasing numbers of contextual elements or that the contextually driven lexical decision process relies on a speech-related recoding system that is hindered by contextual elements filling up short-term memory.

SUMMARY AND CONCLUSIONS

One of the original purposes of this chapter was to see how the word-recognition process changes when various types of contextual information are provided to the subject. We have seen that, as in isolated word recognition, visual characteristics such as stimulus quality and memory-related factors such as word frequency play an important role in word recognition in context. Moreover, the addition of contextually constrained stimulus-presentation conditions has made it possible to discover the points during processing at which these factors have their influence. It is clear that as contextual constraint builds up there are more and more opportunities for top–down generated expectancies to exert their influence upon recognition, whereas structural considerations such as orthographic regularity can still influence the process in a bottom–up manner. It therefore appears that experimentation with isolated words has given us an important set of variables to examine in contextually constrained situations and that we have only just begun to understand how these variables operate and interact in the complex process of natural reading.

ACKNOWLEDGMENTS

The research reported in this chapter was supported by National Science Foundation grant #BNS76-82337 to the first author. We gratefully acknowledge the assistance of Debbie J. Dickstein and Deborah Kasman in executing the experiments and in preparing the figures.

REFERENCES

Becker, C. A. Allocation of attention during visual word recognition. *Journal of Experimental Psychology: Human Perception and Performance*, 1976, 2, 556–566.

Becker, C. A. *The costs and benefits of semantic context in visual word recognition.* Paper presented at the annual meeting of the Psychonomic Society, San Antonio, Tex., November, 1978.

Becker, C. A. Semantic context and word frequency effects in visual word recognition. *Journal of Experimental Psychology: Human Perception and Performance*, 1979, 5, 252–259.

Becker, C. A., & Killion, T. H. Interaction of visual and cognitive effects in word recognition. *Journal of Experimental Psychology: Human Perception and Performance*, 1977, 3, 389–401.

Biemiller, A. Relationships between oral reading rates for letters, words, and simple text in the development of reading achievement. *Reading Research Quarterly*, 1977–1978, 13, 223–253.

Broadbent, D. E. Word-frequency effect and response bias. *Psychological Review*, 1967, 74, 1–15.

Bouma, H. Visual recognition of isolated lower-case letters. *Vision Research*, 1971, 11, 459–474.

Cattell, J. M. *Philosophical Studies*, 1885, 2, 635–650.

Collins, A. M., & Loftus, E. F. A spreading-activation theory of semantic processing. *Psychological Review*, 1975, 82, 407–428.

Cosky, M., & Gough, P. B. *The effect of context on word recognition.* Paper presented at the meeting of the Midwestern Psychological Association, Chicago, May, 1973.

Doehring, D. G. Acquisition of rapid reading responses. *Monographs of the Society for Research in Child Development*, 1976, 41 (2, Serial No. 165).

Fischler, I., & Bloom, P. A. Automatic and attentional processes in the effects of sentence contexts on word recognition. *Journal of Verbal Learning and Verbal Behavior*, 1979, 18, 1–21.

Fischler, I., & Goodman, G. O. Latency of associative activation in memory. *Journal of Experimental Psychology: Human Perception and Performance*, 1978, 4, 455–470.

Forster, K. I. Visual perception of rapidly presented word sequences of varying complexity. *Perception & Psychophysics*, 1970, 8, 215–221.

Foss, D. J., & Harwood, D. A. Memory for sentences: Implications for human associative memory. *Journal of Verbal Learning and Verbal Behavior*, 1975, 14, 1–16.

Frederiksen, J. R. *Word recognition in the presence of semantically constraining context.* Paper presented at the annual meeting of the Psychonomic Society, San Antonio, Tex., November 1978.

Gibson, E. J., & Levin, H. *The psychology of reading.* Cambridge, Mass.: MIT Press, 1975.

Gibson, E. J., Pick, A. D., Osser, H., & Hammond, M. The role of grapheme-phoneme correspondence in the perception of words. *American Journal of Psychology*, 1962, 75, 554–570.

Huey, E. B. *The psychology and pedagogy of reading.* New York: Macmillan, 1908.

LaBerge, D., & Samuels, S. J. Toward a theory of automatic information processing in reading. *Cognitive Psychology*, 1974, 6, 293–323.

Mason, M. Reading ability and letter search time: Effects of orthographic structure defined by single-letter positional frequency. *Journal of Experimental Psychology: General*, 1975, *104*, 146-166.

Massaro, D. W., Venezky, R. L., & Taylor, G. A. Orthographic regularity, positional frequency, and visual processing of letter strings. *Journal of Experimental Psychology: General*, 1979, *108*, 107-124.

McClelland, J. L. Letter and configuration information in word identification. *Journal of Verbal Learning and Verbal Behavior*, 1977, *16*, 137-150.

Meyer, D. E., & Schvaneveldt, R. W. Facilitation in recognizing pairs of words: Evidence of a dependence between retrieval operations. *Journal of Experimental Psychology*, 1971, *90*, 227-234.

Meyer, D. E., Schvaneveldt, R. W., & Ruddy, M. G. Loci of contextual effects on visual word-recognition. In P. M. A. Rabbitt & S. Dornic (Eds.), *Attention and performance V*. London: Academic Press, 1975.

Mitchell, D. C. Personal communication, January 24, 1979.

Mitchell, D. C., & Green, D. W. The effects of context and content on immediate processing in reading. *Quarterly Journal of Experimental Psychology*, 1978, *30*, 609-636.

Morton, J. The effects of context on the visual duration threshold for words. *British Journal of Psychology*, 1964, *55*, 165-180.

Morton, J. Interaction of information in word recognition. *Psychological Review*, 1969, *76*, 165-178.

Morton, J. A functional model of memory. In D. A. Norman (Ed.), *Models of human memory*. New York: Academic Press, 1970.

Neely, J. H. Semantic priming and retrieval from lexical memory: Evidence for facilitatory and inhibitory processes. *Memory & Cognition*, 1976, *4*, 648-654.

Neely, J. H. Semantic priming and retrieval from lexical memory: Roles of inhibitionless spreading activation and limited-capacity attention. *Journal of Experimental Psychology: General*, 1977, *106*, 226-254.

Neisser, U. *Cognitive psychology*. New York: Appleton-Century-Crofts, 1967.

Perfetti, C. A., Bell, L. C., Hogaboam, T. W., & Goldman, S. R. *Verbal processing speed and reading skill*. Paper presented at the meeting of the Psychonomic Society, Washington, D.C., November 1977.

Perfetti, C. A., & Hogaboam, T. The relationship between single word decoding and reading comprehension skill. *Journal of Educational Psychology*, 1975, *67*, 461-469.

Rubenstein, H., Garfield, L., & Millikan, J. A. Homographic entries in the internal lexicon. *Journal of Verbal Learning and Verbal Behavior*, 1970, *9*, 487-494.

Rumelhart, D. E. Toward an interactive model of reading. In S. Dornic (Ed.), *Attention and performance VI*. Hillsdale, N.J.: Lawrence Erlbaum Associates, 1977.

Samuels, S. J., Begy, G., & Chen, C. C. Comparison of word recognition speed and strategies of less-skilled and more highly skilled readers. *Reading Research Quarterly*, 1975-1976, *11*, 72-88.

Schuberth, R. E., & Eimas, P. D. Effects of context on the classification of words and nonwords. *Journal of Experimental Psychology: Human Perception and Performance*, 1977, *3*, 27-36.

Schuberth, R. E., Spoehr, K. T., & Lane, D. M. Effects of stimulus and contextual information on the lexical-decision process. *Memory & Cognition*, in press.

Schvaneveldt, R., Ackerman, B. P., & Semlear, T. The effect of semantic context on children's word recognition. *Child Development*, 1977, *48*, 612-616.

Spoehr, K. T. Phonological encoding in visual word recognition. *Journal of Verbal Learning and Verbal Behavior*. 1978, *17*, 127-142.

Stanners, R. F., Jastrzembski, J. E., & Westbrook, A. Frequency and visual quality in a word-nonword classification task. *Journal of Verbal Learning and Verbal Behavior*, 1975, *14*, 259-264.

Stanovich, K. E., & West, R. F. Mechanisms of sentence context effects in reading: Automatic activation and conscious attention. *Memory & Cognition,* 1979a, *7,* 77-85.

Stanovich, K. E., & West, R. F. The effect of orthographic structure on the word search performance of good and poor readers. *Journal of Experimental Child Psychology,* 1979b, *28,* 258-267.

Sternberg, S. Two operations in character-recognition: Some evidence from reaction-time measurements. *Perception & Psychophysics,* 1967, *2,* 45-53.

Sternberg, S. The discovery of processing stages: Extensions of Donders' method. *Acta Psychologica,* 1969, *30,* 276-315.

Thompson, M. C., & Massaro, D. W. Visual information and redundancy in reading. *Journal of Experimental Psychology,* 1973, *98,* 49-54.

Tulving, E., & Gold, C. Stimulus information and contextual information as determinants of tachistoscopic recognition of words. *Journal of Experimental Psychology,* 1963, *66,* 319-327.

Tulving, E., Mandler, G., & Baumal, R. Interaction of two sources of information in tachistoscopic word recognition. *Canadian Journal of Psychology,* 1964, *18,* 62-71.

West, R. F., & Stanovich, K. E. Automatic contextual facilitation in readers of three ages. *Child Development,* 1978, *49,* 717-727.

6

Exploring the Nature of a Basic Visual-Processing Component of Reading Ability

Mark D. Jackson
Bell Laboratories

James L. McClelland
University of California, San Diego

Reading is a complex act requiring the integration and interaction of a number of basic cognitive processes. Understanding this complexity is an interesting and challenging pursuit in itself. In our own studies, an additional motivation for analyzing reading is to identify those component processes that determine reading proficiency. By examining the determinants of reading ability, we aim to extend our knowledge of the interactions of basic cognitive processes in reading and provide input for the task of devising effective methods of improving reading skill.

An individual's ability to read, as well as the ability to perform a variety of complex cognitive tasks, may be determined by a small number of basic cognitive skills. For example, general language-comprehension processes may largely determine our ability to understand language both when reading and listening (Perfetti & Lesgold, 1978). Better readers tend to have better comprehension of text both when listening and reading (Jackson, 1980; Jackson & McClelland, 1979). In fact, individual differences in the ability to understand language when listening can account for a large portion of the differences between the same individuals in their ability to read.

In recent years, a view of reading ability has emerged claiming that reading proficiency is almost totally dependent on these general language-comprehension skills (Goodman, 1970; Smith, 1971). If this view is correct, reading ability should not depend on any processes unique to reading per se. In contrast, our research has uncovered a basic visual processing skill that influences reading ability. Better readers, we have discovered, appear to have faster access to information in memory for visual symbols. This faster access allows them to encode more information from each reading fixation. In the remainder of this chapter, we summarize the evidence for this memory access difference between skilled and less-skilled readers and consider whether this visual processing skill is specific to reading. Also, we examine the question of whether this difference in memory-access speed is the result of different degrees of reading practice or is independent of practice.

Before considering the results of our experiments, we wish to emphasize a few characteristics of our subject population. As we are primarily interested in the component skills of more proficient readers, our subjects have been college undergraduates. One potential disadvantage of examining this relatively homogenous population is that the range of reading skills may be much smaller than we would expect to find in the general population. However, our experience has shown that large, stable individual differences in reading skill exist between these proficient readers.

To examine the relative component skills of readers within this population, we test the reading ability of a large sample of subjects and select the top and bottom quartiles (ranked by effective reading speed) as our groups of skilled and less-skilled readers.[1] We compare the performance of these groups on tasks designed to tap component reading processes. The reading tests consist of short stories similar in length and style to selections found on standardized reading and aptitude tests. Each story has a corresponding set of short-answer comprehension questions chosen to minimize the likelihood that the reader may know the correct answer prior to reading the test passage. In different studies we have used other reading tests and found that our subject rankings and experimental results are very stable across reading tests.

EVIDENCE OF A VISUAL ENCODING SKILL

Reading differs from listening in the processes that map the sensory input of letters and words on the page to the representations in memory that serve as input to the language-comprehension processes. These encoding processes begin with the visual pattern of print on the retina and result in a representation of the letters and words contained in that pattern. Because of limitations in our visual acuity, we can encode only a limited number of letters in any one eye fixation. In order to read one or more lines of text, the reader makes a number of eye fixations separated by very brief saccades. Although reading proficiency may be sensitive

---

[1]Effective reading speed is calculated by multiplying reading speed (in words per minute) by comprehension (percentage correct on a comprehension test). Effective reading speed is used as an index of the reader's speed of understanding, taking into account both the extent of the reader's comprehension and the speed at which the level of comprehension was reached.

to the pattern of eye fixations across the page of text, the control of eye movements during reading does not appear to be a significant determiner of reading ability (Tinker, 1965). Rather, the pattern of eye fixations may be automatically driven by language-comprehension processes anlayzing inputs over a number of fixations (Kolers, 1976; O'Regan, 1975; Rayner, 1975). Also, McConkie and Zola (1979) have reported evidence to suggest that the information that is integrated across fixations are the results of encoding the stimulus into letters, words, and other levels of representation.

The available evidence suggests that better readers are able to process more text *per* reading fixation. The efficient reader makes fewer fixations per line of text while spending the same aount of time per fixation (Buswell, 1922; Huey, 1908). Thus, better readers may be processing more text from each reading fixation. From a methodological standpoint, it is difficult to measure exactly how much text a reader is encoding from each fixation while reading without actually disrupting the reading process itself (but see, McConkie, Zola, Wolverton, & Burns, 1978). However, when good and poor readers are presented with simple five-word sentences under tachistoscopic conditions approximating a reading fixation, better readers are able to report more words and letters than poorer readers (Jackson & McClelland, 1975). Although this result suggests that better readers encode more information from each presentation, this task leaves open the possibility that better readers merely are better at guessing unrecognized letters based on the sentence context.

To test the ability to encode information from a single fixation—independent of differences in the ability to fill in missing information—we presented readers with simple sentences under the same tachistoscopic conditions followed by a probed forced-choice test. A typical stimulus sentence presented to the subject was:

Jane wore a plaid scarf

followed by the test alternatives:

Jane wore a ᵖˡᵃⁱᵈ⁄ₚₗₐᵢₙ scarf.

Subjects were required to choose which of two test words was presented in the stimulus sentence. The choices differed by a single letter, and both choices fit the sentence context. The choice word and critical letter location were equally likely to occur in any position in the sentence. If subjects had not seen the critical letter and had to guess which word was presented, they would choose either word with equal probability. However, we found that better readers identified the correct word more often than poorer readers, indicating that they had encoded the critical letter more often. Thus, better readers were able to pick up more information from the briefly presented sentences.

When reading, the amount of text encoded from any one fixation may depend on the efficiency of language-comprehension processes analyzing information gained from successive fixations. However, the visual processes responsible for the better-reader advantage on these tachistoscopic tasks appear to operate on units smaller than sentences or words. Using the same tachistoscopic presentation to approximate a reading fixation, we found that better readers could report more letters from a string of *unrelated consonants* than less-skilled readers. Although the ability to report unrelated items is influenced by the span of short-term memory, recent studies indicate that skilled and less-skilled readers do not systematically differ in their short-term memory *capacity* (Jackson & McClelland, 1979; Perfetti & Goldman, 1976). Rather, better readers were able to *encode* more letters from the briefly presented string. Thus, the visual-processing advantage underlying performance differences in these tasks is independent of language-comprehension processes and effects the encoding of single letters.

VISUAL ENCODING PROCESSES

Comparisons of skilled and less-skilled readers have consistently failed to yield any differences in visual sensory function that could account for the differences in performance we observe on these tasks. No systematic differences have been found between mature readers in their sensitivity to light (Buswell, 1922), parafoveal sensitivity (Jackson & McClelland, 1975), or sensitivity to lateral or temporal masking (Jackson & McClelland, 1979). Rather, the performance differences indicate a visual encoding difference that lies within the stages of processing that identify the letters and words represented in the sensory pattern.

A basic claim of many recent models of reading is that the recognition of patterns in the visual input depends on a hierarchical organization of subprocesses (Estes, 1975; LaBerge & Samuels, 1974; McClelland, 1976; Rumelhart, 1979). These models claim that the recognition of letters and words is achieved by recognizing configurations of subpatterns. Encoding of patterns at one level of analysis (i.e., letters) serves as the input to recognition of patterns at the next level of organization (i.e., letter clusters or words). Thus, the sensory pattern of a line of text may be analyzed for simple configural features, letters, letter clusters, and words.

The speed or efficiency at which information can be processed through this hierarchy may determine how much information can be encoded in a fixed amount of time. Studies by McClelland (1976) and Turvey (1973) suggest that as new information enters the visual-processing hierarchy, the processing of previous input is disrupted at each level of analysis or organization. During a reading fixation, information that travels through the hierarchy to more abstract levels— before lower-level information is disrupted by masking or dissipated by decay—will have a greater chance of becoming available for report. Better readers may be able to encode more letters and words from a brief fixation because they analyze the input pattern faster at any or all levels of representation in the recognition hierarchy.

To tap the speed of the visual-encoding processes, we tested skilled and less-skilled readers with a number of simultaneous matching tasks. In each task, the subject is presented a pair of items and is required to respond "same" or "different" as quickly as possible. By varying the stimulus items or the basis for comparison, we can index the relative speeds of different encoding processes by examining subject reaction times for making the correct response. In one matching task, the stimuli were letters, and subjects were required to respond "same" if the letters were either physically identical or identical in name, as in the paradigm developed by Posner (Posner, Lewis, & Conrad, 1972). In another task, the display elements were words, and subjects were required to respond "same" if the words were synonyms. In two other versions, the display elements were words or pronounceable pseudowords, and subjects were required to respond "same" if the words had the same sound (i.e., were homonyms). Examples of same and different stimulus pairs for each task are shown in Fig. 6.1. Thus, these tasks attempted to reflect the processes of forming visual-letter codes, letter-identity codes, semantic-word codes, and verbal codes.

The reaction-time results for these tasks (see Table 6.1) clearly indicate a processing speed difference between skilled and less-skilled readers for tasks requiring letter or word identification. Better readers were faster than poorer readers for each task. However, the smaller difference between groups for the physical letter-match trials was partially due to differences in accuracy level. The skilled-reader group was significantly less accurate than the less-skilled group, so their faster reaction times primarily reflect differences in accuracy criterion and not faster processing of the stimulus items. For the letter name-match trials and

Task	Same	Different
Letter		
Physical	AA	—
Name	Aa	Br
Synonym	ABRUPT SUDDEN	AGED STAY
Homonym	BARE BEAR	RARE REAR
Homophone	PEEN PEAN	PREN PRAN

FIG. 6.1. Examples of same and different stimulus pairs for letter- and word-matching tasks.

TABLE 6.1
Mean Reaction Times for Good and Poor
Readers

| | Reaction time | | |
Task	Good	Poor	Difference
letter			
physical	492	558	66
name	586	694	108
synonym	822	993	171
homonym	983	1132	149
homophone	1221	1365	144
dot pattern	1256	1230	−26

the other tasks, accuracy for the two groups was not significantly different, or better readers were slightly more accurate. Thus, we can infer that the faster reaction times of the skilled readers on the letter- and word-identification tasks reflect faster access to identity codes of the items in memory.

The presence of a reaction-time advantage for the skilled readers on *each* of the tasks suggests the possibility that better readers may be faster than poorer readers on any reaction-time task or any speeded task that requires a comparison of two visual items. To test this hypothesis, subjects were tested on a matching task that required a visual comparison but did not require access to memory codes. In this task, subjects were presented with two unfamiliar dot patterns and required to respond "same" if the two patterns were physically identical. The "different" patterns differed by the placement of a single dot. Unlike the pattern of results from the letter- and word-matching tasks, reaction times for better readers were not faster than reaction times for poorer readers. This result is consistent with the view that the better-reader advantage on the letter and word tasks is not due to more efficient visual comparison processes or general response time.

The correlation of reaction time and reading ability was highest for the letter name-match trials and the synonym task (see Table 6.2). Regression analyses indicated that the letter name-match reaction time accounted for the correlations between reading ability and each of the other reaction-time tasks. Thus, these results suggest that the speed of identifying the names of letters (i.e., the speed of accessing the names for the letters in memory) accounts for the better-reader advantage in each reaction-time task requiring letter identification. If letter identification is a component of word identification, as claimed by the hierarchical models of reading, then faster access to letter codes should be a source of individual differences in any task requiring word identification. Faster access to letter-identity codes in memory would give better readers an encoding advantage in the tachistoscopic presentation tasks because more letters and words would become available for report before processing of the stimulus was disrupted by the postexposure mask or subsequent stimulus.

TABLE 6.2
Correlations of Reading Ability and Reaction Time

	Letter		Word		
	Physical	Name	Synonym	Homonym	Homophone
Effective reading speed	.33	.47	.45	.21	.22

As suggested earlier, this visual encoding component of reading ability may be independent of general language-comprehension determiners of reading ability. In fact, in two independent comparisons (Jackson, 1980; Jackson & McClelland, 1979), reaction-time performance on the letter name-matching task was not significantly correlated with performance on tests of general language comprehension ($r = .17$ and $r = .16$). Also, regression analyses have indicated that general language-comprehension skills and the relative speed of accessing memory for letter-name codes (as measured by letter name-match reaction time) account for independent components of reading ability.

Although the reaction-time tasks clearly are tapping a visual encoding difference between readers in memory access speed, these tasks do not clearly define the nature of this visual memory access component of reading ability. Is this memory access difference between readers specific to the processing of letters, or does a systematic individual difference exist in the speed of accessing memory for any meaningful visual stimulus? To address this question, Jackson (1980) compared reaction times of skilled and less-skilled readers for a picture category matching task. The stimulus items were pictures of common objects. The objects were chosen from six categories such as vegetables, kitchen utensils, or modes of transportation. On each trial, a pair of pictures were presented, and subjects had to decide whether the objects belonged to the same or different categories. Reaction time for making the correct response is primarily dependent on the speed of accessing the representation in memory for the objects.

The results were strikingly similar to the reaction-time results for the letter name-matching tasks: Better readers showed roughly the same 100 msec reaction-time advantage over poorer readers for making the correct response (see Table 6.3). The correlations of category-match reaction time with reading ability and general language-comprehension skill paralleled those for letter name-match reaction time as well. Category-match reaction time was significantly correlated with effective reading speed ($r = .29$) but not correlated with comprehension performance ($r = .09$).[2] The similar pattern of results for both the object-matching and letter-matching tasks indicates a basic difference between readers

[2]Although the degree of correlation with reading ability is less than previously reported correlations for letter- and word-matching reaction times (Jackson & McClelland, 1979), the range of reading abilities in this sample of subjects was smaller.

TABLE 6.3
Mean Reaction Times for Category and New
Character Tasks[a]

| Task | Reaction Time | | |
	Skilled	Less-Skilled	Difference
new characters			
physical matching	404	406	2
name matching			
session 1	1023	1134	111
session 2	835	925	90
category	821	925	104

[a] From Jackson (1978).

in their speed of accessing memory codes for visual input (see Morrison, Giordani, & Nagy, 1977). Individual differences in speed of access to letter-identity codes are only one instance of the effects of this underlying difference in memory access.

MEMORY ACCESS AND PRACTICE

The category-match, letter name-match, and word-match results indicate a basic speed difference between skilled and less-skilled readers in the process of accessing information in memory for a meaningful visual pattern. When reading, this processing difference enables better readers to encode more letters in the brief duration of an average reading fixation. However, better readers can encode other meaningful visual patterns faster as well; their processing advantage is not restricted to alphabetical stimuli. This situation raises an interesting question as to how this memory-access difference developed. One possibility is that better readers achieved relatively faster memory-access processes for letters through additional reading practice. Also, one would have to assume that this increased efficiency transferred to the processing of other visual patterns with associated memory codes. The reverse order of events is much less likely, i.e., that better readers developed faster memory access for all patterns through additional processing of many visual patterns and that this skill applies to reading and letters as well. A more likely alternative is that the better-reader memory-access advantage does not result from more practice, or at least is independent of practice or familiarity with the particular items being encoded.

A conclusive test of the hypothesis that the better-reader memory-access advantage is independent of differences in amount of practice or training requires a comparison of subjects before and after they begin to read. By measuring their relative memory-access speed as they practice reading, we can get some indication of the relationship between individual differences in visual memory-access speed and amount of training or practice. Such a longitudinal study has not been performed. However, Jackson (1980) has examined the question of whether the better-reader advantage depends on the amount of familiarity with the particular visual items being tested. Using the same simultaneous matching format of the letter matching task, skilled and less-skilled readers were tested using a new character set that neither group had seen before the experiment. Examples of the new character pairs are shown in Fig. 6.2. In one version of this task, the pair of characters presented on each trial were either physically identical or different, and subjects responded "same" or "different" on the basis of the physical identity of the pair. As shown in Table 6.3, no difference in reaction time was found between the groups of readers. Also, the correlation of physical-match reaction time and reading ability was small and not significant ($r = .17$). This result strongly reinforces the conclusion that the differences between readers on letter- and word-matching tasks are due to differences in memory-access speed and not due to general reaction-time differences or differences in general visual-processing speed.

After completing the physical-match task with the new characters, each subject learned names for a second set of novel characters. The second set of

NAME

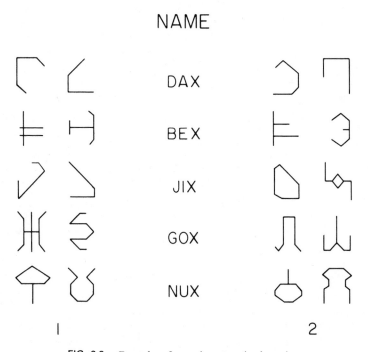

FIG. 6.2.   Examples of new character stimulus pairs.

characters was divided into five pairs, with both members of each pair assigned the same three-letter name. Examples of the nonsense names are shown in Fig. 6.2. During a learning phase, subjects were presented each character and its corresponding name twice, one character at a time, followed by a test on the names of each character. On the average, both groups of readers took an equal number of learning trials to reach criterion. After learning the names of the characters, subjects were tested on a name-match version of the character-matching task. On each trial the pair of characters was physically different, but on half the trials the characters had the same name, exactly analogous to the letter name-matching task. Each subject was tested on two successive days, and the results are shown in Table 6.3. As was the case with alphabetical letters, better readers had faster reaction times for deciding whether the novel characters had the same name. Furthermore, the size of the better-reader advantage was about the same for familiar alphabetical letters and unfamiliar novel characters. Although both groups of readers improved their reaction time by approximately 200 msec on the second day of testing, the speed advantage for better readers was roughly the same. The correlation of character name-match reaction time and reading ability was if anything better ($r = .48$) than the correlation of letter name-match reaction time with reading ability previously reported. Thus, the better-reader advantage in their speed of accessing the names of the characters in memory does not depend on the amount of practice or familiarity with the visual items being encoded.

SUMMARY

The evidence for a strong relationship between general language comprehension skills and reading ability is well-documented and compelling. Although one may have suspected that reading ability was determined in part by the efficiency of visual information processes, the evidence indicating the role of visual encoding processes in determining reading fluency has been lacking. Our research has uncovered a visual processing advantage that influences reading ability independently of general language-comprehension processes. This reading component appears to lie within the stages of visual encoding that access representations in memory for visual patterns or symbols. During reading, memory-access speed may influence reading proficiency by determining the number of letters and words that can be encoded in a brief reading fixation. However, the advantage in memory-access speed demonstrated by better readers is not limited to the processing of alphabetical letters. Rather, as demonstrated with the picture category-matching task, the same better-reader speed advantage is present when the task required the recognition of common objects.

Perhaps the most surprising characteristic of the individual differences in visual memory access speed is the lack of dependence on practice or familiarity with particular items being encoded. Better readers show an equivalent reaction-time advantage over less-skilled readers at processing familiar and unfamiliar characters. Two possible paths for the evolution of this difference between mature readers remain. One possibility is that better readers always had faster access to memory representations for visual patterns, and the size of their advantage over less-skilled readers remains about the same as overall encoding efficiency improves with practice.

The alternative ties the better-reader advantage to amount of practice. To make this hypothesis work, one could claim that improved memory-access speed results from practice encoding letters while reading and/or from practice accessing memory from visual inputs of pictures, objects, and other visual symbols. By this account, the improved speed gained from reading practice must transfer to the encoding of all new visual patterns. This implies that a poorer reader might reduce the difference in memory-access speed compared to a better reader through increased visual encoding practice. However, because the access-speed difference exists between mature adults with extensive amounts of practice with both reading and other forms of visual encoding, the prospect for dramatic improvement appears remote. There may be particular stages in the process of learning to read when the amount of encoding practice influences memory-access speed. If so, differences in practice between readers at those times may determine relative differences in visual memory-access speed that affect encoding processes and reading ability from that time on.

In any case, important questions still need to be answered before we can address the implications of this visual memory access component of reading ability for methods of teaching and improving reading. One particularly promising line of investigation is to examine further the reaction-time results indicating individual difference in memory access in light of the speed–accuracy tradeoff (SAT) function (Pachella, 1974; Wickelgren, 1977). The SAT shows the relationship of response latency to response accuracy. Mean reaction time and accuracy for any one task is a measure of only one point on the SAT curve. The parameters of the SAT function may indicate important dynamic characteristics of the underlying information processes (Jackson, 1978; McClelland, 1978). Examining the SAT function for reading tasks may shed more light on the interactions of component-recognition processes and language-comprehension processes.

ACKNOWLEDGMENTS

The research reported in this chapter was supported by NSF grant BNS 76–16830 to the second author and was carried out while the first author was at the University of California, San Diego.

REFERENCES

Buswell, G. Fundamental reading habits: A study of their development. *Supplementary Educational Monographs,* 1922, *21.*

Estes, W. The locus of inferential and perceptual processes in letter identification. *Journal of Experimental Psychology: General*, 1975, *1*, 122–145.

Goodman, K. Reading: A psycholinguistic guessing game. In H. Singer & R. Ruddell (Eds.), *Theoretical models and processes of reading*. Newark, Del.: International Reading Association, 1970.

Huey, E. *The psychology and pedagogy of reading*. New York: Macmillan, 1908; Cambridge, Mass.: MIT Press, 1968.

Jackson, M. *Memory access and reading ability*. Unpublished doctoral dissertation, University of California, San Diego, 1978.

Jackson, M. Further evidence for a relationship between memory access and reading ability. *Journal of Verbal Learning and Verbal Behavior*, 1980, *19*, 683–694.

Jackson, M., & McClelland, J. Sensory and cognitive determinants of reading speed. *Journal of Verbal Learning and Verbal Behavior*, 1975, *7*, 194–227.

Jackson, M., & McClelland, J. Processing determinants of reading speed. *Journal of Experimental Psychology: General*, 1979, *108*, 151–181.

Kolers, P. Buswell's discoveries. In R. Monty & J. Senders (Eds.), *Eye movements and psychological processes*. Hillsdale, N.J.: Lawrence Erlbaum Associates, 1976.

LaBerge, D., & Samuels, J. Toward a theory of automatic information processing in reading. *Cognitive Psychology*, 1974, *6*, 292–323.

McClelland, J. Preliminary letter identification in the perception of words and nonwords. *Journal of Experimental Psychology: Human Perception and Performance*, 1976, *1*, 80–91.

McClelland, J. *On the time relations of mental processes: A framework for analyzing processes in cascade* (Tech. Rep. 77). La Jolla, Cal.: Center for Human Information Processing, 1978.

McConkie, G., & Zola, D. Is visual information integrated across successive fixations in reading? *Perception & Psychophysics*, 1979, *25*, 221–224.

McConkie, G., Zola, D., Wolverton, G., & Burns, D. Eye movement contingent display control in studying reading. *Behavior Research Methods and Instrumentation*, 1978, *10*, 154–166.

Morrison, F., Giordani, B., & Nagy, J. Reading disability: An information processing analysis. *Science*, 1977, *196*, 77–79.

O'Regan, K. *Structural and contextual constraints on eye movements*. Unpublished doctoral dissertation, Cambridge University, 1975.

Pachella, R. The interpretation of reaction time in information processing research. In B. Kantowitz (Ed.), *Human information processing: Tutorials in performance and cognition*. New York: Halsted Press, 1974.

Perfetti, C., & Goldman, S. Discourse memory and reading comprehension. *Journal of Verbal Learning and Verbal Behavior*, 1976, *15*, 33–42.

Perfetti, C., & Lesgold, A. Discourse comprehension and sources of individual differences. In M. Just and P. Carpenter (Eds.), *Cognitive processes in comprehension*. Hillsdale, N.J.: Lawrence Erlbaum Associates, 1978.

Posner, M., Lewis, J., & Conrad, C. Component processes in reading: A performance analysis. In J. Kavanagh & I. Mattingly (Eds.), *Language by ear and by eye*. Cambridge, Mass.: MIT Press, 1972.

Rayner, K. The perceptual span and peripheral cues in reading. *Cognitive Psychology*, 1975, *7*, 65–81.

Rumelhart, D. Toward an interactive model of reading. In S. Dornic (Ed.), *Attention and performance VI*. Hillsdale, N.J.: Lawrence Erlbaum Associates, 1979.

Smith, F. *Understanding reading*. New York: Holt, Rinehart & Winston, 1971.

Tinker, M. *Basis for Effective Reading*. Minnesota: University of Minnesota Press, 1965.

Turvey, M. On peripheral and central processes in vision: Inferences from an information processing analysis of masking with patterned stimuli. *Psychological Review*, 1973, *80*, 1–52.

Wickelgren, W. Speed–accuracy tradeoff and information processing dynamics. *Acta Psychologia*, 1977, *41*, 67–85.

7 Recoding of Printed Words to Internal Speech: Does Recoding Come Before Lexical Access?

William P. Banks
Evelyn Oka
Pomona College

Sherrie Shugarman
Claremont Graduate School

This chapter is concerned with the question of whether people in the process of analyzing visually presented words for meaning translate them mentally to some form of internal speech. We use "internal speech" to refer to the general class of speechlike mental representations that have been proposed and "speech recoding" to refer to the various mechanisms proposed for translating to internal speech. We do this because we do not intend to review evidence that bears on the decision between phonetic, phonemic, articulatory, acoustic, or other models of recoding and mental representation. Our concern is in deciding whether or not speech recoding takes place in reading, and the question of the form speech recoding takes seems a secondary issue.

The topic of speech recoding has at least two sources of interest. The first comes from questions about mental representations in cognitive processing in general. The second—and the specific motivation for this article—comes from questions about how we read. We note that the general implications of speech recoding for cognitive theorizing are quite important. The early evidence for speech recoding in memory for visually presented items (Conrad, 1962, 1964; Glanzer & Clark, 1962, 1963; Harris & Haber, 1963) constituted, we think, an important event in the history of cognitive psychology. This research showed that the internal representation of a stimulus may be in a form entirely different from that in which it was presented. Furthermore, nontrivial operations that are not immediately observable must exist to make the translation to the internal representation. The effect of these demonstrations was to show that the simpler stimulus-response formulations of mental processing were inadequate. Cognitive theory had to find other mechanisms. These recoding experiments, then, form one of the major historical origins of cognitive theorizing. In dealing with our topic of recoding in reading, we hope readers keep in mind the importance of many findings for the general issues as well as for mental processing in reading. If speech recoding turns out to be an unessential or only occasional process in normal reading, it still is an aspect of processing in other tasks and thus has importance for cognitive theory.

THE LOCUS OF SPEECH RECODING
IN READING

We think that the crucial question is not whether speech recoding occurs in reading, but rather at what level it occurs. There is a good deal of evidence (discussed later) that supports recoding in reading and in experimental tasks that simulate reading or a component of it. However, the evidence that recoding takes place in a number of cognitive tasks other than reading should arouse our suspicions. Do we have support for recoding in *reading* or in the *memory* of what was just read? If it is in reading proper, does it take place when we initially access the meanings of words in the text, or does it take place at some other point, after a strictly visual analysis of word meaning? If translation to a speech code took place before words were "looked up" in memory it would imply that the mental lexicon was organized on the basis of speech codes and that translation of a visual symbol is necessary for (or, at least, facilitates) the search for the meaning of the symbol. Translation to a speech code *after* the meaning is determined would reasonably take place if short-term memory is best suited for storing internal speech codes, as many have suggested. The decision as to where speech recoding takes place is, then, a matter of some importance in understanding how we read. A number of researchers have contributed very clear analyses of the stage at which recoding could take place in reading (e.g., Kleiman, 1975; Levy, 1977; Massaro, 1975; Rayner & Posnansky, 1978; and Smith, 1971). In the following discussion of speech recoding hypotheses, we draw on these analyses and attempt to integrate them.

A diagram can help organize the assumptions about the different possible loci of speech recoding as well as make it easy to see their interrelations (Fig. 7.1). It is difficult to avoid the flowchart schema, possibly because we have an underlying approach that deals with reading in terms of information flow. However, it should be understood that Fig. 7.1 is not intended to be a model of reading. It is only a diagram of global stages or processes that take place in reading. They are organized to make discussion of speech recoding easier, not to give a "working model" of reading, and the global schema of the figure suffices to organize most of the questions about speech recoding in reading.

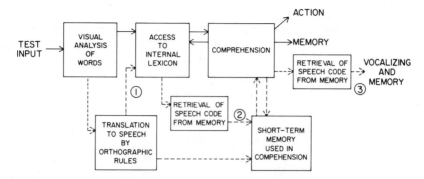

FIG. 7.1.   Schema showing possible roles of speech recoding in reading. Solid
lines depict strictly visual analyses; dashed lines depict analyses involving speech
recoding. Speech recoding at point 1 is prior to lexical access, at 2 is in short-term
memory used in reading, and at 3 is after reading altogether.

Figure 7.1 distinguishes four different processing components of reading:
visual analysis of words, access of the meaning of words in the "mental lexicon," comprehension of text, and memory for what was comprehended. In this
diagram the solid lines connect the stages that would be involved if strictly visual
analysis was applied to words, if the results of this visual analysis were used to
locate the word meanings in the mental lexicon, if the comprehension of text
used the looked-up word meanings, and if the comprehended message directed
action or was stored in abstract form in memory. This hypothetical sequence of
events is essentially what Kleiman (1975) terms the direct pathway hypothesis.
Several other researchers and students of reading have also referred to strictly
visual analysis as "direct" (Smith, 1971, in particular), but we must point out
that even the most direct visual analysis probably requires stimulus processing as
complex as that proposed by speech recoding models (Rayner & Posnansky,
1978; Smith & Spoehr, 1974). The only truly direct model of visual perception is
template matching (Neisser, 1967), and it is unlikely that words are recognized
by matching a perceptual image to a memory template.

The dashed lines show connections to possible speech recoding stages. The
first of these stages is the translation to a speech code before look-up in the
mental lexicon. This translation would be based on orthographic decoding rules.
If recoding takes place here, the important conclusion would be that the mental
lexicon is organized according to the speech codes of words and that reading,
even in the skilled reader, is parasitic on speech in the way it accesses information in semantic memory. Recoding at this stage is termed the lexical access
hypothesis by Kleiman (1975).

The second place for recoding is the loop that begins immediately after access
to the mental lexicon. If a speech code was generated only at this point, it would
be based on stored information about the sound of the word rather than on the

orthography of the visually available stimulus (Forster & Chambers, 1973). The speech code input to short-term memory could also come directly from a spelling-to-sound translation, as shown by the dashed arrow from the first translation mechanism. The purpose of speech recoding at this stage is to provide short-term memory with a speechlike representation, to hold for the use of the comprehension process. A temporary storage medium for ongoing speech seems to be a necessity, given that comprehension requires the listener to make relations between units separated in time. It is possible that in rapid reading (with very few regressive eye movements) the same speechlike medium of storage would also be used. Recoding at this stage is termed the working memory hypothesis by Kleiman (1975).

The third possible mechanism that might explain speech recoding effects lies in the memory for text after it is comprehended, as shown by the third recoding point in Fig. 7.1. The translation to internal speech could occur only at this stage, after reading was complete, and still some acoustical effects in reading tasks would be found. We note, however, that although this recoding stage and the recoding for memory used in comprehension are logically separable, researchers have not often attempted to distinguish these two loci. In most of what follows, we simply distinguish between evidence for speech recoding before and after lexical access.

We cover some of the evidence on speech recoding with the intention of determining whether speech recoding in reading comes before or after lexical access. Inasmuch as most investigators concede that there is evidence for speech recoding at some point after lexical access, there is little need to pursue the later stages of recoding. We therefore concentrate on the following question: *Is there any evidence at all for speech recoding before lexical access?* To answer this question, which seems to be the critical one, we need to consider whether the available findings that give evidence for speech recoding can all be explained by events occurring after lexical access. Our review looks at a number of separate categories of evidence on this point. We also attempt to show how a variety of experimental results and common observations about speech recoding can be described in terms of the schema in Fig. 7.1. We cover here only topics that are particularly important to our main question or that have specific importance in relation to the schema in Fig. 7.1.

Evidence on Speech Recoding

Short-Term Memory.   As mentioned, speech coding in short-term memory was discovered early in modern cognitive research, and the existence of such coding is well documented. A large body of research has been generated on speech recoding at the level of short-term memory. Because we are mainly interested in tasks more specifically related to reading than short-term memory—and because this literature does not help decide whether recoding can come *before* lexical access—we do not cover this area. We refer the reader to Crowder's (1976) excellent and thorough review of speech coding in short-term memory. Reviews of this topic oriented toward reading are found in Conrad (1972) and Massaro (1975).

"Inner Speech" While Reading.   It is a common observation that readers hear a "voice" or a stream of inner speech while reading. Huey (1908/1968) states: "although [inner speech] is . . . foreshortened and incomplete . . . in most of us, . . . [it] is a constituent part of the reading of by far the most people [p. 117]." Roger Brown (1970), in commenting on T. G. R. Bower's (1970) experimental attempt to show reading does not require speech recoding, begins by noting a very definite sort of speech recoding in his own silent reading of Bower's article. As Brown (1970) puts it: "As I read these sentences they came to me in Bower's familiar Scots accent and that seemed quite a thing for the eye alone to have accomplished [p. 178]." We find experimental support for this sort of recoding in the work of Kosslyn and Matt (1977). They showed that the speed of silent reading of a passage was strongly influenced by the speaking rate of the person said to have written it, whose voice the subjects heard before they read the passages to themselves. If the supposed author of the passage was a fast speaker, they read it quickly; if the author spoke slowly, they read it slowly. In a series of six experiments, Kosslyn and Matt convincingly make the case that the effect on reading speed comes from the speaking rate of the author and not from other factors. It is as though the readers translate to inner speech at some point in the comprehension process, and the inner speech to which they translate is an image of the writer's voice.

The fact that mature readers are sensitive to strictly acoustical properties of written speech also points to recoding to inner speech at some level in reading. If we did not recode to speech we would not enjoy reading most poetry silently; we would have to read it aloud to appreciate the meter, rhyme, and relation between sense and sound that distinguish poetry from prose. A lack of speech recoding would also cause us to miss puns and many other forms of wordplay that authors deliberately put in their writings, knowing they will be understood. But perhaps the most telling sort of acoustical property in written prose concerns aspects of style that derive from the sound the prose would have if read aloud. Masters of style know how to use the characteristic rhythms of their native tongue, alliteration, and contrast of sounds effectively, and readers are sensitive to these aspects of prose. Few of these speech-derived properties of style create regular visual patterns. Without speech recoding of a text at some level, these stylistic niceties would be overlooked by the silent reader.

Although all these observations support a role for inner speech in silent reading, they do not tell us where in the reading process the speech coding takes place. It seems reasonable to place this sort of inner speech at a level after lexical access because it encompasses phrases and other units larger than the word. The nuances of accent, rhythm, and style do apply to single words, but they generally operate across groups of words. At best we can say that the inner speech phenomena do not give good evidence for recoding prior to lexical access.

Proofreading. Corcoran (1967) and Corcoran and Weening (1968) have shown a sort of speech coding in a proofreading task by demonstrating that spelling errors that delete nonpronounced letters (e.g., *k* in *knight*) were less likely to be detected than spelling errors that delete pronounced letters. Corcoran's (1967) interpretation of this finding is that both a visual image and an acoustical image of the word are examined for spelling. When the misspelling is apparent only in the visual image, there is one less source of information (or, indeed, a conflict between visual and auditory information) and thus a greater likelihood that the misspelling will be overlooked than when the auditory image is also altered by the misspelling. This finding implies that translation to a speech code takes place. However, to conclude from this finding that speech recoding took place in reading, we would need to understand mental processing in a proofreading task. Proofreading certainly has much in common with reading, but even if speech recoding takes place in normal reading, the process of detecting spelling errors might operate directly on graphemic spelling units (cf. Gibson, Pick, Osser, & Hammond, 1962; Spoehr & Smith, 1973), without any translation to internal speech. The misspellings that preserved the sound would, if this hypothesis is true, create a graphemically proper spelling group or syllable in most cases, whereas the incorrect sounds would not. Thus, the misspelling could be detected by a strictly visual analysis. In fact, in Corcoran and Weening's study (1968) many of the nonhomophonic misspellings are orthographically illegal. This criticism probably also applies to the Corcoran (1967) proofreading study where subjects searched for a missing letter *e* in words in text and were more likely to note their absence when they were pronounced than when they were not. In most cases, dropping a silent *e* leaves a legal spelling but dropping a pronounced *e* does not.

Even if we were satisfied that speech recoding was necessary to account for the proofreading effects, we would not know what locus of recoding they implied. The effects could result from lexical access through a speech code because homophonic misspellings would retrieve the appropriate meaning. The effects could also come from a search, after lexical access, of the auditory image in a short-term memory. Also, it is possible that people do not read for meaning in proofreading but rather adopt a search strategy that uses an acoustic representation not used in reading.

Experiment 7b in this chapter addresses several deficiencies in previous proofreading tasks that attempted to determine whether a phonological or visual representation was used in reading. In this experiment, subjects read for meaning and were asked to judge afterward which words in a test list had been misspelled in the task. This technique has the disadvantage of requiring memory for—as well as recognition of—misspellings, but there is no reason to believe that misspellings that preserved the speech code would be forgotten any faster than those that did not. The experiment also included careful control for visual similarity. As is shown later, it gives no evidence for acoustical recoding.

Lexical Decision and Related Tasks. These tasks require subjects to judge whether singly presented strings of letters are words or not, or sometimes whether they belong to a certain category if they are words. These could be viewed as one-word-at-a-time proofreading tasks. Of course, they are even less like real reading than proofreading, but they do allow better experimental control and measurement.

MacKay (1972; cf. also MacKay, 1968) compared detection of phonologically compatible misspellings (homophonic ones, such as *werk* for *work*) with incompatible ones (e.g., *wark* for *work*) under two conditions. In the 1972 study subjects were required simply to report exactly what they saw in the tachistoscope. In the set condition of this study subjects were first verbally told the word they would see, either correctly or incorrectly misspelled, and they then saw a tachistoscopic presentation of the word or one of its misspellings. In the no-set condition the same words and misspelled words were presented, but no cue was given beforehand. The set condition therefore tested reporting of a particular word, whereas the no-set condition required subjects to decide which, if any, word was presented.

MacKay's measure of detection of misspelling was the proportion of incorrectly spelled words reported exactly as they were misspelled in the tachistoscope. (The measure is thus different from the more typical two-alternative word–nonword decision used in most of these tasks and may, therefore, have different properties.) The results showed that the set condition facilitated detection of incompatible misspellings but not compatible ones. However, both sorts of misspellings were detected equally well in the no-set condition.

MacKay's results could be viewed as showing a difference in processing between detection of misspelling of an expected word and reporting a literal string without prior context. The difference in processing seems to be that a speech code is used in the one case (detection of misspelling) and not in the other. Does this effect provide evidence for recoding before lexical access? MacKay's explanation of the effect goes somewhat beyond the schema of Fig. 7.1, but it does imply a preaccess locus. MacKay's main point is to reject passive models of word recognition (such as is suggested by Fig. 7.1), and he proposes an input-testing theory by which perception results from active testing of stimuli against internally generated hypotheses. Lexical access would not be a passive look-up in the mental lexicon but a test based on the ongoing comprehension of the text. To the extent that MacKay's task simulates reading, he has shown that the test forming the basis of lexical access can use a speech code. As a qualification of this conclusion we note that MacKay's results could come from a strategy of verifying spelling by pronunciation, without any reliance on lexical access. There is no need to determine the meaning of the words in the set condition in which the possible speech coding effects were found. MacKay (personal communication) points out one complication to this qualification. This is that subjects in the set condition (and only in this condition) gave wrong responses that spelled words more often when a non-target word was presented than subjects in the no-set condition did. It was as though they knew the stimulus was a word but did not know which word it was. This result implies that subjects processed more than just phonology because they apparently discriminated words from nonwords, but it still does not necessarily mean that they accessed meaning or that they used an acoustical representation to determine the meaning of words.

Results apparently supporting speech coding prior to lexical access were reported by Meyer, Schvaneveldt, and Ruddy (1974a). They presented subjects with pairs of letter strings and asked them to respond "yes" if both spelled words, "no" otherwise. This research followed other experiments using this task that showed a facilitation in decision time for "yes" responses if the two words were semantically or associatively related. This experiment sought to determine the effect of acoustical and visual similarity between the words. They found an interference between the visual and acoustical form of the words such that *freak-break,* for example, took longer to accept as a word pair than *fence-hence.* Meyer et al. attribute this finding to inappropriate speech codes induced in the conflict condition. In our example with the *freak-break* pair, the word *break* would be internally pronounced as *breek* (or *freak* as *frake*) and so cause slow or errorful responses because it would be classified as a nonword on the basis of the speech code. The effect implicates speech coding prior to lexical access because an incorrect speech code could only affect processing in this task by disturbing lexical access, or so it would seem. Massaro (1975) has argued, however, that interference between the visual and speech-coded aspect of the words could take place after a purely visual lexical access. This interference would be such that the acoustical nonword *breek* in our example would slow the correct response to the visually looked-up word *break.* Massaro's argument still depends on lexical access by a speech code, we think, because the nonword *breek* could not be recognized as a nonword unless lexical access was attempted with the speech code.

Another of Massaro's criticisms (1975) seems more valid. Subjects could not fail to notice that a large proportion of word pairs, like *hence-fence,* rhyme. Could the failure to rhyme somehow slow performance for pairs like *freak-break?* Massaro does not provide a mechanism for the slowing of responses in such cases. We propose as a possible mechanism that subjects may develop a strategy of checking for rhymes. If nonwords never rhymed with anything in the experiment (which is likely), then rhyming pairs in the experiment are definitely words, whereas nonrhymes may or may not be. Words whose pronunciation is ambiguous (as in *freak-break*) could well seem like nonwords by this strategy. If the pronunciation checks went on in parallel with lexical access it could produce the observed pattern of RT's and errors, without any need for lexical access by a speech code. Whether or not our proposal is valid, it does point up the difficulty of drawing inferences about reading from tasks of this kind. We cannot be sure that they do not simply tap some experiment-specific strategy rather than fundamental aspects of mental processing in reading.

In a study that does employ a task something like reading and that is widely cited as giving evidence against speech recoding, Baron (1973) instructed subjects to judge the meaningfulness of phrases. The phrases contained either orthographically and phonetically incorrect words or visually incorrect but phonetically correct (homophonic) words. For example, a homophonic error is in the phrase *dont dew it,* and an orthographic one is in *new I cant.* Baron (1973) hypothesized that if recoding occurred, the correct sound of the homophonic errors would interfere with rejecting the sentence as meaningful, and the homophonic errors would have longer reaction times than the orthographic errors. If no recoding took place, then the decision would be based on only the visual features of the string, and there would be no difference between homophones and nonhomophones. Baron's results rejected the speech-coding hypothesis.

Three main problems mar this study. First, subjects were presented all stimuli prior to the actual testing in order to learn what "meaningful" meant. This preexposure may have allowed subjects to learn specific errors and thus eliminated differences between stimulus classes. A second problem is the use of real words as misspellings. The reaction times may all measure the same process: time to access an anomalous lexical item and reject the string as meaningless. If lexical access of the word created by the misspelling is faster than the access of its homophone, the homophonic errors will rarely have a chance to slow processing, and the two classes of misspelling will give the same results. The final problem in Baron's study was a higher percentage of errors in the homophonic condition (5.1%) than in the control condition (2.4%). A speed-accuracy trade-off may be indicated here (cf. Pachella, 1974). The pattern of reaction times may have been different had the accuracy been the same in the two critical conditions.

Despite the flaws in Baron's investigation, it remains one of the most frequently cited pieces of evidence against recoding. It therefore seemed imperative to replicate it in a way that avoids these flaws. Experiments 8 and 9 in this chapter replicate the experiment in two slightly different ways, and both, it turns out, support Baron's conclusions.

The first six experiments reported in this chapter seek to improve on some of the discrete-trial lexical decision tasks, or at least to approach the question of speech recoding with a slightly different set on the part of the subject. In these experiments subjects made a decision about the semantic category of a word rather than about its status as a word or nonword, as in lexical decision tasks. Although subjects may make word–nonword decisions in normal reading for meaning, there is no reason for them to do so. A category decision seems closer to word processing in reading than a word–nonword decision does. These experiments also attempt to control in various ways for visual similarity between target and nontarget words. With very few exceptions (such as *I* and *eye*) homonyms are similar to each other visually. Careful construction of visually similar alternatives is needed to make sure that what seems like a homophonic effect is not really an effect of visual similarity.

Effects of Syllabic Structure in Letter Detection

Performance in detection of single letters in multiletter arrays is better when the letters spell a word than when they do not. We are not reviewing the extensive literature on this topic because it does not bear directly on the question of speech recoding in lexical access (see Baron & Thurston, 1973; Bjork & Estes, 1973; Massaro, 1975; Smith & Spoehr, 1974; Thompson & Massaro, 1973; Wheeler, 1970). However, one series of studies on recognition of letters in words reports phonological effects and is relevant to the question of speech recoding in processing of words (Spoehr, 1978; Spoehr & Smith, 1973, 1975). If a translation to a speech code is made early enough in processing to be used in tachistoscopic letter detection experiments, it could also be available early enough to be used in lexical access.

The most important contribution of the Spoehr and Smith research is the analysis of syllabic and orthographic effects in letter detection. Apparently subjects do not simply search a letter string for a target but rather organize the string into syllabic groups by very definite orthographic rules before searching for the target. However, even though the syllabic organization ultimately has its roots in the spelling-to-sound rules of English, the syllabic effects in tachistoscopic word perception could come from strictly visual analysis. On the other hand, Spoehr's (1978) finding that tachistoscopic detection accuracy is an inverse function of the length of the phonological code seems to be more direct evidence for translation to a speech code in this task. Unfortunately for the hypothesis of speech coding before lexical access, Spoehr's analysis of the phonemic length effect supports speech coding for memory better than speech coding prior to any search of the array for the target. Spoehr, noting that most of the experiments showing syllabic or phonological effects require subjects to wait before responding, systematically varied the interval between stimulus and response to see how the effect of phonemic length varied over the interval. Her results show very clearly that the phonological length effect "develops" over time. If response alternatives are given immediately after the offset of the array and up to .1 sec afterward, the stimuli longer in terms of a speech code (more syllables and/or more phonemes) actually give slightly better performance than the shorter ones. But at .25 sec the effect reverses, and for intervals out to 2 sec the phonological length effect previously found with an uncontrolled but relatively long interval between presentation and response is replicated (cf. Spoehr, 1978). It seems then, that search of the string for the target letter can use either a visual or a speech-coded representation, that in the very early stages of processing a visual representation is used, but that requiring that the decision be deferred causes subjects to store a speech code of the stimulus in memory while waiting.

The Argument from Alphabetical Writing

One a priori argument that readers translate written text to an internal speech code is the existence of alphabetical writing systems. These systems encode speech into writing in a fairly direct way, and it is not implausible that readers may convert the writing back to speech in decoding it. This argument gains some plausibility from considerations of how children learn to read. If the new reader had to learn each word as a separate visual pattern, the task would seem to be excessively difficult. Fortunately, children already know how to decode spoken language by the time they begin to learn to read, and a relatively simple system exists for recoding written words to their spoken form. Instead of learning the meaning of many thousands of different visual patterns, the beginning reader only has to master a system containing at most a few hundred rules about pronunciation. It seems likely that the spelling-to-sound rules of alphabetical written languages account for the rapid progress a new reader o. these languages can make. By the second grade, for example, an average reader of English may read as many words as a scholar of Mandarin, a language whose written form is not alphabetical (Rozin & Gleitman, 1977).

To be fair, however, we must recognize that the argument from alphabetical writing or from economy of learning gives weak support to the notion that adult readers recode to speech. Beginning readers might depart from phonological translation of words very soon after learning them, even if they did use the economical recoding strategy in the first place. It is also possible that the relatively rapid learning of an alphabetical language comes about because the orthographical regularities create visual patterns that are easy to learn, without any need for acoustical translation. On the other hand, the argument that speech recoding need *not* take place because idiographic languages do not have spelling-to-sound correspondence is also very weak. Speech coding could still take place, and in fact Tzeng, Hung, and Wang (1977) have shown that it does in short-term memory for visually presented Chinese characters for Chinese-speaking subjects.

Altered Systems of Alphabetical Writing

If lexical access uses a speech code, text that is altered in some way but is still pronounced correctly should be no harder to read than unaltered text. Following this reasoning, Bower (1970) used Greek letters to symbolize English words for Greek-English bilinguals. Because his subjects found it very difficult to read this material he concluded that speech recoding was not used in reading. Smith (1973) in arguing against speech coding in silent reading pointed out that homophonic misspellings in text slow reading greatly, as for example, in the frequently cited sentence (a variant of one LaBerge, [1972] used to make the same point): *The none tolled hymn she had scene a pare of bear feat inn hour rheum.*

The difficulty of reading in these examples could come from a customary reliance on visual rather than auditory codes, but it could also be due to a number of other factors. One of these is conflict between the visual and auditory aspects of the oddly spelled words. This conflict would exist because *both* the visual and auditory aspects of the words are used. In normal reading they do not conflict, but in these cases they do. The fact that reading is possible at all in these examples shows that phonological access to the lexicon can be used. The interference would thus be a kind of Stroop (1935) interference in which the way the word is spelled interferes with processing how it sounds.

A second reason for poor reading performance with oddly spelled materials may be related to the very great difficulty practiced readers have in learning new orthographies (Baron, 1976; Brooks, 1977). The difficulty may, therefore, have nothing to do with the question of speech recoding in normal reading but rather with speed of deriving a speech code from the altered orthography.

Speed of Reading Aloud

Several experiments have used speed of reading words out loud as a tool by which to examine the speech recoding hypothesis. These studies tend to argue against recoding, although there are some contradictions between them. Forster and Chambers (1973), Frederiksen and Kroll (1976), and Baron and Strawson (1976) have all found that subjects can pronounce singly presented words faster than nonwords. If a speech code was generated prior to lexical access, however, words and nonwords should be pronounced with equal speed. The faster pronunciation of words than nonwords seems to indicate, therefore, that the speech code is generated after lexical access (at the second loop in Fig. 7.1), possibly by retrieval from memory rather than by translation from orthography. The nonwords would have to be decoded to speech by processes of orthographic analysis, which by this account must be slower than retrieval of a speech code after lexical access. The problem with this account is that pronunciation time for words, while faster than for nonwords, shows the same functions of number of letters and syllabic structure as the nonwords (Frederiksen & Kroll, 1976). It seems likely, then, that the same decoding strategy is used in both cases.

Why, then, are words read faster than nonwords? There are a number of possibilities. One could be an optional check of the internal lexicon that is performed by most subjects in parallel with (or following) phonological decoding. If a semantic representation is found, the orthographically derived speech code is checked against the speech code in memory, and the word is pronounced. If not, the orthographic decoding is rechecked, and then the nonword is pronounced. Parallel access of the lexicon simultaneously with orthographic translation might also produce faster response for words than nonwords if, on some trials, the speech code for a word was retrieved (after a purely visual lexical access) before the orthographic translation was finished (as suggested by Forster & Chambers, 1973). Still another possibility is that familiarity or some other uncontrollable difference between words and nonwords slowed the pronunciation of nonwords.

Frederiksen and Kroll compared pronunciation latency for words and nonwords to see if the same effects of number of letters and syllabic structure on RT are found in a lexical decision task as in naming. This tests whether phonological coding takes place prior to lexical access because the lexical decision task requires lexical access. Thus, if a phonological code is used to access word memory, the time to perform the lexical decision task for a word or nonword should show effects of stimulus structure similar to those observed in pronunciation latency. The RT to decide on nonwords did increase with number of letters, as it did for pronunciation latency, thus suggesting that phonological recoding did take place for them, but the RT for words was invariant with length. None of the effects of syllabic structure found in the pronunciation task were reliable, but it is not reported whether the RT effects were at least correlated across the tasks. It is possible that the effects were, overall, in the same direction in both tasks, but simply not reliable in the second. (Forster and Chambers did find a reliable correlation between the two tasks for words.) The effects found in the pronunciation task might be stronger than those found in the lexical decision task because a full speech code, with a complete motor component, is not generated for the decision task or because a visual code is used more often in the lexical decision task. In either case, the magnitude of the correlation would be reduced. Nevertheless, despite these possible interpretations, the results do imply that speech recoding as measured in a pronunciation task is not a necessary component of lexical access. At best, we can say that speech recoding may take place sometimes before lexical access.

Bradshaw and Nettleton (1974) also found evidence against phonological recoding using stimuli similar to those of Meyer et al. (1974a) in a pronunciation task. Subjects were shown heterophone pairs like *mown-down* and had to read the first, the second, or both aloud. There was an interference in reading heterophone pairs relative to nonheterophones but only when both words had to be pronounced. If one of the two was read silently it did not interfere. Thus, an interfering phonological code was not generated in silent reading as it was in reading aloud. It is possible, however, that this interference effect in pronunciation is peculiar to vocalization and has nothing to do with lexical access. Meyer et al. (1974a) did, after all, show heterophonic interference in lexical access without any vocalization by the subjects.

Finally, Rayner and Posnansky (1978) studied how times for the naming of a picture varied as a function of the composition of a string of letters printed in the middle of the picture. They were mainly interested in the visual properties of the string of letters, and they found evidence for a visual-features stage model of word analysis. They also found evidence for speech coding of letter stings in that the nonwords *burd* and *byrd,* for example, facilitated naming time for a picture of a bird almost as much as the word *bird* did. However, they point out that the pronunication task may have induced speech recoding even though recoding is not normally a part of reading. Also, there is no evidence that lexical access took place in this task. Consequently, any evidence found here for speech recoding does not decide the issue of whether it comes before or after lexical access.

Interference Between Reading and Irrelevant Vocalizing

If inner speech of some sort is necessary in reading, and if concurrent vocalizing (such as shadowing, counting, repeating "the," etc.) interferes with inner speech, then concurrent vocalizing should slow reading down. Huey (1908/1968) reported that experiments had been performed at Cornell showing that "some readers" could still read while "whistling or doing other motor tasks that would hinder inner speech [p. 117]," but these experiments did not settle the issue of recoding. The modern research on interference between reading and vocalizing attempts to see what components of the reading process are susceptible to interference by vocalizing and therefore normally use inner speech.

Two studies, Kleiman (1975) and Levy (1977), used the concurrent interference approach to determine whether speech coding occurs before or after lexical access. Kleiman's first experiment presented subjects with pairs of words and had them judge, in different conditions, whether they had the same spelling after the first letter, the same sound, or the same meaning. Subjects made these judgments while shadowing digits (repeating auditorily presented digits aloud). Shadowing slowed the spelling and meaning judgments both by about .12 sec, but it slowed the same sound judgments by .372 sec. We note only one minor question about these results, namely that the sound judgment task was harder in the first place and may have been more susceptible than the others to interference of any kind. Kleiman's second experiment supported the proposition that the spelling judgment task does not involve speech recoding and so could serve as a baseline that measures the effect of shadowing on a process other than speech coding. His third experiment showed that shadowing slows a phonemic search task and a grammatical or semantic acceptability task (in which the meaningfulness of a string of words was judged) by about the same amount. In the third experiment a spelling judgment and a category judgment were slowed much less than the phonemic and grammatical judgment task. If the grammatical judgment requires both lexical access and comprehension of a string of words, and category judgment requires only lexical access, the fact that comprehension shows more interference than category judgment indicates that the interference affects the component that only comprehension has, namely, postaccess short-term memory. The small amount of interference shown by the category task does not exceed that of the spelling task. Therefore it probably comes from generalized interference with processing rather than from interference with lexical access.

Levy (1977) has also shown interference between vocalizing (her subjects counted aloud) and comprehension of text. Her experiments are not intended to test whether speech recoding occurs before or after lexical access. The results are compatible with a postaccess locus of speech recoding. Interestingly, her vocalizing task did not interfere with comprehension of sentences that subjects *heard,* only with those that they *read.* Possibly, then, the verbal task interferes with generation or retrieval of an internal speech code rather than with memory for the speech code once it is obtained.

Suppression of Covert Vocalization

Hardyck and Petrinovich (1970), in an important and widely cited study, monitored the minute subvocal muscular activity of the larynx in subjects who were reading silently. They found an increase in subvocal activity when the passage became difficult. When subjects, trained by biofeedback techniques to suppress subvocal activity, stopped the activity while reading, their comprehension of the difficult passages dropped. The most plausible interpretation of these results is that some sort of speech recoding takes place and that it probably occurs after lexical access, in the short-term memory used during comprehension. Lexical access in difficult material would not seem to be harder than in easy material (unless more low-frequency words were included), but the demands for integration of material in short-term memory would certainly be increased.

EXPERIMENTS ON SPEECH RECODING

The experiments that follow address several different issues in speech recoding. Experiments 1–6 show, in separate visual search tasks and discrete-trial RT tasks, that homophones of members of target categories are difficult to reject as members of those categories. These experiments were initially conceived as a test of Morton's (1970) hypothesis that speech codes are generated only after lexical access. The experiments seem to require immediate processing of stimuli, with no need for storage in a short-term memory before responding, and therefore homophonic confusions can be taken as evidence for speech recoding in lexical access, at least for judgments of category membership.

The extension to lexical access through speech recoding in reading is a question requiring further experiments. Experiments 7–9 use homonyms and look-alikes as spelling errors in reading material to test whether speech recoding occurs in reading as it does in processing single words. Experiment 7 uses a proofreading task in which misspellings are either visually similar to the correct word or homophonic with it. The experiment very carefully matches look-alikes and homophones and compares performance in active proofreading with memory for errors. The experiment is designed to avoid some of the problems with proofreading tasks previously mentioned in the discussion of proofreading.

Experiments 8 and 9 replicate Baron's (1973) study without the flaws discussed in the section on lexical decision tasks. The results indicate that Baron's findings did not depend on the flaws of his study, and his conclusion that speech recoding does not come before lexical access in reading simple sentences stands.

EXPERIMENTS 1 AND 2:
HOMOPHONIC CONFUSION IN VISUAL SEARCH

Experiment 1

Method

The paradigm employed in Experiments 1 and 2 was a Neisser-type search task (Neisser, 1963, 1967). Subjects scanned lists of 50 words for the name of an animal. One target was randomly placed in each list at one of the 50 possible positions. Four different types of lists were used in experimental sessions, each type containing a different kind of distractor set as discussed later.

Materials. An IBM 360 computer was used to generate and print in upper-case letters 50 lists of each of the four types used in experimental trials and 150 of the type used in practice sessions. Every list contained one animal name (the target) randomly chosen from a set of 50. Each list had a target placed on a different one of the 50 lines. Each list also contained a fixed set of 19 irrelevant "filler" words randomly positioned on the list, as well as 30 more words drawn from one of four sets. The set to which these 30 words belonged defined the type of list that was constructed. One of the sets consisted of homonyms and some near homonyms of target words, and search lists containing these 30 words were termed homonym distractor lists. A second set contained words that were ortho-graphically similar to targets but that were neither homonyms nor rhymes of targets. Search lists containing these 30 words were termed look-alike distractor lists. A third set contained words that are commonly associated with particular animals or with the taxonomic category in general (e.g., *zoo, nest, claw*), and lists that contained these 30 words were termed associative distractor lists. Finally, there was a set of 30 randomly selected words that bore no obvious relationship to the targets. This set contributed to the random distractor search lists.

All words were less than eight letters long. The computer program randomly selected the target, combined it with the 19 fillers and the appropriate set of 30, and randomly shuffled these 50 words. The lists were printed in five columns of ten rows.

Subjects.   Subjects were two female Pomona College undergraduates who volunteered their time.

Procedure.   Subjects viewed the lists at a comfortable reading distance through a pane of 50% reflective glass that formed the aperture of a one-field tachistoscope. The experimenter mounted each list behind the one-way glass and turned on a signal light that told the subject that she could begin a trial when she wished. To begin searching the list the subject operated a switch that simultaneously started a Standard Electric centisecond timer and illuminated the list behind the glass so that it became visible. When the subject located the target she pronounced it into a microphone, and a voice-operated relay stopped the timer and extinguished the light in the tachistoscope.

Subjects had five practice sessions and then five experimental sessions, lasting about 15–30 min each, and usually held on consecutive days. Subjects were instructed to search always from the top. They were told that accuracy of search was more important than speed.

On the five practice sessions lists with random distractors (not the same distractors as in the five experimental sessions) were used. Subjects scanned 30 computer-generated lists during each practice session. They scanned 40 on each of the five experimental sessions. Of these 40 daily lists, 10 were from each of the four different stimulus sets. The 40 lists were randomly presented so that at all times the subjects were unaware of what type of list they were about to scan. Lists on which subjects made errors were repeated later in the session.

Results and Discussion

Regression coefficients were determined for each subject on each type of experimental list over all 5 experimental days. List position (from 1 to 50) of the target was treated as the abcissa value, and latency of response (in msec) was the corresponding ordinate. In all cases, correlation coefficients exceeded .9, and most r's were greater than .95.

Mean regression coefficients, averaged for the two subjects, are plotted in Fig. 7.2. Overall differences among search rates for the four list types are significant, with $F(1, 3) = 9.01$, $p < .05$. So few errors were obtained that their distribution is meaningless.

Subsequent analysis by Duncan's new multiple range test shows that the random distractor lists are scanned significantly faster (the regression coefficient is smaller) than the other three types at $p < .05$ and faster than homonym distractor lists at $p < .01$. Both look-alike distractor and associative distractor

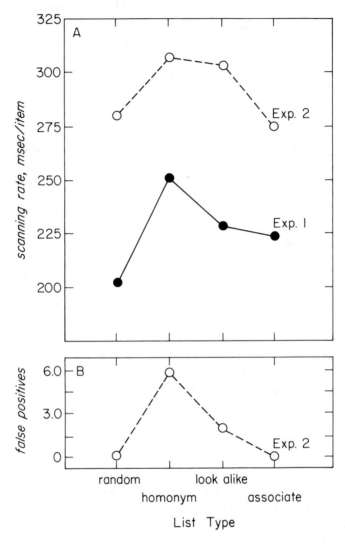

FIG. 7.2. Scanning rates (Experiments 1 and 2) and false positives (Experiment 2) for searching lists for names of animals. The lists contained as nontargets either random words, homonyms of possible targets (e.g., *hoarse* for *horse*), words that look like possible targets (e.g., *loin* for *lion*), and words associated with the target category (e.g., *zoo, fur, hoof,* etc.).

types are searched faster than homonym distractor lists at $p < .05$, but they do not differ from each other.

Experiment 2

The use of a voice-operated relay in Experiment 1 may have induced the subjects to read subvocally. Thus, acoustical confusions may have resulted from response processes in the task rather than from processes mediating the visual perception of the words. Experiment 2 replicates Experiment 1 with a manual rather than verbal response. In addition, Experiment 2 uses a larger set of targets, equates Thorndike–Lorge word frequency for all sets, and has a more stringent criterion of orthographic similarity than Experiment 1.

Method

The procedure used in Experiment 2 is the same as that of Experiment 1 except that the subject released a button to stop the clock and extinguish the lights. The subject then told the experimenter the target he or she had found. Four new subjects were used. They were Pomona College students, two males and two females.

The lists were constructed in the same way as those in Experiment 1, but they used stimulus sets that were all matched for Thorndike–Lorge G frequency. The criteria for orthographic similarity were more stringent, requiring that a stimulus differ from the corresponding target either by the addition, subtraction, or substitution of only one internal letter or by having the positions of two letters in the word switched. (Actually, 6 of the 30 look-alikes—because of the need for frequency matching—had a changed internal letter plus a switch of letters.) The target set of animal names was expanded to 150. Practice lists were the same lists used for training in Experiment 1.

Results and Discussion

The slopes for each subject on each day were cast in a subjects × treatments × days factorial design. Both the improvement over days (F [3, 12] = 17.74, $p < .01$) and the differences among list types are significant, with F (3, 9) = 7.20, $p < .01$. The effect of distractor type did not vary over days. Mean slope coefficients, averaged over subjects and days, are plotted by the broken line in the upper half of Fig. 7.2.

Subsequent analysis by Dunnett's t test shows that both homonym distractor lists ($t = 4.59$) and look-alike distractor lists ($t = 4.02$) are scanned more slowly than random distractor lists at $p < .0025$, one-tailed. Differences between associate distractor and random distractor lists and between homonym distractor and look-alike distractor lists yield t's less than 1.0. The stringent criterion for constructing look-alikes may have caused orthographic similarity effects to be nearly as strong as homonymic effects or at least to have reduced the difference between the two categories.

The distribution of false positives follows a pattern similar to that of the latency data. The overall differences are significant in a Freedman two-way analysis of variance by ranks test, with $\chi_r^2 = 10.80$, $p < .0016$. A binomial test shows that homonym distractor list errors are more frequent than look-alike distractor list errors at $p < .004$. Medians of the false positives are shown in the lower half of Fig. 7.1.

EXPERIMENTS 3–6: HOMOPHONIC EFFECTS IN JUDGMENTS OF CATEGORY MEMBERSHIP

Experiments 3–6 use stimuli similar to those of Experiments 1 and 2 but present them one at a time and measure the RT for the classification. This procedure allows us to collect RT's for decisions about particular words rather than for lists as a whole, and therefore allows the use of inferential statistics that estimate the generalizability of effects over the population of words as well as subjects (cf. Clark, 1973). The discrete-trials technique also gives a converging method for studying the homonymic effect. It is possible that list scanning induces subvocal reading and recoding into short-term memory before the decision. The discrete-trial technique should be free of this effect.

Experment 3

Method

Stimulus words were presented one at a time, and subjects were instructed to throw one of two miniature toggle switches (mounted on a 2″ × 3″ × 4″ hand-held box) to indicate their "yes" (it is a target) or "no" (it is not a target) decision. The yes switch was always on the right; the no switch was on the left. The subjects were free to choose whatever hand(s) or fingers they wished for making the responses. The experimenter warned the subject before presenting each stimulus, which stayed in view until the subject responded. Stimuli that led to an error were repeated later in the session.

The 90 experimental stimuli in Experiment 3 consisted of 45 animal names (targets) randomly selected from the 150 of Experiment 2, plus 15 members of the four sets of 30 distractor words used in Experiment 2 to generate the experimental lists. The words chosen for this experiment were closely matched in frequency and number of letters. For training sessions, 150 stimuli were prepared, of which 50 were words, 50 were nonsense syllables, and 50 were numbers. In the training task, subjects responded "yes" to words and "no" to everything else. All stimuli were typed in capital letters in the pica type of a portable typewriter.

Subjects were 14 males and females, all native English speakers, ranging in age from 18 to 31 years. Their education varied from 11th grade to postlaw degree training. All passed a spelling test on the words that had appeared as homonyms in the experiment.

Results

The RT's to reject distractors of different types are plotted in Fig. 7.3. The effect of distractor type is reliable when tested over subjects and words within type (as suggested by Clark, 1973), with an F' (3, 90) = 8.20, $p < .01$. The

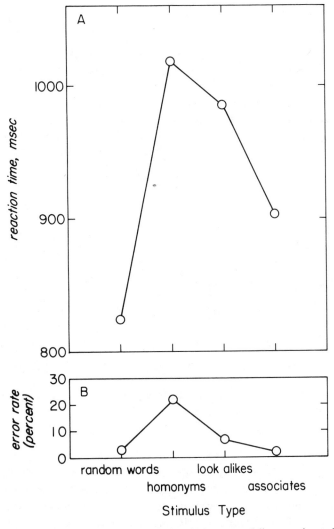

FIG. 7.3. Reaction times and error to reject singly presented distractors in a task in which subjects responded positively to names of animals and negatively to all other stimuli. Distractors are similar to those in Experiments 1 and 2 (shown in Fig. 7.2).

mean square error for this effect is 24 msec (over subjects and stimuli), and given this as the basis for a simple least significant difference test, all means are reliably different at $p < .05$ or better, except for look-alikes and homonyms, which fall short of the critical difference. Errors, however, also plotted in Fig. 7.3, show a strong difference between homonyms and look-alikes, reliable beyond the .01 level by a binomial test.

Experiment 4

Method

Experiment 4 replicates Experiment 3, with these exceptions: There was one training session of 75 stimuli (words, nonsense syllables, and numbers) and one experimental session of 90 stimuli. The experimental stimuli were of the same four types as before (random, homonyms, look-alikes, and associates), but the taxonomic category for targets was now "A Part of the Human Body." There were 14 of each distractor type, matched for frequency. All homonyms were perfect, and all look-alikes met the stringent criteria for orthographic similarity that were used in Experiments 2 and 3. There were 34 body-part targets.

Subjects were two male and two female Pomona students, paid for their time in the experiment.

Results and Discussion

The reaction times and errors are seen in Fig. 7.4. Reaction times to reject nontargets on the experimental task were cast in a subjects × treatments design. The stimulus type ($F [3, 9] = 4.32, p < .05$) variable is significant by this analysis, but it falls short by the quasi-F analysis, with $F' (1, 43) = 2.49$. Differences among the error rates show a large effect of homonyms but are not reliable by a χ^2 test.

Experiment 5

This experiment was performed to make sure that the category task, and not some peculiar property of homonyms, was responsible for the effects in the previous experiments.

Method

Experiment 5 was given to Experiment-4 subjects on the next 2 consecutive days. During each experimental session, subjects viewed 71 randomly presented stimuli. On both days the sets were identical, but the yes–no task differed from one day to the other. During one session, subjects decided whether or not each stimulus was an animal. During the other, they decided whether each was a body part. Both task order and stimulus arrangement were counterbalanced across subjects by blocks.

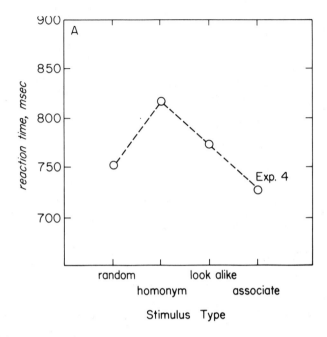

FIG. 7.4. Reaction times as in Fig. 7.3, but with body parts as the positive category.

The stimulus set had 19 of each target type (animals and body parts), plus 11 each of animal homonyms, body-part homonyms, and random words. The latter three sets were matched for frequency.

Results and Discussion

Reaction times to reject nontarget were cast in a subjects × homonym type × question (or task) design. (Targets of both types and random words were deleted from the data in this analysis.) No effects are reliable except for the interaction between homonym and question type, with $F (1, 50) = 4.60$, $p < .05$. (This effect is *not* reliable by a quasi-F analysis; $F = 1.76$.) The upper half of Fig. 7.5 shows this interaction, with a plotting of random word rejection latencies for comparison.

The false positives, shown in the lower half of Fig. 7.5, follow a similar pattern. The interaction between homonym and question type is significant in a Fisher Probability Test at $p = .00054$. Random words, also plotted, are accompanied by no errors.

Experiment 6

This experiment replicates Experiment 5 with look-alike distractors as well as homonyms. In this experiment the look-alike distractors were all nonwords,

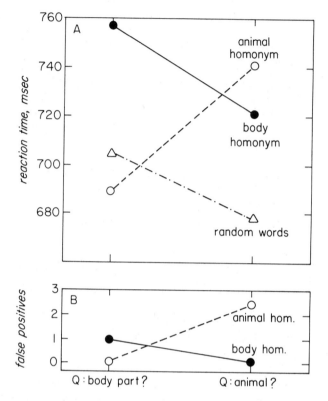

FIG. 7.5. Reaction times (and errors) for rejecting homonyms of animal names and names of body parts (and for random words) under two different conditions, one where the target category is animal names and one where it is body parts.

rather than words as in the previous experiments, so that they could be made extremely similar to category members. These look-alikes were created by substitution of one letter by a highly similar alternative (R for B, P for R, M for N, etc.). The homonyms were all English words. Each look-alike was matched with one homonym with a common category member. Thus, for example, a look-alike for DEER was DEEB, and the homonym was DEAR. This matching was used to prevent any variance due to the accessibility of the particular category member from contaminating the results.

Method

Subjects, in a single session, saw a set of 52 stimuli twice, once deciding in each case whether it was the name of a body part and once deciding whether it was an animal. The set contained 11 names of animals, 11 body parts, and 8 each of the following four categories: look-alikes for animals, look-alikes for body parts, homonyms for animals, and homonyms for body parts. Words were all typed in upper-case pica and presented in the same tachistoscope used in Experiment 3. There were 20 subjects, all male and female Pomona College students paid $2 for their participation. Half of the subjects answered the body-part question first and half the animal question. Subjects knew they were being timed in the task but were instructed that accuracy was more important than speed.

Results

Figure 7.6 shows the reaction time to reject the four critical types of distractor for each of the two questions. Clearly, the question type stringly influences the RT to reject both kinds of distractor (the RT's to animal names and body parts were not analyzed). The overall interaction is reliable by a quasi-F analysis with F' (1, 22) = 17.8, p <.001. The effect of question type is also separately reliable for look-alikes alone, with F' (1, 32) = 6.04 (p <.05), and for homonyms alone, with F' (1, 20) = 13.56 (p <.01). The size of the interaction for homonyms was 43 msec per point, but it was only 20 msec for look-alikes. The effect of question type was thus a bit greater for homonyms than look-alikes, pointing to a greater effect of acoustical than visual similarity. The difference, however, falls short of reliability, with F' = 1.8.

Error rate for false positives to homonyms of members of the target category was 8.3% and for homonyms not members of the category, 3.1%. Errors for the

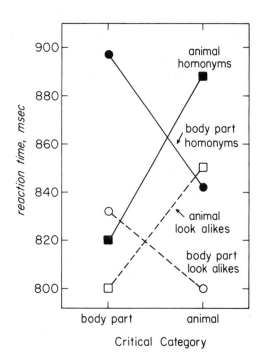

FIG. 7.6. Same as Fig. 7.5, but with distractors that are orthographically similar to members of the target category (look-alikes) as well as those that are homonyms of targets.

look-alikes related to the target category were 7.3% and for look-alikes not related, 2.6%.

Discussion of Experiments 1–6

Taken as a whole, these experiments give some evidence that a homophone of a member of a semantic category is difficult to classify as a nonmember of the category. The fact that the homophones were more difficult to reject than words visually similar to members of the target category indicates some effect of acoustical similarity over and above the orthographic similarity that usually accompanies homophony.

We note that the difference between homonyms and look-alikes appears not to be a robust one, certainly not as great as the difference between these two categories and random words or associate distractors. However, it is a difference that held up over the five experiments that tested for it here; those plus one more (a previous version of Experiment 3 not reported here) makes six out of six, giving $p = .016$ for the difference. There are at least two factors that may make the homophonic effect seem less than it is. First is the conservatism of the quasi-F statistic. Second is the conservative procedure that we are forced to use in generating look-alikes. Because we have no quantitative metric for the visual similarity between words, we must make the look-alikes even more similar to targets than the homophones are by intuitive criteria. The homophones are therefore acoustically identical to targets but not as visually similar as the look-alikes, whereas the ideal compairson would have them exactly equated for visual similarity. If there is an effect of visual similarity—which we do not doubt—it will tend, therefore, to reduce the difference between homonyms and look-alikes.

Experiment 7

Method

Experiment 7 has two parts (which we call 7a and 7b) using similar materials in different tasks with two separate groups of subjects. Both used a 455-word passage taken from a sample reading comprehension test (Brownstein & Weiner, 1967). In the first half of the passage 17 words were misspelled. Of these, 10 were critical words in both experiments. These critical words each had two misspellings, a homophonic one and an orthographically similar one that changed the same letters as the homophonic one but that was not pronounced like the correct spelling. The reading passages were prepared in two versions, each with five of the ten critical words misspelled with the homophone and the other five misspelled with the look-alike. In one version the five homophonic misspellings were the words misspelled with the look-alike in the other, so that the nature of the misspelling was perfectly counterbalanced across the two versions.

This counterbalancing was necessary because words in some positions are more likely to be noticed than words in other positions, and both homonyms and look-alikes should be in every position.

Subjects participated in groups and were given 1½ min to read the passages. When the time was up they made a slash where they were reading. Protocols from subjects who did not get beyond the last misspelling were not scored. After they stopped reading they were given a comprehension test of four multiple-choice items and a spelling test in which they spelled words dictated to them. Protocols from subjects who missed more than one of the comprehension items or any of the spelling words were discarded. Both experiments used students in classes who volunteered to stay after class to perform the task. Volunteer groups ranged from 12 to 30. In each group approximately half of the subjects got one version of the passage and half got the other. Experiment 7a used 60 subjects at Pomona College, of whom 4 had their data removed from analysis for some reason. Experiment 7b began with 61 subjects at Stanford University, of whom 5 gave unusable data.

Experiments 7a and 7b differed mainly in that 7a was a true proofreading task in which subjects circled or underlined spelling errors while reading, whereas 7b had no proofreading but asked subjects to judge after reading the passage whether some words were misspelled. The test of memory for misspellings in Experiment 7b came immediately after the passage and before the comprehension and spelling tests. Subjects were given a list of 23 words, of which 10 were the critical ones, 7 were the noncritical misspelled ones, and 7 were words that appeared in the text but were not misspelled. They had to circle "yes" (it was misspelled) or "no" (it was not) after each word and then gave a confidence rating of their judgment on a three-point scale. These judgments were used to generate five points on a memory operating characteristic from which a measure of memory for the two kinds of misspellings uncontaminated by response bias could be computed (cf. Banks, 1970). A second difference between the two experiments was in the construction of look-alikes and homonyms and the choice of critical words. Experiment 7b substituted new critical words for those that subjects nearly always found in 7a, and 7b designed both misspellings so that only one letter was changed or deleted or two letters interposed.

Results—Experiment 7a

This proofreading task gave some evidence for homophonic confusions and therefore for speech recoding. Subjects detected 54% of the homophones and 66.4% of the look-alikes. When tested over the subjects as the only sampling variable, the effect is reliable, with $F(1, 54) = 12.4$, $p < .001$. However, when tested over both words and subjects, $F' < 1.0$. Furthermore, only 6 out of the 10 critical words showed more misses for the homophonic version than the look-alike version.

Results—Experiment 7b

This experiment gave no evidence at all for homophonic confusions being greater than visually similar ones. In terms of raw percentage of "yes" for the misspellings, the homophonic version had 52.3%, and the look-alikes had 54.0%—a very small and unreliable difference. The signal detection analysis showed almost identical operating characteristics for the homophones and look-alikes, with a mean d' of 1.02 for homophones and 1.05 for look-alikes. The noncritical misspelled words had a d' of .85. Performance on the delayed test in Experiment 7b seems in the same range of accuracy as that in 7a, but the memory for misspellings shows less of a difference between look-alikes and homophones than the proofreading task.

It is difficult to imagine that subjects in Experiment 7b noticed more look-alike misspellings than homophones but forgot the look-alikes more rapidly so that their performance on the memory test was the same for the two categories. It seems more likely that the set induced by proofreading in 7a favors detection of homophones over look-alikes, whereas the more normal reading for meaning presumably employed in Experiment 7b does not. Of course, some of the items were changed from 7a to 7b, but it seems unlikely that the change could have affected the results greatly.

Experiments 8 and 9

These experiments replicate Baron (1973) with the flaws mentioned earlier in the section on lexical decision tasks corrected. Baron's experiment required subjects to judge whether errors had occurred in brief, stereotyped phrases such as *don't do it*. He found homophonic spelling errors (such as *dew* for *do* in the example) to be detected as quickly as look-alikes. However, the study has at least three problems: (1) subjects had considerable exposure to the material before testing (and so may not have read the phrases but only recognized in testing the correct and incorrect ones); (2) all misspellings were themselves words (and so might access their own lexical representation quickly and be rejected without any confusions with the possible correct word); (3) subjects, although rejecting homophonic errors quickly, also made more errors on the homophones than look-alikes. If we were looking only at accuracy and not speed, we would have come to a conclusion exactly opposite to Baron's. The RT effects could be due to a speed-accuracy trade-off (Pachella, 1974); if errors across conditions were equal, the homophones might have had slower RT's.

Experiments 8 and 9 were similar to Baron's experiment. Simple sentences were used, and a single critical word in each was changed to either a homophonic nonword misspelling or an orthographically similar misspelling, also a nonword.

The chief difference between Experiments 8 and 9 is that in 8 the look-alikes were designed to look like the correct spelling of the critical word. They were identical to the correct word except for a change of a single internal letter to an orthographically similar one. In Experiment 9 they were similar to the homophonic misspelling, differing from them by only the change of one internal letter. The uncertainty about handling the problem of the orthographic similarity of the homophones to the correct words prompted the use of these two different ways of controlling for the visual similarity. In Experiment 8 the look-alike distractors tested for the effect of orthographic change per se, but they were generally more similar orthographically to the correct spelling than the homophonic misspellings were. In Experiment 9 the look-alikes, being similar to the homophones, had approximately the same degree of orthographic similarity to the correct spellings as the homophones did. In this experiment, if the homophones took longer to reject than the correct words, it would be because of the added confusability conferred by acoustical similarity and not because of uncontrolled differences in visual similarity.

Both experiments had the same design. Each subject was timed judging the correctness of 36 critical sentences and 24 filler sentences. The fillers contained semantic anomalies (e.g., *Drinking wine makes you sober*) to make sure subjects read sentences for meaning and did not simply search for misspellings. The fillers also contained the number of positive and negative sentences needed to equate "yes" and "no" responses over the experiment. Before the subjects began the experimental trials they judged a series of 18 practice sentences with half positive and half negative responses. The nine negatives included misspelled words and semantic anomalies.

The 36 critical sentences that a subject saw were taken from a master set of 108. To create the master set we first chose 12 words to be the critical words. We then took one homophonic misspelling from Rubenstein, Lewis, and Rubenstein's (1971a) list and generated orthographically similar misspelling for each word. Then we wrote three sentence frames for each critical word. For example, one critical word in Experiment 9 was *broom,* the two misspellings were *brume* and *breme,* and the three sentence frames corresponding to this critical word were: (1) *A new————sweeps floors clean.* (2) *The witch rode her————.* (3) *The dustpan and————are dirty.* Each of the three versions of the word was put in each sentence frame in the master list, creating nine combinations, which multiplied by the 12 critical words, gives the master set of 108. Each subject saw only one sentence frame combined with one of the three versions (correct, homophonic, and look-alike spellings) of the critical word. Thus, they saw three sentence frames for each critical word, for a total of 36 per subject. There were, however, three groups of subjects, and each of them saw a different 36 sentences so that every one of the 108 was seen by some subjects.

To test for any effects of subjects seeing versions of words several times, we arranged the sequence of tests of the critical sentences in three blocks, with a different version of each critical word in a different block. In this way cumulative familiarity effects if they exist would show up as an interaction of words with blocks, and if such an interaction was found, the first block, being free of such effects, could be analyzed separately.

Subjects were male and female Pomona College students, paid $1 for the approximately 30 min the experiment took. There were 15 subjects in Experiment 8 and 9 subjects in Experiment 9. To discourage errors they were given one more dollar, from which 25¢ was deducted for each error. Feedback and admonishments were given on every trial that led to an error. On his or her fifth error a subject was given $1, and the experiment was terminated.

Results—Experiment 8

Baron's (1973) conclusions were essentially supported. Subjects required a mean of 1.996 sec to reject the sentences with look-alike misspellings and 1.884 sec to reject those with homophonic misspellings. The RT to accept the correct sentences was 2.886 sec. The F' (1, 20) of 25.5 for the overall effect is reliable beyond the .01 level. Subsequent analysis showed that RT's for look-alikes and homophones were equal, and both differed from the RT to accept the correct sentences. There were no interactions of any kind with blocks that approached reliability.

No subject made more than four errors in the 60 trials. Sentences with look-alike errors led all other sentence types with 13.9% errors. Homophonic misspellings had 5% errors, and correct sentences had 2.3% errors. There was thus no contamination by a speed-accuracy trade-off in this experiment.

Results—Experiment 9

Baron's conclusions were once more supported. Sentences with look-alike misspellings took 1.987 sec to reject, and those with homophonic misspellings took 1.779 sec. The F' (1, 11) for the effect is only 2.9, falling short of reliability. There did happen to be a speed-accuracy trade-off, with a total of two errors for the look-alikes and five for the homophones (equal to 1.9% and 4.6%, respectively). However, if we look only at data from the subset of subjects who made no errors, the same pattern of results is found (every subject but one took longer to reject the look-alikes than the homophones). In this case, with such a small absolute number of errors, the observed proportions are probably too variable to give good evidence for a speed-accuracy trade-off.

In sum, it seems that Baron's (1973) conclusion is correct. In the processing of simple sentences, there is no evidence at all that homophonic misspellings are harder to reject than well-matched misspellings that are not homophonic. In fact, they seem a bit *easier* to dismiss as incorrect! If they had been harder to reject, we would have had evidence that possibly supported speech coding before lexical access, but we clearly do not have such evidence.

CONCLUSIONS

Research on speech coding in reading and tasks similar to reading gives, we think, very good evidence that inner speech is an important part of mental processing in normal reading. However, the evidence shows, just as clearly, that recoding does *not* take place prior to lexical access. The recoding of material in internal speech seems to be used in an active memory for text that is used in comprehension. To put this conclusion another way, we would say that reading uses a primarily visual analysis of the written words and determines their meaning on the basis of orthographic structure without any need to convert the words to a speech code to recognize them. The task of reading, however, usually requires that more than one word at a time be kept active or "in circulation" until the meaning, which usually requires integration of information from several words, can be determined. Speech recoding seems to be one mechanism by which words are kept available for short periods. Another possible role for speech recoding in reading, but one that seems not to have been studied, might be as a mechanism for determining the supersegmental phonemes, rhythms, and stress patterns that mark phrase boundaries in speech but are not noted in written text, at least not in English. This role for recoding might actually be more useful than its possible role in maintaining a short-term memory trace.

Our Experiments 1–6 do give evidence for speech recoding in a category judgment task, but comparing them with Experiments 7–9, we see some possible problems in generalizing to reading from discrete-trial tasks in which words are processed singly. The homophonic confusion effects of Experiments 1–6 simply were not found in Experiments 8 and 9. It seems likely that the evidence for speech recoding comes from strategies specific to the tasks in Experiments 1–6 and tells us little about the processing in reading. This same criticism applies to many of the discrete-trial single-word experiments we reviewed. Also, comparing Experiment 7a, a proofreading plus reading task, with Experiment 7b, which did not require proofing while reading, we may suspect that even the requirement to look for errors while reading may introduce speech-recoding strategies that are not used in normal reading.

In sum, we think the hypothesis that speech recoding is used normally by mature readers to determine the meaning of words in text should be laid to rest. There is some evidence against it, and every piece of evidence seemingly for it is better attributed either to processes of recoding that occur after meaning is determined or else to paradigm-specific strategies that are unlikely ever to be used in reading.

ACKNOWLEDGMENTS

This research was supported by National Science Grant BNS 17742 and by Pomona College research funds. The authors thank Robin Mermelstein and Lance Rips for their assistance and advice in data analysis.

Experiments 1, 2, 4, and 5, were conducted with the collaboration of Michael NcCarthy, who was a student at Pomona College when they were performed. Garielle Greisbach, also a student at Pomona, assisted with experiments 3 and 6.

REFERENCES

Banks, W. P. Signal detection theory and human memory. *Psychological Bulletin*, 1970, *74*, 81-99.

Baron, J. Phonemic stage not necessary for reading. *Quarterly Journal of Experimental Psychology*, 1973, *25*, 241-246.

Baron, J. Mechanisms for pronouncing printed words: Use and acquisition. In D. LaBerge & S. J. Samuels (Eds.), *Basic processes in reading: Perception and comprehension*. Hillsdale, N.J.: Lawrence Erlbaum Associates, 1976.

Baron, J., & Strawson, C. Use of orthographic and word-specific knowledge in reading words aloud. *Journal of Experimental Psychology: Human Perception and Performance*, 1976, *2*, 386-393.

Baron, J., & Thurston, I. An analysis of the word-superiority effect. *Cognitive Psychology*, 1973, *4*, 207-228.

Bjork, E. L., & Estes, W. Letter identification in relation to linguistic context and masking conditions. *Memory & Cognition*, 1973, *1*, 217-223.

Bower, T. G. R. Reading by eye. In H. Levin & J. P. Williams (Eds.), *Basic studies on reading*. New York: Basic Books, 1970.

Bradshaw, J. L. Three interrelated problems in reading: A review. *Memory & Cognition*, 1975, *3*, 123-134.

Bradshaw, J. L., & Nettleton, N. C. Articulatory interference and the MOWN-DOWN heterophone effect. *Journal of Experimental Psychology*, 1974, *102*, 88-94.

Brooks, L. Visual pattern in fluent word identification. In A. S. Reber & D. L. Scarborough (Eds.), *Toward a psychology of reading*. Hillsdale, N.J.: Lawrence Erlbaum Associates, 1977.

Brown, R. Psychology and reading: Commentary on chapters 5 to 10. In H. Levin & J. P. Williams (Eds.), *Basic studies on reading*. New York: Basic Books, 1970.

Brownstein, S. C., & Weiner, M. *Baron's how to prepare for the Graduate Record Examination*. New York: Barron's Educational Series, 1967.

Clark, H. H. The language-as-fixed-effect fallacy: A critique of language statistics in psychological research. *Journal of Verbal Learning and Verbal Behavior*, 1973, *12*, 335-359.

Cohen, G. The psychology of reading. *New Literary History*, 1972, *4*, 75-90.

Conrad, R. As association between memory errors and errors due to acoustic masking of speech. *Nature*, 1962, *193*, 1314-1315.

Conrad, R. Acoustic confusions in immediate memory. *British Journal of Psychology*, 1964, *55*, 75-84.

Conrad, R. Speech and reading. In J. F. Kavanagh & I. G. Mattingly (Eds.), *Language by ear and by eye: The relationship between speech and reading*. Cambridge, Mass.: MIT Press, 1972.

Corcoran, D. W. J. Acoustic factors in proofreading. *Nature*, 1967, *214*, 851-852.

Corcoran, D. W. J., & Weening, D. L. Acoustic factors in visual search. *Quarterly Journal of Experimental Psychology*, 1968, *20*, 83-85.

Crowder, R. G. *Principles of learning and memory.* Hillsdale, N.J.: Lawrence Erlbaum Associates, 1976.

Forster, K. I., & Chambers, S. M. Lexical access and naming time. *Journal of Verbal Learning and Verbal Behavior,* 1973, *12,* 627-635.

Forster, K. I., & Dickinson, R. G. More on the language-as-fixed-effect fallacy: Monte Carlo estimates of error rates for F_1, F_2, F', and *min* F'. *Journal of Verbal Learning and Verbal Behavior,* 1976, *15,* 135-142.

Frederiksen, J. R., & Kroll, J. F. Spelling and sound: Approaches to the internal lexicon. *Journal of Experimental Psychology: Human Perception and Performance,* 1976, *2,* 361-379.

Gibson, E. J., Pick, A., Osser, H., & Hammond, M. The role of grapheme-phoneme correspondence in the perception of words. *American Journal of Psychology,* 1962, *75,* 554-570.

Glanzer, M., & Clark, W. H. Accuracy of perceptual recall: An analysis of organization. *Journal of Verbal Learning and Verbal Behavior,* 1962, *1,* 289-299.

Glanzer, M., & Clark, W. H. The verbal loop hypothesis: Binary numbers. *Journal of Verbal Learning and Verbal Behavior,* 1963, *1,* 301-309.

Goodman, K. S. Behind the eye: What happens in reading. In H. Singer & R. B. Ruddell (Eds.), *Theoretical models and processes of reading.* Newark, Del.: International Reading Association, 1976.

Hardyck, C., & Petrinovich, L. Subvocal speech and comprehensive levels as a function of the difficulty level of reading material. *Journal of Verbal Learning and Verbal Behavior,* 1970, *9,* 647-652.

Harris, C. S., & Haber, R. N. Selective attention and coding in visual perception. *Journal of Experimental Psychology,* 1963, *65,* 328-333.

Huey, E. B. *The psychology and pedagogy of reading.* Cambridge, Mass.: MIT Press, 1968. (Originally published, 1908).

Kleiman, G. Speech recoding in reading. *Journal of Verbal Learning and Verbal Behavior,* 1975, *14,* 323-329.

Kosslyn, S. M., & Matt, A. M. C. If you speak slowly, do people read your prose slowly? Person-particular speech recoding during reading. *Bulletin of the Psychonomics Society,* 1977, *9,* 250-252.

LaBerge, D. Beyond auditory coding: A discussion of Conrad's paper. In J. F. Kavanagh & I. G. Mattingly (Eds.), *Language by ear and by eye: The relationship between speech and reading.* Cambridge, Mass.: MIT Press, 1972.

LaBerge, D., & Samuels, S. J. Toward a theory of automatic information processing and reading. *Cognitive Psychology,* 1974, *6,* 293-323.

Levy, B. A. Reading: Speech and meaning processes. *Journal of Verbal Learning and Verbal Behavior,* 1977, *16,* 623-638.

MacKay, D. G. Phonetic factors in the perception and recall of spelling errors. *Neuropsychologia,* 1968, *6,* 321-325.

MacKay, D. G. Input testing in the detection of misspellings. *American Journal of Psychology,* 1972, *85,* 121-127.

Massaro, D. *Understanding language.* New York: Academic Press, 1975.

Manelis, L. The effect of meaningfulness in tachistoscopic word perception. *Perception & Psychophysics,* 1974, *16,* 182-192.

Meyer, D. E., Schvaneveldt, R. W., & Ruddy, M. G. Functions of graphemic and phonemic codes in visual word-recognition. *Memory & Cognition,* 1974, *2,* 309-321. (a)

Meyer, D. E., Schvaneveldt, R. W., & Ruddy, M. G. Loci of contextual effects on visual word-recognition. In P. Rabbitt & S. Dornic (Eds.), *Attention and performance V.* New York: Academic Press, 1974. (b)

Morton, J. A functional model for memory. In D. A. Norman (Ed.), *Models of human memory.* New York: Academic Press, 1970.

Neisser, U. Decision time without reaction time: Experiments in visual scanning. *American Journal of Psychology*, 1963, *76*, 376–385.

Neisser, U. *Cognitive psychology*. New York: Appleton-Century-Crofts, 1967.

Pachella, R. G. The interpretation of reaction time in information-processing research. In B. H. Kantowitz (Ed.), *Human information processing: Tutorials in performance and cognition*. Hillsdale, N.J.: Lawrence Erlbaum Associates, 1974.

Rayner, K., & Posnansky, C. Stages of processing word identification. *Journal of Experimental Psychology: General*, 1978, *107*, 64–80.

Rozin, P., & Gleitman, L. R. Reading II: Alphabetic principle. In A. S. Reber & D. L. Scarborough (Eds.), *Toward a psychology of reading*. Hillsdale, N.J.: Lawrence Erlbaum Associates, 1977.

Rubenstein, H., Garfield, L., & Millikan, J. A. Homographic entries in the internal lexicon. *Journal of Verbal Learning and Verbal Behavior*, 1970, *9*, 487–494.

Rubenstein, H., Lewis, S. S., & Rubenstein, M. A. Evidence for phonemic recoding in visual word recognition. *Journal of Verbal Learning and Verbal Behavior*, 1971, *10*, 645–657. (a)

Rubenstein, H., Lewis, S. S., & Rubenstein, M. A. Homographic entries in the internal lexicon: Effects of systematicity and relative frequency of meanings. *Journal of Verbal Learning and Verbal Behavior*, 1971, *10*, 57–62. (b)

Rubenstein, N., Richter, M. L., & Kay, E. J. Pronounceability and the visual recognition of nonsense words. *Journal of Verbal Learning and Verbal Behavior*, 1975, *14*, 651–657.

Smith, E. E., & Spoehr, R. T. The perception of printed English: A theoretical perspective. In B. H. Kantowitz (Ed.), *Human information processing: Tutorials in performance and cognition*. Hillsdale, N.J.: Lawrence Erlbaum Associates, 1974.

Smith, F. *Understanding reading*. New York: Holt, Rinehart & Winston, 1971.

Smith, F. *Psycholinguistics and reading*. New York: Holt, Rinehart & Winston, 1973.

Spoehr, K. T. Phonological encoding in visual word recognition. *Journal of Verbal Learning and Verbal Behavior*, 1978, *17*, 127–141.

Spoehr, K. T., & Smith, E. E. The role of syllables in perceptual processing. *Cognitive Psychology*, 1973, *5*, 71–89.

Spoehr, K. T., & Smith, E. E. The role of orthographic and phonotactic rules in perceiving letter patterns. *Journal of Experimental Psychology: Human Perception and Performance*, 1975, *1*, 21–34.

Stroop, J. R. Studies of interference in serial verbal reactions. *Journal of Experimental Psychology*, 1935, *18*, 643–662.

Thompson, M. C., & Massaro, D. W. Visual information and redundancy in reading. *Journal of Experimental Psychology*, 1973, *98*, 49–54.

Tzeng, O. J. L., Hung, D. L., & Wang, W. S-Y. Speech recoding in reading Chinese characters. *Journal of Experimental Psychology: Human Learning and Memory*, 1977, *3*, 621–630.

Whaley, C. P. Word-nonword classification time. *Journal of Verbal Learning and Verbal Behavior*, 1978, *17*, 143–154.

Wheeler, D. D. Processes in word recognition. *Cognitive Psychology*, 1970, *1*, 59–85.

8 Some Aspects of Language Perception by Eye: The Beginning Reader

Carol A. Fowler
Dartmouth College
and Haskins Laboratories, New Haven, Ct.

Reading is prototypical neither of ordinary visual perception nor of ordinary language understanding, its two major evolutionary and ontogenetic forebears. Instead it is a hybrid activity. Although it depends on seeing and its goal is to comprehend linguistic messages, it requires capabilities, skills, and knowledge characteristic of neither basic function when accessed alone. More particularly, reading involves a special kind of seeing because the stimulus for perception is a written *linguistic* message. Furthermore, it requires, at the very least, a special mode of access to procedures for language understanging because written linguistic messages are visible rather than audible. To a large degree, developing these new modes of seeing and understanding language is the problem of reading acquisition. Here we consider both of these special skills in more detail as a way of characterizing the nature of reading itself and the problem of reading acquisition in particular.

READING AS A SPECIAL KIND OF VISUAL PERCEPTION

First consider the way in which reading is a special kind of visual perception, beginning with a characterization of "ordinary visual perception." The necessary conditions for seeing are: visible objects or events in the environment ("distal stimuli"); light structured by the visible objects and events ("proximal stimuli"); and an observer who is sensitive to some of the light's structure. Except for certain human artifacts, including writing systems, the distal stimuli are three-dimensional objects often undergoing some transformation in their relationship to the observer. The proximal stimuli for these four-dimensional events are patterns of intensity and wavelength of light transforming in time (cf. Gibson, 1966, 1979).

One important problem for an investigator of visual perception is to discover how a proximal stimulus provides information about significant properties of objects and events to sentient observers. A solution to the problem has two salient aspects: (1) specifying how it is that structured light can serve a message function for an organism; (2) specifying the particular correspondences between distal and proximal stimuli. A second problem for an investigator is to describe just how stimulation by structured light eventuates in the perception of distal stimuli.

What is important to the concerns of investigators of reading is that solutions to *both* problems are incomplete at best, and perhaps they differ in fundamental ways when the distal stimulus is a written message rather than another kind of object or event in the environment. To understand this, let us first ask how the proximal stimulus serves its message function. Next let us consider the nature of the relationship between message and referent in ordinary seeing and in reading, and finally examine the "how" of perceptual processing itself.

Environments impose structure on radiant light. The structure is specific to the special properties of the environment and, in part, that is why it can specify environmental properties to a sensitive observer. Although environments may vary infinitely, and therefore so can proximal stimuli, in both instances the infinite possibilities are bounded. This is critical to the message function served by the proximal stimulus. Variety in the environment is bounded because terrestrial surfaces, objects, and events are limited in kind and because the reflection of light from them is governed by physical law. Consequently, the set of all proximal stimuli is also bounded; light can be structured only in limited ways by the limited kinds of distal stimuli.

In principle, one could write a grammar only capable of generating all the proximal stimuli that the earth can offer a visual system. Such a grammar would characterize the concept "light reflected from terrestrial surfaces, objects, and events." From this perspective, each actual proximal stimulus would be a grammatical instance of an infinite (but restricted) set of possible stimuli, more or less as a sentence in a language is a grammatical instance of an infinite (but restricted) set of possible utterances.

The foregoing specifies the conditions under which physical systems take on a message function and thereby can provide information about something other than themselves (Pattee, 1973, 1976; Polanyi, 1958, 1968). A set of organized constraints (grammatical rules, however embodied) restrict the possible arrangements of components of a system (i.e., the light rays) to a subset of arrangements that otherwise would be possible. The limited arrangements that can occur *thereby* take on new significance. In particular, they provide information about the source of the grammatical restrictions (i.e., the distal stimulus).

All of our perceptual systems are sensitive to grammatically coded proximal stimuli of this sort.

The grammatical system just described is a physical grammatical system, and consequently, the relationship between distal referent and proximal stimulation is primarily a necessary one. Moreover, because it is necessary, the significance of proximal stimuli for a perceiver is sharply constrained. Thus, for example, a gradient of texture in the proximal stimulus *must* provide information about something related to the slant of environmental surfaces if it provides any information at all; it could not provide information about the pigmentation of those surfaces instead.

Orthographies and linguistic grammars are at once fundamentally similar and fundamentally different from physical grammars. They are similar in providing an organized set of restrictions (orthographic rules, phonological rules, rules of syntax) on arrangements of a set of components (letters, phonological segments, words). The arrangements of components that do occur thereby take on a message function that they would not have in the absence of the restrictions; they provide information about something other than themselves. A fundamental difference between physical and linguistic grammars of course is that in the latter (at linguistic levels superordinate to the phonetic level, as discussed later) the proximal stimulus-referent relationship is conventional rather than tightly constrained by the necessary correspondence between proximal and distal stimuli. This has an enormously important practical consequence. Whereas proximal stimuli can readily provide information only about events that are "here and now" (excepting proximal stimuli owing to the recent inventions of various kinds of cameras), the content of linguistic messages is freed from that dependence. Whereas proximal stimuli are structured by the environment and provide information about the environment's structure, linguistic utterances are structured by a talker according to conventional rules, and they provide information about anything at any time that can be humanly conceived. The price we pay for this freedom is the requirement that we learn a large set of labels, rules, and correspondences.

To summarize this description of the conditions for ordinary seeing and reading: The two functions are alike in involving the extraction of content from coded media, but they are fundamentally different because in the one case the content is related necessarily to its encoded form, whereas in the other case the relationship is conventional.

This distinction may well be critical in shaping the perceptual styles characteristics of ordinary visual perception and reading. It is certainly the case that "ecological" theories of visual perception, developed almost exclusively by consideration of natural stimuli (rather than two-dimensional human artifacts; see e.g., Gibson, 1966, 1979; Turvey & Shaw, 1979) are substantially different from theories of visual information processing based exclusively on the perception of two-dimensional forms. A major difference in the theories lies in their treatment of the source of perceived meanings. The ecological approach considers the significance of distal objects to be *given* in the stimulation as it relates to a perceiver. The information-processing approach considers the meaning to be *assigned* to stimulation by the perceiver on the basis of stored knowledge. This difference in the theories may stem from the fact that the one theoretical approach concerns itself with physical grammars and the other with conventional ones.

The difference between ordinary visual perception and reading along the dimension of necessary versus conventional meanings places reading squarely in the domain of linguistic functions. To the extent that procedures for extracting meaning from linguistic (conventional) codes are special (and thereby, perhaps, the evolution of left-hemisphere "language centers" is rationalized), reading, but not ordinary seeing, must invoke those special procedures. Reading then may be an extraordinary, rather than a prototypical, instance of visual perception.

Before contrasting reading with ordinary language understanding, let us briefly consider a final way in which reading may involve a special kind of seeing. This pertains to the "how" of perceptual processing. Letters are two-dimensional stimuli that—at least when they are investigated—tend to be presented perpendicularly to the viewer's line of sight. Natural objects are three dimensional, and they are observed at various orientations relative to the perceiver's line of sight. Two-dimensional forms perpendicular to the line of sight are the only distal stimuli for which the corresponding proximal stimuli constitute near literal copies. Consequently, they may provide the only stimuli for which theories of visual information processing are applicable. Typically, in these theories, stimuli are said to be identified when detected features (of the proximal stimulus) are matched to something like lists of features (presumably of the distal form) in long-term store (e.g., Estes, 1977; LaBerge & Samuels, 1974; Neisser, 1967). Even if this sort of "visual information-processing" model is accurate, it may in fact *only* model letter and word perception. It is not evident that it can characterize the perception of natural environments.

READING AS A SPECIAL KIND
OF LANGUAGE UNDERSTANDING

The foregoing discussion sought to establish reading as a special kind of visual perception primarily because the stimulus for perception in reading is linguistic and hence meaningful by convention. Now we consider the role of language in reading and suggest that reading requires not only a special kind of seeing, but also a special kind of language understanding just because in reading the linguistic message is presented visually rather than auditorily.

The special properties of reading as an instance of language understanding may be most apparent in the beginner rather than the experienced reader—not so much because the speical properties are only characteristic of beginners, but because they are made salient by the difficulties exhibited in acquiring them. Consequently, the discussion and the research that follows focuses on the beginning reader.

Language perception by eye is unlikely to be analogous in all respects to language perception by ear. This is suggested in part by several observations that point to the spoken language as a biological property of the human species, in contrast to the written language, which is an acquired property only of some human cultures. Thus, spoken languages are universal among human societies, but written languages are relatively rare. Moreover, we know of many biological adaptations to speech (e.g., Lenneberg, 1967; Lieberman, 1975), but none to reading. Perhaps this is why the spoken language is fairly impervious to developmental disruption (e.g., Lenneberg, 1967), whereas reading is susceptible to it. Finally, among human cultures many fluent talkers are illiterate, but very few people read a language fluently that they neither produce nor perceive by ear.

The near inevitability of spoken-language learning in contrast to reading acquisition may be due in part to peripheral differences in the auditory and visual systems as kinds of input channels. Children cannot as readily avoid being bombarded with speech as they can avoid the written language because their auditory system is less directionally sensitive than their visual system, and their ears have no analogues to eyelids. Hence, spoken-language learning can be ongoing and may even occur incidentally while the child is doing other things. But reading acquisition only takes place during the limited times of the day when the child focuses his or her eyes on the printed word.

However, in addition to these differences in the conditions under which speech and reading acquisition may take place, Mattingly (1979) and Liberman (e.g., Liberman, Liberman, Mattingly, & Shankweiler, 1980) have identified certain demands on the reader's linguistic abilities that they believe are imposed or promoted uniquely by the problem of perceiving language by eye. In their view, these special demands—which they call "linguistic awareness" and "phonological maturity"—may account, on the one hand, for the elusiveness of the alphabetical principle in the history of writing systems and, analogously on the other, for the frequent failures of learning to read among children.

Linguistic Awareness

Skilled readers differ strikingly both from illiterate adults (Morais, Cary, Alegria, & Bertelson, 1979) and from prereading children (e.g., Liberman, Shankweiler, Fischer, & Carter, 1974) along a dimension that Mattingly (1972, 1979) has called linguistic awareness. Linguistic awareness refers to a language user's explicit (or accessible) knowledge of the structure of his or her language as assessed, most typically, by tasks that require deliberate manipulation of linguistic units. In contrast to skilled readers, illiterate adults and prereading children perform poorly on tasks that require access to the more atomic units of the language.[1] Thus, for example, they find it difficult to count the syllables in a word, and many are unable to count the phonemes in a monosyllable—despite their proficiency in producing and perceiving these units under ordinary conditions. In addition, prereading children are reported to have difficulty providing rhymes for familiar words (Calfee, Chapman, & Venezky, 1972; Venezky, Shiloah, & Calfee, 1972) and acquiring "secret languages" such as pig Latin (Savin, 1972). Performance on tests of linguistic awareness improves with literacy (Liberman et al., 1974) and correlates highly with measures of reading skill independent of experience in reading (Liberman, Shankweiler, Liberman, Fowler, & Fischer, 1977; Zifcak, 1977). Moreover, among Zifcak's subjects on whom IQ scores were available, phoneme segmentation abilities correlated highly ($r = .78$) with a measure of word-reading skill, whereas the potentially confounding variable, IQ, was not significantly related ($r = .33$) to the same measure.

These experimental findings demonstrate a close association between linguistic awareness and reading, but not between awareness and speaking or listening. Although the significance of this special association is not yet clear, it is worthy of consideration because the association itself suggests a mode of language understanding by eye that, at the level of the meaningless units of the language, is distinct from language understanding by ear.

Of course, one reason why the nonreading users of the spoken language have little or no explicit facility with linguistic units may be just that they are expert rather than novice users of the spoken language. Evidence from several different domains indicates that the attentional demands of a task diminish substantially with practice and expertise. Thus, components of a task (e.g., riding a bicycle, typing, playing the piano) that require the undivided attention of a novice are performed "automatically" and effortlessly by the expert. This process of automatization is characteristic of perceiving (e.g., LaBerge & Samuels, 1974) as well as skilled activity. Moreover, its investigation in the domain of perceiving has revealed an attentional shift with expertise on tasks involving hierarchically organized units such as features, letters, and words in reading. With practice, attention is shifted gradually away from the smaller less significant units to the larger meaningful units that they constitute (e.g., Drewnowski & Healy, 1977; Healy, 1976).

We might suppose that infants acquiring the units of language are aware of phonetic features, segments, and syllables. At the very least, focal attention to these units may be required in order for the infant to learn the unique phonological and syllabic inventories of the language and the distribution of each

---

[1]The data used in the study by Morais et al. were collected in Portugal where the literacy rate is lower than in the U.S. Therefore, the investigators were able to compare two groups of adults, one literate and the other not, who were reasonably matched on dimensions other than literacy.

phoneme's allophonic variation. If focal attention is equivalent to explicit aware-ness (e.g., Posner & Warren, 1972), then perhaps infants are aware of the units of their language.

With practice, the child may gradually be able to shift attention away from the mechanics of talking and listening and focus it instead on the meaningful units that the phonemes constitute. This automatization process may be complete well before children begin to learn to read so that they enter the reading situation no longer aware of the lower level units of their language.

The difficulty experienced in focusing on these units once again as the child learns to read may be not unlike the difficulty experienced by a skilled pianist who tries to introspect on individual finger movements, or by the subject in a letter-cancellation experiment searching for individual letters in meaningful prose.

Alternatively, however, linguistic awareness may develop for the first time when reading is acquired. It may not be necessary during language acquisition in part because human infants are *born* experts in perceiving phonetic segments by ear (cf. Liberman, Studdert-Kennedy, 1978).

The view that humans are endowed with special capacities for perceiving the phonetic units of the language derives from several sources. One is the literature on hemispheric specialization for language. Perhaps foremost among human biological adaptations to language (see Lenneberg, 1967; Lieberman, 1975) is the specialization typically of the left cerebral hemisphere for linguistic process-ing. Humans show both neuroanatomical (Witelson & Pallie, 1973) and be-havioral (Entus, 1977) correlates of hemispheric specialization from birth. In-deed, there is no convincing evidence that specialization later develops in any significant way.

Moreover, some research on callosalized (Levy, 1974; Zaidel, 1974) and normal (Studdert-Kennedy & Shankweiler, 1970; Studdert-Kennedy, Shank-weiler, & Pisoni, 1972) individuals implicates phonetic perception among the linguistic processes for which the left hemisphere is specialized. Zaidel's research indicates, for example, that the right hemisphere is unable to identify meaningless monosyllables (/ba, da, ga, pa, ta, ka/) differing in one or two phonetic features, even though it can handle some meaningful words and phrases.

The special character of phonetic perception by ear has been fairly clearly established by the work of A. Liberman and his colleagues (e.g., Liberman, Cooper, Shankweiler, & Studdert-Kennedy, 1967; Liberman & Pisoni, 1977; Liberman & Studdert-Kennedy, 1978). The term "phonetic perception," as it is used by Liberman and others, refers to a sensitivity on the part of a perceiver of speech to acoustical "cues" that specify their articulatory source. Thus, a per-ceiver hears as equivalent—and even indistinguishable—two very different cues (e.g., a silent gap and spectral information) if and only if they specify generation by equivalent articulatory gestures. Similarly, perceivers distinguish a given

acoustical cue in different contexts if in the different contexts it specifies generation by different articulatory gestures. Research on infants suggests that they
share some of these characteristics of phonetic perception (e.g., Eimas, Siqueland, Jusczyk, & Vigorito, 1971; Fodor, Garrett, & Brill, 1975; see Pisoni, 1977
for a review). If infants do share these perceptual characteristics, they may never
need to focus attention on phonetic segments before they learn to read, because
they are born experts in phonetic perception.

A related reason for an absence of awareness of segments in speaking or
listening proposes that these processes require only a practical knowledge of
segments (Ryle's "knowing how") simply because the segments are prescribed
to perceivers by acoustical stimulation. On the other hand, reading requires
something akin to explicit knowledge ("knowing that") because grapheme/
segment correspondences are arbitrary and tend to be learned by rote association.
Thus, it seems possible that the essential distinction between speech perception
and reading that promotes the development of linguistic awareness only for
reading is the same as that between ordinary visual perception and reading
discussed earlier. In the present instance, the difference lies in the necessary
relationship between acoustical stimulation and its phonetic significance on the
one hand, and the conventional relationship between optical stimulation and *its*
phonetic significance on the other. Thus, the acoustical signal for /b/ *has* to
sound more or less as it does; we cannot learn to make it sound, say, like /s/, nor
to make it signify anything other than a bilabial stop. In contrast, although a
written *b* has to look the way it does, it need not signify /b/; it could, in another
alphabet, signify /s/.

This discussion suggests not only why awareness of segments need not develop during acquisition of language, but also why it does develop with experience in reading. The basic units of an alphabetical orthography correspond in a
more or less regular way to the sound units (phonetic, phonological, or
morphophonological) of the spoken language. Although it is a matter of some
debate whether children ought to be encouraged to take notice of (and to exploit)
these correspondences between sound and spelling, the facts of linguistic awareness suggest that children do at least notice them. Their purpose (or their
teachers' purpose) presumably is to enable them to exploit the ruleful sound-
spelling relationships in their reading of unfamiliar words. That is, an alphabetical orthography enables a reader to "sound out," and hence to read and
understand, words known by sound, but not by sight. It may be for this purpose
that the beginning reader develops a special sensitivity to the sound system of a
language.

As to why this sensitivity entails explicit access to the sound units, Liberman
and her colleagues (e.g., 1980) suggest that the innate "speech decoder" that is
responsible for "automatic" phonetic perception by ear cannot help out when
language is input to the eyes. Alternatively, we might simply recognize that
phonetic segments are prescribed to a sensitive perceiver by an acoustical signal

but are not prescribed to a sensitive naive perceiver by an alphabetical orthography. Consequently, in order to learn to assign sounds to spellings, children may need to develop explicit concepts of the sounds for which, heretofore, they have had only a practical knowledge.

To summarize the discussion of linguistic awareness, we have reviewed evidence that language perception by ear and eye differ in the nature of the encounter that each promotes between the perceiver and the meaningless units of language. We have suggested that explicit confrontation with the phonetic units is promoted in order to relate them by conventional rule to orthographic symbols. In reading, language users enter the realm of conventional (rather than necessary) grammars one step further down in the hierarchy of linguistic units than they do in listening. The optical stimuli for phonetic segments, in contrast to the corresponding acoustical stimuli, specify the segments by arbitrary association.

Phonological Maturity

Mattingly (1979) and Liberman et al. (1980) propose a second difference between language perception by ear and eye, this one having to do with the degrees of "phonological maturity" that each process encourages.

An ideal speaker/hearer's stored knowledge of the words and morphemes in a language is said to include, among other things, just that phonological information about the word's pronunciation that is not predictable by a general rule. This style of storing lexical representations minimizes the amount of information that must be stored and best captures the underlying regularities of the phonological system of the language. Thus, for example, the words *heal* and *health* are said to be stored as /hēl/ and /hēl + θ/ respectively, even though one is realized phonetically as /hiyl/ and the other as /helθ/. A "laxing" rule changes /hēlθ/ to /helθ/, whereas "diphthongization" and "vowel-shift" rules change /hēl/ to /hiyl/. This abstract mode of representation captures the morphological relatedness of the two words even though that relatedness is not so evident in their phonetic realizations.

If all of this is the case, then the phonological (or morphophonological) form of a word as it is indexed in the "mental lexicon" may well differ from its spoken form. And, of course, the written form of a word often deviates from its spoken form. According to Chomsky (1970), however, the written and morphophonological forms often correspond rather closely.

In Chomsky's view, for the ideal speaker/hearer, the English orthographic system is nearly optimal because it tends to map most neatly onto the morphophonological rather than the phonetic forms of words when the two forms are different. (Witness *heal* and *health*.) Given this correspondence, readers can map written words directly onto their lexical representations of them—a feat that would be more difficult if the spellings were phonetic, and hence deviant from the lexical representations.

Of course, we should be cautious about accepting this proposal that the English orthography is nearly optimal for a reader. For one thing, the claim of near optimality seems suspect given that its achievement was not by design, but more by virtue of different rates of phonological and orthographic change through history. Second, we do not know to what degree language users approximate ideal speaker/hearers.

In respect to the first consideration, as Francis (1970) points out, the correspondence of spelled words to the morphophonological rather than the phonemic forms of words is due to the sound system of the language having evolved faster than the writing system and not, evidently, to its being as preferred system of letter-sound correspondence. Apparently, English spelling once closely approximated the phonemic level of representation. However, as the sound system evolved, the spelling system remained relatively fixed. The current morphophonological forms of words as proposed by Chomsky and Halle (1968) closely approximate the historically earlier surface phonemic forms. Inasmuch as written words do the same, they resemble the putative underlying forms of words represented in the mental lexicons of ideal speaker/hearers.

In regard to the second consideration, we do not know very much about the lexical representations of adults. However, some evidence suggests that prereading children do not very closely approximate the ideal speaker/hearers previously characterized. Read's work (1971; see also Zifcak, 1977) on the invented spellings of young children suggests a surprising sensitivity to some *phonetic* detail that adults typically ignore. Thus, for example, children may spell the word *bend* conventionally, but often omit the *n* in *bent*. This probably occurs because the /n/ in /bent/ is quite short acoustically and phonetically relative to the /n/ in /bend/. Likewise, some children recognize that the vowel in *bent* is nasalized in contrast to that in *bet*. Adults tend to be insensitive to both of these phonetic facts.

Additionally, Read finds that in their spelling of vowels, children spell /iy/ and /i/ with the letter *e* and /ay/ and /a/ with the letter *i*. These choices seem to be based on a phonetic similarity between the sounds themselves and the letter names (/iy/ for *e* and /ay/ for *i*). The pairings of /iy/ and /i/ and of /ay/ and /a/ are phonetically quite sensible, but they violate the pairings that an ideal speaker/hearer would choose based on morphophonological lexical entries. Thus, an ideal speaker/hearer would use the same vowel grapheme in spelling *heal* and *health,* but Read's data suggest that a child would spell them *hel* and *halth.* Likewise, the ideal speaker/hearer would spell the second vowels of *divine* and *divinity* with the same letter, whereas Read's subjects would choose *i* and *e*, respectively.

There is evidence of a developmental change in the direction of the ideal speaker/hearer with experience in reading. Some data from Moskowitz (1973) suggest that children do eventually develop a sensitivity to the more abstract pairings of vowels compatible with those of Chomsky and Halle's ideal speaker/

hearer. This occurs between the ages of 7 and 9, and Moskowitz suggests that it probably is provoked by experience with the writing system itself. For example, children learn for the first time that *heal* and *health* are related morphophonologically because they see that the two words are spelled similarly, even though the vowel sounds are different. Familiarity with words like these (e.g., *please, pleasant, extreme, extremity,* etc.) may lead children to learn the vowel-shift rule (which changes the underlying /hɛl/ to /hiyl/, for example). Consequently, as in Moskowitz's study, at the age of 7 but not before, children more easily learn spoken nonsense word pairs that conform to the rule than those that do not conform.

Thus, with experience in reading, language users may acquire increasing "phonological maturity." That is to say, they begin to acquire information that they otherwise would not about the morphophonological regularities of language. A consequence (though by no means a necessary one) of learning that certain phonetically different word pairs are morphologically related and hence, perhaps, of learning the vowel-shift rule, may be that they revise their lexical representations of these word pairs. Thus, their lexicon may come more nearly to approach that of an ideal speaker/hearer. Whether or not this happens, increased phonological maturity leads readers to *see* the sound system of their language (and probably to hear it as well) in a way that they did not hear it before they learned to read.

THE ROLE OF THE SOUND SYSTEM OF THE LANGUAGE IN READING

The foregoing discussion proposed that reading marshals two familiar processes—visual perception and language understanding—in the service of its aims but adjusts the familiar styles of each process in accommodating one to the other. Thus, in reading, processes of visual perception detect two-dimensional forms to which they assign significance by conventional rule. Assignment of meaning by convention is characteristic of supraphonetic linguistic processes, but it contrasts with ordinary visual perception. For their part, processes of language understanding accommodate to graphic rather than acoustical input. The accommodations seem to be of two kinds. One, linguistic awareness, may be to the conventional relationship between a graphic form and its phonetic significance. The second accommodation, phonological maturity, is to the close relationship between graphic representations of lexical forms and the abstract morphophonological representations of words. Apparently, readers accommodate to this by acquiring (or achieving access to) information about morphological relatedness among words.

I have presumed that the phonetics and the phonology of the language are important in the reading process. I suggested earlier that the facts of linguistic awareness imply this, at least among beginning readers. Here, I suggest why I think that the sound system must be critically involved in the reading process independently of level of reading skill.

In the discussion that follows, I consider two issues. First is whether or not the phonology can be bypassed in reading—that is, whether reading can be a purely visual process. I suspect that, on close examination, this issue can be resolved. The second issue concerns the role or roles of phonological information in reading. Two roles are commonly proposed: One is to mediate visual access to the lexicon; a second is to provide a useful form for the short-term storage of textual material until enough is available to support syntactic analysis.

Can The Phonology Be Bypassed in Reading?

I doubt that the phonology can be bypassed in reading for the following reasons.

A universal linguistic unit among spoken languages, and therefore among written languages as well, is the sentence or phrase. A phrase consists of *words* in some grammatical relationship to each other. For virtually all language users, words have three defining properties: a grammatical class, a meaning, and a phonological form. Presumably, these jointly constitute the "lexical entry" for a word. Eventually a fourth property, the graphic form of the word, may be added when the language user learns to read.

Language understanding by ear or by eye implies lexical access because it involves detecting the grammatical relationships among words (not among un-labeled meanings) in a sentence or phrase. Given that words are accessed in language understanding, the phonological form of a word is accessed because it is a necessary part of a word. Let us consider these claims in more detail.

Even among conventional symbol systems, language is extraordinary in its capacity to convey intended messages. Among the special properties of language that enable it to convey messages reliably are two of its linguistic units: the sentence and the word. To understand the power of these units to convey mes-sages, let us first consider a different conventional system for conveying mean-ings, which lacks words and sentences, and then consider what is gained by a system that has them.

One conventional system is "semasiography." (I take this example from Gleitman & Rozin [1977] who describe it more fully. Their sources are Direnger [1962], Gelb [1952], and Jensen [1969].) In a semasiographic system, meanings are conveyed directly by pictures or objects—that is, the pictures or objects refer directly to concepts but not to words or sequences of words. Instances in our culture may be some highway signs, such as a deer running or a vehicle on a steep incline. These signs convey ideas—warnings in these examples—but they do not convey the ideas by calling forth a necessary sequence of words that has the prescribed meaning. Rather, the viewer goes directly to meaning. Thus, motorists might use different words if asked to characterize the meanings of the signs, but one hopes the content of their different descriptions would be the same.

Semasiography works well to convey simply and stereotyped meanings. However, in the absence of a grammar, it tends to break down when the message to be conveyed is complicated and has no associated stereotyped depiction. Hence, it is severely restricted in usefulness as a writing system.

Among other properties that make languages more powerful than semasiographic systems are the words of the language and their participation in sentences. For a language user who learned to talk before learning to read, a word is essentially a phonological form to which a meaning (or meanings) and a grammatical classification have been attached by convention. Neither a meaningless label, an unlabeled meaning, nor a meaningful, but agrammatic, label can be a word of any language.

The phonological form of the word is analogous to the visible form of the picture in semasiography. It is the public instantiation to which public (i.e., conventional) meanings can be attached. It differs most importantly from the pictures in having a form class and in participating in grammatical structures.

I should perhaps point out that it is not necessary that the physically instantiable form (the label) to which a meaning or meanings and a form class are attached be phonological. For signers, it is gestural; for individuals who learn to read, but not to speak, it is graphic. What is critical is that there be a physically instantiable form to which semantic information and form class can be attached. The form has to be physically instantiable to enable its public meanings to be learned. For individuals who first learn to speak the language, the form is phonological.

For their part, sentences are collectives of words, but, due to the rules of grammar that restrict the kinds of collectives that can occur, they are quite distinct from word aggregates. In English, the rules of grammar constrain, among other things, the orderings of form classes that can constitute a sentence. The orderings that are allowed thereby take on a new significance that they would not have in the absence of grammatical constraints. In particular, the orderings convey information about the grammatical relationships among the words in a sentence and hence about the relationships among the events, objects, and ideas that the words signify. Thus, *the dog chased the cat* means something different from *the cat chased the dog,* and both mean much more than the excluded ordering *chased the the cat dog.* Due to grammatical constraints, like those on word order, languages have the productivity that semasiographies tend to lack. An indefinitely large number of sentences can be produced from the lexical entries and grammatical constraints that are understandable to any other person who commands approximately the same entries and rules.

This indicates that individual word meanings conjointly with the grammatical relations among the words of a sentence largely determine the message that a sentence conveys. Clearly, for perceivers of speech or written language to perceive an intended message, it is critical that they access both the words of the sentence themselves and the grammatical relations among the words. Inasmuch as *words* must be accessed rather than unlabeled meanings, it may make no sense to ask whether a reader goes directly to meaning. What a reader has to do, directly or not, is go to *words*—that is, to lexical entries, and lexical entries include phonological, grammatical, and, for a skilled reader, orthographic information as well as a meaning or meanings.

To summarize, I have suggested that a special property of language is its capacity for generating an indefinite number of reliably understandable messages. They are conveyed by sentences, which are words in particular grammatical relationships to each other. Hence, for perceivers to exploit the power of language to convey novel, understandable messages, either written or spoken, they must not go directly to meanings, but instead must access the appropriate lexical entries of words. Among the defining properties of a word for users of the spoken language is its phonological form. Hence, accessing a word means accessing its phonological form among other things. Similarly, detecting the grammatical relationships among the words of a sentence *means* detecting the grammatical relationships among phonological forms to which meanings and grammatical classifications are attached.

One may argue that the situation changes when an individual learns to read. A consequence of learning to read may be that meanings and form classes attach themselves to orthographic forms. This is no doubt the case, but it does not imply that the phonological information is absent from the lexical entry that includes orthographic information.

When language users learn to read, they learn a new way that words may be produced—namely, orthographically. This may mean one of two things. Most obviously, readers may add information about the orthographic forms of words to their lexical entries, which already include phonological, grammatical, and semantic information. Alternatively, they may acquire a whole new lexicon of words, this one addressed orthographically in contrast to the old one, which is addressed phonologically. In the first case, accessing the lexicon, whether by ear or by eye, implies accessing the graphic and phonological forms of a word along with its attached meaning and form class. The second would mean that in reading, graphic, semantic, and syntactic information is accessed, whereas in listening, phonological, semantic, and syntactic information is accessed.

The second alternative is highly uneconomical both in terms of storage and in its requirement that a whole new lexicon of words be learned, but it cannot be ruled out a priori. However, some *association* between the lexical entries of corresponding graphic and phonological words apparently must be proposed. If there were none, we would have to predict for example that a language user who reads *rob* does not know whether or not he or she has read the graphic word corresponding to /rab/ or to /stiyl/. Nor would children benefit from someone *telling* them what a word is that they cannot read. Indeed, oral reading would be very difficult—much more so than silent reading, which would not involve the phonologically addressed lexicon. Moreover, we might guess that the connotative meanings of corresponding written and spoken words are sometimes different because the nature of an individual's encounters with the written and spoken forms need not be the same. All of these proposals seem highly unlikely.

If we acknowledge at the very least an association between the separate lexicons for written and spoken words, it would seem that the proposal is more unwieldy than (but is not testably different from) a view that there is one lexicon containing both graphic and phonological information. Therefore, we might as well propose that there is one lexicon containing both kinds of information. If so, even when a word is addressed graphically, its phonological form is accessed.

For the reasons given, it seems highly likely to me that phonological information is accessed during reading. The interesting questions to ask concern its role or roles, if any, in reading beyond the necessary one of serving as a word property in sentence understanding. I now consider two roles that are commonly proposed, namely mediating lexical access and providing useful information for the short-term storage of text.

Lexical Access

The role of speech coding in lexical access has received a great deal of attention in the literature on skilled reading but much less in the literature on beginning reading. On intuitive grounds, it seems likely that readers can access lexical entries in either of three general ways. They can use the orthographic form of a word to "address" the lexicon directly, or they can translate the orthographic form either by association or by rule into its corresponding phonological form, which may then serve as the address. The first mode of lexical access would seem easiest for a skilled reader because it is the most direct. The third mode of access (rule based) would seem *least* efficient because it involves several spelling-to-sound translations. The second mode of access, involving a translation by holistic association of a written to a spoken word, would seem to have little to recommend unless the lexicon is more readily accessed by phonological than orthographic probes. In any event, Klapp's (1971) findings suggest that this route is used at least under conditions that preclude the use of sound/spelling correspondences.

In fact, the experimental literature offers a variety of conclusions as to the relative importance of the various modes of lexical access. Skilled readers are found to use either or both of the indirect (phonological) routes in some tasks (e.g., Erickson, Pollack, & Montague, 1970; Klapp, 1971) even when the usage probably causes a performance decrement (Rubenstein, Lewis, & Rubenstein, 1971). Other investigators report that readers use the direct route (e.g., Baron, 1973; Green & Shallice, 1976; Kleiman, 1975), use both routes concurrently

(Meyer, Schvaneveldt, & Ruddy, 1974), have individual preferences for one or the other access mode (Baron and Strawson, 1976), and, finally, adjust their style of access depending on the properties of the set of words used in the experiment (Davelaar, Coltheart, Besner, & Jonasson, 1978; Hawkins, Reicher, Rogers, & Peterson, 1976). If these data permit any summary at all, it is that skilled readers have some flexibility in the way that they use orthographic representations to access the lexicon (cf. Levy, 1978).

One might expect dependence on spelling-to-sound rules to diminish with expertise in reading. The main advantage that this route would seem to confer is in reading words that are familiar by sound but unfamiliar by sight. The general relationship rules between orthographic and phonological units allow readers to "sound out" unfamiliar words. They can then exploit the phonological route to the lexicon that is used in listening to speech. Most written words are familiar to skilled readers however, and one might expect this indirect route to the lexicon to be unpopular with them.

But this does not seem to be the case, at least when words are read aloud. Baron and Strawson (1976) compared reading times for lists of two kinds of real English words. One list included words spelled according to regular English sound-spelling correspondences (e.g., *chant, fresh*). The other list included irregular words (*sword, cough*). Reading times were substantially longer for the list of irregular words.

Moreover, Baron and Brooks (reported separately in Baron, 1977; Brooks, 1977) find an advantage for the spelling-to-sound route that *develops* with fluency. The investigators devised two alphabets of unfamiliar symbols and sets of six-word written and spoken vocabularies. In one condition, the artificial alphabet was a cipher on the English alphabet. Therefore, the association between sound and spelling was as regular as it was in the English words used in the experiment. The second condition included the same six-word written and spoken sequences as the first, but they were randomly paired. This writing system had the same letter sequences as the first, and thus was as regular orthographically (i.e., had the same positional redundancies) as the first writing system, but the sequence of letters in a word had no regular relationship to the word's pronunciation. On each of 400 trials, subjects were shown the six written words of one spelling system in an order that varied across trials, and their reading times were measured.

Curiously, reading times for words with regular spelling-to-sound correspondences were slower than irregular words over the first 200 trials, but they were significantly *faster* over the last 200. The results suggests, counterintuitively, that exploitation of spelling-to-sound regularities facilitates *fluent* word reading even after practice that one might expect to promote holistic written-to-spoken word associations. Additional studies reported by Brooks (1977) replicate this outcome.

Given these outcomes obtained from skilled readers and from beginning adult readers of artificial orthographies, we may ask what children do when they first learn to read and as they become increasingly skilled. Probably they should be capable both of direct and of indirect access techniques. Some words, many of them common (e.g., *have, said*), do not conform to English spelling-to-sound rules and must be read either by accessing the lexicon directly or by learning to pair the word name to its orthographic form. However, these procedures by themselves will not suffice for the beginner. For one thing, they impose an enormous burden on the child's ability to memorize word shape and name pairs by rote. Second, they provide no means of reading the many unfamiliar words that the child will encounter except by guessing from context. Inasmuch as children know few words by sight, they have little context from which to guess. Thus, even though phonological coding is slower than other procedures (but only at first according to Brooks and Baron), it has the important advantage of enabling children to read most of the words that they know by sound, but not by sight.

If the spelling-to-sound route to the lexicon is indeed important to the beginner, then we should be able to discover evidence of its use in reading behavior. In particular, we should see a growing practical knowledge of sound/spelling correspondences with experience that continues if necessary even after formal instruction in reading has ended, and we should find a relationship between use of that knowledge and reading skill. More generally, we might expect to find a difference between successful and less successful beginning readers in the extent to which they are able to make efficient use of the phonological route to the lexicon. Next, because this route to the lexicon implies a sensitivity to the internal structure of a word, we should find a relationship between reading ability and linguistic awareness as it was characterized earlier. Several lines of research begin to provide support for these expectations.

With regard to the first expectation—that the child's practical knowledge of sound/spelling relationships will increase with fluency—a recent study provides supportive evidence. The study shows that readers at several levels of expertise, from beginning to skilled readers, all are sensitive to the sound/spelling correspondences of English to a degree that is closely related to independent measures of their word-reading skill (Fowler, Shankweiler, & Liberman, 1979; see also Venezky & Johnson, 1973). Moreover, their knowledge of sound/spelling correspondences grows with expertise beyond the early years of reading training. This is expected, if, as the Brooks and Baron studies suggest, the rule-based phonological route to the lexicon is advantageous even for fluent readers.

In the study, groups of 20 second-, third-, and fourth-grade children and a group of 20 adults were asked to read a list of approximately 100 nonsense words. In the list, 34 different vowel spellings (e.g., *a, ay, ea,* etc.) were represented where possible in the initial, medial, and final positions in the syllable. Responses to the vowel spellings were scored according to whether or not they represented a sound/spelling correspondence that occurs in English. (Thus, the response /deyb/ to *dabe* would be a correct response, but /dib/ would not.)

Nonsense words cannot be read by means of a visual route to the lexicon. Nor, because they are unfamiliar, are they likely to be read by holistic association of name to shape. Instead, they encourage a letter-sound decoding strategy. By using a list of nonsense words, then, we expected to obtain a relatively pure measure of word-decoding skill that we could then compare to skill in reading real words, on which use of the decoding strategy is optional.

All four groups of subjects were substantially above chance in their assignments of sound to spelling. Moreover, the data revealed an orderly increase in performance with reading experience that extended even beyond the fourth grade. This indicates that readers continue to add to their knowledge of spelling-to-sound regularities even after they have achieved fluency. At each grade, performance on this test correlated highly (range .77 to .91) with a measure of real-word reading skill. This means that between 59 and 83% of the variance in real-word reading performance is accounted for by variability in nonsense reading ability. This in turn may mean that the word decoding strategy demanded by the nonsense reading task is used even when real words are read.

This interpretation is also suggested by an examination of the errors made by the readers on lists of real words (Fowler, Liberman, & Shankweiler, 1977). In one list of words, 19 consonant phonemes were presented equally often in the initial and final positions of CVC monosyllables. In all three grades, children made twice as many errors on final than on initial consonants. This remained true when possible differences in the complexity of initial and final consonant spellings were taken into account. Because the same phonemes occurred in the initial and final positions of the syllable, we attributed the differential error rates to differences in *position* and not to the sounds or spellings that tend to occur in the two positions. This differential error rate for initial and final consonants suggested a left-to-right reading strategy in which the child attempted to assign sounds to individual letters or letter groups. Immature segmentation abilities would lead children to have more difficulty the further into the syllable they progressed (cf. Liberman et al., 1980).

We can be sure that they did attempt to transform the graphic structure of the written words on this list into its corresponding phonological (or phonetic) structure (rather, say, than to sound out the first letter and to guess randomly at the rest) because the errors on final consonants patterned phonetically. That is, the errors tended to bear a close phonetic relationship to the correct sound. In particular, in all three grades—second, third, and fourth—the errors tended to share a much closer relationship to the correct sound than would be expected if the children's responses been made randomly with respect to the correct sound.

Together, these studies suggest that children do exploit the spelling-to-sound route of access to the lexicon in their reading both of unfamiliar (nonsense words) and of more familiar words.

A third study (Mark, Shankweiler, Liberman, & Fowler, 1977) suggests that good and poor readers are distinguished by the extent to which they rely on phonological information when they read isolated words. The study was patterned after others (Hyde & Jenkins, 1969; Morris, Bransford, & Franks, 1977) showing that the nature of a subject's interaction with an acquisition list of words determines the kind of information about the list items that will be remembered. We expected good and poor readers to differ in the extent to which they made deliberate use of phonological information when they read a list of words, and we expected this differential attention to phonological information to influence what they later remembered about the words.

In the study by Mark et al., groups of good and poor second-grade readers were given lists of words to read aloud. Following that, they were unexpectedly given a new list of words to read that included the words they had just read and an equal number of foils. Some of the foils rhymed with the "old" words, and some did not. The rhymes were selected to be no more visually similar to their corresponding old words than were the nonrhyming foils to theirs. The children were asked to identify the words in the recognition list as old or new.

The recognition test was not expected by the children. Hence, we assume that differences in numbers of false positives to the nonrhyming and rhyming foils assess the salience of phonological information for the readers during the acquisition period and do not reflect any intentional effort to store the words in short-term memory. Thus, differences between good and poor readers on this measure assess differences between the groups in the relative salience of phonological information about the acquisition list of words.

The results were that good but not poor readers made significantly more false positive responses to rhyming than to nonrhyming foils. Similarly, good but not poor readers made fewer false negative responses to target words that followed their rhyming foils than to targets that followed their nonrhyming foils. This pattern of results indicates a more enduring memory among the superior readers for phonological information about the words that they had read. In line with the interpretation of the earlier studies on which this one was based, we attribute the difference to differential attention to the phonological properties of the acquisition list by the good and poor readers.

We suggested, finally, that the phonological route to lexical access in which spelling-to-sound correspondences are exploited requires a sensitivity on the readers' part to the internal sound structure of the word. Because of that, we might expect to find a relationship between a child's sensitivity to the sound structure of words and measures of his or her reading skill. As noted earlier, several studies have found a strong correlation between performance on Liberman's phoneme segmentation task and measures of isolated-word reading skill (Helfgott, 1976; Liberman et al., 1974; Zifcak, 1977). Zifcak found phoneme segmentation performance to be the best predictor of word-reading abilities (r = .78) among a set of predictors including invented spellings, chronological age, and IQ. IQ showed only a moderate correlation with phoneme segmentation (r = .40) and a nonsignificant relationship to word-reading skills (r = .33).

Together, the collection of studies described here suggests the importance of the child's ability to use phonological information about a word in the reading of isolated words. Now we can move on to consider a second role of phonological information in reading—in the short-term storage of text awaiting syntactic analysis.

Short-Term Memory

Some facts about grammatical utterances suggest that processes of comprehension work on chunks of words rather than sequentially on individual words as they are given to the perceiver. Because of that, short-term storage may be involved in sentence understanding. One fact of language that suggests this is the occurrence of embedding in sentences; another is pronominalization.

In sentences with embedded clauses, close grammatical relationships may obtain between words that are far apart (e.g., "The *subjects,* all native speakers of English, *participated* in the experiment for course credit"). For perceivers to extract the intended grammatical relationships among words in sentences like this, they have to hold several words of the sentence's surface-structure form in storage until there is a coherent chunk to process. The memory system with the requisite capacity and duration for the storage task probably is phonological short-term memory. (See Baddeley [1978], who argues that the role of the phonological component of short-term memory is somewhat more restricted than usually supposed. He proposes that the "articulatory" component to short-term memory is useful under conditions of information overload, but is not essential to sentence comprehension. However, embedded sentences may provide sentence-internal conditions of overload that require the use of phonological short-term memory.)

The facts of pronominalization lead to a similar conclusion. Writers and talkers use pronouns when they are able to assume that the reader or listener can recover the pronoun's referent. Thus, the sentences in 1 are natural, but those in 2 are not.

1. John broke the expensive vase. He tripped over it on his way out the door.
2. John broke the expensive vase. John tripped over the expensive vase on John's way out the door.

In Chafe's view (e.g., 1974), talkers and writers use pronouns when they assume that the receiver of the message is currently "thinking about" the pronoun's referent. Indeed, pronominalization is only feasible if something like this takes place. That is, we must assume that the reader or listener keeps old information in mind when taking in new information. A likely means of preserving old information is phonological short-term memory.

More generally, at the very least, any properties of language that require the temporary preservation of stretches of sentence surface structure for their comprehension imply that phonological information is also preserved. This is so because the surface-structure form of a sentence is a sequence of words or morphemes, and a property of these linguistic units is their phonological form.

Several lines of evidence suggest that the short-term memory system involved in the comprehension of text preserves phonological information or something similar (e.g., phonetic, acoustical, or articulatory information). One source of evidence is the letter-cancellation paradigm first used by Corcoran (1966; see also Locke, 1978). Letter-cancellation studies show that readers with normal hearing persist in their dependence on phonological information about written text even when it impairs their performance on a letter-cancellation task. Not surprisingly, congenitally deaf readers show no dependence on phonological information (Locke, 1978).

Moreover, when preservation of phonological information is made difficult for a reader, sentence comprehension may suffer (e.g., Levy, 1977). The reason seems to be that the reader is unable to preserve the surface structure of the stored sentence (Levy, 1978). This information is necessary for the extraction of grammatical meanings.

Finally, a recent experiment by Tzeng, Hung, and Wang (1977) shows that even skilled readers of the Chinese logographic writing system depend on phonological information when their task is to read sentences for meaning. In a logographic orthography, written symbols stand for morphemes directly—that is, they stand for *meaningful* units of language, not for meaningless units of sound as do the primitive units of an alphabet. Therefore, if any writing system were to promote a "purely visual" style of reading, it would be the logographic system. As I have suggested, however, purely visual reading probably is not possible given the requirement that words rather than unlabeled meanings be read. The study of Tzeng et al. suggests that phonological information is indeed accessed by readers of logographic writing systems (see also Erickson, Mattingly, & Turvey, 1977) and that it serves a role in the extraction of grammatical content.

The role of short-term memory in reading would seem to be magnified for beginning readers because their progress through written text is relatively slow. Thus, we would expect to find evidence of dependence on phonological short-term memory in reading even at its earliest stages and, as in the reading of isolated words, a relationship between dependence on phonological short-term memory and reading skill.

Mohan (1978) has used Corcoran's e-cancellation procedure to test the role of phonological coding in the child's reading of text. His subjects were kindergarteners, second-, third-, and fifth-grade children. Each child was asked to cancel all of the *e*'s in a prose passage selected according to the child's level of reading experience. As expected, the prereading kindergarteners failed to differentiate among silent *e*'s, pronounced *e*'s, and *e*'s in *the*. In contrast, third and fifth graders missed significantly more *e*'s in *the* than in other words, and more silent than pronounced e's. Second-grade readers missed more e's in *the* than in other words; they also missed more silent e's than pronounced e's, but this difference was nonsignificant.

In an unpublished study of my own, good and poor readers in the second grade were asked to read a prose passage for meaning and to cancel any letter e that they say while reading. Among these second graders, in contrast to Mohan's, the silent-e effect was highly significant. Although the good readers missed fewer pronounced e's and more silent e's than the poor readers, the interaction between reading group and silent-e effect did not approach significance. (A very large difference between the groups was observed on proportion of e's missed in *the*. Good readers missed 66% of e's in *the*, whereas poor readers missed only 28%. It is unlikely that this difference has to do with coding differences between the groups, but rather it relates to the units of text on which each group tends to focus its attention. See Drewnowski, [1978].) Together, this study and Mohan's suggest that phonological information is accessed and attended to in the processing of text by beginning readers as early as the second grade.

Several studies point to phonological coding in memory and comprehension as a locus of important differences between good and poor beginning readers (e.g., Liberman et al., 1977; Vellutino, Pruzek, Steger, & Meshoulam, 1973). Although it is unlikely that phonological coding is the only locus of difference between successful and unsuccessful beginning readers (e.g., Drewnowski, 1978), it does seem to be an especially salient one, as Vellutino points out in his recent review (1977).

Using the Conrad paradigm (e.g., Conrad, 1972), we have found that good and poor readers differ in their degree of reliance on phonological information in memory (Liberman et al., 1977; Shankweiler, Liberman, Mark, Fowler, & Fischer, 1979). In these studies, sets of five letters are presented for recall. The letter sets are presented either visually or auditorily, and they are either phonetically confusable (e.g., *BZTVC*) or nonconfusable (e.g., *HKLRY*). In *either* modality, good readers are much more severely affected by the confusability of rhyming letters than are poor readers. We have interpreted this to suggest that poor readers are less able than good readers to use phonological information in memory, regardless of the input modality of the to-be-remembered items.

The differences in memorial performance between good and poor readers apparently does not extend beyond memory for verbal material, however. Liberman and Shankweiler (1979) report that good and poor beginning readers perform equally well on recognition tests of nonsense figures and faces but unequally on a recognition test of nonsense words.

Finally, a recent study by Mann, Liberman, & Shankweiler (1980) demonstrates a relationship between reading skill and sentential memory. In this study, good and poor readers were tested on recall of sentences. The words of some sentences were phonologically confusable, whereas those of others were not.

The good readers' recall performance was found to be affected more substantially by the confusability variable than was the recall results of poor readers. This replicates the results on letters and extends the finding to grammatical sentences. Collectively, the foregoing studies strongly suggest that the meaningless units of language—that is, the phonetic or phonological units—are normally involved in the procedures surrounding the memory and comprehension of text. This is true across all levels of reading experience, and it even holds for readers of nonalphabetical orthographies. That this is so is not surprising given that the written language is the spoken language translated into a visible medium, and the critical linguistic information for a perceiver is provided by words and their grammatical interrelations.

ACKNOWLEDGMENTS

The preparation of this paper as well as the research on which it was based was supported by NIH grant HD 01994 to Haskins Laboratories.

REFERENCES

Baddeley, A. The trouble with levels: A reexamination of Craik and Lockhart's framework for memory research. *Psychological Review,* 1978, *85,* 139–152.

Baron, J. Phonemic stage not necessary for reading. *Quarterly Journal of Experimental Psychology,* 1973, *25,* 241–246.

Baron, J. Mechanisms for producing printed words. In D. LaBerge & S. J. Samuels (Eds.), *Basic processes in reading: Perception and comprehension.* Hillsdale, N.J.: Lawrence Erlbaum Associates, 1977.

Baron, J., & Strawson, C. Use of orthographic and word-specific knowledge in reading words aloud. *Journal of Experimental Psychology: Human Perception and Performance, 1976, 2,* 386–393.

Brooks, L. Visual patterns in fluent word identification. In A. S. Reber & D. Scarborough (Eds.), *Toward a psychology of reading.* Hillsdale, N.J.: Lawrence Erlbaum Associates, 1977.

Calfee, R., Chapman, R., & Venezky, R. How a child needs to think to learn to read. In L. W. Gregg (Ed.), *Cognition in learning and memory.* New York: Wiley, 1972.

Chafe, W. Language and comprehension. *Language,* 1974, *50,* 111–133.

Chomsky, N. Phonology and reading. In H. Levin & J. Williams (Eds.), *Basic studies on reading.* New York: Basic Books, 1970.

Chomsky, N., & Halle, M. *The sound pattern of English.* New York: Harper & Row, 1968.

Conrad, R. Speech and reading. In J. Kavanagh & I. Mattingly (Eds.), *Language by ear and by eye: The relationships between speech and reading.* Cambridge, Mass.: MIT Press, 1972.

Corcoran, D. An acoustic factor in letter cancellation. *Nature,* 1966, *210,* 658.

Davelaar, E., Coltheart, M., Besner, D., & Jonasson, J. Phonological recoding and lexical access. *Memory & Cognition,* 1978, *4,* 753–758.

Direnger, D. *Writing.* New York: Praeger, 1962.

Drewnowski, A. Detection errors on the word "the": Evidence for the acquisition of reading levels. *Memory & Cognition,* 1978, *6,* 403–409.

Drewnowski, A., & Healy, A. Detection errors on "the" and "and": Evidence for reading units larger than the word. *Memory & Cognition,* 1977. *5,* 636–647.

Eimas, P., Siqueland, E., Jusczyk, P., & Vigorito, J. Speech perception in infants. *Science,* 1971, *171,* 303–306.

Entus, A. Hemispheric asymmetry in processing of dichotically presented speech and nonspeech by infants. In S. Segalowitz & F. Gruber (Eds.), *Language development and neurological theory.* New York: Academic Press, 1977.

Erickson, C., Pollak, M., & Montague, W. Implicit speech: Mechanisms in perceptual coding. *Journal of Experimental Psychology,* 1970, *884,* 502–507.

Erickson, D., Mattingly, I., & Turvey, M. Phonetic activity in reading: An experiment with Kanji. *Language and Speech,* 1977, *20,* 384–403.

Estes, W. On the interaction of perception and memory in reading. In D. LaBerge & S. J. Samuels (Eds.), *Basic processes in reading: Perception and comprehension.* Hillsdale, N. J.: Lawrence Erlbaum Associates, 1977.

Fodor, J., Garrett, M., & Brill, S. Pi ka pu: The perception of speech sounds by prelinguistic infants. *Perception & Psychophysics,* 1975, *18,* 74–78.

Fowler, C., Liberman, I., & Shankweiler, D. On interpreting the error pattern in beginning reading. *Language and Speech,* 1977, *20,* 162–173.

Fowler, C., Shankweiler, D., & Liberman, I. Apprehending spelling patterns for vowels: A developmental study. *Language and Speech,* 1979, *22,* 243–252.

Francis, W. N. Linguistics and reading: A commentary on chapters 1 to 3. In H. Levin & J. Williams (Eds.), *Basic studies on reading.* New York: Basic Books, 1970.

Gelb, I. J. *A study of writing: The foundations of grammaticality.* Chicago: University of Chicago Press, 1952.

Gibson, J. *The senses considered as perceptual systems.* Boston: Houghton-Mifflin, 1966.

Gibson, J. *The ecological approach to visual perception.* Boston: Houghton Mifflin, 1979.

Gleitman, L., & Rozin, P. The structure and acquisition of reading I: Relations between orthographies and the structure of language. In A. Reber & D. Scarborough (Eds.), *Toward a psychology of reading.* Hillsdale, N.J.: Lawrence Erlbaum Associates, 1977.

Green, D., & Shallice, T. Direct visual access in reading for meaning. *Memory & Cognition,* 1976, *4,* 753–758.

Hawkins, H., Reicher, G., Rogers, M., & Peterson, L. Flexible coding in word recognition. *Journal of Experimental Psychology: Human Perception and Performance,* 1976, *2,* 380–385.

Healy, A. Detection errors on the word "the": Evidence for reading units larger than letters. *Journal of Experimental Psychology: Human Perception and Performance,* 1976, *2,* 235–242.

Helfgott, J. Phonological segmentation and blending skills of kindergarten children: Implications for beginning reading acquisition. *Contemporary Educational Psychology,* 1976, *1,* 157–169.

Hyde, T., & Jenkins, J. Differential effects of incidental tasks on the organization of recall of a test of highly associated words. *Journal of Experimental Psychology,* 1969, *82,* 472–481.

Jensen, H. *Sign, symbol and script* (3rd rev. ed.). New York: Putnam, 1969.

Klapp, S. Implicit speech inferred from response latencies in same–different decisions. *Journal of Experimental Psychology,* 1971, *91,* 262–267.

Kleiman, G. Speech recoding in reading. *Journal of Verbal Learning and Verbal Behavior,* 1975, *14,* 323–339.

LaBerge, D., & Samuels, S. J. Toward a theory of automatic information processing in reading. *Cognitive Psychology,* 1974, *6,* 293–323.

Lenneberg, E. *Biological foundations of language.* New York: Wiley, 1967.

Levy, B. A. Reading: Speech and meaning processes. *Journal of Verbal Learning and Verbal Behavior,* 1977, *16,* 623–628.

Levy, B. A. Speech analysis during sentence processing: Reading and listening. *Visible Language,* 1978, *12,* 81–102.

Levy, J. Psychobiological implications of bilateral asymmetry. In S. Dimond & G. Beaumont (Eds.). *Hemisphere function in the human brain*. New York: Halsted Press, 1974.

Liberman, A., Cooper, F., Shankweiler, D., & Studdert-Kennedy, M. Perception of the speech code. *Psychological Review*, 1967, *74*, 431-461.

Liberman, A., & Pisoni, D. Evidence for a special speech perceiving subsystem in the human. In T. Bullock (Ed.), *Recognition of complex acoustic signals*. Berlin: Dahlem Konferenzen, 1977.

Liberman, A., & Studdert-Kennedy, M. Phonetic perception. In R. Held, H. Leibowitz, & H.-L. Teuber (Eds.), *Handbook of sensory physiology, Vol. VII: Perception*. Heidelberg: Springer-Verlag, 1978.

Liberman, I., & Shankweiler, D. Speech, the alphabet, and teaching to read. In L. Resnick & P. Weaver (Eds.), *Theory and practice of early reading*. Hillsdale, N.J.: Lawrence Erlbaum Associates, 1979.

Liberman, I. Y., Liberman, A., Mattingly, I., & Shankweiler, D. Orthography and the beginning reader. In J. F. Kavanagh & R. L. Venezky (Eds.) *Orthography, Reading and Dyslexia*. Baltimore: University Park Press, 1980.

Liberman, I., Shankweiler, D., Fischer, F. W., & Carter, B. Explicit syllable and phoneme segmentation in the young child. *Journal of Experimental Child Psychology*, 1974, *18*, 201-212.

Liberman, I. Y., Shankweiler, D., Liberman, A., Fowler, C., & Fischer, F. W. Phonetic segmentation and recoding in the beginning reader. In A. S. Reber & D. Scarborough (Eds.), *Toward a psychology of reading*. Hillsdale, N.J.: Lawrence Erlbaum Associates, 1977.

Lieberman, P. *On the origin of language*. New York: Macmillan, 1975.

Locke, J. Phonemic effects in the silent reading of hearing and deaf children. *Cognition*, 1978, *6*, 175-187.

Mann, V., Liberman, I. Y., & Shankweiler, D. Children's memory for sentences and word strings in relation to reading ability. *Memory & Cognition*, 1980, *8*, 329-335.

Mark, L., Shankweiler, D., Liberman, I., & Fowler, C. Phonetic recoding and reading difficulty in beginning readers. *Memory & Cognition*, 1977, *5*, 623-629.

Mattingly, I. Reading, the linguistic process and linguistic awareness. In J. Kavanagh & I. Mattingly (Eds.), *Language by ear and by eye: The relationships between speech and reading*. Cambridge, Mass.: MIT Press, 1972.

Mattingly, I. *Reading, linguistic awareness and language acquisition*. Paper presented at Conference on Linguistic Awareness and Cognitive Clarity, Victoria, B.C., June 1979.

Meyer, D., Schvaneveldt, R., & Ruddy, M. Functions of graphemic and phonemic codes in visual word recognition. *Memory & Cognition*, 1974, *2*, 309-321.

Mohan, P. Acoustic factors in letter cancellation: Developmental considerations. *Developmental Psychology*, 1978, *14*, 117-118.

Morais, J., Cary, L., Alegria, J., & Bertelson, P. Does awareness of speech as a sequence of phones arise spontaneously. *Cognition*, 1979, *7*, 323-332.

Morris, C., Bransford, J., & Franks, J. Levels of processing versus transfer appropriate processing. *Journal of Verbal Learning and Verbal Behavior*, 1977, *16*, 519-533.

Moskowitz, B. On the status of vowel shift in English. In T. Moore (Ed.), *Cognitive development and the acquisition of language*. New York: Academic Press, 1973.

Neisser, A. *Cognitive psychology*. New York: Appleton-Century-Crofts, 1967.

Pattee, H. The physical basis and origin of hierarchical control. In H. H. Pattee (Ed.), *Hierarchy theory: The challenge of complex systems*. New York: Braziller, 1973.

Pattee, H. H. Physical theories of biological coordination. In M. Grene & E. Mendelsohn (Eds.), *Topics in the philosophy of biology*. Dordrecht, The Netherlands: Reidel, 1976.

Pisoni, D. Speech perception. In W. K. Estes (Ed.), *Handbook of cognitive processes*. Hillsdale, N.J.: Lawrence Erlbaum Associates, 1977.

Polanyi, M. *Personal knowledge*. Chicago: University of Chicago Press, 1958.

Polanyi, M. Life's irreducible structure. *Science*, 1968, *160*, 1308-1312.

Posner, M., & Warren, R. Traces, concepts and conscious construction. In A. Melton & E. Martin (Eds.), *Coding processes in human memory*. Washington, D.C.: Winston, 1972.

Read, C. Pre-school children's knowledge of English phonology. *Harvard Educational Review*, 1971, *41*, 1-34.

Rubenstein, H., Lewis, S. S., & Rubenstein, M. Evidence for phonemic recoding in visual word recognition. *Journal of Verbal Learning and Verbal Behavior*, 1971, *10*, 645-657.

Savin, H. What a child knows about speech when he starts to read. In J. Kavanagh & I. Mattingly (Eds.), *Language by ear and by eye: The relationships between speech and reading*. Cambridge, Mass.: MIT Press, 1972.

Shankweiler, D., Liberman, I., Mark, L., Fowler, C. & Fischer, F. W. The speech code and learning to read. *Journal of Experimental Psychology Human Learning and Memory*, 1979, *5*, 531-545.

Studdert-Kennedy, M., & Shankweiler, D. Hemispheric specialization for speech perception. *Journal of the Acoustic Society of America*, 1970, *48*, 579-594.

Studdert-Kennedy, M., Shankweiler, D., & Pisoni, D. Auditory and phonetic processes in speech perception: Evidence from a dichotic study. *Cognitive Psychology*, 1972, *3*, 455-466.

Turvey, M., & Shaw, R. The primacy of perceiving: An ecological reformulation of perception as a point of departure for understanding memory. In L.-G. Nilsson (Ed.), *Perspectives on memory research: Essays in honor of Uppsala University's 500th anniversary*. Hillsdale, N.J.: Lawrence Erlbaum Associates, 1979.

Tzeng, O., Hung, D., & Wang, W. Speech recoding in reading Chinese characters. *Journal of Experimental Psychology: Human Learning and Memory*, 1977, *3*, 621-670.

Vellutino, F. Alternative conceptualizations of dyslexia. *Harvard Educational Review*, 1977, *47*, 334-353.

Vellutino, F., Pruzek, R., Steger, J., & Meshoulam, U. Immediate visual recall in poor and normal readers as a function of orthographic linguistic familiarity. *Cortex*, 1973, *9*, 368-384.

Venezky, R., & Johnson, D. Development of two letter-sound patterns in grades one through three. *Journal of Educational Psychology*, 1973, *64*, 109-115.

Venezky, R., Shiloah, Y., & Calfee, R. *Studies of prereading skills in Israel* (Tech. Rep. No. 22). Madison: Wisconsin Research and Development Center in Cognitive Learning, 1972.

Witelson, S., & Pallie, W. Left hemispheric specialization for language in the newborn: Neuroanatomical evidence of asymmetry. *Brain*, 1973, *96*, 641-647.

Zaidel, E. *Language, dichotic listening and the disconnected hemispheres*. Paper presented at the 15th annual meeting of the Psychonomic Society, Boston, November 1974.

Zifcak, M. *Phonological awareness and reading acquisition in first grade children*. Unpublished doctoral dissertation, University of Connecticut, 1977.

9 What Good Is Orthographic Redundancy?

Marilyn Jager Adams
Bolt Beranek and Newman Inc.

Across the literature on visual word recognition, one of the most widely respected features of English orthography is its sequential redundancy. The fact of this redundancy can be demonstrated statistically (Shannon, 1948). Its psychological reality is evidenced by the relative ease with which good readers can encode sequentially redundant nonwords as compared to arbitrary strings of letters (e.g., Adams, 1979a; Baron & Thurston, 1973; Gibson, Pick, Osser, & Hammond, 1962; Johnston & McClelland, 1974; Krueger, 1979; Massaro, Venezky, & Taylor, 1979; Mewhort, 1974; Miller, Bruner, & Postman, 1954). Its psychological importance is implicated by evidence that this advantage is generally depressed or absent among poor readers (e.g., Adams 1979b; Frederiksen, 1978). Not surprisingly, means for recognizing and taking advantage of orthographic redundancy have come to reside at the core of many current theories about the knowledge and processes involved in word recognition (e.g., Adams, 1979a; Estes, 1975a,b; Johnston, 1978; LaBerge & Samuels, 1974; Massaro, 1975; McClelland, 1976; Rumelhart & Siple, 1974; Smith, 1971).

The purpose of this chapter is not to challenge the assumption that orthographic redundancy is of central importance to the word-recognition process. It is instead to ask why. What advantage does the reader gain from orthographic redundancy, and why would such redundancy be built into a written language in the first place?

THE PROBLEM

In a message with no sequential redundancy, the probability with which any element will occur is independent of the identities to preceding elements. Sequential redundancy, then, corresponds to the extent to which knowledge of one element or fragment of a message can help predict what the next element will be. Such redundancy greatly reduces the criticality of any one element to the message as a whole. As it allows the recipient of a message to predict ensuing elements, it reduces the amount of care and effort that need be allocated to their decoding. As it allows the recipient to detect and correct anomalous elements, it reduces the consequence of errors in transmission or reception. Thus, wherever the signal is noisy or the receiver has limited processing capacity (or is otherwise error prone), redundancy may be critical to the accurate communication of a message. In particular, sequential redundancy offers obvious advantages in the case of most oral language situations.

A moment's reflection makes clear that English orthography carries considerable redundancy. For example, if a word begins with *t,* its second letter will probably be an *h,* an *r,* a *w,* or a vowel, and there are substantial differences among the likelihoods of these alternatives as well. However, the advantages of sequential redundancy are not obvious in the case of orthography. First, spelling errors and obfuscating noise are rare in printed text. Second, written text (unlike speech) is permanent, and readers (unlike listeners) can therefore process and reprocess any fragment of a message for as long as they need. Third, when errors in letter or word recognition do occur, redundancy at the syntactic and semantic levels may provide sufficient means for coping (see Smith, 1973). Thus, orthographic redundancy would not seem to be essential for containing errors in written communication.

Further, when concern is turned from letter identification to word identification, it can be argued that the sequential redundancy of English orthography is actually disadvantageous for the reader. Because of sequential redundancy, each letter of an English word yields a certain amount of information as to what the next letter will be. But in direct proportion to this interletter facilitation, the amount of information a letter can provide as to what the *word* will be must be reduced. This point may be best illustrated through the extreme case. Suppose a reader has encountered a *q* in an English text. She or he may be virtually certain that the next letter will be a *u.* Yet confirming that the next letter is indeed a *u* will not bring the reader any closer to knowing what the word will be. With respect to word identification, the sequence *qu* provides no more information than does the single letter *q.*

The sequential constraints of English are also quite costly in terms of notational efficiency. Shannon (1948) has estimated the redundancy of English orthography to be 50%. Note that this figure pertains strictly to orthography; it does not include semantic or syntactic redundancy. In other words, our texts are roughly twice as long as they need be, solely because of the way we spell. An alternate way to appreciate the burden of redundancy is to consider how concise our orthography could be without it. From an alphabet of 26 letters, we could generate over 475,254 unique strings of 4 letters or less, or 12,376,630 of 5 letters or less. Alternatively, we could represent 823,543 unique strings with an alphabet of only 7 letters, or 16,777,216 with an alphabet of only 8. For comparison, the total number of entries in *Webster's New Collegiate Dictionary* (1977) is only 150,000. By eliminating redundancy, we could thus realize a substantial savings in our orthographic code, and we could do so even while leaving considerable margin for systematically locating our words in the letter space. For example, words could be designated so as to minimize orthographic overlap or to create clusters corresponding to semantic, syntactic, or phonetic similarities.

All such considerations aside, the facts remain that English orthography is highly redundant and that sensitivity to this redundancy seems to be well developed among good readers. The remainder of this chapter is directed toward the task of puzzling out why this should be so. Each of the sections to follow takes up one class of explanations of the utility of orthographic redundancy and explores its adequacy.

THE ROLE OF SPELLING-TO-SOUND CORRESPONDENCES

The redundancy of our written language is due in large measure to the fact that it is alphabetical. Only certain sequences of phonemes are permissible within our spoken language, and even among those some occur far more frequently than others. To the extent that orthographic redundancy is a consequence of spelling-to-sound correspondences, our question becomes: Are spelling-to-sound correspondences useful to the reader, and can they explain the apparent utility of orthographic redundancy?

Smith (1973) has argued that our alphabetical system is designed primarily for the benefit of the writer, and further that: "anything tending to make writing easier will make reading more difficult [p. 117]." To be sure, our alphabetical system has certain drawbacks for the reader. In particular, phonemes, or the elementary speech sounds to which our letters refer, do not occur as discrete elements in our spoken language. Rather, as Rozin and Gleitman (1977) put it, they are "shingled" together in the continuous sound wave of speech. The mapping of spelling to sound, therefore, requires an explicit and somewhat artificial analysis of our aural language. Indeed, there is considerable evidence that such analysis is especially difficult for young children (Liberman, Shankweiler, Liberman, Fowler, & Fischer, 1977; Rozin & Gleitman, 1977) and, more generally, that the phoneme, as a psychological unit, is relatively inaccessible to consciousness even for adults (Savin & Bever, 1970; Warren, 1971). Compounding this problem, the letter-to-phoneme correspondence of English is by no means one-to-one. Efforts to systematize the relationship have resulted in hundreds of correspondence rules (e.g., Berdiansky, Cronnell, & Koehler, 1969, cited in Smith, 1973; Hanna & Hanna, 1959; Wijk, 1966). Thus, as simple and elegant as the alphabetical principle might seem to mature readers of English, phonics may stand as a linguistically abstruse and cumbersome technique for the novice (see Gleitman & Rozin, 1977; Rozin & Gleitman, 1977).

But our alphabetical system also has much to recommend it. Chomsky (1970) has argued that disillusionment with the efficiency of the system derives from a myopic understanding of the spelling-to-sound correspondences that it captures. Phonemes, he argues, are but a superficial aspect of the language. Neither linguistic theory nor psychological evidence provides reason to believe that they are functionally significant. When our spelling-to-sound correspondences are traced to the broader phonological and lexical structure of our language rather than to phonemes, Chomsky sees the system as a nearly optimal means of representing the spoken language. The orthography conveys the phonological information necessary to access a word's morphemic segments. The orthography omits (thereby incurring much of its reputation as irregular) such phonological nuances as stress placement and the phonetic variants of the vowels, which in any case are given once the deep representation of the word has been found—they are integral to the system for producing and understanding speech. Thus, according to Chomsky, the difference in the sound of the medial vowel in Arab versus Arabian, Canada versus Canadian, or melody versus melodious does not reflect irregularity of our spelling-to-sound system, but regularity of our phonological system.

Of course, there are also the traditionally cited advantages of our alphabetical system. First, the possibility of "sounding out" visually unfamiliar words affords an important degree of independence for the beginning reader. Second, an alphabetical system is purported to hold a mnemonic advantage for the reader and writer over scripts, such as Chinese, that are not based on phonology. In support of this contention comes the observation that although the average English-speaking high-school student can read about 50,000 words, the Chinese scholar can rarely name more than 4000 logograms (Rozin & Gleitman, 1977).

Given the nature of our written language, a more direct argument can be made for the mnemonic importance of spelling-to-sound correspondences. Let me relate this argument in the way I came to appreciate it. Many schools for deaf children in this country teach reading through phonics. On first learning this, I was dismayed: How counterproductive and egocentric of us to make written English parasitic on the spoken English which the children generally do not have. It seemed to me that for deaf children, any useful dependence between the modalities should run in the opposite direction—that spoken English, if it need be taught at all, should be built upon preestablished knowledge of written English. Then it came to me.

Imagine that I set before you the task of learning a notational system for the English language. Within this system, words would be represented by ordered sets of just a few elementary symbols. More specifically, let us suppose that the system included 26 such symbols but, just to make it interesting, let's say that some 90% of the time I would only use 15 of them (computed from Mayzner & Tresselt, 1965). Let us further imagine that the composition of the symbol set has been essentially arbitrary: The individual elements have no a priori iconic significance; they were not designed with an eye toward maximizing visual discriminability; they are, in themselves, completely meaningless; and they are unrelated to the sounds or articulatory structures of the words in whose representations they occur. Thus, the only basis you have for memorizing the words within this system is in terms of the specific, ordered sets of elements by which I designate them. Half of the words I would present would be quite short, consisting of 7 elements or fewer; the remainder could be indefinitely long although relatively few would exceed 15 elements (Miller, Newman, & Friedman, 1958). The criterion for passing is that you, like the average American high-school student, learn the combinations and permutations of elements corresponding to at least 50,000 words.

What an awful task. And yet, the system I have just described corresponds very closely to our own system of writing. The major difference is that my system lacks any symbol-to-phoneme correspondences, and that is, of course, the point. However fuzzy one's knowledge of the spelling-to-sound (or spelling-to-articulation) correspondences of English, it must be of invaluable assistance in learning the identities and orders of the letters comprising English words. It is no wonder that poor reading and poor phonological recoding skills are found to be so highly correlated among young readers (e.g., Barron, 1978b; Jorm, 1979; Liberman, et al., 1977).

It has been suggested that the shapes of whole words offer an alternate set of cues for word identification (e.g., Johnson, 1975; Smith, 1971; also see review by Woodworth, 1938). In defense of this notion, Brooks (1977) has shown that if words are presented to students in distinctive typographies, learning is facilitated. Perhaps this would be a useful technique for teaching deaf children to read. On the other hand, Groff (1975) has shown that given normal typography, the visual configurations of words are poor clues to their identities. And, in any case, the shapes of words or frequent letter clusters evidently do not contribute to word identification by mature readers (Adams, 1979a).

In short, if the alphabetical nature of written English is the source of orthographic redundancy, it may also be its defense. Even if Smith's (1973) contention were true in the extreme—that is, even if spelling-to-sound correspondences proved to be critical *only* for the writer—that would be justification enough for the existence of orthographic redundancy. However, I am convinced that spelling-to-sound correspondences are at least as important to the reader, and it follows that orthographic redundancy must also be.

Even so, a full explanation of the apparent role of orthographic redundancy in word recognition cannot be discovered through considerations of spelling-to-sound correspondences. Although they lead to the conclusion that orthographic redundancy is (indirectly) useful for the reader, they do not imply that it is *used* by the reader. Direct phonemic translation of the written word depends only on knowledge of the relationships between spelling and sound. Phonological translation, as Chomsky (1970) would have it, additionally requires knowledge of underlying morphology and the relationships among sounds. Knowledge of the relationships among the letters of a written word is inherently required by neither approach. Rather, for both, orthographic redundancy is incidental to the end product of the translation process as it is but a concomitant of the sound structure of the language.

Of course, if spelling-to-sound translations were found to be an integral and automatic component of the world-recognition process, the apparent role of orthographic redundancy would, by corollary, be explained. But again we have hit a dead end. Lexical access apparently does not depend on phonological recoding, even among young children (see reviews by Barron, 1978a and Spoehr, 1980).

This is not to say that phonological recoding is not involved in skilled reading. To the contrary, there is increasing evidence that it is. However, its function seems primarily one of facilitating retention for the words of the text until the complete phrase or sentence in which they occur has been read and comprehended (Barron, 1978a; Kleiman, 1975; Levy, 1975, 1978), and it appears to be a consequence rather than an antecedent of lexical access (Forster & Chambers, 1973; Stanovitch & Bauer, 1978). That such recoding occurs among readers of Chinese (Tzeng, Hung, & Wang, 1977) suggests that it can be mediated by processes that are not at all associated with spelling-to-sound correspondences. There is some evidence that even among readers of English phonological recoding does not proceed by any direct path from letter-to-sound (Glushko, 1980).

Considerations of spelling-to-sound correspondences raise another more subtle question about the orthographic redundancy of English. Namely, of what value are vowels? As the six primary vowels comprise roughly 39% of the letters in English text (from Mayzner & Tresselt, 1965), they contribute heavily to its redundancy—more heavily, in fact, than can be defended in the interest of spelling-to-sound correspondences. It is the vowels that are responsible for the majority of spelling-to-sound irregularities of English. Indeed, the descriptive advantage of Chomsky's (1970) approach to spelling-to-sound correspondences derives largely from his dismissal of much of the variation in vowel-to-phoneme mapping as irrelevant to, or at least beyond the province of, our alphabetical system.

Given the amount of redundancy that is carried by the vowels, one might further suspect that they contribute especially little information with respect to the identities of words. Confirming this suspicion, Miller and Friedman (1957) found that when English passages were abbreviated by removing all of the vowels and spaces, people could regenerate them almost perfectly. In contrast, when a similar proportion of random letters was removed, median reconstruction accuracy was less than 20%. It is interesting to note that in reformed alphabets, such as UNIFON and the i/t/a, the number of different vowels is more than tripled. In this way the reformed alphabets simultaneously offer a means of reducing the redundancy attached to the vowels and of increasing their phonemic significance (see Aukerman, 1971).

It may be that vowels contribute minimally to word identification in spoken language as well. It is, after all, the vowel sounds that vary most noticeably across dialects. However, a certain variety of vowel sounds is essential in spoken language, as it allows the listener to estimate the size of a speaker's vocal tract and, in turn, to convert acoustical into phonemic information (Gerstman, 1967). Clearly no parallel function is possible or necessary in written language, which leads one to wonder why vowels need be represented in the script at all. They typically are not represented in the otherwise "alphabetical" Semitic scripts. Indeed, they were not represented in the Semitic ancestor of our own script.

Such reservations are peaked by the observation that the task of segmenting vowels from consonants is the most troublesome prerequisite to learning an alphabetical script (e.g., Gleitman & Rozin, 1977; Liberman et al., 1977). Maybe vowels really are more a hindrance than a help to the reader. Alternatively, given that the vowels seem to contribute little else of value to our orthography, perhaps they hold a critical clue with respect to the role of redundancy in word recognition. We return to this possibility in a later section of this chapter.

SEQUENTIAL REDUNDANCY AND LETTER IDENTIFICATION

It has often been suggested that sequential redundancy is used by skilled readers to facilitate letter recognition (Adams, 1979a; Broadbent, 1967; Estes, 1975a,b; Massaro, 1975; Morton, 1969; Rumelhart & Siple, 1974; Smith, 1971). The essential quality of a redundant string is, after all, that its elements do not occur independently of one another. The task of visual feature identification in reading could be substantially reduced if it were complemented or guided by knowledge of interletter constraints. According to this view, people with keener sensitivity to the sequential redundancy of our orthography should be better readers, not because they have overlearned their phonics but because they invest less effort in visual feature extraction.

The hypothesis that sequential predictability enhances perceptibility finds support from the many demonstrations that pseudowords are more readily perceived than unrelated strings of letters (for a review, see Adams 1979a). However, more refined evidence of such facilitation has been hard to come by. Several investigators have measured the speed with which people can search through more and less constrained nonwords for prespecified target letters (Gibson, Tenney, Barron, & Zaslow, 1972; James & Smith, 1970; Krueger, 1970a, b; Krueger, Keen, & Rublevich, 1974; Massaro et al., 1979). The advantages of this paradigm are that it minimizes confoundings of guessing and memory. Its major disadvantage, with respect to the issue at hand, is that the visual processing it requires may be so much more cursory than that required for word recognition as to preclude meaningful comparisons. In any case, the results from these studies have been mixed, and even when faster search times have been found with more tightly structured strings, the effect has been quite small (Krueger, 1970a; Krueger et al., 1974; Massaro et al., 1979).

Results from studies requiring more thorough visual processing have been no more positive. Broadbent and Gregory (1968) and Owsowitz (1963, cited in Broadbent & Gregory, 1968) found that bigram frequency had no significant effect on tachistoscopic recognition thresholds for high-frequency words. Moreover, for low-frequency words, the bigram effect was significant but backwards: Low frequency words with low brgram counts were perceived significantly *more* readily than those with high bigram counts. Analogous results have been obtained by Rice and Robinson (1975) through a lexical decision task. Reducing paradox to confusion, Biederman (1966) and Rumelhart and Siple (1974) found low-frequency words with high bigram frequencies to be more perceptible than those with low bigram frequencies. Finally, filling in the spectrum of possible results, McClelland and Johnston (1977) found virtually no effect of bigram frequency on the perceptibility of either words or pronounceable nonwords under either full-report or forced-choice procedures.

It seems that, excepting the robust pseudoword/nonword difference, facilitative effects of orthographic redundancy on performance have consistently been found only through experimental tasks involving relatively heavy memory requirements (Krueger, 1970a; Massaro & Taylor, 1980; Massaro et al., 1979; Miller, Bruner, & Postman, 1954). But, given the well-known relation between information and memorability (Miller, 1956), it is difficult to ascribe such effects to perceptibility.

Even so, our failure to demonstrate that the perceptibility of words and pseudowords varies with sequential predictability cannot be taken as evidence against the notion of interletter facilitation. Elsewhere (Adams, 1979a), I have proposed a model of word recognition that would predict no such trend, even though one of its central assumptions is that sequential redundancy facilitates letter recognition. The reason for this seeming contradiction is that the model carries the additional assumption that letter recognition is facilitated by lexical knowledge. As letter-cluster frequency and word frequency are highly correlated, these two sources of knowledge normally work together to facilitate word perception. In effect, they provide redundant information about redundant information. The problem with studies like these is that they have necessarily focused on the exceptions to this rule—on the cases in which lexical and orthographic knowledge yield conflicting biases. To develop this explanation more completely, it is necessary to consider the model in some detail.

The basis assumption of the model is that the perception of an orthographic string consists in the activation of appropriate letter- and word-recognition units in memory. Facilitative effects of orthographic and lexical familiarity are built into the model through the old idea that any two units in memory that are reportedly activated at the same time become associated such that the activation of one facilitates the activation of the other.

The network of letter-recognition units is schematized in Fig. 9.1. The circles in Fig. 9.1 represent letter-recognition units, and the arrows represent the associations between them. The solid circles correspond to units receiving activation

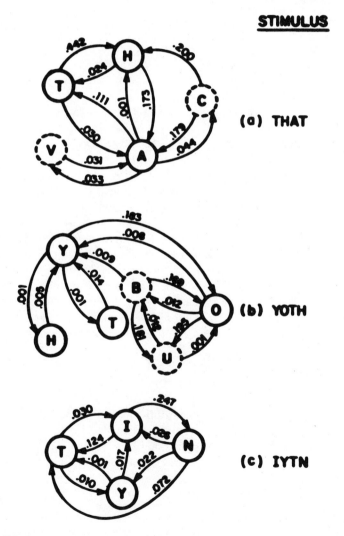

FIG. 9.1.   Schematic of the associated letter network. From Adams (1979a).

both directly from the stimulus and indirectly through other activated units in the network; the broken circles correspond to units receiving indirect activation only. The fraction of activity relayed by one unit to another is supposed to depend on their history of cooccurrence; within the model these weightings are estimated as interletter transition probabilities (from Mayzner & Tresselt, 1965). The directions of the arrows between the units are not meant to constrain the flow of activity but merely indicate the direction of the transition. For example, when the H unit in Fig. 9.1(a) is activated, the facilitation of the T unit is weighted by .442 for T's to the immediate left of the H and by .024 for T's to the immediate right.[1]

The relation between the letter- and word-recognition units is schematized in Fig. 9.2. Like the interletter associations, the associations between the letter and word units are supposed to be bidirectional. As any letter unit becomes activated, it relays activation to every word unit to which it belongs; as any word unit becomes activated, it proportionately and reciprocally relays activation to the letter units corresponding to each of its component letters. The strengths of the associations between the letter and word units are assumed to be a function of word frequency; the weightings given are from Carroll, Davies, and Richman's (1971) Standard Frequency Index.

A critical assumption of the model is that processing occurs concurrently within and across all levels. Visual features are extracted from the letters of the stimulus in parallel, but with a left-to-right bias in attention, and each feature is mapped onto all compatible letter-recognition units. As soon as any unit in memory becomes activated in the least, it relays proportionate activation to all of its associates.

Thus, if the system consisted only of the letter-recognition network, a strong effect of sequential redundancy would be predicted. For strings composed of highly probable bigrams, like those in Fig. 9.1(a) and 9.1(b), the relevant letter-recognition units would simultaneously receive direct visual activation from the stimulus and strong indirect activation from each other. In contrast, for strings composed of unlikely bigrams, as in Fig. 9.1(c), facilitation through interletter association would be minimal, and perception would depend almost entirely on direct activation from the stimulus.

It is because of the influence of the word-recognition units that the bigram effect is expected to be invisible in experiments like those described earlier in this section. For high-frequency words, the priming afforded by the word-recognition units should be so strong as to obscure any differences owing to bigram probability. In contrast, for low-frequency words, associations between the letter- and word-recognition units should act to undermine the facilitative effects of high bigram frequency. After all, if the bigrams comprising a low-frequency word or

---

[1]If this model is correct, it suggests another explanation for the failure of studies like McClelland and Johnston's (1977) to obtain significant effects of orthographic structure. Specifically, the strength of the interletter facilitation should depend, not on simple bigram frequency, but on the conditional probability of the ordered bigram given the occurrence of either of its component letters.

STIMULUS

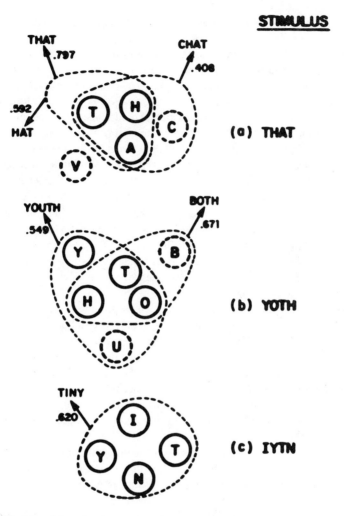

FIG. 9.2.   Schematic of the associated lexical network. From Adams (1979a).

pseudoword have occurred frequently, it must be because they have occurred in many other words or at least in a few high-frequency words. Thus, the priming they elicit from the word-recognition units will be misleading—it will act to disperse activation counterproductively across the letter-recognition network. As a consequence, despite the advantage they may accrue through the network of interletter associations, low-frequency words with high bigram frequencies may be expected to require at least as much visual attention as low-frequency words with low bigram frequencies. Notably, the model nonetheless predicts that low-frequency words will be more perceptible than strings of unrelated letters because the latter receive no facilitation through either type of association, but lots of interference from both.

SEQUENTIAL REDUNDANCY AND LETTER ORDER

Estes (1975a,b, 1977) has hypothesized that an important function of sequential redundancy is to help readers encode the order of the letters in an orthographic string. The motivation for this hypothesis stems from evidence that the visual system's capacity for processing spatial information is, in itself, too limited to support the speed and accuracy with which skilled readers can recognize words.

According to Estes (1972), the visual system's primary means of encoding the location of information in the visual field is in terms of the input channel through which it is passed from the retina to the feature detectors, but the density of these input channels is limited, especially beyond the fovea. Thus, when letters are arrayed closely together, and especially when this happens toward the periphery of the field, their features will necessarily be shipped through the same input channel. As a consequence, there will be no sensory basis for distinguishing their respective locations. In keeping with this theory, Estes, Allmeyer, and Reder (1976) have shown that when subjects are restricted to a single visual fixation and asked to report unrelated letters from a densely packed visual array, the frequency of positional errors increases significantly toward the periphery of the field. In support of their hypothesis that such positional uncertainty arises from sensory limitations (e.g., rather than from memory limitations), they also found that the frequency of transposition errors did not decrease when viewing time was extended from 150 to 2400 msec. Using much briefer exposure durations (5 to 74 msec) and foveal displays, I have also found evidence that different processes are responsible for the extraction of identity and positional information from an orthographic string and, moreover, that it takes the system less time to encode item information accurately than to encode positional information accurately (Adams, 1979a).

Importantly, in letter-recognition experiments with normal adult readers, transposition errors occur frequently only when the stimuli are strings of unrelated letters; transposition errors all but disappear when the stimuli consist of words, pseudowords, or frequent bigrams (Adams, 1979a; Estes, 1975a; Johnston, 1978; McClelland, 1976). That is, performance with unrelated strings of letters is typically consistent with the evidence that the visual system's capacity for processing spatial information is both crude and sluggish; performance with sequentially constrained strings of letters is not. The hypothesis that good readers use knowledge of sequential redundancy to compensate for positional uncertainty in letter perception follows easily.

These theories also carry several implications with respect to problems that are likely to beset readers with poorly developed knowledge of sequential redundancy. First, such readers are liable to transpose letters frequently unless the print is sufficiently large or spaced out to ensure that no two letters will share the same visual input channel. (We note the time-honored practice of setting primers in large type.) Second, given smaller print and no knowledge of sequential redundancy, the only means a reader would have of avoiding transpositional errors would be to fixate on words repeatedly. (We note that a characteristic difference between better and worse readers is in the number of times they fixate on each word while reading connected prose [Kolers,1976].) Letter reversals and transpositions are frequently observed among very poor readers but have traditionally been interpreted as evidence of neurological dysfunction, or so-called "primary dyslexia." The present theories suggest that these behaviors may reflect nothing more than inadequate knowledge of sequential redundancy. In keeping with this possibility I have recently found experimental evidence suggesting that letter ordering difficulties are very common among below average readers in general—if less extreme than among "dyslexics" (Adams, 1979b).

This experiment involved sixteen paired high-school volunteers who were divided into eight good and eight poor readers on the basis of their performance on the Nelson–Denny Reading Comprehension Test. The mean percentile scores for the good and poor readers were 95.6% and 47%, respectively. All subjects were shown two series of quadrigrams at very brief exposure durations. Their task was to report all of the letters of each quadrigram in the correct order, by guessing if necessary. One of the series of quadrigrams consisted of nonwords only—that is, of quadrigrams with very low bigram frequencies. The other series consisted of equal numbers of high-frequency words, pseudowords with high-positional bigram frequencies, and nonwords, randomly interspersed. The nonwords and pseudowords that were presented to any one subject were in fact anagrams of the words presented to another, such that the composition of the quadrigrams, in terms of single letters, was fully controlled across subjects.

The rationale for this design grew from Aderman and Smith's (1971) demonstration that the functional units in the perception of printed English may be either single letters or spelling patterns, depending on the perceiver's set or expectations. In particular, it was assumed that when the stimulus series consisted of nonwords alone, the subjects' functional perceptual units would be single letters. Performance should, in this case, reflect the subjects' basic ability to extract identity and order information from the stimulus. In contrast, when nonwords were interspersed with words and pseudowords, subjects should tend to use orthographic patterns as the functional perceptual units. If, as hypothesized, a basic role of orthographic knowledge is that of rectifying the perception of letter order, then its application should result in an active misordering of the letters of the nonwords. Moreover, if a characteristic difference between good and poor readers is in their knowledge of orthographic redundancy, then the good readers should be more prone than the poor readers to misorder the letters of the nonwords in the mixed condition.

The results of this experiment were wholly consistent with these expectations. The good readers were significantly worse at reporting the letters of nonwords in their correct positions when the nonwords were intermixed with words and pseudowords than when they were presented alone; for the poor readers there was no difference. Moreover, in the mixed condition, poor readers were significantly less accurate than good readers at identifying and ordering the letters of pseudowords, but they were every bit as accurate as the good readers with words. Although the latter contrast corroborates the hypothesis that good and poor readers tend to differ in their sensitivity to orthographic structure as distinct from whole, familiar words, the results of the experiment corroborate the hypothesis that such sensitivity is directly related to the encoding of letter order information.

ORTHOGRAPHIC REDUNDANCY AND THE PERCEPTION OF MULTISYLLABIC WORDS

In the last two sections, I presented arguments that knowledge of orthographic redundancy facilitates the encoding of the identities and the order of letters in orthographically regular strings. These arguments suffer a common drawback, however, with respect to explaining the utility of orthographic redundancy. Specifically, it seems that any facilitation that orthographic redundancy might provide is superfluous if the reader is visually familiar with the word as a whole. In the experiment (Adams, 1979b) described in the last section, the effect of orthographic knowledge on the encoding of letter order was apparent only for nonwords and pseudowords; correctly identified letters of words were almost never misordered by either good or poor readers. Similarly, in the section on orthographic redundancy and letter recognition, the only reliable evidence that recognition of one letter may prime or facilitate the recognition of its most likely neighbors came from comparisons of people's performance with pseudowords and nonwords.

Nevertheless, in this section I argue that orthographic redundancy is an essential property of our written language. I contend that knowledge of orthographic redundancy is critical to the skilled reader and that its utility derives primarily from the two types of facilitation described earlier. However, I argue that the primary domain of its utility is in the reading of multisyllabic words.

To begin this argument, let us reconsider the value of vowels. To the extent that vowels are not phonemically informative, the English writing system is not really an alphabet but rather some hybrid between an alphabet and a syllabary. Of what advantage, we might ask, is such a hybrid over a straightforward syllabary? After all, it has been repeatedly argued that syllables are psychologically more accessible than phonemes for both children and adults (e.g., Liberman et al., 1977).

A general explanation offered by Gleitman and Rozin (1977) is that the desirability of syllabic script is a function of representational efficiency. Thus, for classical Chinese, in which the number of syllables approaches the number of words, a syllabary offers little savings over a logography. In contrast, for Japanese, which can be adequately represented with about 50 syllabic signs, a

syllabary offers tremendous economy over a logography. A syllabary would be more economical than a logography for English as well. However, English is estimated to consist of as many as 5000 distinct syllables (Rozin & Gleitman, 1977). Thus, strictly in terms of the number of symbols or, equivalently, the amount of rote memorization required, our alphabet of 26 letters is far more manageable than a pure syllabary would be.

But why vowels? With the exception of relatively few institutionalized perversities of our spelling system (e.g., *kn——*, *——ght, wr——*), the differences in the predictability with which one consonant follows another can be traced to the sound structure of the language. For example, the fact that *d* more frequently precedes *r* than *n* is a consequence of the alphabetical principle; it is a relatively faithful reflection of the way we talk. With respect to consonants, then, orthographic redundancy can be seen as a concomitant of phonemic information. However, as previously discussed, the same cannot be said for vowels. In the interest of phonological information, it would seem that a well-designed alphabet ought to include either more vowels than are included in our own alphabet, or none at all. Yet I believe that the primary function of vowels within our writing system is orthogonal to their phonological significance. Their primary function is that of preserving the syllable as a perceptual unit, and as such derives directly from the redundancy they carry.

The importance of vowels to the decipherment of our script can be illustrated through variations on the technique that has so often been used to argue their superfluousness:

Th bsc dmnstrtn s tht txt s stll mr r lss lgbl whn th vwls hv bn rmvd.

Th prps f th frst vrtn n ths thm s t dmstrt tht th trnsprnc f th nttn dcrss prcptsl whn th txt s cmprsd f rltvl nfrqnt wds nd bcms vrtll mpntrbl f wds r nt smntcll r sntctcll prmd, vz. prcpn, Drcl, trnp, cstnt, nnsns.[2]

Th* p*rp*s* *f th* s*c*nd v*r**t**n *n th*s th*m* *s t* d*m*nstr*t th*t th* *mp*rt*nc* *f v*w*ls c*nn*t b* f*lly *xpl*'*n*d *n t*rms *f th**r ph*n*m*c s*gn*f*c*nc*, f*r th* l*g*b*l*ty *f th* t*xt *s *lm*st c*mpl*t*ly r*c*v*r*d *f th* v*w*ls *r* n*t *m*tt*d b*t r*pl*c*d w*th s*m* ph*n*m*c*lly n*ns*gn*f*c*nt s*mb*l, *nd th*s *s tr** *v*n f*r l*ng, *nfr*q**nt, *nd c*nt*xt*t**lly *npr*d*ct*bl* w*rds, v*z. d*ff*d*l, h*rps*ch*rd, r*ct*ngl*, br*nt*s**r*s.

The idea that syllabic encoding is an important component of the word-recognition process has been gaining support in recent years (e.g., Rozin &

---

[2]The purpose of the first variation on this theme is to demonstrate that the transparency of the notation decreases precipitously when the text is comprised of relatively infrequent words and becomes virtually impenetrable if words are not semantically or syntactically primed, viz. porcupine, Dracula, turnip, castanet, nonsense.

Gleitman, 1977; Spoehr & Smith, 1973, 1975; Stanners, Neiser, & Painton. 1979; Taft, 1979). Most of this research has focused on the role of syllabic units in the processes of phonological recoding or lexical access. Although a few investigators have suggested that the syllable influences the very course of perception (e.g., Gibson et al., 1962; Smith & Spoehr, 1974), this notion has always been shackled with a parsing problem. Specifically, to perceive the letters of a word in syllabic units, one would seemingly need to know where the syllables begin and end before knowing what they were. Where the units of perception are letters or words, unitization could be based on the physical cue of interitem spaces, but no obvious physical cue exists in the case of syllables.

Nevertheless, Mewhort and Beal (1977) have developed evidence that the syllabic structure of a word does indeed guide the visual processing of its letters. In Mewhort and Beal's first experiment, the stimuli were eight-letter words, such as *OBTAINED*. The letters of the words were arrayed, one-by-one, from left-to-right or right-to-left, for 5 msec each; the interstimulus interval, or the time between the offset of one letter and the onset of the next, varied across trials from 0 to 250 msec. Regardless of the order in which the letter appeared, subjects were able to recognize the words almost perfectly with 0 msec interstimulus interval. However, as the interstimulus interval was lengthened, word-recognition accuracy declined by about 50% in the left-to-right condition. That is, subjects' word-recognition processes were somehow disrupted by the nonsimultaneity of the letters. In the right-to-left condition, the number of words that subjects recognized correctly fell nearly to zero with increases in the interstimulus interval. Moreover, this decline in accuracy was mirrored by a shift toward encoding the letters from right-to-left. This suggests that the word-recognition system may be inherently biased toward accepting information in left-to-right order. Alternatively, the subjects' difficulty in the right-to-left condition might have resulted not from the spatial order of letter presentation per se, but from a consequent disruption in their ability to recognize or exploit the sequential dependencies of the string.

To evaluate these explanations, Mewhort and Beal included two more conditions in the experiment. These conditions were like the first two except that the stimulus words were spelled backward, e.g., *DENIATBO*. Thus, when these backward words were arranged from left-to-right, the spatial order of letter encoding was normal, but the sequences of letters were reversed; when arrayed from right-to-left, the sequences of letters were normal, but the spatial order of encoding was reversed. Mewhort and Beal's subjects recognized virtually none of the backward words at 0 msec interstimulus interval, regardless of whether the array stepped from left-to-right or right-to-left. For the left-to-right arrays, there was virtually no improvement in performance with increases in the interstimulus interval. For the right-to-left arrays, the proportion of correctly recognized words approached .50 as the interstimulus interval was increased, and again, this change in report accuracy was mirrored by a shift toward encoding the letters in a

right-to-left order. In short, the results of these conditions indicate that the word-processing system is biased for left-to-right input but that, regardless of the spatial direction of input, the probability of recognizing a word under letter-by-letter presentation conditions depends strongly on whether the letters are encoded in the order or sequence in which they normally occur.

In a previous study, Mewhort (1974) obtained a virtually identical pattern of results using pseudowords instead of words. Mewhort and Beal's effects, therefore, cannot be attributed to the meaningfulness or holistic familiarity of the stimuli. Nor can they be attributed to differences in the subjects' ability to recognize the individual letters of the strings: Mewhort (1974) found that performance was invariant across comparable experimental conditions with first-order approximations (i.e., nonwords with no sequential redundancy). By process of elimination, Mewhort and Beal's results would seem to reflect people's dependence on structural properties of the strings.

Following Smith and Spoehr (1974), Mewhort and Beal hypothesized that their effects reflected a disruption of the subjects' ability to parse the strings into syllabic units during scanning. To test this idea, they repeated the first two conditions of their first experiment, sequentially presenting fragments of words from left-to-right or right-to-left. However, in this experiment, the fragments were not single letters but groups of letters. For half the subjects, the letter groups corresponded to syllables (e.g., *in-dus-try, spe-ci-fic*); for the other half, they did not (e.g., *ind-ust-ry, sp-eci-fic*). Mewhort and Beal found that, except at 0 msec interstimulus interval where accuracy was generally very high, performance was more accurate with the syllabic groups of letters than with the nonsyllabic groups of letters regardless of the spatial order of presentation. Moreover, very few errors occurred in the left-to-right syllabic condition at any interstimulus interval. This consistently high level of accuracy contrasted not only with the performance in the other conditions of this experiment, but also with the performance with left-to-right letter-by-letter presentation of forward words in Mewhort and Beal's first experiment. The data thus lend strong support to the hypothesis that the syllable is a fundamental unit of encoding in word perception.

Finally, to ascertain whether the syllabic effect accrued in the course of scanning or afterwards as the result of short-term memory operations, Mewhort and Beal ran one more experiment. As before, the words were arrayed in syllabic or nonsyllabic letter groups. But this time, the letter groups were arranged in vertical columns instead of horizontal rows. This procedure was intended to preclude normal left-to-right scanning but nonetheless ensure that the letters be entered into short-term memory, group-by-group or syllable-by-syllable. Mewhort and Beal found that across interstimulus intervals of 0 to 625 msec, mean word-recognition accuracy hovered between 20% to 40%. Further, there was no difference in accuracy between the syllabic and nonsyllabic conditions. It thus seems that normal scanning is critical to the word-recognition process. And, adding Bryden's (1970) evidence that the recognition of strings of unrelated letters is not impaired by such a vertical format, it seems, in particular, that normal scanning is critical to the reader's ability to recognize and exploit the syllabic structure of an orthographic string. By implication, the word-recognition system must indeed have some preliminary means of segregating syllables or identifying syllable boundaries.

I would like to suggest that such automatic preliminary syllabification is mediated by the reader's knowledge of orthographic redundancy. In particular, I would like to suggest that it could be mediated by a network of associated letter units like that proposed in the word-recognition model described earlier (Adams, 1979a). Again, within that model, it is assumed that letters of an orthographic string, or more precisely the features of those letters, are encoded in parallel but with a left-to-right bias in attention. When any given letter unit in memory is stimulated, it will prime or relay activation to all other units with which it is associated. The strengths of an association between two letter units is assumed to be a direct function of the relative frequency with which one has followed or preceded the other in the reader's experience. Thus, the effect of the interletter priming will be that the unit corresponding to each of the component letters of a highly redundant sequence will simultaneously receive strong activation from the units corresponding to its neighbor on either side as it receives visual activation from the stimulus. In this way, the perception of the entire sequence will be greatly facilitated. Moreover, because the associations are between *ordered* pairs of letters, the perceived letters will become encoded in memory as a cohesive, ordered sequence. In contrast, when the transition probability from one letter to another is relatively low, the association between them will be weak. In this case, there will be little interfacilitation between them in the course of perception, and, once perceived, there will be little cohesion between their internal representations.

Provided that interletter transition probabilities, or equivalently sequential redundancy, is relatively high within syllables and low between them, the workings of such a network would automatically produce syllabic parsing in the course of letter perception. The syllabic structure of a word would be given by the relative strengths of the associations between the units corresponding to adjacent letters. Because of their mutual facilitation, the letters within a given syllable will be perceived almost concurrently. In contrast, because the first letter of a new syllable will not enjoy the same degree of facilitation and because the allocation of attention tends from left-to-right, its perception will lag in time. In addition, the strong associations within a syllable will reinforce perception of, and memory for, the order of the letters within the syllable. This is especially important for long words because, as Wolford (1975) has demonstrated, the tendency toward perturbations in letter order increases when there are no spaces between letters (as there are between words) and with distance from the fovea. The associations between letter-recognition units will provide little reinforcement with respect to the order of an adjacent pair of weakly associated letters. However, if such pairs only occur at syllable boundaries, this will cause little difficulty: Each of the letters will be securely ordered within the syllable to which it belongs, and the spatial order of the syllables will be given by the temporal order in which they are perceived. Thus, just as Mewhort and Beal (1977) have theorized, syllabic parsing is held to occur during scanning; the system is supposed to encode the syllables from left-to-right and, in so doing, to convert their spatial order into a temporal one.

Of course, the viability of this schema really rests on the assumption that orthographic redundancy is higher within than between syllables. And this is where, at last, the importance of the vowels may be discovered. Because of their very redundancy they ensure the integrity of the syllable. The vowel corresponds to the vocalic center of the syllable, and every written English syllable must include at least one. Because the vowels constitute nearly 40% of the letters in running text and because there are so few of them, the left-to-right transition probability from any given consonant to a vowel is bound to be relatively high. A quick glance at Mayzner and Tresselt's (1965) table of bigram frequencies confirms this conjecture.

On the assumption that syllable boundaries will be located where the associations between adjacent letters are weakest, the significance of this observation is that the system will never try to delimit as a syllable any string that does not include a vowel. More specifically, the implication is that the system will virtually never locate a syllable boundary in the midst of a CV pair. In contrast, as the vowels are relatively indifferent as to what letters they may precede, the associative link between a VC pair is generally expected to be of intermediate strength. Inasmuch as it is the relative strengths of the interletter associations to which the system responds, this means that the system will tend to parse strings consiting of [...VCV...] into [...V-CV...]. That is, the system will recognize such words as *major, preface,* and *cumulate* as consisting of multiple syllables and will parse them as *ma-jor, pre-face,* and *cu-mu-late.*

If the probability that a consonant will be followed by one of the six major vowels is quite high, then the probability that it will be followed by any one of the twenty other letters of the alphabet must be quite low. Again, a glance at Mayzner and Tresselt's table confirms that, with a few predictable exceptions (e.g., *ck, gh, ng, th*), the frequency with which any consonant is followed by any other consonant is much lower than the frequency with which it is followed by any vowel. This means that the associative linkage of an orthographic string will be especially weak between consonant pairs. Thus, the system will typically parse [...VCCV...] strings as [...VC-CV...]. For example, *rabbit* and *advent* will be encoded as *rab-bit* and *ad-vent.*

Because some consonant pairs are quite frequent and because there is considerable entropy in the VC pairs, I suspect that the system will parse some [...VCCV...] strings as [...V-CCV...]. However, the most frequent consonant bigrams correspond either to single phonemes (e.g., *ch, th*) or to phonemes that are frequently coarticulated (e.g., *st, fr, bl*). Thus, when [...V-CCV...] parsings do occur, they are more likely to capture than to distort the true syllabic structure of the word.

Finally, when more than two consonants occur in sequence, the system will locate the syllable boundary within the least likely pair. For many such cases, the pair that spans the syllable boundary will be much less likely than any of the others, because unlike the others it will be relatively free of coarticulation constraints. Thus, *sumptuous, thoughtful,* and *franchise* will be encoded as *sumptuous, thought-ful,* and *fran-chise.*

In short, the potential of this schema for syllabifying long words in the course of perception looks very good from an armchair perspective. Even so, a great advantage of the schema is that the way in which it would parse any given word can be objectively specified through straightforward Bayesian statistics. Although we have not yet tested the theory in this way, we hope to do so in the near future.

From here, it looks as though the parsings that this schema will yield are generally the same as those posited by Smith and Spoehr's (1974) theory. Nevertheless, I believe that this schema improves on Smith and Spoehr's grammar in several ways. First, the assumption that syllabic parsing proceeds concurrently with letter identification—that it is mediated by the same knowledge and processes that guide the organization of visual features into letters—is consistent with Mewhort and Beal's (1977) findings that syllabic structure influences the scanning process. In contrast, according to Smith and Spoehr's theory parsing begins only after visual feature extraction has been completed. Second, the hypothesis that syllable boundaries are located on the basis of the relative strength of the associations between letters obviates the need for classifying letters as consonants or vowels prior to their identification. I have always felt that the latter requirement injected a hint of circularity into Smith and Spoehr's theory. The notion that syllable boundaries correspond to weak associative links is also more flexible than Smith and Spoehr's grammar of permissible consonant–vowel sequences. Under Smith and Spoehr's theory, less common parsings, such as [...V-CCV...] instead of [...VC-CV...], can only be obtained through sequential application and testing of secondary parsing rules. In contrast, under the present schema either of these parsings may be produced immediately; which of them is, will depend on the relative transition probabilities between the pairs of letters. Further, Smith and Spoehr's theory has general difficulty with syllable boundaries that fall within a pair of vowels. The present schema is expected to have difficulty parsing words like *naive* and *react,* where the syllable boundary falls within a very common vowel digraph. But then, people have difficulty with these words, too (Adams, Huggins, Starr, Rollins, Zuckerman, Stevens, & Nickerson, 1980). On the other hand, the present schema should have no difficulty in splitting relatively infrequent vowel digraphs, such as those in *chaos, giant, duet,* and *creosote.*

The algorithm of parsing words as a function of relative transition prob-abilities is qualitatively different from Taft's (1979) parsing principle. According to Taft (1979), the system should: "include in the first syllable as many conson-ants following the first vowel of the word as orthotactic factors will allow without disrupting the morphological structure of that word [p. 24]." Whether the pre-sent schema can compete with Taft's principle in predicting empirical results has yet to be learned. However, there is at least one class of words that, though troublesome for Taft's principle, would be correctly and readily parsed by the present schema. Examples of this class are: *cowlneck* versus *cowlick, cornice* versus *corncob,* handsome versus *handsbreadth, country* versus *countless,* and *costly* versus *costive.*

The schema is not expected to do a perfect job at parsing words into syllables. But then, it doesn't need to if, as increasing evidence suggests, words are stored in memory in both holistic and in morphologically decomposed states (e.g., Gibson & Guinet, 1971; Murrell & Morton, 1974; Osgood & Hoosain, 1974; Stanners, Neiser, Hernon, & Hall, 1979; Stanners et al., 1979; Taft & Forster, 1975). Top-down influences from the lexicon should compensate for ambiguities left by the parsing process.

In any case, if the hypothesis I have offered approaches reality, it carries some fairly satisfying theoretical implications. First and foremost with respect to the theme of this chapter, it provides an explanation for the utility of orthographic redundancy. Second, it provides an explanation for the correlation between knowledge of orthographic redundancy and reading proficiency. Third, we have long appreciated the fact that written English is both an alphabet and a logog-raphy. The present hypothesis fills in the gap. It suggests, as Rozin and Gleitman (1977) have suggested before, that written English is in reality a three-tiered system: It is at once an alphabet, a logography, and a syllabary. This insight adds meaning to our knowledge that logographies and syllabaries have not, in history, been abruptly displaced by alphabetical scripts but instead have evolved gradually into them.

ACKNOWLEDGMENTS

The writing of this chapter was supported by National Institutes of Education Contract No. MS-NIE-C-400-76-0116 to Bolt Beranek and Newman Inc. and the University of Il-linois. I would like to thank B. C. Bruce, A. W. F. Huggins, and R. S. Nickerson for their critical readings of the manuscript and Mary Tiernan and Florence Maurer for their help in preparing it.

REFERENCES

Adams, M. J. Models of word recognition. *Cognitive Psychology,* 1979, *11,* 133–176. (a)
Adams, M. J. Some differences between good and poor readers. In M. L. Kamil & A. J. Moe

(Eds.), *Reading research: Studies and applications.* Clemson, S.C.: National Reading Conference, 1979. (b)

Adams, M. J., Huggins, A. W. F., Starr, B., Rollins, A., Zuckerman, L., Stevens, K., & Nickerson, R. *A prototype test of decoding skills* (BBN Report No. 4316). Bethesda, Md.: The National Institute of Child Health & Human Development, 1980.

Aderman, D., & Smith, E. E. Expectancy as a determinant of functional units in perceptual recognition. *Cognitive Psychology,* 1971, *2,* 117–129.

Aukerman, R. C. *Approaches to beginning reading.* New York: Wiley, 1971.

Baron, J., & Thurston, I. An analysis of the word-superiority effect. *Cognitive Psychology,* 1973, *4,* 207–228.

Barron, R. W. Access to the meanings of printed words: Some implications for reading and for learning to read. In F. B. Murray (Ed.), *The recognition of words.* Newark, Del.: International Reading Association, 1978. (a)

Barron, R. W. Reading skill and phonological coding in lexical access. In M. M. Gruneberg, P. E. Morris, & R. N. Sykes (Eds.), *Practical aspects of memory.* London: Academic Press, 1978. (b)

Berdiansky, B., Cronnell, B., & Koehler, J. Spelling-sound relations and primary form-class descriptions for speech comprehension vocabularies of 6-9-year olds. Southwest Regional Laboratory for Education Research and Development, Technical Report No. 15, 1969. (Cited in Smith, 1973).

Biederman, G. B. The recognition of tachistoscopically presented five-letter words as a function of digram frequency. *Journal of Verbal Learning and Verbal Behavior,* 1966, *5,* 208–209.

Broadbent, D. E. Word-frequency effect and response bias. *Psychological Review,* 1967, *74,* 1–15.

Broadbent, D. E., & Gregory, M. Visual perception of words differing in letter digram frequency. *Journal of Verbal Learning and Verbal Behavior,* 1968, *7,* 569–571.

Brooks, L. Visual pattern in fluent word identification. In A. S. Reber & D. L. Scarborough (Eds.), *Toward a psychology of reading.* Hillsdale, N.J.: Lawrence Erlbaum Associates, 1977.

Bryden, M. P. Left–right differences in tachistoscopic recognition as a function of familiarity and pattern orientation. *Journal of Experimental Psychology,* 1970, *84,* 120–122.

Carroll, J. J., Davies, P., & Richman, B. *Word frequency book.* New York: American Heritage, 1971.

Chomsky, N. Phonology and reading. In H. Levin & J. P. Williams (Eds.), *Basic studies on reading.* New York: Basic Books, 1970.

Estes, W. K. Interactions of signal and background variables in visual processing. *Perception & Psychophysics,* 1972, *12,* 278–286.

Estes, W. K. The locus of inferential and perceptual processes in letter identification. *Journal of Experimental Psychology: General,* 1975, *104,* 122–145. (a)

Estes, W. K. Memory, perception, and decision in letter identification. In R. L. Solso (Ed.), *Information processing and cognition: The Loyola symposium.* Hillsdale, N.J.: Lawrence Erlbaum Associates, 1975. (b)

Estes, W. K. On the interaction of perception and memory in reading. In D. LaBerge & S. J. Samuels (Eds.), *Basic processes in reading.* Hillside, N.J.: Lawrence Erlbaum Associates, 1977.

Estes, W. K., Allmeyer, D. H., & Reder, S. M. Serial position functions for letter identification at brief and extended exposure durations. *Perception & Psychophysics,* 1976, *19,* 1–15.

Forster, K. I., & Chambers, S. M. Lexical access and naming time. *Journal of Verbal Learning and Verbal Behavior,* 1973, *12,* 627–635.

Frederiksen, J. R. Assessment of perceptual decoding and lexical skills and their relation to reading proficiency. In A. M. Lesgold, J. W. Pellegrini, S. D. Fokkems, & R. Glaser (Eds.), *Cognitive psychology and instruction.* New York: Plenum Press, 1978.

Gerstman, L. Classification of self-normalized vowels. *IEEE Transactions on Audio and Electroacoustics,* 1967, *AU-16,* 78–80.

Gibson, E. J., & Guinet, L. Perception of inflections in brief visual presentation. *Journal of Verbal Learning and Verbal Behavior,* 1971, *10,* 182–189.

Gibson, E. J., & Levin, H. *The psychology of reading.* Cambridge, Mass.: MIT Press, 1975.

Gibson, E. J., Pick, A., Osser, H., & Hammond, M. The role of grapheme-phoneme correspondence in the perception of words. *American Journal of Psychology,* 1962, *75,* 554–570.

Gibson, E. J., Tenney, Y. J., Barron, R. W., & Zaslow, M. The effect of orthographic structure on letter search. *Perception & Psychophysics,* 1972, *11,* 183–186.

Gleitman, L. R., & Rozin, P. The structure and acquisition of reading I: Relations between orthographies and the structure of language. In A. S. Reber & D. L. Scarborough (Eds.), *Toward a psychology of reading.* Hillsdale, N.J.: Lawrence Erlbaum Associates, 1977.

Glushko, R. J. Principles for pronouncing print: The psychology of phonography. In C. Perfetti & A. Lesgold (Eds.), *Interactive processes in reading.* Hillsdale, N.J.: Lawrence Erlbaum Associates, 1980.

Groff, P. Research in brief: Shapes as cues to word recognition. *Visible Language,* 1975, *9,* 67–71.

Hanna, J. S., & Hanna, P. R. Spelling as a school subject: A brief history. *National Elementary Principal,* 1959, *38,* 8–23.

James, C. T., & Smith, D. E. Sequential dependencies in letter search. *Journal of Experimental Psychology,* 1970, *85,* 56–60.

Johnson, N. G. On the function of letters in word identification: Some data and a preliminary model. *Journal of Verbal Learning and Verbal Behavior,* 1975, *14,* 17–29.

Johnston, J. C. A test of the sophisticated quessing theory of word perception. *Cognitive Psychology,* 1978, *10,* 123–153.

Johnston, J. C., & McClelland, J. L. Visual factors in word perception. *Perception & Psychophysics,* 1973, *14,* 365–370.

Johnston, J. C., & McClelland, J. L. Perception of letters in words: Seek not and ye shall find. *Science,* 1974, *184,* 1192–1194.

Jorm, A. F. The cognitive and neurological basis of developmental dyslexia: A theoretical framework and review. *Cognition,* 1979, *7,* 19–33.

Kleiman, G. M. Speech recoding and reading. *Journal of Verbal Learning and Verbal Behavior,* 1975, *14,* 323–339.

Kolers, P. A. Buswell's discoveries. In R. A. Monty & J. W. Senders (Eds.), *Eye movements and psychological processes.* Hillsdale, N.J.: Lawrence Erlbaum Associates, 1976.

Krueger, L. E. Search time in a redundant visual display. *Journal of Experimental Psychology,* 1970, *83,* 391–399. (a)

Krueger, L. E. Visual comparison in a redundant display. *Cognitive Psychology,* 1970, *1,* 341–357. (b)

Krueger, L. E. Features versus redundancy: Comments on Massaro, Venezky, and Taylor's "Orthographic regularity, positional frequency, and visual processing of letter strings." *Journal of Experimental Psychology: General,* 1979, *108,* 125–130.

Krueger, L. E., Keen, R. H., & Rublevich, B. Letter search through words and nonwords by adults and fourth-grade children. *Journal of Experimental Psychology,* 1974, *102,* 845–849.

LaBerge, D., & Samuels, S. J. Toward a theory of automatic information processing in reading. *Cognitive Psychology,* 1974, *6,* 293–323.

Levy, B. A. Vocalization and suppression effects in sentence memory. *Journal of Verbal Learning and Verbal Behavior,* 1975, *14,* 304–316.

Levy, B. A. Speech Processing during reading. In A. M. Lesgold, J. W. Pellegrino, S. D. Fokkems, & R. Glaser (Eds.), *Cognitive psychology and instruction.* New York: Plenum Press, 1978.

Liberman, I. Y., Shankweiler, D., Liberman, A. M., Fowler, C., & Fischer, F. W. Phonetic segmentation and recoding in the beginning reader. In A. S. Reber & D. L. Scarborough (Eds.), *Toward a psychology of reading.* Hillsdale, N.J.: Lawrence Erlbaum Associates, 1977.

Massaro, D. W. Primary and secondary recognition in reading. In D. W. Massaro (Ed.), *Understanding language: An information processing analysis of speech perception, reading, and psycholinguistics.* New York: Academic Press, 1975.

Massaro, D. W., Venezky, R. I., & Taylor, G. A. Orthographic regularity, positional frequency, and visual processing of letter strings. *Journal of Experimental Psychology: General,* 1979, *108,* 107–124.

Mayzner, M. S., & Tresselt, M. E. Tables of single-letter and digram frequency counts for various word-length and letter position combinations. *Psychonomic Monograph Supplements,* 1965, *1* (Whole No. 2), 13–32.

McClelland, J. L. Preliminary letter identification in perception of words and nonwords. *Journal of Experimental Psychology: Human Perception and Performance,* 1976, *2,* 80–91.

McClelland, J. L., & Johnston, J. C. The role of familiar units in perception of words and nonwords. *Perception & Psychophysics,* 1977, *22,* 249–261.

Mewhort, D. J. K. Accuracy and order of report in tachistoscopic identification. *Canadian Journal of Psychology,* 1974, *28,* 383–398.

Mewhort, D. J. K., & Beal, A. L. Mechanisms of word identification. *Journal of Experimental Psychology: Human Perception and Performance,* 1977, *3,* 629–640.

Miller, G. A. The magical number seven, plus or minus two. *Psychological Review,* 1956, *63,* 81–97.

Miller, G. A., Bruner, J. S., & Postman, I. Familiarity of letter sequences and tachistoscopic identification. *Journal of General Psychology,* 1954, *50,* 129–139.

Miller, G. A., & Friedman, E. A. The reconstruction of mutilated English texts. *Information and Control,* 1957, *1,* 38–55.

Miller, G. A., Newman, E. B., & Friedman, E. A. Length-frequency statistics for written English. *Information and Control,* 1958, *1,* 370–389.

Morton, J. Interaction of information in word recognition. *Psychological Review,* 1969, *76,* 165–178.

Murrell, G. A., & Morton, J. Word recognition and morphemic structure. *Journal of Experimental Psychology,* 1974, *102,* 963–968.

Osgood, C. E., & Hoosain, R. Salience of the word as a unit in the perception of language. *Perception & Psychophysics,* 1974, *15,* 168–192.

Owsowitz, S. E. The effects of word familiarity and letter structure familiarity on the perception of words. Rand Corporation Publications, No. P-2820, 1963. (Cited in Broadbent & Gregory, 1968.)

Reicher, G. M. Perceptual recognition as a function of meaningfulness of stimulus material. *Journal of Experimental Psychology,* 1969, *81,* 274–280.

Rice, G. A., & Robinson, D. O. The role of bigram frequency in perception of words and nonwords. *Memory & Cognition,* 1975, *3,* 513–518.

Rozin, P., & Gleitman, L. R. The structure and acquisition of reading II: The reading process and the acquisition of the alphabetic principle. In A. S. Reber & D. L. Scarborough (Eds.), *Toward a psychology of reading.* Hillsdale, N.J.: Lawrence Erlbaum Associates, 1977.

Rumelhart, D. E., & Siple, P. Process of recognizing tachistoscopically presented words. *Psychological Review,* 1974, *81,* 99–118.

Savin, H. B., & Bever, T. G. The nonperceptual reality of the phoneme. *Journal of Verbal Learning and Verbal Behavior,* 1970, *9,* 295–302.

Shannon, C. E. A mathematical theory of communication. *The Bell System Technical Journal,* 1948, *27,* 379–423.

Smith, E. E., & Spoehr, K. T. The perception of printed English: A theoretical perspective. In B. H. Kantowitz (Ed.), *Human information processing: Tutorials in performance and cognition.* Hillsdale, N.J.: Lawrence Erlbaum Associates, 1974.

Smith, F. *Understanding reading.* New York: Holt, Rinehart & Winston, 1971.

Smith, F. *Psycholinguistics and reading.* New York: Holt, Rinehart & Winston, 1973.

Spoehr, K. T. Word recognition in speech and reading: Toward a single theory of language processing. In P. D. Eimas & J. L. Miller (Eds.), *Perspectives on the study of speech*. Hillsdale, N.J.: Lawrence Erlbaum Associates, 1980.

Spoehr, K. T., & Smith E. E. The role of syllables in perceptual processing. *Cognitive Psychology*, 1973, *5*, 71-89.

Spoehr, K. T., & Smith, E. E. The role of orthographic and phonotactic rules in perceiving letter patterns. *Journal of Experimental Psychology: Human Perception and Performance*, 1975, *104*, 21-34.

Stanners, R. F., Neiser, J. J., Hernon, W. P., & Hall, R. Memory representation for morphologically related words. *Journal of Verbal Learning and Verbal Behavior*, 1979, *18*, 399-412.

Stanners, R. F., Neiser, J. J., & Painton, S. Memory representation for prefixed words. *Journal of Verbal Learning and Verbal Behavior*, 1979, *18*, 733-743.

Stanovich, K. E., & Bauer, D. N. Experiments on the spelling-to-sound regularity effect in word recognition. *Memory & Cognition*, 1978, *6*, 410-415.

Taft, M. Lexical access via an orthographic code: The basic orthographic syllabic structure (BOSS). *Journal of Verbal Learning and Verbal Behavior*, 1979, *18*, 21-39.

Taft, M., & Forster, K. I. Lexical storage and retrieval of prefixed words. *Journal of Verbal Learning and Verbal Behavior*, 1975, *14*, 638-647.

Tzeng, O., Hung, D., & Wang, W. Speech recoding in reading Chinese characters. *Journal of Experimental Psychology: Human Learning and Memory*, 1977, *3*, 621-630.

Warren, R. M. Identification times for phonemic components of graded complexity and for spelling of speech. *Perception & Psychophysics*, 1971, *9*, 345-349.

Webster's New Collegiate Dictionary. Springfield, Mass: G. & C. Merriam Co., 1973.

Wijk, A. *Rules of pronunciation for the English language*. London: Oxford University Press, 1966.

Wolford, G. Perturbation model for letter identification. *Psychological Review*, 1975, *82*, 184-199.

Woodworth, R. S. *Experimental psychology*. New York: Holt, 1938.

10 Language Structure and Optimal Orthography

William S.-Y. Wang
Univeristy of California, Berkeley

SPEECH AND SCRIPT

When we study the spoken languages of the world—and there are by now many hundreds of reliable descriptions available—we are always impressed by the fact that all these languages are, to echo a phrase of Greenberg (1963): "cut from a common pattern [p. 255]." No doubt a large part of this common pattern can be explained by reference to the properties of the human organs that produce or perceive these sounds. In particular, many of the phonetic universals that have been extracted from numerous studies are clearly due to the mechanical limitations of the mouth—its range and rate of movement.[1]

In contrast to spoken language, the written languages of the world exhibit more major differences. Inasmuch as their development (and probably their emergence as well) is largely based on speech, the scripts are all correlated with the preexisting units of the spoken language. But the exact nature of this correlation varies across languages.

THE UNITS OF SPOKEN LANGUAGE

The units of interest to us here cut across two dimensions: phonology and syntax. Phonologically, the smallest unit is the feature, which corresponds roughly to the independent gestures of the articulators. There are no more than three or four

---

[1]In Wang (1971a), I discuss some of the articulatory and perceptual factors that constrain the structure of speech sounds.

dozen of these features in all that play distinctive roles in human speech. These features bundle up vertically to form segments, which average some 100 msec in duration. So, although we cannot hear the features singly, we are able to hear them in bundles cooccurring in individual segments, such as in tape recordings.

These segments can be classified according to a variety of criteria. The elucidation of such criteria has been the primary concern of phonological theory over these five decades. Linguists commonly recognize three classes of segments: phones, phonemes, and morphophonemes—in the order of increasing abstractness.[2] One dichotomy that holds for all languages is that between consonants and vowels (see Greenberg, 1962). This distinction is relevant for some scripts, where the symbols for consonants dominate the line, but the symbols for vowels are essentially appended to the consonants and are mostly optional. This is no doubt due to the greater amount of information contained in the consonants, which typically outnumber the vowels by ratios of 3 or 4:1. Such is the case with several Semitic scripts, as well as Semitic-inspired systems of writing in South and Southeast Asia.

The segments connect together in time into larger sequences: the mora and the syllable. The distinction between these two can be seen in the Japanese kana script. An utterance like *ko-m-ba-n* contains two syllables but four moras because each of the nasal consonants counts as an additional mora. As the kana is based on the mora rather than the syllable, the word is written with four kana symbols, i.e., こ ん ば ん. The corresponding kanji, however, contains just two logographs because the Chinese script is based on the syllable, of which there are two, namely, *kom-ban,* 今 晚. Similarly, geminate consonants and vowels constitute independent moras, as in *yu-k-ku-ri* or *o-ba-a-sa-n.*

Occurring parallel in time with the segments of the syllable are a special class of features, which are sometimes called the suprasegmental features.[3] As the name suggests, the range of these features goes beyond single segments but extends over entire syllables. A classic example of suprasegmental features is the tone in Chinese, as illustrated in Fig. 10.1.

Inasmuch as suprasegmentals do not "line up" neatly with the consonants and vowels in temporal succession, they have been represented differently in alphabetical scripts. The official Chinese spelling, Pinyin, adopted by the First National People's Congress on February 1958, writes tones as diacritic marks over vowels (see Wu, 1958).

Along the syntactic dimension, we should distinguish morphemes from words. In English script, spaces are largely determined on the basis of words. So,

---

[2]For a critical review of recent developments in phonological theory, see Wang (1972). It should be clear by now that earlier attempts to "abolish the phoneme" by some proponents of generative phonology have not been successful and that a phonemic level, intermediate between the phonetic and the morphophonemic, is necessary and useful for both theoretical and practical reasons.

[3]The most comprehensive discussion of these features is Lehiste (1970).

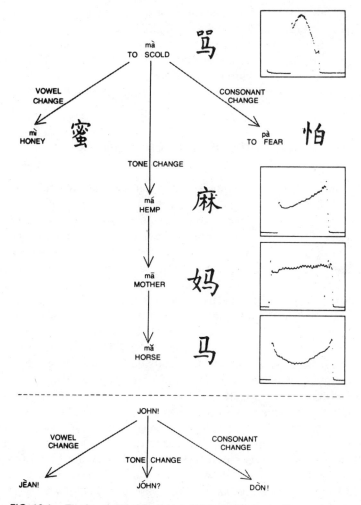

FIG. 10.1.   The four tones of the Peking dialect of Chinese are illustrated on the segments *ma*. The curves depict changes in the pitch of the author's voice. Adapted from Wang (1973).

man, gentleman, gentlemanly, ungentlemanly, and *ungentlemanliness* are each written as a single word, even though the last word contains five morphemes, whereas the first contains only one. In Chinese script, on the other hand, the spacing is based on the morpheme. Hence, a word like *tricycle* has three morphemes in Chinese, "three-wheel-vehicle," and is therefore written with three characters. There have been sporadic attempts to introduce into Chinese script a few characters each of which is a polymorphemic word, such as 書 for *library*, but such attempts have never met with much success. The standard way of writing *library* is with three characters for three morphemes functioning as a single word, literally "picture-book-building."

Also within the syntactic dimension, it is useful to distinguish the contentives (i.e., the major parts of speech) from the functives (i.e., the various classes of grammatical particles). In Japanese and Korean, for example, most contentives are written in logographs, whereas the functives are in kana or hangul.

THE UNITS OF WRITTEN LANGUAGE

In all writing systems, we can discern a spatial unit that we can refer to as a "frame," a deliberately neutral term. A rather superficial difference among scripts is that in some the frames move horizontally in rows, whereas in others they move vertically in columns. Furthermore, the frames within rows may move from left-to-right as in English. from right-to-left as in Hebrew, or even alternate in direction in boustrophedon fashion as in some ancient Greek inscriptions. Similarly, the columns may go from left-to-right conversely.

Another superficial difference has to do with the gross shape of the symbols, which is frequently due to the nature of the early writing instruments. Thus, the Tibetan script is linear and angular, whereas the Burmese script is curvilinear and round. Both are derived from the alphabets of India. The difference is due to the fact that early Burmese writing was frequently done with stylus on palm leaves, and so straight lines that might cut into the leaves were avoided.

These differences are superficial in the sense that they are consequences of historical accidents without intrinsic importance. Over the last several decades, for instance, Chinese printing, which used to go in columns from right-to-left, has been gradually shifting to rows from left-to-right. This has been motivated, at least in part, by the greater convenience the latter format offers in incorporating such items as English words or Arabic numerals. As an example, the major newspaper of China, the *Renmin Ribao,* is printed in this format.

Three types of units may go into the individual frames. The letters of the alphabet correspond most closely to the segments of spoken language. The symbols of the syllabary correspond most closely to the mora or the syllable. And the logograph, or the Chinese character, corresponds either to the morpheme or to a combination of morpheme plus syllable. (The name for "character" in Chinese is *hanzi*—Han character—after the Han dynasty, which flourished some 2000 years ago. This name has been adopted together with the characters, though the pronunciation for the name has been changed through the centuries. In Japanese it is *kanji;* in Korean it is *hanja.*)

Diacritic marks are simple graphs that do not have their own frames. Rather, they are superimposed on other units to modify their phonetic values. In this respect, they correspond most closely to the distinctive features in speech. Familiar examples here include the three accent marks written over French vowels to adjust their articulatory height or the tilde written over the Spanish ñ to mark palatal pronunciation.

These examples are of diacritics used with alphabets. They can be also used with syllabaries. In Japanese kana, for instance, there is a diacritic that changes all the *h* syllables into *p* syllables, so it corresponds to the feature "+stop." There is another diacritic that changes *h-, t-, k-,* and *s-* syllables into *b-, d-, g-,* and *z-* syllables, respectively. We saw an example of this diacritic earlier in the kana for *ko-m-ba-n.* Here the diacritic corresponds to the feature "+voiced."

By far the most extensive use of diacritic marks can be found in hangul, the Korean alphabet.[4] All the 9 basic vowels of Korean plus the 11 glide-vowel sequences are essentially built on the letter for the high front vowel /i/ or on the letter for the high back unrounded vowel /u/. The letter for /i/ is a single vertical stroke I. With one diacritic, ├, it becomes /a/; add another diacritic, ╞, and it palatalizes into /j/. Similarly, the letter for /u/ is a single horizontal stroke —. With one diacritic, ⊥, it becomes /u/; add another diacritic, ⊥⊥, and it palatalizes into /ju/. This pattern is followed for the approximately 20 vowel complexes in the language.

Diacritics are also used in the letters for Korean consonants. Stop consonants in Korean have been of special interest to linguists because they form an unusual set of three series: plain, aspirated, and tense (Kim, 1965). In the hangul, the aspiration is indicated by a diacritic on the letter for the plain stop, whereas tenseness is indicated by doubling the letter.

This extensive and systematic use of diacritics is unusual in written languages. Of all current writing systems, the Korean script probably comes closest to a feature representation of speech. Furthermore, the shapes of some hangul letters had been designed to mirror the corresponding shapes of the tongue during articulation. Considering that the system was invented in 1443 during King Sejong's reign and long before phonetics became a science, it was indeed a remarkable achievement (Taylor, 1980).

Another unusual aspect of hangul is the way in which the letters are stacked together. Although the hangul letters constitute an alphabet, they are not written in successive frames as in most alphabetical writings. Instead, like a syllabary, each frame contains a syllable, which in turn is constructed in different ways according to the shapes of the various hangul letters. Hence, the script is at once a syllabary (in that its frames correspond to syllables) and an alphabet (in that its letters correspond to segments).

When one examines the shapes of the hangul letters, the similarity to hanzi becomes quickly apparent. Indeed, most of the letters appear to be simple adaptations from the strokes of hanzi. Moreover, the method of stacking the letters into

---

[4]I am indebted to Dr. Namgui Chang for explaining various matters in Korean linguistics over these several years.

syllables within each frame appears to be an adaptation from the construction of hanzi.

Figure 10.2 gives some examples to illustrate these similarities. Corresponding to the letters in hangul, which represent phonetic segments, the components of a hanzi frame come from a much larger set, some of which represent entire morphemes and are hence much more complex in form. Thus, the top hanzi, meaning *bright,* has two components: The left means *sun* and the right means *moon.*

In both orthographies, the tendency is toward maintaining a square frame. So in hangul when the vowel letter is vertical, the consonant is stacked on horizontally (as in the example in row 1, *ka*). And when the vowel letter is horizontal, the consonants are stacked on vertically (as in the example in row 2, *nun*). The situation is roughly opposite that of Semitic orthographies, where the optional vowels are appended to the consonant instead. A more important difference, of course, is that in hangul both the vowels and the consonants are always written, whereas the vowels are optional in Semitic orthography.

Because the components in hanzi do not represent the segments in a Chinese syllable, there is greater flexibility in their spatial arrangement within a frame. Thus, the word *begin* used to be written in two ways: 启 or 启. And the word *neighbor* was either 隣 or 鄰. Such variations are not functional but may be aesthetic. With the orthography reform of the 1950s, such variations have been greatly reduced. So the two words exemplified here are now written 启 and 邻.

	HANZI	HANGUL	PHONETIC
1) HORIZONTAL	明	가	k | a
2) VERTICAL	曼	느	n / m / n
3) MIXED	然	산	s a / n
	琶	닭	t a / l k

FIG. 10.2.   The hangul syllables are constructed from segments according to the same principles as Chinese characters from the components. These examples show some of the ways a frame is filled.

THE SPREAD OF HANZI IN ASIA

The influence that the Chinese language has had on its neighbors makes an interesting story. As China has been the hub of Asian civilization for many centuries, the spoken vocabulary has been borrowed extensively by all the neighboring languages. The script, the logographs or hanzi, however, has extended only eastward, but not westward. In the southwest, for instance, the Tibeto-Burman languages, members of the Sino-Tibetan family and therefore genetically related to Chinese, have developed scripts akin to the Devangari alphabet of Sanskrit. In the northwest, some dialects of the Chinese language itself were written not in logographs but in various indigenous alphabets. In the north, Chinese script was borrowed into Korean and then into Japanese through Korea, although these are Altaic languages with drastically different morphological and syntactic structures. And in the south, it was borrowed into Vietnamese, a language of the Mon-Khmer family, again not genetically related to Chinese.

It is a bit of a paradox that the languages to the west often did *not* borrow the Chinese script, even though some of these are genetically related to Chinese as well as more similar structurally. However, those languages that *did* borrow the Chinese script are not genetically related and are structurally quite different. This is exactly what we would not have predicted on optimal linguistic grounds.

Yet another counterlinguistic development is that Vietnamese, which is much closer to Chinese in its spoken language than Japanese or Korean, was the first to abandon the logographs in favor of a Western alphabet. (According to Miller [1976], this was in the 17th century; North Korea stopped using the logographs at the end of World War II.) From these historical lessons, it is apparent that in adopting or abandoning an orthography, linguistic criteria can be and are often overruled by more powerful sociopolitical factors.

Although Japanese and Korean have very similar structures, they differ extensively from Chinese. Chinese is a tone language; Japanese and Korean are not. Chinese morphemes are virtually all monosyllabic; Japanese and Korean morphemes are predominately polysyllabic. Chinese has essentially no morphological inflections; Japanese and Korean have very elaborate inflectional systems based on suffixes. They share these features with other Altaic languages.

The fact that Chinese are virtually all monosyllabic morphemes provides a happy fit with the hanzi. Some of the suffix morphemes, such as *men, er, de, le,* and a few others, often reduce and telescope into the preceding stressed syllable in casual speech. But these are few in number, and speakers are typically unaware of the reduction. Furthermore, the great majority of the morphemes maintain a constant shape for lack of inflection (i.e., free from the kind of English variation found in *sing : sang* and *mouse : mice*. So there is a remarkable degree of regularity in this correspondence: A line of n hanzis usually represents n morphemes and is read with n syllables.

For Japanese and Korean, however, the match between speech and script was much less than optimal. Both languages developed supplementary native scripts to support the logographs, and both these scripts are derived from the logographs. But here the parallels cease because the two scripts are based on quite different principles. The Koreans borrowed some strokes from the logographs and constituted an alphabet, the hangul, about 500 years ago. About 1000 years ago, the Japanese selected a few dozen logographs on the basis of their sounds, stripped these down graphically, and constituted a syllabary, the kana. In both cases, symbols that arose in China for their semantic associations were modified and used for phonetic associations.

Figure 10.3 shows the hanzi from which the two kinds of kana were originally derived. Although both types of kana are extensively used in everyday Japanese orthography, katakana is used more frequently in the transcription of proper names or unassimilated foreign words. The katakana is on the top half of Fig. 10.3, and the more cursive hiragana is on the lower half. Each column is made up

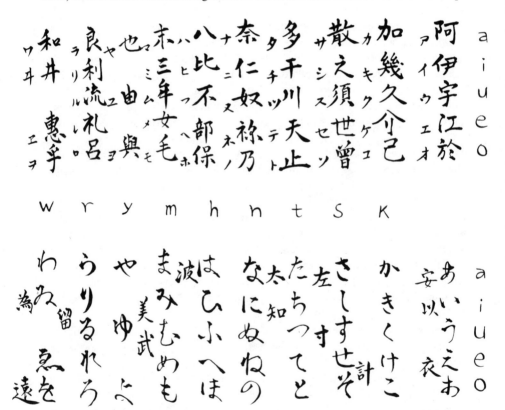

FIG 10.3.   The hanzi sources for the two types of Japanese Kana: katakana (top) and hiragana (bottom).

of five symbols, corresponding to the five vowels in Japanese. These vowels are shown in small phonetic symbols to the right. The next column shows the five hanzis, which have been simplified to form the five kanas to their left.

Moving in Fig. 10.3, each pair of columns represent another set of five Japanese moras sharing the same initial consonant. For example, the second pair of columns, counting from the right, show the hanzis and the kanas for the moras *ka, ki, ku, ke, ko*. The next pair of columns show the kanas with the consonant *t;* the next pair with *s;* and so on. The ordering of the consonants, shown in columns going from left to right, *k, s, t, n, h, m, y, r, w,* unambiguously indicates an Indic influence during the invention of the kanas.

In the lower half, the hiragana is written to the right of the hanzi. Only the hanzi sources that differ from the katakana are included.

It is common for different communities to create new logographs for items not covered by the stock of imported hanzis. Li (1956) has provided an analysis of the indigenous logographs used in Wuming, a Tai language spoken in southern China. The same phenomenon can be seen in the major dialects as well, where indigenous logographs are often found in the regional literature. Typically these logographs are constructed according to the same organizational principles as the basic hanzis. Recently, Cheng (1978) made the interesting observation that the educational level of the speech community has an influence on the response made in choosing or designing the new logographs.

STRUCTURE OF HANZI

How far back we date a writing system depends in part on where we draw the line between the script and its precursor. According to Schmandt-Besserat (1978), the earliest precursor of writing dates back to symbols used in Western Asia some 11,000 years ago. The earliest Chinese graphs generally acknowledged to be true writing are found on shells and bones that date back some 3400 years. Judging by the extent these shell-and-bone logographs are already conventionalized, it is reasonable to infer that true writing emerged considerably earlier, though at present we have no way of knowing exactly when. The archaeological excavations at Banpo (near Xi-an), which started in the 1960s, have uncovered pottery with etchings that appear ancestral to the characters of the shell-and-bone logographs (Ho, 1976). This would indicate that the earliest extant Chinese writing dates back some 6000 years, perhaps a little earlier than the Sumerian script of Asia Minor, which heretofore has been accepted as the earliest specimen of true writing in the world (Gelb, 1952).

The oldest extant dictionary of logographs is the Shuowen Jiezi (121 A.D.). In this compilation of 9353 logographs, the author Xu Shen used two principles of organization that are still referred to even today. One principle divides the logographs into six categories according to the way the logograph is formed. These are: (1) xiangxing (pictographs); (2) zhishi (simple ideograms); (3) huiyi (complex ideograms); (4) jiajie (phonetic loans); (5) xingsheng (phonograms); and (6) zhuanzhu (derivatives).

Although there is disagreement about some of these categories, it is clear that the pictographs are designed to have an iconic relation with the objects they represent. Ideograms are frequently formed by putting pictograms together to suggest an idea (e.g., the combination of moon and window to mean "bright" or two men confronting each other to mean "fighting"). For ideograms, the components are used for their semantic associations.

Typically, phonograms are also made up of two or more components. One of the components, however, is not used for its semantic content but for its phonetic value. So given a phonogram with two components, the reader gets a hint as to its meaning from one component (called the signific) and as to its pronunciation from the other component (called the phonetic).

The category of phonograms turns out to be the most popular. In a Qing dynasty (1644–1911AD) study of the Shuowen Jiezi by Wang Jun, it is estimated that 82% of the logographs are phonograms (Zhou, 1978). Ten centuries later, in a monograph compiled by Zheng Qiao, the dictionary was increased to 24,235 logographs. Of these, phonograms increased to 90%, with 7% ideograms, and 3% pictograms (Tsien, 1962). These percentages are based on dictionary frequencies, which would differ of course from frequencies obtained from actual texts.

It is often stated that the Chinese script is nonphonetic. Given such a high ratio of phonograms, we can see that such a statement is not true for most of the logographs. Rather, the method of phonetic notation is holistic, and not atomistic. An alphabet tells us that morpheme x should be pronounced as segment 1, followed by segment 2, followed by segment 3, and so on. Diacritics provide information even finer than that of segments. A syllabary tells us that morpheme x should be pronounced as syllable 1, followed by syllable 2, followed by syllable 3, and so on. Hashimoto (1980) has commented judiciously on this issue:

> ... segmentation of speech sounds of one language can and should in general be carried out to and only to the level which the grammar of the language requires. That is to say, a sound segment is divided and isolated because and only because there is in the phonology of the language at least one rule which refers to it. Any finer division is obviously an oversegmentation, and any less fine division obscures the phonological structure of the language [p. 154].

A phonogram, on the other hand, tells us simply that morpheme x should be pronounced like morpheme y. Inasmuch as the phonetics in the phonograms are usually familiar logographs, this method of phonetic notation works well most of the time. As the shapes of the logographs evolve, however, various problems arise. Let us briefly consider a current example.

In recent decades, the Chinese government has officially simplified the shapes of numerous logographs in order to promote literacy and ease in writing. It is estimated that before these simplifications, the average number of strokes per logograph was about six or seven; after simplifications, the average dropped down to four or five. In the process of simplification many new phonograms were created, but some are ambiguous in that they contain phonetics that have different pronunciations, such as 迁开 .

We would expect that in time these ambiguous phonograms will bring about a change in pronunciation of the logographs. For a transitory period, there will be two competing pronunciations, and eventually the one that is suggested by the phonetic will be adopted.

Xu Shen's other principle of organization in the Shuowen Jiezi has to do with grouping the logographs into an accessible series. The author proposed a set of 54% components, each one of which labels a group. These components, which serve this special function, have the special name of *radicals*. Many of them are symbols for common classes of objects such as water, fire, gold, woman, etc., and frequently they are the significs in phonograms.

The set of radicals that is best known today was first used by Mei Ding-Zuo in his 1615 dictionary, Zihui, which contains 214 radicals. In some of the dictionaries recently published in China, such as the Xinhua Zidian, the set has been further reduced to 187.

The radicals remain the most prevalent basis for imposing an order on the thousands of logographs that are used in dictionaries, library catalogs, print shops, or telegraph offices. When confronted with a logograph, the standard procedure for finding it in a dictionary is to turn to the section determined by its radical and locate it in a list that is arranged according to the number of strokes.

Some 10 to 20 strokes are used in the construction of logographs, the exact number depending on how one defines "stroke." Given this number and the fact that an average logograph contains four or five strokes, it is tempting to see the parallels with English, where there are 26 letters in the alphabet, and the average word contains four or five letters. The information content in terms of bits-per-stroke in Chinese appears to be quite comparable to that of bits-per-letter in English.

One aspect of the construction of logographs that is not apparent from the printed page is the manner in which the strokes are applied. Namely, there is a strict sequence in the application of strokes for the majority of logographs. In English, the ordering of letters is obvious in words such as *top, pot,* and *opt* because the letters follow each other in a single linear dimension. Although the logograph is two dimensional, the order in which the strokes are added is an important part of its construction, which plays a significant role in a kind of manual memory for the user. Often in the process of recalling or verifying a logograph, a person will trace it in the air following a fixed order of strokes.

No doubt this fixed order assures a certain uniformity in the ultimate appearance of the logographs. The general order is from top to bottom and from left to right. Sometimes the order can be used to disambiguate logographs that contain exactly the same set of strokes. The words *master* and *jade,* for instance, each contain three horizontal strokes, one vertical stroke, and one dot. For the word *master,* however, the dot is applied before the other four strokes, whereas for the word *jade* the dot is applied last.

THE FUTURE OF HANZI

Discussions on writing systems by authors in the Western world—from 17th-century missionaries to modern linguists—all too often present the bias that the alphabet in some undefined way is the ultimate triumph of all orthographies. Thus, it is not surprising, though it is regrettable, to find these careless words in a recent article from anthropology, a discipline that has traditionally prided itself on *not* being ethnocentric. The anthropologists Washburn and McCown write (1978): "Various forms of picture writing were used for more than two thousand years before the alphabet was invented. Even today, in China and Japan, non-phonetic writing may be used. Many millions of man hours have been spent unnecessarily because people did not understand the phonetic basis of the language they were using [p. 292]."

Whatever the practical merits of hanzi, it is generally acknowledged that within the tradition of Chinese scholarship, the understanding of "the phonetic basis of the language they were using" came quite early. According to Hummel (1940), the discovery that: "changes in sound were regular, and could be recovered with a fair degree of certainty [p. 169]" was made in China almost 3 centuries before the Neogrammarians reached similar conclusions in Leipzig. This knowledge in no way leads automatically to the conclusion that Chinese should be written with the Latin alphabet.

Occasionally, this alphabet bias is even detectable in the writings of modern Chinese scholars.[5] As a recent example, in discussing the problems of hanzi Xi (1979) made the following remark: "The best method of thoroughly improving such a situation, of course, is to change over to a spelling system [p. 392]."

However, in view of the fact that scientific investigations on hanzi are barely beginning, such a suggestion would seem grossly premature (Tzeng & Hung, 1980; Tzeng, Hung, & Wang, 1977; Tzeng, Hung, Cotton, & Wang, 1979). In recent years, there have been a variety of interesting findings in connection with hanzi, including the low incidence of reading disorders in Japan, the preservation of kanji over kana in aphasics, and the success in teaching hanzi to dyslexic American children in Philadelphia.

---

[5]This also applies to the popular press. Note this sentiment from the *Remin Ribao* (1980): "hanzi nanren, nanji, nanxie, bixu gaige; er yao gaige, dei zou pinyinhuade daolu." Roughly transalted: "Hanzis are difficult to learn, remember, and write, they must be reformed; the reform must take the path of phoneticization."

The hanzi constitutes a remarkable historical monument because of the light it can shed on the cultures of China over a span of several millenia. The investigations by T'sou (1981) on the role of woman in ancient times, and by Yau (1978) on element ordering in gestural languages through an analysis of the early hanzi are but some recent examples of how this resource may be creatively utilized.

In addition, the hanzi is an extremely fertile area for the study of the processing of linguistic information by the human nervous system, and it appears that a method of writing with the properties of hanzi has some unique advantages, which we are only beginning to become aware of. It may yet turn out that this ingenious scheme upon which most hanzis are based—that of presenting cues simultaneously to both the sound *and* the meaning of the word—provides the most rational foundation for most orthographies.

It has been pointed out repeatedly in the literature that the hanzi has been a bottleneck in efforts to construct typewriters, to organize literature in a large information system, and so on in ways that seem easy and convenient for alphabets. But these problems may simply be due to the fact that the level of word-processing technology has lagged behind the demands of the hanzi. The past decade has been an outburst of developments in word-processing technology, in both hardware and software, with powerful input, output, and editing capabilities. With an adequate supporting technology, the high potential of the hanzi may well be realized in the near future.

ACKNOWLEDGMENTS

An earlier version of this chapter was presented to the Conference on Communicating by Language: Orthography, Reading and Dyslexia, Bethesda, Md., September 1978. My thanks go to the organizers of that conference, J. Kavanagh and R. Venezky, for their encouragement and stimulation and to Ovid Tzeng, for numerous enlightening conversations.

REFERENCES

Cheng, R. Taiwanese morphemes in search of Chinese characters. *Journal of Chinese Linguistics,* 1978, *6,* 306-314.
Gelb, I. J. *A study of writing* (2nd ed.). Chicago: University of Chicago Press, 1952.
Greenberg, J. H. Is the vowel-consonant dichotomy universal? *Word,* 1962, *18,* 73-81.
Greenburg, J. H. *Universals of language.* Cambridge, Mass.: MIT Press, 1963.
Hashimoto, M. J. Typogeography of phonotactics and suprasegmentals in languages of the East Asian continent. *Computational Analyses of Asian and African Languages,* 1980, *13,* 153-164.
Ho, P. T. *The cradle of the east.* Chicago: University of Chicago Press, 1976.
Hummel, A. W. Phonetics and the scientific method. *Annual Report of the Libraries of Congress: Division Orientalia,* 1940.
Kim, C. -W. On the autonomy of the tensity feature in stop classification. *Word,* 1965, *21,* 339-359.

Lehiste, I. *Suprasegmentals*. Cambridge, Mass.: MIT Press, 1970.

Li, F. K. *Wuming tuyu,* (The language of Wuming.) Taipei: Institute of History and Philology. *Monograph*. A. 19, 1956.

Miller, R. A. *The Japanese language*. Chicago: University of Chicago Press, 1976.

Renmin Ribao (People's Daily). Peking, March 11, 1980.

Schmandt-Besserat, D. The earliest precursor of writing. *Scientific American*, 1978, *233*, 50–59.

Taylor, I. *The Korean writing system*. In P. A. Kolers, M. Wrolstad & H. Bouma (Eds.), *Processing of Visible Language 2*. New York: Plenum Press, 1980.

Tsien, T. -H. *Writing on bamboo and silk*. Chicago: University of Chicago Press, 1962.

T'sou, B. K. Y. A sociolinguistic analysis of the logographic writing system of Chinese. *Journal of Chinese Linguistics* 9. 1–19, 1981.

Tzeng, O. J. L., & Hung, D. L. Reading in a nonalphabetic writing system: Some experimental studies. In J. F. Kavanagh & R. L. Venezky (Eds.), *Orthography, reading and dyslexia*. Baltimore, Md.: University Park Press, 1980.

Tzeng, O. J. L., Hung, D. L., Cotton, B., & Wang, W. S. -Y. Visual lateralization effect in reading Chinese characters. *Nature*. 1979, *282*, 499–501.

Tzeng, O. J. L., Hung, D. L., & Wang, W. S. -Y. Speech recoding in reading Chinese characters. *Journal of Experimental Psychology: Human Learning and Memory*, 1977, *3*, 621–630.

Venezky, R. L. Principles for the design of practical writing systems. *Anthropological Linguistics*, 1970, *12*, 256–270.

Wang, W. S. -Y. The basis of speech. In C. E. Reed (Ed.), *The learning of language*. New York: Appleton-Century-Crofts, 1971. (a)

Wang, W. S. -Y. Review of Chinese characters and their impact on other languages of East Asian by S. H. Liu. *Modern Language Journal*, 1971, *55*, 187–188. (b)

Wang, W. S. -Y. Approaches to phonology. In T. A. Sebeok (Ed.), *Current trends in linguistics*. The Hague: Mouton, 1972.

Wang, W. S. -Y. The Chinese language. *Scientific American*, 1973, *228*, 50–60.

Washburn, S. L., & McCown, E. R. Human evolution and social science. In S. L. Washburn & E. R. McCown (Eds.), *Human evolution: Biosocial perspectives*. Menlo Park, Cal.: Benjamin/Cummings, 1978.

Wu, Y. -Z. *Report on the current tasks of reforming the written language and the draft scheme for a Chinese phonetic alphabet*. Paper delivered at the Fifth Session of the First National People's Congress, Beijing, February 1958.

Xi, B. -X. Cong lingyi jiaodu kan shengpangde biaoyin gongneng. *Zhongguo Yuwen*, 1979, *152*, 388–392. (Beijing).

Yau, S. -C. Element ordering in gestural languages and in archaic Chinese ideograms. *Cah. de Linguistic Asie Orientale*, 1978 *3*, 51–65.

Zhou, Y. -G. Xiandai hanzizhong shengpangde biaoyin gongneng wenti. *Zhongguo Yuwen*, 1978, *146*, 172–177.

11 Linguistic Determinism: A Written Language Perspective

Ovid J. L. Tzeng
Daisy L. Hung
University of California, Riverside

LINGUISTIC DETERMINISM AND VISUAL INFORMATION PROCESSING

The invention of written symbols to represent spoken language was a great achievement in human history. With the advent of writing, communication was expanded and the limitations of space and time (which are usually imposed upon oral communication) were overcome. There have been many writing systems for many different types of spoken languages. The basic design principles can be divided into two different categories. One category includes a progression from the early semasiography, which expresses a general idea in picture drawings rather than a sequence of words in a sentence, to logographs with each symbol expressing a single particular morpheme. The concept underlying the development of this type of orthography is the mapping of written symbols directly onto meaning. The second category of writing system includes a progression from the rebus system (a representation of a word or phrase by pictures that suggest how it is said in the spoken language, e.g., 👁🐝 for *idea*) to syllabaries, and then to the alphabet. The concept behind this type of orthography is sound writing. Undoubtedly, the evolution and persistence of a certain type of writing depends to a great degree on the special characteristics of its corresponding spoken language (a review of the development of various types of writing systems can be found in Hung & Tzeng, in press). Inasmuch as spoken languages differ considerably, diversity in writing systems is to be expected.

The diversity of writing systems raises an important question: Is the acquisition of reading skill either facilitated or hindered depending on how the spoken language is represented in print? This question has become a major concern among reading specialists (e.g., Gibson & Levin, 1975; Gleitman & Rozin, 1977; Liberman, Liberman, Mattingly, & Shankweiler, 1980) as well as cognitive psychologists (Biederman & Tsao, 1977; Lukatela & Turvey, 1980; Park & Arbuckle, 1977; Tzeng & Hung, 1980; Tzeng, Hung, & Garro, 1978; Tzeng, Hung, & Wang, 1977) who are interested in the effect of orthographic differences on visual information processing. It is not unreasonable to conjecture that human information-processing strategies may differ when the information is presented in different formats. For example, it has been suggested that the meaning of words and pictures are recovered via different processing routes (Paivio, 1971). Thus, depending on how meanings are represented in print (i.e., what type of writing system is used), a reader may have to develop different processing strategies in order to achieve reading proficiency. Hence, by comparing experimental results on reading behavior across languages as well as across different writing systems, we should be able to gain some insight into the various intricate processes involved in reading.

The proposal that reading different writing systems may entail different processes, which in turn impose different problems for the beginning reader, in a sense argues for a view of linguistic determinism. However, it differs from the renowned Whorfian (Whorf, 1956) hypothesis in its particular emphases on the formation of written language (rather than spoken language per se) and on processing differences (rather than production differences, which would argue for a view of linguistic relativity). The idea of such an orthography-based linguistic determinism is not new. In fact, Miller (1957), in his review of Newman's (1956) *The World of Mathematics,* has pointed out the importance of notational design in the history of mathematics. In Miller's words (1957): "In order to study the interaction of thought and symbol it is not necessary to travel with Whorf to the Zuñi Indians; the language of mathematics is rich with excellent examples. Why are Arabic numbers so superior to Roman? What do Cartesian coordinates enable us to do that was never done without them? [p. 39]." Similarly, drawing upon the interaction between symbolic innovations and mathematical advancement, we (Tzeng & Hung, 1979) have put forth the hypothesis that a notational system can be good or bad in that it may enhance or retard our thinking processes. We can readily appreciate the convenience of Arabic-numeral notation if we attempt to multiply two not too large numbers represented by Roman-numeral notation. Had it not been for the adoption of the new and more versatile ideographic symbols, many branches of mathematics could never have developed because no human mind could grasp the essence of their operation in terms of the phonograms of ordinary language or of the complex Roman numerals (Jourdain, 1956). So, sometimes our thinking is blocked not because we lack the necessary mental power, but because the graphemic symbols used to represent certain concepts happen to be clumsy and thus require a great deal of mental resource (central-processing capacity) in order to hold them in our working memory, let alone to further operate on them.

To illustrate this argument, let us take a look at an interesting example from the history of calculus, where notation is all important. Most of us are aware of the fact that calculus was invented independently by Newton and Leibnitz, but few of us realize that mathematical symbols used in most calculus texts today were the deliberate design of Leibnitz. Although undoubtedly the greatest talent and thinker of his time, Newton's notational system for calculus did not measure up to his inferential power. In retrospect, we may be able to see why his system failed to meet the challenge of later mathematical developments. For example, Newton's x, $\ddot{x}$, $\dddot{x}$, $\overset{2}{x}$, $\overset{3}{x}$, $\overset{n}{x}$ are not as neat as Leibnitz's dx, d^2x, d^4x, dx^2, dx^3, dx^n. It is easy to see that $\overset{n}{x}$ is more difficult to distinguish from x^n than dx^n is from d^nx. Similarly, Newton's $Py^r + Hy^{r-1} + hy^{r-2}$ can be written in Leibnitz's notation as $Pd^ry + Hd^{r-1}y + h^{r-2}y$. In this case, the problem with Newton's system is that in the fluxionary notation the position of r, $r-1$, $r-2$ introduces ambiguity because the symbols may be mistaken for indices of P, H, h.

But such perceptual factors, important as they can be, may only be secondary. It is the conceptual advantage of Leibnitz's notational system that makes him the most successful and influential builder of symbolic notation that the science has ever had. Take the example of the notation for the derivative dx/dy. Although not especially desirable typographically, the symbol nevertheless commands at the present time a wider adoption than its many rivals. The main reasons for this are the flexibility of the symbols, the ease with which one passes from the derivative to the differential by the application of simple algebraic processes, and the intuitional suggestion of the characteristic right triangle that has dy and dx as the two perpendicular sides. In fact, these symbols readily call to mind ideas that reach to the very heart of geometric and mechanical applications of calculus. British mathematicians, honoring Newton, refused to use Leibnitz's notation, and for that they had to face grave consequences. According to Jourdain (1956), one of the greatest experts on the history of mathematics:

> . . . for considerably more than a century, British mathematicians failed to perceive the great superiority of Leibnitz' notation. . . . Thus, while. . . . Continental mathematicians were rapidly extending knowledge by using the infinitesimal calculus in all branches of pure and applied mathematics, in England comparatively little progress was made. It was not until the beginning of the nineteenth century that there was formed, at Cambridge, a Society to introduce and spread the use of Leibnitz' notation among British mathematicians [p. 59].

This historical account emphasizes the importance of notational design, and we may add another commentary note: It is just not enough to have good ideas without also having good notations.

Such a linguistic-deterministic view of notation inevitably leads to a further claim. That is, metaphorically speaking, a good notational system, once formed, seems to have an independent existence and an intelligence of its own. Not only does it provide a framework for us to operate on certain mathematical concepts, it also opens up a host of unforeseen opportunities and directions for the further development of these concepts. In some sense, these notational symbols are much wiser than their inventors. Bertram Russell cogently puts it this way: "...A good notation has a subtlety and suggestiveness which at times make it seem almost like a live teacher (cited in Newman, 1956, *p.* 1856)." Humans stand alone in history as the sole creatures on earth to invent written symbols and to benefit from them also. It is curious and pitiful that psychologists have paid little attention to such an intricate symbol-thought interaction.

Another important aspect of our orthography-based linguistic determinism is its emphasis on processing rather than on production differences. That is, we are not arguing that the ultimate semantic structures would differ just because different notational systems are used to create them. After all, mathematical computation should be understood to be completely independent of the particular way it is physically realized. But this in no way denies the possibility that the same understanding may be achieved via different mental processes. For instance, a text can be analyzed into a set of coherent propositions, which in turn can be represented in either a graphic layout with connecting nodes (Rumelhart, Lindsay, & Norman, 1972) or a sequential list of arguments and relations (Kintsch, 1974). A similar text base can be recovered from either representation. However, these different representations have different functional values and may require different processing assumptions (Anderson, 1978). Therefore, a linguistic determinism with emphasis on processing rather than production differences needs not necessarily lead to the conclusion of linguistic relativity.

Such a hypothesis of linguistic determinism should not be limited to the area of mathematics where the advancements involve only a handful of talented mathematicians. The hypothesis should include equally strong statements concerning the design of writing systems, and its predictive power should be easily applicable to the behavior in reading various types of scripts. After all, written languages are no more than special types of notations. Unlike spoken languages, which are part and parcel of our organismic structure, they are the intentional creation of human beings to expand the act of communication. Sliding our tongues and maneuvering air through our superlaryngeal tracts are no more foereign to us than programming one's own arms to move, wave, grasp, or make gestures. Using written language to communicate, on the other hand, requires the utilization of something external to us: conventional notation systems invented by human beings. Inasmuch as these new notational symbols are arbitrary inventions external to our organismic structure, both accommodation and assimilation processes must have worked at their extremes in order for us to achieve efficiency in manipulating them. For example, our visual system is biologically wired (Fowler, Chapter 8, this volume) for the perception of three-dimensional objects. The invention of written language requires a totally new visual information-processing strategy. We are now required to extract linguistic substance out of a two-dimensional arrangement. In this sense, we have to accommodate to its linguistic characteristics. Different writing systems have different script-speech relationships. Our visual information-processing system has to adjust to cope with these variations. As long as a nontrivial relationship between the orthographic structure and our cognitive strategy is exhibited, a linguistic determinism is implicated. Thus, the validity of our hypothesis about notational design can be tested by examining the effect of orthographic variations on visual information processing. Before we review empirical data bearing on this issue, let us take a look at various script-speech relationships embedded in different writing systems.

RELATIONS BETWEEN SCRIPT AND SPEECH

The relationship between written scripts and spoken languages seems so close that one would expect that anyone who is able to speak and see should be able to read. But this simply is not the case. For all normal children, learning a spoken language seems to require no special effort. However, learning to read requires a relatively long period of special training and depends heavily on intelligence, motivation, and other sociocultural factors. Even with so much effort being directed toward the acquisition of reading skills, not every child can learn how to read. Gleitman and Rozin (1977) have summarized the state of affairs by saying: "The problem with reading is not a visual perceptual problem; the problem is rather that the eye is not biologically adapted to language [p. 37]."

There is a general consensus that written languages evolved much later than spoken languages and that, in some way, the former attempted to mimic the latter. In fact, except for the earlier semasiography (dating back at least as far as 20,000 B.C.), which used pictorial representations to refer directly to meaning, most of today's writing systems are parasitic on their corresponding spoken language in various forms. Inasmuch as their development is based largely on speech, the scripts are all correlated with the preexisting units of the spoken languages. But the exact nature of the correlation varies across languages. That is, because there are many levels of representation for spoken language, the transcription of visual symbols into spoken language can be achieved in many different ways. Let us examine these relationships more closely.

If we look back at the history of writing, we soon discover that the appearance of various types of writing systems proceeds in a certain direction. In a sense, the transcription initially starts at the deepest level, the conceptual gist (e.g., picture drawings). Then it gradually shifts outward to the surface level, the sounds. At each step, the unique and concrete ways of representing meaning give way to a smaller but more general set of written symbols. In other words, the efficiency of writing is achieved at the cost of sacrificing the more direct link to the underlying meaning, and consequently, the grapheme-meaning relationship becomes more and more abstract. Some concrete examples can make this clearer.

Ancient people wrote (or more precisely, carved) on rocks, tortoise shells, cave walls, and the like to communicate. These drawings were usually pictures of objects, which immediately evoked meaningful interpretations. A general idea (sememe), rather than a sequence of words in a sentence, is expressed by object drawing. Thus, in this sense, semasiography "writes" concepts directly without the mediation of spoken language. Obviously, picture writing has apparent shortcomings: (1) not everyone is capable of drawing well; (2) it is difficult to draw pictures that express abstract concepts; (3) different ways of arranging objects within a picture result in different interpretations; (4) an unambiguous picture (e.g., a map telling the location of food resources) can be read by anyone, including enemies who may speak a different language. Thus, new systems had to be invented.

The next step is important and shows insight. Instead of expressing a general idea by drawing, written symbols were invented to represent the spoken language directly. First, there were pictograms carried over from the previous stage of picture drawing. Then, there were ideograms, which were frequently formed by putting several pictograms together to suggest an idea. For instance, putting two trees together side by side could mean *woods,* and stacking three trees together could mean *forest.* But even with this new invention, there were still difficulties with the formation of characters to represent abstract concepts.

This need led to the invention of phonograms that were typically made up of two or more components, one of which was used not for its semantic content but for its phonetic value. The reader gets a hint as to the character's meaning from the semantic component (called the signific) and as to its sound from the phonetic component. With these three methods and combinations thereof, virtually an infinite number of characters can be created to represent all the words used in the spoken language. This is exactly how the Chinese logographic system was formed. Similar principles were also used in ancient Egyptian Hieroglyphika and Hieratika.

It should be noted that linguistically logographic symbols map onto spoken language at the morphemic level. Such a one-to-one grapheme-morpheme relationship requires that for all imaginable linguistic terms there must be distinctive characters corresponding to the underlying morphemes. The inevitable consequence is that one has to learn and memorize thousands of these distinctive characters before he or she is able to read. Thus, from the very beginning, literacy in a logographic system took a tremendous amount of both visual discrimination and memorization. Students deficient in performing these tasks usually lag behind their classmates in schoolwork, reading included.

For some languages, only short steps are needed in going from phonograms, to the rebus system, and then to the syllabary system in which every written symbol denotes a syllable in the spoken language. Thus, a relatively small set of syllable-based symbols can be used to transcribe an infinite number of spoken sentences. Economical writing is accomplished, and the unit of written language coincides with that of the spoken language (Gleitman & Rozin, 1977). However, there immediately arises the problem of homophones, which are indeed a nuisance even with the contextual cues provided (Venezky, 1970). Japanese syllabaries resolve the problem of homophones by retaining Chinese logographs (called kanji), which are used primarily for content words, and by using kana syllabic symbols mainly for grammatical purposes (called hiragana) and for transcribing foreign words (called katakana). As these three types of scripts have distinctive writing styles, the problem of homophones is further reduced by visual cues. On the other hand, all of the difficulties associated with logographic script arise once again. It is no wonder that over the last 30 years, the Japanese government has been making every effort to eliminate the use of Chinese characters in their writing. However, the close grapheme-morpheme relationship represented in Chinese characters does have enough intrinsic value in facilitating visual reading that these attempts to abandon Chinese characters have not been very successful. Ironically, instead of reducing the number of kanji characters, the Ministry of Education was forced to increase their allowable list of frequently used characters by five.

Other Indo-European syllabaries moved to an alphabetical system with the number of written symbols further reduced. A full alphabet, marking vowel as well as consonant phonemes, developed over a period of 200 years during the first millenium B.C. in Greece (Kroeber, 1948). The transition from the syllabary system to the alphabetical system marks another gigantic jump with respect to the script-speech relationship. As a sound-writing script, an alphabetical system with its further reduced set of graphic symbols (i.e., letters or letter groups) maps onto speech at the level of the phoneme, a linguistic unit smaller than the syllable but larger than the articulatory feature. The problem of homophones is solved in some languages (e.g., English) by simultaneously taking into account the lexical root of each word. As a consequence, the grapheme-sound relationship becomes opaque. As C. Chomsky (1970) points out:

> English orthography represents linguistic knowledge on different levels. In particular, there is a phonological level and a morphological level. The same sound can often be represented by different letters. Which letters are chosen is then decided on a morphological basis: e.g., "sign" could be spelled sign, syne, cyne, etc. If it relates to "signature" in meaning, then its spelling must be sign [p. 305].

Thus, the grapheme-speech relationship embedded in an alphabetical system is characterized as a morphophonemic representation.

There is an important contrast between logographic and alphabetical scripts with respect to how symbols are stacked together to represent the spoken language graphically. For example, in Englsh script, spaces are largely determined on the basis of words, whereas in Chinese script the spacing is based on morphemes, and each morpheme is in fact a syllable (Wang, Chapter 10, this volume). Perceptually, the grapheme-sound mapping in Chinese is discrete, whereas in English script the relation is continuous and at a more abstract level. This difference may have different implications for beginning readers of these two scripts. For Chinese children, the written array is dissected syllable-by-syllable and thus has a one-to-one correspondence with the syllabic boundaries of the spoken language. Because of the multilevel representation, a reader of English, on the other hand, may have to go through a morphophonemic process in which: (1) words are first parsed into morphemes; and then (2) symbol-sound relationships can apply (Venezky, 1970). Furthermore, phonological rules are necessary in order to derive the phonetic form (e.g., to get /sain/ for sign). These processes seem very abstract and hence may be quite difficult for a beginning reader to go through.

As we look back at these historical changes, we see that the evolution of written scripts does appear to take a single direction: At every advance, the number of symbols in the script decreases, and as a direct consequence, the abstractness of the relationship between script and speech increases. This pattern of development seems to parallel the general trend of cognitive development in children. Results from two independent lines of research are of particular interest to us. First, anthropological studies (Laboratory of Comparative Human Cognition, 1979) have shown that children's conceptualization of the printed arrays in a text proceeds from pictures, to ideas, to syllables, and finally to "wordness." Second, according to Gibson (1977), one of the major trends in children's perceptual development is the increasing specificity of correspondence between what is perceived and information contained in stimulation. This occurs as a beginning reader progresses from the whole to the differentiation of the whole, and then to the synthesis of the parts to a more meaningful whole. In a sense, the ontogeny of cognitive behavior seems to recapitulate the evolutionary history of writing systems. Certainly, this cannot be a simple biological coincidence (cf. Gleitman & Rozin, 1977). Such parallelism indicates the importance of a match between the reader's cognitive ability and the task demands imposed by the specific orthographic structure of the script to be read. Once again, these theoretical analyses lead us to conclude a linguistic determinism advocated earlier. Now we should search for its empirical support.

EFFECTS OF ORTHOGRAPHIC VARIATIONS
ON VISUAL INFORMATION PROCESSING

We have reviewed the historical background for the development of various types of written scripts. We have also briefly discussed the linguistic status of each of the major orthographies in terms of its embedded script-speech relationship. Our concern now is to what extent these orthographic variations affect our visual information processing. Several major issues have been investigated by cognitive psychologists and reading researchers. Let us critically review these issues and their associated studies with respect to our hypothesis of linguistic determinism.

Reading Disability

Although the problem of reading disability is pervasive in languages adopting the alphabetical principle (e.g., English, German etc.), the rarity of reading disability in school children has been reported in languages adopting syllabic and logographic systems (Makita, 1968; Tzeng & Hung, 1980). Makita attributes the success of Japanese initial reading instruction to the fact that kana scripts have a one-to-one grapheme-sound correspondence. Sakamoto and Makita (1973) further show that many Japanese children learn kana symbols without formal instruction before they enter school.

On the other hand, Tzeng and Hung (1980) attempt to account for the success of Chinese instruction in terms of linguistic considerations. They point out that Chinese, as a logographic script, is meant to express a single particular morpheme while ignoring many grammatical marking elements (e.g., *I want go* instead of *I wanted to go*). That is, the character remains the same regardless of syntactic changes. In Chinese, the character-speech mapping is morphosyllabic in nature. Thus, for Chinese children, learning to read simply means learning to associate each spoken syllable with a particular character of a designated meaning. In general, the orientation and the number of strokes that form the basis of a character bear no relationship to the sound of the spoken word. Even though the majority of modern Chinese characters are phonograms (Wang, Chapter 10, this volume), the success rate of using a base character to sound out another character is estimated to be low (less than 39% according to an analysis by Zhou, 1978). This lack of symbol-to-sound correspondence provides beginning readers with a most straightforward way (and probably the only way) to master thousands of distinctive characters, namely, rote memorization. This situation is very different from learning an alphabetical script by extracting orthographic regularities embedded in written words in order to figure out the letter-sound correspondence rules. Therefore, beginning readers of Chinese (at a time when the number of characters to be memorized is still limited) face a more concrete learning situation than those who are learning the alphabetical writing system. The ease of acquiring the logographic system is further attested by a widely cited study in Philadelphia where a group of second-grade school children with serious reading problems that had resisted acquisition even after extensive tutoring by conventional methods were able to make rapid progress in learning and reading materials written in Chinese characters (Rozin, Poritsky, & Sotsky, 1971).

Although the evidence seems impressive, one has to be cautious when interpreting results reported in the aforementioned studies. The study reported by Makita (1968) and the one cited in Tzeng and Hung (1980) were both crude survey reports. Questionnaires were sent to school teachers, and predesignated questions were framed in a manner far from satisfactory. Moreover, in both Japan and Taiwan—where literacy is highly valued and where social pressures keep schools conscious of their public image—a simple survey on reading disability can never tell the whole story. For one thing, Makita claimed that kana is easy to learn because it maps onto the sound at the syllable level. However, linguistic analysis shows that kana actually maps onto the sound at the mora level (Wang, Chapter 10, this volume), a smaller but more abstract unit than the syllable. And there is a report that Japanese children do have problems dealing with mora (Sakamoto, 1980). Furthermore, different countries have different criteria for reading disability.

Thus, the evidence provided by Makita and by Tzeng and Hung, in the absence of appropriate cross-cultural control, cannot be intrepreted too enthusiastically. Rozin et al.'s (1971) data are interesting, but methodological weaknesses make them less impressive than at first appearance. Other criticisms have been advanced in Tzeng et al. (1977). It is important to understand that learning a limited number of Chinese characters does not qualify a person as a successful learner of Chinese. The essential difficulty of learning Chinese scripts lies in its huge number of distinctive characters. Rozin et al.'s success in teaching second-grade nonreaders in English to read "first-grade" or lower materials in Chinese is hardly surprising.

Overall, there seem to be hints that the problem of reading disability may indeed be related to the orthographic structure of the written scripts. Nevertheless, stronger evidence with appropriate cross-cultural controls still remains to be established.

Neuropsychological Differences

We have mentioned that Japanese uses three different scripts to represent text, and a fluent reader has to know all three types. Sasanuma and her associates (for a more detailed review of Sasanuma's work, see Hung & Tzeng, in press) have presented evidence showing that the ability of Japanese aphasic patients to use kanji and kana scripts may be selectively related to the specific type of aphasic disorder. Careful examination of the patients' performance suggested that impairment of kana processing typically occurred in the context of the overall syndrome known as Broca's aphasia, whereas impairment of kanji was characteristic of Gogi (word-meaning) aphasia. The implication is that phonetic-based scripts such as kana and logographic-based scripts such as kanji require different brain locations in their visual information processing.

But this structural interpretation may not be necessary. Empirical research with Chinese characters by Tzeng et al. (1977) and the ongoing research into the relationship between reading and speech by the Haskins group (Liberman, Shankweiler, Liberman, Fowler & Fischer 1977) point to the importance of the auditory short-term store as necessary to primary linguistic activity such as comprehension. In addition, the research indicates that morphological information may require phonetic storage at an intermediate stage of processing. The results reported by Sasanuma and her associates (Sasanuma, 1974; Sasanuma, Itoh, Mori, Kobayashi, 1977) may be interpreted not as independent neural processing of the phonetic and morphemic components, but as differential realization of two levels of linguistic awareness (Erickson, Mattingly, & Turvey, 1972). Although clinical evidence such as that just mentioned is limited in generalizability, the observation of selective impairment of reading kanji and kana scripts among the Japanese aphasic patients nevertheless demonstrates that each script imposes differential task demands.

Sasanuma's (1974) findings quickly prompted another series of studies concerned with whether the visual lateralization effect (i.e., hemispheric dominance) would show differential patterns depending on whether phonetic scripts (e.g., Japanese kana, English alphabet, etc.) or logographic scripts (e.g., Chinese logographic and Arabic numerals) are employed as stimuli. The term "lateralization" refers to the different functions of the left or right cerebral hemispheres. Mishkin and Forgays (1952) tachistoscopically exposed English words to either the right visual field (RVF) or left visual field (LVF) and found a differential accuracy of recognition that favored words presented to the RVF, suggesting a left hemisphere superiority effect. On the other hand, research investigating whether the asymmetric visual field effects are subject to the influence of variations in the orthographic structure generally reports a different pattern. For instance, processing Yiddish words has been found to show a left visual field advantage, and the habit of visual scanning during reading was suggested to assume an important role in the visual half-field experiment (Orbach, 1953).

The unique styles of kanji and kana symbols provide a testing ground for theories of cerebral organization. Hirata and Osaka (1967) and Hatta (1976) found a superior performance of the left hemisphere in the processing of kana symbols. This result is similar to those obtained with alphabetical writing. Recently, Hatta (1977) reported an experiment measuring recognition accuracy of kanji characters and found a LVF (right hemisphere) superiority for kanji characters both high and low in familiarity. Also using a recognition procedure, Sasanuma, Itoh, Mori, and Kobayashi (1977) presented kana and kanji words to normal subjects and found a significant RVF superiority for the recognition of kana words but a nonsignificant trend of LVF superiority for kanji characters. Thus, it seems that for sound-based symbols such as English words and Japanese kana scripts, a RVF-LH superiority effect is to be expected in a tachistoscopic recognition task, whereas a LVF-RH superiority effect is to be expected for the recognition of kanji logographs.

Controversy immediately arises concerning the reliability of the kanji effect. Previous experiments conducted by Kershner and Jeng (1972) and by Hardyck, Tzeng, and Wang (1977) with Chinese subjects reported significant RVF superiority effect in the processing of Chinese characters. Thus, the cerebral orthography-specific localization hypothesis proposed by Hatta (1977) is questionable. A recent study by Tzeng et al. (1979) shed light on this issue. They found that, in fact, the LVF superiority was only obtained with recognition of single characters; a RVF advantage similar to that obtained with alphabetical materials was observed when two or more characters that make up a linguistic term were used. Tzeng et al. interpreted these differential visual lateralization effects as reflecting the function-specific property of the two hemispheres and rejected the orthography-specific localization hypothesis. This interpretation was further supported by Elman's (personal communication) results showing that even with single characters, only the simple naming task showed a LVF right hemisphere dominance; a more complicated grammatical classification task showed a left hemisphere dominance. Therefore, the evidence for differential brain functions in processing phonetically based and logographic scripts does seem to be strong insofar as these functions are interpreted with respect to differential demands imposed by the scripts.

Differential Processing Mechanisms and the Behavioral Consequences

One research issue concerns whether different processing mechanisms are activated in reading different scripts and the behavioral consequences, if any, of being literate in various writing systems. With respect to the first question, Besner and Coltheart (1979) have provided positive answers by showing that making quantitative comparisons between two numbers may engage different processing mechanisms depending on whether these numbers are presented in Arabic numerals (logographic symbols) or in spelled-out English letters. Their data showed that comparing two Arabic numerals was subject to the interference of size incongruence, whereas comparing two spelled-out numbers was not. Similar size-incongruence interference occurs in a comparative judgment task (Paivio, 1975) when the two to-be-compared items are presented in picture form but not as spelled-out words. These findings indicate that different lexical retrieval routes are activated in order to perform the comparative judgment task (Paivio, 1975). Thus, depending on how meanings are represented in print, a reader may have to develop different processing strategies in order to achieve proficiency.

To tap into these different processing mechanisms, Turnage and McGinnies (1973) asked Chinese and American College students to study a list of 15 words in a serial learning paradigm. They also manipulated the input modality of the stimulus presentation. It was found that Chinese students learned the character list faster when it was presented visually, whereas American students learned the word list faster when it was presented auditorily. The finding on the Chinese characters opposes the famous modality effect (Crowder, 1978) in which auditory presentation of English words results in better recall than does visual presentation. The interpretation offered by Turnage and McGinnies (1973) is that Chinese logographs contain more characters with similar sounds but different meanings than is the case for English, and this characteristic of the orthographic structure may favor learning through the visual mode.

Turnage and McGinnies' (1973) study involved two different language populations wherein both the scripts and the spoken language differed. The script may not be the determining factor, but rather the visual modality advantage could have been a result of differences in spoken languages. However, this interpretation was soon ruled out by a study comparing the learning rate of Korean words written in either Chinese characters or Korean hangul (an alphabetical script, see Wang, Chapter 10, this volume). Koreans can transcribe their spoken language in either script. Park and Arbuckle (1977) examined the memory of Korean subjects for words written in these two types of systems. They found that words presented in logographic script were remembered better than words presented in alphabetical script on recognition and free recall but not on paired-associate recall or serial anticipation. Thus, there is indeed an intrinsic difference with respect to the processing mechanism for these two scripts, and these differences do not appear to be associative in nature.

But the most impressive line of research thus far has been provided by Scribner and Cole (1978) in their ethnographic study on the cognitive consequences for tribal Vai (in Africa) adults of becoming literate in Vai or Arabic. An analysis of the process of reading the Vai syllabary indicated that special task demands are imposed by the script. Vai is a tone language, but tonal information is not marked in the script. Furthermore, no word boundaries or punctuation are indicated in writing a text, so the reader must group the syllables together to form words, and then again integrate these into meaningful linguistic units. On the other hand, the Arabic script is an alphabetical system that is learned mainly through a rote memory process (the students don't understand or speak Arabic). When students of these two rather different scripts were tested in various cognitive tasks, Vai and Arabic literates did not differ in their ability to comprehend the words strings, but Vai literates were superior on the picture reading and syllable integration tasks, which mimicked their normal reading activities. In contrast, Arabic literates performed better than Vai literates on the incremental memory task, which presented task demands most similar to their normal reading activities.

These results indicate not only that different scripts impose different task requirements for achieving proficiency, but also that strategies developed to meet these requirements are transferable to situations with similar task requirements. Therefore, Scribner and Cole (1978) provide rather strong evidence for our hypothesis that becoming literate in certain scripts can have a long-lasting effect in molding the information-processing system.

Speech Recoding in Reading

When people read to themselves, do they recode the visual input into some sort of speechlike code (i.e., articulatory, acoustic, or both)? The existence of such recoding is no longer in doubt (Baron & Treiman, 1980; Tzeng & Hung, 1980). The question now facing us is why. What factors encourage its use and what factors discourage it? Orthographies vary considerably in the demands they place on the reader. According to Liberman et al., (1980), one of the aspects of such variations is the depth of the orthography, which can be defined as the relative distance between an orthography and its phonetic representation. For example, compared with Vietnamese, English is a rather deep orthography and thus demands greater phonological development on the reader's part. It is quite possible that differences in orthographies along this dimension affect the use of speech recoding in silent reading. If the written forms on the page stand in a regular relationship to the sounds of language, the reader may use the grapheme-sound rules to help derive the meanings of words. Such a path would be difficult for readers of Chinese to follow, but it would be very possible for readers of English. Therefore, we would expcet English readers to engage in speech recoding more than Chinese readers (Treiman, Baron, & Luk, 1981).

The investigation into the relationship between the degree of speech recoding and the depth of orthography is an important one. By finding differences among orthographies along the dimension of grapheme-sound regularity, we can demonstrate the existence of some speech recoding in at least one of the orthographies studied. For example, Treiman et al.'s (1981) finding that more speech recoding occurs in alphabetical than in logographic scripts (as indexed by longer reaction times and/or more mistakes in judging homophone sentences) enables us to conclude that some speech recoding does occur in reading alphabetical scripts. Once this fact is established, we can begin to provide accounts of the possible pathways (causal links among mental representations) between representations of print, speech, and meaning. For researchers who attempt to build cognitive models in terms of reading behavior, knowing the effect of the orthographic structure on the relations of these pathways should be one of their ultimate goals. So far, we know that whether or not a certain path will be bypassed or activated depends on the orthographic structure of the script one is reading. But the precise relationships are still far from clear.

Bilingual Processing

Our final issue concerns research in bilingual processing. In the past, bilingual studies have always dealt with spoken languages. There has been little concern with the possibility that experimental results may be contaminated to various degrees by variations in the orthographic structure. Recently, Biederman and Tsao (1979) reported a study in which they found that a greater interference effect was observed for Chinese subjects engaging in a Chinese-version Stroop-color naming task than for American subjects in an English-version. They attributed this difference to the possibility that there may be fundamental differences in the perceptual demands of reading Chinese and English.

Prompted by the intriguing finding of Biederman and Tsao (1979), Fang, Tzeng, and Alva (in press) went one step further and ran a modified version of the Stroop experiment. They asked Chinese-English bilingual subjects to name colors in either Chinese or English on a Chinese version or an English version of the Stroop test. They found a reduction of the interference effect in the interlanguage condition (i.e., responding in Chinese on the English version or vice versa) as compared to the intralanguage condition. Fang et al. also conducted another experiment using Spanish-English bilinguals with either an English or Spanish version Stroop test. Again the reduction of the Stroop interference was observed in the interlanguage condition as compared to the intralanguage condition. When data were further analyzed they found that although both experiments showed a reduction of interference in the interlanguage condition, the magnitude of reduction was greater in the Chinese-English experiment than in the Spanish-English experiment. Inasmuch as Spanish and English are both alphabetical scripts, switching languages does not change the processing demands. However, as English and Chinese represent two different orthographic structures, switching from one to the other may prevent subjects from employing the same processing mechanism and consequently cause them to be released from the Stroop effect.

Fang et al. (in press) also made an interesting observation. Using Dyer's (1971) and Preston and Lambert's (1969) bilingual data, they recalculated the magnitude of reduction of the Stroop interference from the intra- to the interlanguage condition. All together, there were six types of bilingual subjects: Chinese-English, Japanese-English (kanji and kana), French-English, German-English, Hungarian-English, and Spanish-English bilinguals. Fang et al. ranked these bilingual data according to the magnitude of reduction from intra to interlanguage condition. The result is as follows: Chinese-English, Japanese-English (with kanji), Japanese-English (with kana), Hungarian-English, Spanish-English, German-English, and French-English. This ordering suggests that the magnitude of reduction (from intra- to interlanguage) depends on the degree of similarity between the orthographic structures of the two tested languages. Thus, bilingual processing is definitely affected by the orthographic factor, and it seems fair to say that the curious neglect of the orthographic factor in previous bilingual research is an unfortunate mistake. How can we resolve the independent versus interdependent lexica issue without taking into account variations in the orthographic structure?

CONCLUSION

The theoretical concern for the relationship between language and thought has a long history, spanning from Aristotle's classical view that thought determines language to the Whorfian (1956) hypothesis that language determines thought. In between these extreme views is Watson (1930), the behaviorist, who claims that thought is language. Empirical evidence and philosophical speculations for or against any of these three views has filled many volumes of anthropological, linguistic, philosophical, and psychological publications.

As with many other behavioral phenomena, the final true account seems to be the inevitable *all of the above* (Jenkins, 1969). But such an answer is hardly satisfactory. It amounts to little in the way of scientific accomplishment. We think the difficulty of resolving the language-thought issue does not lie in specifying the relationship between language and thought. Rather, the difficulty emerges as a result of the ambiguity and confusion in the ways one talks about language behaviors on the one hand and thought (product or process?) on the other. Without specifying the precise meaning of these terms, how can we expect to make any sensible statement concerning the relationship between language and thought? It is no wonder that one camp argues for thought determinism based on the observation of linguistic universals, and the other camp argues for linguistic determinism based on the observation of linguistic diversities. And how can anyone dismiss Watson's position that language is thought just because he happens to define thought as ''nothing more'' than some reduced form of peripheral activity?

In this chapter, we take the case of written language as our starting point to reexamine the relation between thought and language. Inasmuch as different writing systems have different orthographic structures with respect to the script-speech mapping rules, we can precisely define language variations in terms of various grapheme-meaning schemes embedded in the design of different writing systems. Such a conceptualization enables us to establish three major orthographic designs: the logographic, the syllabary, and the alphabetical orthographies. Further analyses reveal that these three orthographies impose different task demands on their readers. A view of linguistic determinism seems to be indicated.

The next step is to define what we mean by thought process. We should point out that our concern is not with the final product of thinking and that at this point we consider the ultimate semantic structure as irrelevant. We are more interested in whether different processing constraints will be built up in our visual information-processing system when we learn to read different writing systems.

It is true that defining thought categories in terms of end products is not an easy job. But for the specification of processing differences in thinking, we can follow the established paradigms in the information-processing approach to cognition. In fact, we have been able to identify five major issues in information-processing research, which are relevant to the issue of orthography. From the review of previous findings in the literature and from the results of our own experiments, we see that orthographic variations affect cerebral processing, memory functions, problem-solving strategies, lexical access pathways, and the lexical organization of bilingual subjects. In other words, the linguistic-deterministic view does have much empirical support. Let us paraphrase Carroll's (1969, p. 239) statement (which paraphrased Jenkins' statement) in the following way: The human information-processing system has been found to depend on written language to the extent that it happens to use the machinery of that particular communicative system.

REFERENCES

Anderson, J. R. Arguments concerning representations for mental imagery. *Psychological Review*, 1978, *85*, 249–277.

Baron, J., & Treiman, R. Use of orthography in reading and learning to read. In J. F. Kavanagh & R. L. Venezky (Eds.), *Orthography, reading, and dyslexia*. Baltimore, Md.: University Park Press, 1980.

Besner, D., & Coltheart, M. Ideographic and alphabetic processing in skilled reading of English. *Neuropsychologia*, 1979, *17*, 467–472.

Biederman, I., & Tsao, Y. C. On processing Chinese ideographs and English Words: Some implications from Stroop-test results. *Cognitive Psychology*, 1979, *11*, 125–132.

Carroll, J. B. Reflections on language and through: Discussion of Prof. Jenkins' paper. In J. F. Voss (Ed.), *Approaches to thought*. Columbus, Oh.: Merrill, 1969.

Chomsky, C. Reading, writing and phonology. *Harvard Educational Review*, 1970, *40*, 287–309.

Crowder, R. G. Memory for phonologically uniform lists. *Journal of Verbal Learning and Verbal Behavior*, 1978, *17*, 73–89.

Dyer, F. N. Color-naming interference in monolinguals and bilinguals. *Journal of Verbal Learning and Verbal Behavior*, 1971, *10*, 297–302.

Erickson, D., Mattingly, I. G., & Turvey, M. Phonetic coding of Kanji. *Journal of the Acoustical Society of America*, 1972, *52*, 33.

Fang, S. P., Tzeng, O. J. L., & Alva, E. Intra- versus inter-language Stroop interference effects in bilingual subjects. *Memory & Cognition,* in press.

Gibson, E. J. How perception really develops: A view from outside the network. In D. LaBerge & S. J. Samuels (Eds.), *Basic processes in reading: Perception and comprehension*. Hillsdale, N.J.: Lawrence Erlbaum Associates, 1977.

Gibson, E. J., & Levin, H. *The psychology of reading*. Cambridge, Mass.: MIT Press, 1975.

Gleitman, L. R., & Rozin, P. The structure and acquisition of reading: Relation between orthography and the structure of language. In A. S. Reber & D. L. Scarborough (Eds.), *Toward a psychology of reading: The proceedings of the CUNY Conferences*. Hillsdale, N.J.: Lawrence Erlbaum Associates, 1977.

Hardyck, C., Tzeng, O. J. L., & Wang, W. S-Y. Cerebral lateralization effects in visual half-field experiments. *Nature*, 1977, *269*, 705–707.

Hatta, T. Asynchrony of lateral onset as a factor in difference in visual field. *Perceptual and Motor skill*, 1976, *42*, 163–166.

Hatta, T. Recognition of Japanese Kanji in the left and right visual field. *Neuropsychologia*, 1977, *15*, 685–688.

Hirata, K., & Osaka, R. Tachistoscopic recognition of Japanese letter materials in left and right visual field. *Psychologia*, 1967, *10*, 17–18.

Hung, D. L., & Tzeng, O. J. L. Orthographic variations and visual information processing. *Psychological Bulletin,* in press.

Jenkins, J. J. Language and thought. In J. F. Voss (Ed.), *Approaches to thought*. Columbus, Oh.: Merrill, 1969.

Jourdain, P. E. The nature of mathematics. In J. R. Newman (Ed.), *The world of mathematics*. New York: Simon & Schuster, 1956.

Kershner, J., & Jeng, A. Dual functional hemispheric asymmetry in visual perception: Effects of ocular dominance and post-exposural processes. *Neuropsychologia*, 1972, *10*, 437–445.

Kintsch, W. *The representation of meaning in memory*. Hillsdale, N.J.: Lawrence Erlbaum Associates, 1974.

Kroeber, A. L. *Anthropology: Race, language, culture, psychology, prehistory* (new rev. ed.). New York: Harcourt Brace, 1948.

Laboratory of Comparative Human Cognition. What's cultural about cross-cultural cognitive psychology? *Annual Review of Psychology*, 1979, *30*, 145–172.

Liberman, I. Y., Shankweiler, D., Liberman, A. M., Fowler, C., & Fischer, F. W. Phonetic segmentation and recoding in the beginning reader. In A. S. Reber & D. Scarborough (Eds.), *Toward a psychology of reading: The proceedings of the CUNY Conference*. Hillsdale, N.J.: Lawrence Erlbaum Associates. 1977.

Liberman, I. Y., Liberman, A. M., Mattingly, I. G., & Shankweiler, D. Orthography and the beginning reader. In J. F. Kavanagh & R. L. Venezky (Eds.), *Orthography, reading and dyslexia*. Baltimore, Md.: University Park Press, 1980.

Lukatela, G., & Turvey, M. T. Some experiments on the Roman and Cyrillic alphabets of Serbo-Croatian. In J. F. Kavanagh & R. L. Venezky (Eds.), *Orthography, reading, and dyslexia*. Baltimore, Md.: University Park Press, 1980.

Makita, K. The rarity of reading disability in Japanese children. *American Journal of Orthopsychiatry*, 1968, *38*, 599–614.

Miller, G. A. The mathematician who counted. *Contemporary Psychology*, 1957, *2*, 38–39.

Mishkin, M., & Forgays, G. D. Word recognition as a function of retrieval locus. *Journal of Experimental Psychology*, 1952, *43*, 43–48.

Orbach, J. Retinal locus as a factor in the recognition of visually perceived word. *American Journal of Psychology*, 1953, *65*, 555–562.

Newman, J. R. (Ed.). *The world of mathematics* (4 vols.). New York: Simon & Schuster, 1956.

Paivio, A. *Imagery and verbal processes*. New York: Holt, Rinehart & Winston, 1971.

Paivio, A. Perceptual comparisons through the mind's eye. *Memory & Cognition*, 1975, *3*, 635–647.

Park, S., & Arbuckle, T. Y. Ideograms versus alphabets: Effects of script on memory in "biscriptual" Korean subjects. *Journal of Experimental Psychology: Human Learning and Memory*, 1977, *3*, 631–642.

Preston, M. S., & Lambert, W. E. Interlingual interference in a bilingual version of the Stroop color-word task. *Journal of Verbal Learning and Verbal Behavior*, 1969, *8*, 295–301.

Rozin, P., Poritsky, S., & Sotsky, R. American children with reading problems can easily learn to read English represented by Chinese characters. *Science*, 1971, *171*, 1264–1267.

Rumelhart, D. E., Lindsay, P. H., & Norman, D. A. A process model for long-term memory. In E. Tulving & W. Donaldson (Eds.), *Organization of memory*. New York: Academic Press, 1972.

Sakamoto, T. Reading of Hiragana. In J. F. Kavanagh & R. L. Venezky (Eds.), *Orthography, reading and dyslexia*, Baltimore, Md.: University Park Press, 1980.

Sakamoto, T., & Makita, K. Japan, In J. Downing (Ed.), *Comparative reading: Cross national studies of behavior and processes in reading and writing*. New York: Macmillan, 1973.

Sasanuma, S. Impairment of written language in Japanese aphasics: Kana versus Kanji processing. *Journal of Chinese Linguistics*, 1974, *2*, 141–157.

Sasanuma, S., Itoh, M., Mori, K., & Kobayashi, Y. Tachistoscopic recognition of Kana and Kanji words. *Neuropsychologia*, 1977, *15*, 547–553.

Scribner, S., & Cole, M. *Literacy without schooling: Testing for intellectual effect* (Vai Literacy Project, Working Paper 2). Laboratory of Comparative Human Cognition, The Rockefeller University, 1978.

Treiman, R. A., Baron, J., & Luk, K. Speech reading in silent reading: A comparison of Chinese and English. *Journal of Chinese Linguistics*, 1981, *9*, 116–125.

Turnage, T. W., & McGinnies, E. A cross-cultural comparison of the effects of presentation mode and meaningfulness in short-term recall. *American Journal of Psychology,* 1973, *86,* 369–381.

Tzeng, O. J. L., & Hung, D. L. Orthography and reading. Paper presented at the annual meeting of the National Reading Conference. San Antonio, Texas, 1979.

Tzeng, O. J. L., & Hung, D. L. Reading in a nonalphabetic writing system: Some experimental studies. In J. F. Kavanagh & R. L. Venezky (Eds.), *Orthography, reading, and dyslexia.* Baltimore, Md.: University Park Press, 1980.

Tzeng, O. J. L., Hung, D. L., Cotton, B., & Wang, W. S-Y. Visual lateralization effect in reading Chinese characters. *Nature,* 1979, *282,* 499–501.

Tzeng, O. J. L., Hung, D. L., & Garro, L. Reading the Chinese characters: An information processing view. *Journal of Chinese Linguistics,* 1978, *6,* 287–305.

Tzeng, O. J. L., Hung, D. L., & Wang, W. S-Y. Speech recoding in reading Chinese characters. *Journal of Experimental Psychology: Human Learning and Memory,* 1977, *3,* 621–630.

Venezky, R. L. *The structure of English orthography.* The Hague: Mouton, 1970.

Watson, J. B. *Behaviorism* (rev. ed.). New York: Norton, 1930.

Whorf, B. *Language, thought, and reality.* Cambridge, Mass.: MIT Press, 1956.

Zhou, Y. G. To what degree are the ''phonetics'' of present-day Chinese characters still phonetic? *Zhongguo Yuwen,* 1978, *146,* 172–177.

12

Speech Understanding and Reading: Some Differences and Similarities

Raymond S. Nickerson
Bolt Beranek and Newman Inc.
Cambridge, MA 02238

Speech understanding and reading are compared and contrasted. Each is presented as a multifaceted activity in which both bottom-up, analytic, data-driven processes and top-down, inferential, knowledge-driven processes play important roles. Differences between speech understanding and reading are apparent when one focuses on stimuli and the sensory systems that transduce them, but become more blurred when one considers the cognitive activities that must be involved in the determination of meaning. Several notions are presented that are viewed as key to the development of an adequate model of language comprehension. The question of whether reading is necessarily parasitic on speech is considered.

INTRODUCTION

Speech understanding and reading are among the most complex perceptual-cognitive skills that human beings have developed. In some respects these skills are quite different. Speech understanding is universal among people everywhere barring physical or mental disabilities that interfere with its normal development. Reading ability is far from universal and, even among individuals in literate countries, is often poorly developed. Speech understanding is acquired spontaneously, and it would seem effortlessly, during the first few years of life. Reading ability typically is acquired after oral-aural language skills have been fairly well developed, and then only as a result of some considerable deliberate effort. To make this point another way: Speech skills are learned in the absence of any explicit attempts to teach them; if reading skills are not taught, they are not, as a rule, acquired at all.

Written language tends to be grammatically correct, whereas speech—especially conversational speech—can violate the formal rules of grammar in every conceivable way. In the case of speech, the stimulus input is paced largely by the speaker, whereas in the case of reading, readers regulate the input rate for themselves. Conversational speech is a cooperative activity, and the listener can request (or the speaker volunteer) amplifying remarks when they are needed to resolve ambiguities or make the meaning of an utterance clear. Reading is an open-loop activity as far as the writer-reader relationship is concerned; the writer has no opportunity to amplify written material that a reader finds difficult to understand.

But although speech understanding and reading differ in some fundamental ways, they also have much in common. Both spoken and written language represent ways of communicating information and ideas among people. As perceptual activities, both have been considered by some investigators to have special characteristics that are not representative of perception in general. Both involve the interpretation of symbols that are more or less arbitrary in the sense that they bear little apparent relationship to the concepts they symbolize. And neither could occur without the utilization of both bottom–up (or data-driven) and top–down (or knowledge-driven) processes.

Both the spoken and written forms of English, as well as of other Western languages, are based on a representational system that is remarkable in its conceptual simplicity, practicality, and virtually unlimited range of possible expression. The system involves the use of a modestly sized set of basic symbols (26 letters in the case of written English, about 40 phonemes in that of spoken English) and rules for combining these symbols into higher-order linguistic units.

Neither spoken nor written language could be understood apart from the inferential application by the listener or reader of knowledge from at least two sources. First, there is the knowledge that the listener/reader brings to the listening/reading situation. This includes knowledge of the world and of linguistic rules and conventions in general, and knowledge of the speaker/writer—including perhaps certain idiosyncratic modes of expression that he or she may have—and of the topic of communication in particular. Second, there are the cues that can be extracted from one part of the spoken or written signal that may be applied to the decoding or interpretation of other parts.

The necessity of the application of knowledge about language and the world is apparent. Whether spoken or written, the sentence *The batter hit the ball* cannot be understood apart from knowing what a batter and a ball are and also what it means to hit something. More particularly, one must know the special meaning of the word *ball* when it is used to signify something that a batter hits, which probably is different from the type of ball that is shot from a cannon or the type at which one dances and watches one's social etiquette. Also, one must know the meaning of *hit* as it relates to what a batter does to a ball—with the help of a bat—as opposed to what a soprano does when she hits a high note or what the flu does when it hits town. Although the need for the application of such knowledge is obvious, only recently have investigators of language behavior begun to give it the attention it deserves.[1]

Presumably, at some level, speech understanding and reading must tap the same knowledge-application processes and information store. It would be difficult to believe that the information required to understand *The batter hit the ball* is stored twice, once for use in decoding the sentence in written form and once for processing its spoken analog. Similarly, it seems unparsimonious to assume that the processes that access this information are entirely separate for the visual and auditory modes. But at what point in the chain of events that culminate in "understanding" do the speech-understanding and reading processes make use of the same components?

The second type of knowledge that the listener/reader uses, namely that derived from linguistic context, is no less essential than the first. Nor is the importance of its role less apparent. That the interpretation of *ball* in *The batter hit the ball* is contingent on the immediate linguistic context is apparent. Of course, this is equally true whether the sentences are spoken or written.

Thus, although speech understanding and reading differ in many ways, they also have much in common. My purpose in this chapter is to consider some of the differences and similarities between these processes in more detail. This comparison is motivated by both theoretical and practical interests. The theoretical interest is based on the assumption that an attempt to compare and contrast speech understanding and reading should result in a better understanding of both. The development of a theory of either process should be facilitated by a better understanding of how that process differs from or corresponds to the other. A practical interest relates to the question of whether reading ability is best thought of as something to be superimposed on existing speech-understanding skills. How one views the relationship between speech understanding and reading—and the dependence of one on the other—has implications for how one thinks of the problem of teaching reading and, in particular, how one thinks of teaching reading to children whose spoken language is deficient.

The style of the chapter is discursive and much of the content conjectural. The literature is cited to illustrate points and to help identify issues, but no attempt is made to review the relevant research in anything approaching a comprehensive way. The comments regarding both speech understanding and reading are made with English in mind, and in the case of reading, text printed with conventional typography is assumed. Although much of what is said may apply to languages

---

[1]Although the sentence *The batter hit the ball* was not chosen to illustrate the need for linguistic context beyond the immediate sentence to help determine meaning, Bertram Bruce pointed out to me that the sentence by itself is indeed ambiguous. In the context of a story about two playful children, one of whom has a basketball and the other a pan of cookie batter, the sentence could have a meaning quite different from the one intended in the illustration.

other than English that have a written form based on an alphabet, much also is undoubtedly inappropriate for languages that are represented in qualitatively different ways.

THE RECEPTOR SYSTEMS FOR
AUDITORY AND VISUAL LANGUAGE

The eye is designed to acquire information about geometrical properties of the environment; it is a spatially extended transducer whose signals to the brain are determined by the changing patterns of radiant energy falling on a two-dimensional surface. By comparison, the ear is essentially a one-dimensional sensor, responding to moment-to-moment changes in the pressure of air against its interface to the world. To be sure, the fact that we have two ears provides directional and depth components to our perception of sound, but hearing compares very unfavorably with vision as a means of acquiring information about spatial aspects of the world.

Signals from the eye and ear travel to different parts of the cerebral cortex by different routes. The major way stations of the visual system are the lateral geniculate bodies in the hypothalamus (some optic nerve fibers also terminate in the superior colliculi, where connections are made with motor nerves controlling reflex eye movements); those of the auditory system are the cochlea nuclei of the medulla, the inferior and superior colliculi, and the medial geniculate bodies of the thalamus. The primary projection areas for vision and audition, within the occipital and temporal lobes respectively, are known to differ somewhat with respect to the relative density and distribution of different types of cells. The visual cortex, for example, contains within its deeper layers many large Betz-like cells, typical of motor areas, whereas the auditory cortex does not. The significance of such cytological differences for vision and audition are not well understood.

Another major difference between the visual and auditory receptor systems relates to their bandwidths. The eye is far more richly innervated than the ear: It contains more than 130,000,000 receptor cells, whereas the ear contains around 25,000–30,000. there is a similar disparity in the ascending neural pathways: The optic nerve bundle contains approximately 1,000,000 fibers, as compared with about 25,000 in the auditory nerve. Thus, the neuroanatomy of the eye permits it to deliver much more information to the brain per unit of time than does that of the ear. Jacobson (1951 a, b) has estimated the channel capacities of the visual and auditory systems to be about 4,300,000 and 10,000 bits per second, respectively. The bases on which these estimates were derived have been questioned (Luce, 1960), but for our purposes, the accuracy of these numbers is not a primary concern; if each is correct to within an order of magnitude, the point of interest holds, namely that in terms of structure the two systems differ greatly with respect to the amount of information they can acquire and transmit.

Behavioral estimates of the amount of information that can be transmitted by the human being, whether the input channel is visual or auditory, stand in sharp contrast to the estimates of upper limits such as those by Jacobson. Numerous measurements of what people actually transmit when performing highly skilled tasks (speaking, reading, typing, piano playing) have yielded rates less than about 50 bits per second (Miller, 1951; Quastler & Wulff, 1955). Various explanations have been given for this huge disparity between the kind of performance the sensory systems seem capable of supporting and that which the organism as a whole can deliver. Performance is sometimes limited by output constraints (e.g., as in speaking, typing, and piano playing), but the limitations seem to be nearly as severe when little or no overt response is required (e.g., silent reading, listening to speech). We seem to be led to the conclusion that the major bottlenecks in the human being's information-processing capabilities are central in origin and that both the eye and the ear can deliver much more information to the brain than it can process effectively. Alternatively one might assume that the brain processes all incoming information that arrives over the sensory pathways and that the apparent discrepancy between input bandwidth and the limitations of perceptual experience are due to such factors as redundancy in sensory codes and loss of information in the process of input classification.

For purposes of this chapter, the most significant question regarding differences between the visual and auditory systems is whether either of these systems is more suitable for language processing than the other. Noting the difficulty with which most people learn to read relative to the apparent ease with which they acquire speech skills, Gleitman and Rozin (1977) suggest that the explanation is to be found in the biological superiority of the ear-brain system for language-processing functions. The argument has sometimes been made that speech has influenced the evolution of the auditory system or, perhaps more plausibly, that the systems for speech production and for hearing have evolved together, the evolution of each affecting and being affected by that of the other.

A corollary claim is that not only is the auditory system specially adapted to process speech, but that speech signals are processed in a way that is qualitatively different from that in which other auditory stimuli are processed. The notion is that the same auditory stimulus may yield one type of perceptual response if listeners believe they are listening to speech and another type if they do not, hence the distinction between listening in a speech or phonetic, as opposed to an acoustic or auditory, mode. No such distinction has been made in the case of reading and vision.

Six pieces of experimental evidence indicating that the perception of speech differs from the perception of auditory stimuli in general are listed by Wood (1975). Three have to do with hemispheric specialization (differential ear advantages in identification of dichotically presented speech and nonspeech signals, differential ear advantages for temporal order judgments on such signals, and differences in average-evoked potentials during classification of auditory and phonemic dimensions). Following Cutting (1978), we may consider these three as indicants of the same process and reduce Wood's list of evidences to four:

1. The "phoneme boundary effect," whereby speech sounds that vary continuously on some dimension (e.g., frequency of second formant) are perceived as being in one of two phonemic categories and never between them.
2. Differential interference between auditory and phonetic dimensions of the same stimulus in speeded classification tasks.
3. The relative effectiveness of adaptation to speech and nonspeech stimuli in shifting the boundary of the phoneme boundary effect.
4. The various evidences of hemispheric specialization just mentioned.

All of these effects are well documented experimentally. What is less clear now than was once thought to be the case, however, is that any of these effects are unique to the perception of speech. Cutting (1978) has reviewed evidence that all of them have in fact been obtained with nonspeech stimuli and, in particular, with musical sounds. This does not rule out the possibility that the perceptual processes underlying these effects were developed initially to facilitate speech perception, and that they, being available, are used in the processing of some other auditory stimuli—especially those that have certain speechlike properties— as well. An alternative interpretation is that there is nothing qualitatively different about the way the auditory system processes speech from the way it processes other equally complex auditory stimuli.

In summary, the visual and auditory systems differ markedly in many ways, but the implications of these differences for language processing are not clear. Structural differences are most apparent at the level of the transducers, the eye and the ear; they are less obvious and their implications are more poorly understood at the level of the cortex. The systems also differ in terms of the amount of information the receptors can encode and transmit. In particular, the eye is much more richly innervated than the ear. However, functional bandwidth limitations appear to be primarily central for both systems, and it is not clear that those limitations are more severe in the one case than in the other. Although some investigators have argued that the auditory system—having evolved a special sensitivity to properties of speech—is better adapted biologically to language processing than is the visual system, the evidence is not conclusive.

THE STIMULUS

A major difference between speech and written matter lies in the way they relate to time. There is a permanence about written language that speech does not have. One might say that printed matter exists, whereas speech occurs. This difference is one of quality and not only of extent. It is not even appropriate to think of speech as being presented to the listener one word at a time, because even a word does not exist as a whole in the auditory domain at any given instant. It is itself an event that occurs over time.

One important implication of this difference for the nature of the processes by which the speech signal and printed matter are decoded is the fact that the speech-understanding process must have available to it a temporary memory in which inherently ambiguous portions of the speech signal can be stored until the information necessary to disambiguate them has been received. Without such a capability, utterances such as the following could not be understood:

The plane vibrated as it was drawn against the grain of the wood.

The plane vibrated as it accelerated for the takeoff.

Printed matter, at least when it is presented in the conventional way (as opposed to one word at a time), does not impose the same type of short-term storage requirement. The printed page itself constitutes a memory of sorts. When an ambiguity is encountered in the reading of text, it can be returned to—reread—after the disambiguating information is acquired. This is not to say that short-term memory is not used in reading. Clearly it is, but the point is that the permanence of the printed text mitigates its importance somewhat. The medium is less demanding in this respect than is the transient signal in the case of speech.

Short-term memory for auditory stimuli has generally been held to be more robust—of longer duration, more easily refreshed—than short-term memory for comparable visual stimuli. The evidence that people tend to recode visually presented linguistic stimuli into an auditory or articulatory representation when participating in short-term memory experiments is well-known and compelling (Conrad, 1964; Sperling & Speelman, 1970; Wickelgren, 1966). Although a number of experimental results suggest that visual short-term memory may be more persistent than has typically been believed (Kolers, 1974; Kroll, Parks, Parkinson, Bieber, & Johnson, 1970; Nickerson, 1972; Parkinson, Parks, & Kroll, 1971), the greater involvement of auditory short-term memory in the processing and retention of linguistic stimuli is still the prevailing assumption. Conrad (1972) has hypothesized that it is difficult to teach children to read before the age of about 6 because they do not have sufficiently well-developed auditory short-term memories to support comprehension before that age. Lesgold (1974) has also identified limited memory span as an important constraint on the ability of young people to learn to read comprehendingly. A problem with this view is that it leaves one wondering how children manage to learn to understand speech.

The relative permanence of printed text makes possible a considerable degree of parallel processing and backtracking. Reading depends on an active scanning process in which the sensory receptors are moved from point to point in the stimulus field, and the movement activity is controlled by a complex and not thoroughly understood feedback process. Evidence suggests that a competent reader takes in several (perhaps two–five) words at each eye fixation (Buswell, 1937; Huey, 1908). However, measurements of eye movements during reading reveal the occurrence, even with competent readers, of frequent regressive movements (Buswell, 1937). Kolers (1976) points out that in reading the visual system may sample information in an order other than as it appears on the page. Furthermore, one cannot even assume that the information acquired from successive eye fixations is necessarily assimilated in the order in which it is acquired. In Koler's (1976) words: "the order and clarity of the messages that the reader receives from text are properties achieved by some powerful cognitive operations, and are not merely reflections of the message the eye picks up from the printed page. . . . The mind orders, arranges, supplements, and fills out the information the eye delivers to it [p. 392]."

The listener does not have the same problem of rearranging speech, inasmuch as the component sounds of speech are delivered to the ear in the correct order without one's worrying about it. There is a related problem, however. Beginning with Warren, Obusek, Farmer, and Warren (1969), several investigators have demonstrated that people have difficulty reporting the order of the cyclic occurrence of clearly discriminable contiguous sounds when the duration of individual sounds is much less than half a second. Many of the individual sounds of speech are much less than half a second in duration, and the rate of occurrence of these sounds can exceed 10 per second. This being true, one is left with the question of how the order of speech sounds is perceived as meaningful.

There are at least two plausible answers to this question. It may be that the difficulty people have in reporting order in the aforementioned experiments is less indicative of a perceptual limitation than of a problem of output coding (Nickerson & Freeman, 1974). Another possibility is that in the case of speech, the order of individual components is not perceived directly but is to some degree inferred. Although n phonemes can be ordered in $n!$ ways, the number of orderings that would result in meaningful speech is very much smaller than $n!$, and in context it may be very small indeed. Thus, the direct and accurate perception of the order of occurrence of phonemes may not be essential to the perception of speech. An approximate ordering based on an analysis of the physical signal might be refined and made more accurate by the top–down application of knowledge of the constraints of the language and of the specific context in which an utterance is heard.

Although the fact that speech occurs over time and leaves no permanent trace would seem to make the speech signal less suitable than text for either parallel processing or backtracking, something analogous to the latter, at least, must occur. Otherwise, one would not be able to understand utterances in which the meaning of a word is disambiguated by material that follows it in time. Also, misperceptions would sometimes be difficult to account for if one were to assume that words are invariably processed in the order in which they are uttered. Consider, for example, the following case of a listener misinterpreting what a speaker has said:

Speaker: "Are you looking for Carl or Ron?"
Listener: "What?"
Speaker: "Are you looking for Carl or Ron?"
Listener: "Oh! I thought you said, 'You look like you have a collar on.' "

It is easy to see how this misperception might arise if what the listener does is try to come up with an utterance that makes sense, given all the cues at his disposal after the speaker has finished speaking. It is difficult to imagine how he got from what the speaker said to what he heard if he were actually processing each word as it was uttered.

Although the foregoing comments about the implications of the permanence of text relative to the transience of speech recognize the possibility of backtracking and parallel processing, they treat reading as a predominantly linear, or quasilinear, activity. That is, the implied view of the reading task is one in which the reader attempts to move steadily through a text, processing the information in at least the approximate order in which it appears on the page. The permanence of text has another important implication, however, in that it allows the reader to use grossly nonlinear processing strategies to advantage. One can scan a page looking for key words or phrases; skim for gist and then focus selectively on particularly salient segments; reread specific portions of a text in order to clarify points or refresh one's memory; juxtapose in time the reading of noncontiguous segments as one might wish to do, for example, in order to check the consistency of one part of a text with another. Some backtracking must be possible in speech understanding, but the degree of flexibility with respect to nonlinear processing strategies that can be adopted seems obviously much more limited in this case.

There are several other differences between speech and printed text that also relate to the temporal structuring of the one and the spatial structuring of the other. These structures are not independent, but nor are they isomorphic; they depart from isomorphism in several ways. At the level of the basic constituents, the most striking difference is with respect to their relative discreteness. The discrete, and nicely separated, letters of text have no analogs in speech. The phonemes, which some speech scientists view as idealizations of the variable sounds of speech, change gradually from one to another during continuous speech with—in many cases—no clear demarcation between them.

There are also many structural differences between speech and printed text at higher organization levels. First, the boundaries between printed words are clearly marked spatially, whereas the boundaries between spoken words are not clearly marked temporally. Indeed speech that is punctuated with pauses between successive words sounds unnatural.

Second, as conventionally formatted, printed matter has discontinuities at the ends (and beginnings) of lines that are arbitrarily placed with respect to the syntactic and semantic properties of the material. Although speakers often pause, they tend to do so at syntactic junctures rather than at random points in an utterance. The experienced reader takes the line-end discontinuities in stride, but one must wonder to what extent they represent obstacles to the child who is just beginning to learn how to read.

Third, the use of paragraphs represents a type of higher-level organization that is more apparent in text than in speech. An orator may insert longer-than-average pauses at points that mark the transition between major thoughts, but the clue is neither as categorical nor as consistently used as the paragraph structure of text.

Fourth, syllabic structure is apparent in speech but not in text; in speech successive syllables are differentiated by different degrees of stress, whereas conventional orthography does not appear to provide equally distinctive clues to syllabic structure.

Fifth, the prosodic (tonal and temporal) aspects of speech provide cues not only about syllabic structure but about emphasis and syntactic structure more generally. Variations in amplitude, duration, and fundamental frequency signify the relative degrees of emphasis received by different parts of an utterance. Pauses often mark major syntactic boundaries. Punctuation and certain typographical conventions (capital letters, italicized words, underlining) play a role in written language similar in some respects to that played by prosody in speech. With respect to the relative helpfulness of these auditory and visual cues, one can argue both ways. There is a discreteness about those encountered in the reading context that does not characterize those encountered in speech. Punctuation marks either occur or they do not; letters are either capitalized (italicized, underlined) or they are not. In contrast, the prosodic aspects of speech vary more or less continuously and are distinctive only relative to their context. On the other hand, punctuation marks do not occur at all syntactic boundaries, and an oral reader who depends on them exclusively to determine the prosodic characteristics of utterances will not produce normal-sounding speech. Conversely, spontaneous speech contains many tonal-temporal cues to syntactic structure that are not reflected by any of the properties of printed text.

Sixth, prosody also sometimes conveys semantic information that is not represented in text. For example, *Does he speak French or German?* is ambiguous in printed form. A speaker makes the intended meaning clear by saying the final word with either a rising or falling pitch: A rising pitch indicates that the expected answer is either "yes" or "no"; a falling pitch indicates that the speaker knows or assumes that the subject of the inquiry speaks one of these languages, and the question is which one. Other examples of the disambiguating role of prosody are easy to find. Analogous examples of statements that would necessarily be ambiguous when spoken, but unambiguous in written form, are much more difficult to produce.

Finally, speech and written material also differ structurally in a way that is qualitatively different from those previously mentioned. Written material presumably tends to be better organized than speech because writers typically have the opportunity to develop carefully what they want to say, modifying drafts as much as necessary until the material meets with their satisfaction. The speaker, on the other hand, typically produces final copy, as it were, the first time around.

The stimuli for speech understanding and reading might also be compared with respect to redundancy. The redundancy of both spoken and written English has been estimated in a variety of ways, beginning with Shannon's letter-prediction technique (Burton & Licklider, 1955; Newman & Gerstman, 1952; Shannon, 1951). All of the methods that have been used lead to the same general conclusion: English as it is typically used in both speech and writing is highly redundant, perhaps as much as 50%.

The main justification for redundancy in a communication system is the need to compensate for the deleterious effects of noise. In effect, what one does by building redundancy into a message is to send the message, or various parts thereof, more than once, albeit not necessarily in the same way each time. The hope is that if one instantiation of some aspect of the message is obliterated by noise, another may survive. Presumably, the need to compensate for noise is also a primary reason for the redundancy in natural language. Communication seldom occurs in a noise-free environment, and even when it does, the signal that is produced, whether spoken or written, may be less than perfect in a variety of ways.

But if the need to compensate for noise is the main reason for redundancy, should it not be possible to eliminate the redundancy when the signal is relatively noise-free, as, for example, when the message is represented by clearly printed text on a piece of paper that can be read under optimal viewing conditions, or by speech that has been recorded by a professionally trained speaker and is listened to in a relatively quiet environment? One recent attempt to investigate this question has been made by Martin and his colleagues (Bassin & Martin, 1976; Martin & Peterson, 1977; Martin & Sheffield, 1976). In these studies, redundancy was decreased by eliminating whole words from printed or spoken prose. Several elimination rules were used, among them that of eliminating those words that are judged by subjects to be least critical to the understanding of the passages. The resulting stimulus material is reminiscent of what one reads in newspaper headlines, and it is referred to by Martin as "telegraphic prose."

The general finding from these studies has been that comprehensibility decreases as redundancy is decreased. What is not yet clear is whether redundancy can be reduced in such a way that listening or reading efficiency, as indicated by some suitable measure of information assimilation per unit time, can be increased or at least held constant. An impediment to obtaining an unequivocal and quantitative answer to this question is the problem of defining an acceptable measure of information-assimilation rate.

With respect to the question of how speech and written language may differ in redundancy, little is known. Undoubtedly, one can find examples of material with widely varying degrees of redundancy in both cases. It would not be surprising, however, if a careful study of spoken and written language with this question in mind revealed some systematic differences.

To summarize, the differences between the stimuli for speech and reading are many and large. Foremost is the fact that speech occurs in time, whereas text exists in space. This difference has several consequences for the way in which the material is processed. For example, speech and text make different demands on short-term memory and permit different degrees of flexibility with respect to backtracking and parallel processing. Although it is clear that something analogous to regressive eye movements must occur in speech understanding, as when people are forced to reinterpret something they have just heard, data that would permit a comparison of the frequency with which such backtracking occurs in the two modes do not exist. Other major differences between the stimuli of spoken and written language that have implications for how they are processed relate to the relative discreteness of the basic constituents, the organization of higher-level components, and the roles of prosody in speech and punctuation in text. Both auditory and visual language tend to be highly redundant; how they compare in this regard has not been thoroughly studied.

THE PERCEPTUAL UNIT IN
SPEECH UNDERSTANDING AND READING

As we have already noted, both spoken and written English follow an elegantly simple principle of construction: a small set of basic elements (phonemes and letters) and rules for combining those elements into an essentially infinite number of larger units. We have also noted, however, that the concatenation of phonemes in the speech signal does not have the discrete character of a sequence of printed letters. The fact that printed English is made up of sequences of discrete symbols, whereas speech is not, has been characterized by Gleitman and Rozin (1977) as: "the fundamental conceptual problem in early reading acquisition: the alphabetic signs (and their referents, the set of phones and phonemes) and discrete units, while speech itself does not consist of physically segmentable discrete units, but is a continuous, gradually varying event [p. 39]."

Whether it makes sense to speak of phonemes in the speech signal at all has been questioned by some investigators because of the lack of invariance due to coarticulation and contextual effects. However, most speech scientists recognize the existence of phonemes as at least idealizations of individual speech sounds and perhaps also as targets for articulatory gestures. But the problem of phoneme identification within the speech signal is a very difficult one, as developers of speech-understanding systems have discovered, not the least problematic aspect of which is that of determining where one phoneme ends and another begins. In this respect, the speech signal is more similar to cursive script than to printed text. The decomposition of script into individual letters also requires the solution of a segmentation problem and that of coping with various contextual effects.

It seems reasonable to say, therefore, that phonemes and letters have this in common: They represent basic constituent elements from which speech and written language, respectively, can be produced and into which, at least in theory, they can be decomposed. Major differences between them are their relative discreteness and the extent to which they preserve their individual identities when embedded in larger linguistic entities.

Another characteristic that phonemes and letters share is the fact that the role of the one in speech perception and that of the other in reading are both uncertain. A naive model of speech understanding might assume that the first step in the process would be the identification of a sequence of phonemes on which word recognition might be based. However, there are several reasons for concluding that the phoneme is probably not the perceptual unit involved in the decoding of the speech signal. As Miller (1962) has pointed out, a speaker producing words at the rate of 150 per minute, which is within the normal range for conversational speech, is producing individual phonemes at the rate of perhaps 10 to 12 per second. If, as some studies seem to indicate, people are incapable of making more than two or three perceptual judgments per second, the understanding of speech cannot depend on a process of identifying individual phonemes in sequence. Although the unit of perceptual analysis remains a point of controversy, there seems to be fairly general agreement that it must be something larger than the individual phoneme.

Another reason for dismissing the phoneme as the perceptual unit of speech is the fact that no one yet has been able to develop a method for reliably extracting phonemes from the sound pressure wave without recourse to the use of contextual and other higher-order cues (although Cole & Zue, (1980) have demonstrated that a highly practiced observer can come closer to identifying all the phonemes in a sound spectrogram than had commonly been believed). The degree to which the developers of computer programs for recognizing speech have found it necessary to invoke top-down heuristics to get as far as they have on the problem attests to the inherent ambiguity of the cues by which phonemes may be identified (Klatt & Stevens, 1973; Woods, 1978).

What of the role of letter perception in reading? In the absence of evidence to the contrary, it is perhaps natural to assume that individual letters are the units of analysis, given an alphabetical language such as English. To produce written words, one must, after all, produce them letter by letter. And children are taught to think of words in terms of their constituent letters in order to spell them correctly. But there are several reasons—both theoretical and experimental—to question the role of the individual letter as the unit of perceptual analysis in reading. The literature on the issue is large, and it can only be touched upon here.

Kolers (1970) rejects the possibility that reading is based on a serial letter-by-letter identification process on the grounds that the time required to recognize individual letters is too large to be consistent with typical reading rates—an argument similar to that used by Miller to reject the phoneme as the unit of analysis for speech perception. However, to say that individual letters are not processed serially during reading is not to deny the possibility that they are processed individually. It is at least conceptually possible that they are processed individually, albeit in parallel to some degree.

Most of the experimental work relating to this issue has not involved reading tasks per se but, rather, tasks requiring the recognition of briefly exposed letters or words. Generalizing the results of these studies to the reading task itself should be done cautiously. Hochberg (1970) has pointed out that in such experiments the words that are to be recognized appear out of context, they are not fixated as a result of eye movements, and the task requires a response that is not characteristic of the reading process. (Similar observations could be made with respect to many of the studies of auditory word and phoneme perception that purport to be relevant to an understanding of speech perception.) I believe that this cautionary note is valid. Speech understanding and reading will probably be understood only as a result of investigations of speech understanding and reading. However, the results of studies of phoneme and spoken-word recongition, and of letter and printed-word recognition, can be of value for the hints they provide regarding processes that may underlie the higher-level abilities.

It has long been known that a word can be named about as quickly as a single letter. In addition, words can be recognized under conditions in which all the letters in equally long nonword letter sequences cannot be reported (Cattell, 1885/1947; Woodworth, 1938). Although Cattell took these findings as evidence that words are perceived as wholes, they do not rule out the possibility that the underlying process involves a letter-by-letter analysis. Naming time includes components (e.g., retrieval of a name from memory, execution of the motor activity required to emit the name) that would not necessarily be involved in the kind of analysis of letters that might underlie word recognition. Moreover, Cattell considered only the possibility of a sequential letter-by-letter analysis; the assumption that letters are analyzed in parallel would not necessarily lead one to expect the naming of a word to require much more time than the naming of one of its constituent letters.

One proposed explanation of the finding that words can be recognized under conditions in which not all the letters in equally long nonwords can be reported has attributed it to the relative ease with which words—as opposed to random letter strings—can be remembered. (Consider the relative difficulty of remembering the letter string *eohonmpnne* as opposed to the same letters arranged as *phenomenon.*) Smith and Haviland (1972) showed, however, that words and their constituent letters are more accurately reported than nonwords even when the memorability advantage of words is removed by equating both types of stimuli with respect to orthographic redundancy. Subjects in their study were informed that each of the (three) letters in their stimuli (whether words or nonwords) would be one of only two alternatives, e.g., in one set of nonwords the first letter was either *v* or *b,* the second *s* or *d,* and the third *g* or *m.* These investigators took the fact that words were recognized better than nonwords under these conditions as evidence in support of the idea that words are processed as wholes and not on a letter-by-letter basis.

A corollary to the "word-superiority" effect is the finding that an individual letter is likely to be reported more accurately when briefly presented within a word than when presented alone, or within a string of letters that does not form a word. Moreover, this result has been obtained under conditions in which the possible effect of the orthographic redundancy of words was nullified by giving the subject a two-alternative forced-choice test for recognition of a specific one of the letters in the stimulus (Reicher, 1969; Wheeler, 1970). When the stimulus was a word, both alternatives (together with the other letters of the string) formed a word; when it was a nonword, both alternatives formed a nonword. The fact that letters were more accurately reported in word contexts than in nonword contexts under these conditions not only seems to challenge the notion that letter recognition provides the basis for word recognition; it seems to suggest just the opposite possibility, namely that the recognition of a letter may be facilitated by the recognition of the word in which it is contained.

Some theories have held that the perceptual unit for word recognition is not the individual letter, but supraletter features or high-frequency letter combinations (Gibson, Pick, Osser, & Hammond, 1962; Johnson, 1975). A problem for this view, as well as for the whole-word hypothesis, is the finding of a word-superiority effect even with stimuli composed of mixtures of upper- and lower-case letters or of letters of widely different fonts (Adams, 1979; McClelland, 1976), a condition that should be devastating for any process that depends on the detection of familiar visual patterns involving more than a single letter.

Adams (1979) has proposed an account of visual word recognition that assumes that the recognition of individual letters does play an inportant role in the process. Her account also postulates, however, the simultaneous operation of processes that apply information regarding the statistical properties of the language at the level of letter combinations, and it acknowledges the importance of top–down processing even in the recognition of isolated words. Adams' model attributes the word-superiority effect and related findings in part to interactions among letter-recognition processes and in part to the active generation and testing of hypotheses at the word level. Letter recognizers that are frequently activated together are assumed to become mutually facilitative. Because h often follows t, for example, the process of recognizing a t will facilitate the recognition of an h to its right, whereas that of recognizing an h will facilitate the recognition of a t to its left. Thus, words and orthographically regular pseudowords are recognized more readily than orthographically irregular nonwords because these facilitative effects will often be consistent with the letters that are actually there in the former cases but not in the latter case. Words are recognized more readily than regular pseudowords because, simultaneously with the ongoing letter-recognition processes, a process at the word-recognition level is collecting data from the letter recognizers and formulating hypotheses about what the word might be. These hypotheses direct the further gathering of information from the letter recognizers and facilitate the recognition of those letters that comprise the hypothesized word.

In schema-theoretic terms (Adams & Collins, 1979), letter schemata facilitate each other in a way that reflects the statistical dependencies in the language and feed their outputs up to word schemata, which in turn facilitate the further testing of the visual input against specific letter schemata in an effort to fill in the word schemata's remaining empty slots. Words are recognized more readily than pseudowords, and consequently, so are their constituent letters because typically there are no schemata corresponding to entire pseudowords, and their recognition must proceed in exclusively bottom–up fashion. It is important to note that Adams' model implicitly acknowledges the greater recognizability of common spelling patterns and frequently encountered words, but it does not attribute this greater recognizability to familiarity with visual patterns. Indeed, she tested her model with words composed of multiple type fonts in order to rule out this possibility.

Although Adams' (1979) model was developed to account for the recognition of individual words presented in isolation, it is extendible to the process of reading meaningful text. One need only postulate processes directed toward the filling of slots of higher-level (word-combination, phrase, sentence) schemata, operating in parallel with letter- and word-recognition processes, accepting their outputs as bottom–up inputs, and in turn directing the activities of these lower-level hypotheses from the top down.

One of the things that this view suggests is that attempts to find *the* perceptual unit of reading may be doomed to failure because the question of *the* perceptual unit is the wrong one to ask. Maybe perceptual processing occurs at several levels simultaneously. That is at least the conclusion that is drawn in this chapter, and not only with respect to reading but with respect to speech understanding as well. On balance, the results of efforts to identify the perceptual unit of language processing—whether within the context of speech understanding or within that of reading—seem to demonstrate the flexibility and multifaceted nature of the process more than anything else. It seems clear that people do make use of individual letters and phonemes: They are able to distinguish between words that differ with respect to only a single such element. Whole-word shape cues are probably used in reading, as are prosody and other suprasegmental features in the understanding of speech. (Such global cues may be especially important when signal quality is poor as, for example, when one is listening to speech in noise or attempting to read blurred print.) The view of language comprehension that is espoused here, and about which more is said later, takes flexibility to be a fundamental property of the process.

INFORMATION ASSIMILATION

A question of some practical importance is that of the relative efficiency of oral and written language for the purpose of information transmission. The question is probably too general to be answered in any useful way, but there are some observations that can be made.

People normally speak at a rate of between 125 and 175 words per minute (Abrams, Goffard, Kryter, Miller, Sanford, & Sanford, 1944; Gregory, 1969; Maclay & Osgood, 1967). When attempting to talk as fast as possible, some people have been able to attain rates as high as 250 to 275 words per minute. Intelligibility appears to be best for the slower rates within the normal range, to drop off very slightly as the rate is increased to about 150 words per minute, and to fall off more sharply as the rate is increased further. With artificially speeded speech, fairly good intelligibility has been maintained with rates as high as 300 words per minute. It deteriorates quickly for still higher rates, however. No one, to my knowledge, has reported speech to be highly intelligible with any compression algorithm for rates as high as 400 words per minute.

Hochberg (1976) distinguishes conceptually among four different types of reading, which differ, among other ways, in reading rate and level of comprehension. One extreme (Type I) is the kind of reading that depends on a letter-by-letter analysis of individual words; this kind of reading, according to Hochberg, is rarely done by a skilled reader. Obviously, when it is done, it permits only very slow rates. The other extreme (Type IV) is the type of very rapid reading sometimes referred to as "skimming," which makes heavy use of a priori knowledge of the subject matter and works best with highly redundant or familiar material. Rates of over 1000 words a minute may be attainable with this type, but comprehension may be less than complete unless the material is familiar, in which case the amount of new information that is being acquired may be small. Between these extremes are the more common types of reading (Types II and III), which produce intermediate estimated reading rates in the vicinity of 250 and 600 words per minute respectively. Type III reading produces the higher rates by virtue of its greater utilization of whole-word features (such as length) as cues to word identity; this type is also somewhat dependent on the redundancy of the material, but less so than Type IV.

Whether or not one accepts Hochberg's taxonomy, it seems clear that reading rates can vary widely, and the rate at which an individual reads a given text must depend on such factors as general level of reading ability, the difficulty of the material (familiarity to the reader of both vocabulary and subject matter, and the quality of the writing), and the level of comprehension desired. Other factors, such as print size, type font, and page layout, probably also play some role. In contrast, the information-presentation rate in the case of speech is not usually under the listener's control. Rather it is determined by the rate at which people talk, which in most circumstances varies over a remarkably narrow range.

In short, the two major differences between speech understanding and reading with respect to assimilation rates appear to be these: (1) reading is a self-paced activity, whereas listening is not; (2) there is a far greater range of individual differences in assimilation rates in the case of reading than in that of understanding speech.

A few investigators have attempted to assess the relative effectiveness of listening and reading for information acquisition and retention. It is difficult, however, to come up with a meaningful generalization from the results of these studies. Which of the two modes proves to be more effective in any particular case seems to depend on several variables, such as the nature (substance and organization) of the material, the listener/reader's general familiarity with the subject matter, the level of skill as a listener or (especially) reader, and the purpose for which the information is being acquired.

TOP—DOWN PROCESSES IN
LANGUAGE COMPREHENSION

The role of bottom–up or data-driven processes in speech understanding and reading is obvious. One usually does not hear speech unless there is some to hear, or see text unless there is some to see. Moreover, generally what one hears is what was said, and what one sees is what is actually on the page. The role of top–down or knowledge-driven processes may be less apparent a priori, but evidence is accumulating that it is no less real.

To illustrate the interaction between top–down and bottom–up processing in speech understanding, Marslen-Wilson and Welsh (1978) varied degree of contextual constraint, magnitude of phonetic deviation (either one or three features), and position of the deviation within the word (first or third syllable) in both a shadowing and a mispronunciation-detection task. For our purposes, the most notable result from this experiment was that single-feature changes of individual phonemes were detected poorly by either method when they occurred in the context of meaningful speech. This illustrates the potency of the top–down processing for compensating for imperfections in the speech signal. It also illustrates the immediacy of the effect of the interaction between the data-driven and knowledge-driven processes: The result of the interaction is the listener's immediate conscious percept and not secondary perceptual effects following from a reworking of the initial analysis of the input.

Another bit of evidence that what we hear when we listen to speech is determined in part by our knowledge of linguistic rules and conventions at the level of phoneme sequences comes from the phenomenon of "phonological fusion." When different words or phoneme strings are presented simultaneously to the two ears, they will "fuse" under some conditions, producing a perception that is based on a composite of the individual inputs. The pair *pay/lay,* for example, may be perceived as *play,* or *go/row* as *grow* (Cutting, 1975; Day, 1968, 1970). Such fusions do not always occur, but when they do the resulting words (or nonwords) tend to be consistent with the phonological rules of English. For example, if one of the input strings begins with a stop consonant and the other with a liquid, the fused percept will contain these two phonemes with the liquid following the stop and never preceding it, even when the onset of the liquid slightly precedes that of the stop.

Cutting (1975) has demonstrated that semantic, phonemic, and acoustic cues are all influential in determining the fusibility of dichotically presented stimulus pairs. The effect of semantic context seems to be to increase the probability of fusibility of two words, which would have been likely to have been fused even when presented in isolation. The role of semantic factors is also indicated by the fact that fusions tend to occur more frequently when the fused percept is an acceptable English word than when it is not (Day, 1968). Thus, fusions of these sorts are not entirely stimulus determined; what listeners perceive, or at least report, depends in part on knowledge about English phonology that they bring to the task. Cutting also notes that phonological fusion has a visual analog, which apparently was discovered before the work was done in the auditory domain. Rommetveit and his colleagues had found that when letters such as *shar* were presented to one eye and *shap* to the other, subjects often fused the two sets and reported seeing *sharp*. (See Cutting, 1975, for references.)

The necessity of appealing to context for the resolution of inherent ambiguities is apparent in both spoken and written language. Words that sound alike but have different spellings and meanings (*rain, reign; flour, flower*) are obvious illustrations of this point for speech understanding, and those that have more than one pronunciation and meaning (*lead, invalid*) make the case for reading. And, of course, many words with only a single spelling and pronunciation have more than one meaning and therefore must depend on context for disambiguation.

In addition to the fact that the use of contextual information is essential for dealing with the problem of multiple word meanings in both oral and written language, there is a wealth of evidence showing that contextual information can facilitate comprehension even in situations when appeal to it may not be a logical necessity. This facilitative role of context may be viewed as one manifestation of a more general and widely studied phenomenon, namely the influence on perceptual processes of the a priori uncertainty in the mind of the perceiver regarding the nature of the stimulus that one is trying to detect, recognize, or identify.

The results of numerous studies of effects of stimulus uncertainty (for reviews see Garner, 1962; Luce, 1960) illustrate that perceptual performance depends in part on the knowledge the perceiver brings to the task regarding the stimulus (and the potential stimuli). In the cases of speech understanding and reading, not only do listeners bring a wealth of linguistic and world knowledge to the task, they acquire information while listening to or looking at one part of the stimulus sequence that can be used to facilitate the interpretation of subsequent (or preceding) parts. Thus, the same words are more readily recognized within sentence contexts than when presented in isolation (Miller, Heise, & Lichten, 1951; Schuberth & Eimas, 1977; Tulving & Gold, 1963). And the degree to which that context facilitates the perception of a given word depends on how good a basis it provides for predicting that word when the word itself is not presented (Kalikow, Stevens, & Elliott, 1977).

In short, contextual effects are ubiquitous in both speech understanding and reading, as they are in perception more generally. The importance of situational (as opposed to linguistic) context, however, is more apparent in speech understanding than in reading. Speech typically (though not always) is an interpersonal activity occurring in a social setting and involving an interaction between at least two people who share a common spatiotemporal frame of reference. The information that is exchanged via speech is amplified and supplemented with information that is communicated by nonverbal means and by the situation in which the exchange occurs. Ambiguities can be resolved and obfuscations clarified through real-time interactions initiated by the speaker or requested by the listener. Generally, none of these is true of reading.

One consequence of this difference is that there is a greater burden on a writer than on a speaker to make meaning clear. Writers must anticipate all the difficulties of interpretation that readers might have; speakers have the luxury of feeling their way and of being only as precise as listeners' moment-to-moment reactions demand. Another consequence of the fact that a speaker and listener typically share a situational context, whereas a writer and reader do not, is that oral language makes greater use of ellipsis and deixis than does written language. Thus the statement, *I prefer the one on your left,* might be meaningful in a face-to-face conversation, but it would be a strange message to send in a letter.

Even when engaged in telephone conversation, speaker and listener may share a situational context, though to a lesser extent than when talking face to face. Knowledge of each other's identity, for example, permits the unambiguous use of references to *you* and *me.* A common temporal context insures that references to *now, yesterday,* or *next week* will mean the same thing to both parties to the conversation. Locational and societal contexts also may be shared to greater or lesser degrees. Thus, people who live in the same community may make elliptical references to the weather, to common acquaintances, to local events, and so on.

Writers and readers typically cannot be assumed to share situational contexts to the same degree as speakers and listeners, which is not to say that shared situational contexts play no role in producing and understanding written language. Writers typically assume that readers will possess knowledge that is common to their shared culture or subculture. And writing of a more personal nature—personal letters—may make considerable use of shared semiprivate knowledge and common frames of reference.

Both speech understanding and reading are increasingly viewed as multifaceted activities in which both bottom–up, analytical, data-driven processes and top–down, inferential, knowledge-driven processes play important roles. Moreover, the activities are viewed as involving an interaction between the two types of processes, in which the top–down hypotheses that are generated are determined in part by the results of the bottom–up analyses, and the bottom–up processing is guided in part by the expectancies that are imposed from the top. Speech understanding and reading differ with respect to the nature of the contextual and knowledge-based cues they involve, but both require the use of such cues.

TOWARD A MODEL OF
SPEECH UNDERSTANDING AND READING

At least one purpose of written or spoken communication is the transmission of information—the conveying of ideas—from one mind to another. The key questions that need to be answered, if one would understand this process, have to do with relationships between ideas and the symbol systems used to represent them for transmission. How is it that an idea gets translated into a structured sound wave or a pattern of marks on paper, and, conversely, how is it that such patterns get translated back into ideas? One might define degree of comprehension as the degree to which the ideas that the pattern of sounds or marks evokes in the mind of the listener or reader correspond to those that existed in the mind of the speaker or writer who produced those patterns. This may not be a very useful definition, however, because of the difficulty of judging the degree of correspondence between ideas independently of the patterns in terms of which they are represented.

One thing that does seem to be increasingly clear is that the process by which language is understood is an immensely complex one. Also, more and more, speech understanding and reading are being viewed as knowledge-based/problem-solving skills in which listeners or readers attempt to extract from a signal (speech wave or printed text) cues, which when combined with other relevant information at their disposal, will permit them to construct or test a hypothesis as to what the speaker or writer has said. Both involve the generation of hypotheses or expectancies, the directed seeking of information, the making of inferences, or, more generally, the continual search for and utilization of uncertainty-reducing cues concerning what it is that one is listening to or looking at. In this respect, speech understanding and reading are representative of perception more broadly. The perceiver's problem is to construct and test a model of the world in general and of the events in his or her immediate perceptual field in particular.

However, the perception involved in communication puts at least two kinds of demands on the perceiver that perception more broadly defined typically does not. First, communication involves the production of symbols by a "sender" and their reception and interpretation by a "receiver." The receiver's task is only partially completed upon determining what the sender has "said" (whether orally, in writing, or in any other way); the more important problem is understanding what the sender means.

Contemporary investigators of language and linguistic behavior have made a strong case for the importance in communication of the role of intentions, goals, plans, and beliefs (Austin, 1962; Cohen & Perrault, 1979; Griece, 1957; Searle, 1969). To appreciate, in any deep sense, what takes place in a conversation, one must consider such questions as: How does the speaker intend to affect the listeners, to influence their behavior, emotional state, or model of the world?

What does the speaker believe about what the listeners believe, including what the listeners believe about what the speaker believes? What is the nature of the illocutionary act that is performed in the making of an utterance: assertion, request, warning, order, apology? What is the effect of the act: conviction, anger, fright? What kinds of ancillary or "side-effect" information are conveyed by such acts: information about the speaker's beliefs, intentions emotional state?

Most of the discussion of these matters has focused on speech and, in particular, on conversational situations. Much of it is equally relevant, however, to written communication, especially written communication involving a bidirectional exchange (e.g., postal correspondence). In this regard it is important to bear in mind a distinction that is often obscured in comparisons of speech understanding and reading. Such comparisons often fail to distinguish two somewhat independent factors: (1) whether the mode of communication is speech or writing; (2) whether the communication is unidirectional or bidirectional. In particular, sometimes characteristics that are ascribed to writing are more appropriately viewed as characteristics of unidirectional situations or media (e.g., lectures, books). Similarly, properties that are sometimes attributed to speech are really more descriptive of bidirectional media (e.g., conversations, personal letters).

To make the same point in a slightly different way, lectures and books have many similarities, as do conversations and letters; spontaneous speech is likely to differ in certain respects from recitation or oral reading, and the characteristics of written material may differ somewhat depending on whether the writer intended the product to be read aloud. But comparisons between speech and writing often overlook this fact by describing speech as though it were always spontaneous and conversational and writing as though it were always formal and unidirectional.

Rubin (1977) has criticized the method of comparing comprehension of the same passage when it is presented as written text and when it is heard as speech for investigating differences between the comprehension of written and spoken language. Her point is that inasmuch as written language and oral language differ in many respects, it is not clear what can be concluded from experiments in which oral language is presented in written form or written language is presented orally. I believe this point to be well taken. Although it is not necessarily a good reason to avoid making these comparisons, it dictates caution in the interpretation of their results.

A second way in which perception in communication differs from perception more generally stems from the fact that language is often used in figurative or nonliteral ways. Perkins (1978), among others, has discussed how metaphorical writing poses special problems for the reader. In particular, it requires "insightful," as opposed to "careful," reading. Careful reading suffices for the comprehension of what is explicit in text, but not for the understanding of what is there only implicitly or analogically. Perkins (1978) writes: "One needs to learn to read not only the lines, but between the lines. One needs the knack of attending to suggestion and connotation. One must follow out implication and innuendo [p. 133].'' He makes the insightful point that there is a difference between understanding the explanation of a metaphor and understanding (''seeing'') the metaphor. Presumably, what is true of written language in this regard is true of speech as well.

The inferring of intentions and the interpreting of metaphors represent two of the ways in which the understanding of speech or text requires the listener or hearer to go beyond the given. There are others. Reflection on the various roles that inference may play in language understanding leads one to raise the question of what it means to say that something is comprehended or understood. If I read that all men are mortal and that Socrates is a man, yet fail to understand that Socrates is mortal, have I comprehended what I have read? One might answer the question either way. I have understood the individual assertions but failed to see what they imply. Shall we let this pass for comprehension or not? The mortal/Socrates example is perhaps too trivial a reasoning problem to provide a plausible illustration of how what is in a text explicitly may be understood, whereas what is there only implicitly is missed. It is easy to think of more complex and realistic examples, but the simple one suffices to make the point. To what extent must that which is represented in a text only implicitly be appreciated before we can say the text has been understood? Clearly our understanding of understanding must recognize the notion of degree.

The need to invoke the idea of degree of understanding is apparent in many cases other than those involving intentions, metaphors, and syllogistic reasoning. Puns, double-entendres, and innuendos are examples of linguistic forms whose full meanings can be missed without necessarily precluding comprehension to some extent. Allegories are also examples of material that can be understood at different levels or to different degrees. The child's understanding of *The Ugly Duckling, Gulliver's Travels,* or *Don Quixote* may correspond relatively closely to that of an adult at a literal level, but the adult may impose figurative interpretations on such stories that are beyond the child's comprehension.

Another thing that seems fairly clear is that language may be more or less difficult to comprehend for a variety of reasons. Comprehension is bound to be impossible if the signal is of sufficiently poor quality to preclude being decoded into words or if the material is nonsensical (i.e., inherently uninterpretable). But even given a high-quality signal encoding inherently meaningful speech or text, the ease with which the meaning can be extracted is likely to depend on a variety of factors such as: (1) the frequency of words whose meanings the listener/reader does not recognize; (2) the complexity of sentence structure; (3) suprasentential factors such as the ordering of sentences and the progression of ideas; and (4) the conceptual complexity of the subject matter and the listener's/reader's degree of familiarity with it.

The last factor illustrates the importance to comprehension of the world knowledge that listeners/readers bring to the task and into which they incorporate what they hear or read. It is apparent that the ease with which people understand the information that is being conveyed will depend on how that information relates to what they already know. The fact that a child of 12 is usually a more proficient reader than a child of 8 is due in some measure to the greater amount of general world knowledge that the 12-year-old has acquired. Adult readers also differ from one anoother in terms of both general knowledge and language competency, but subject-specific knowledge probably takes on increasing significance in this case. Thus, in general, physics will be read more comprehendingly by a physicist, history by a historian, and economics by an economist, because the subject-specific information that the reader brings to the task in each case facilitates the reading process in at least two ways. First, if one already has stored away much information regarding the subject matter being read, reading will involve not so much the assimilation of new information as the reactivation of familiar concepts. Second, even if the information that is being processed is genuinely new, the reader's subject-specific knowledge provides a context, or frame of reference, into which it can be placed. Historians, for example, reading about a particular historical event for the first time can relate that event to others that they are aware of in a way that an individual who is not knowledgeable in history cannot. What holds for reading in this regard holds, of course, for listening as well.

One might define comprehension as a putting of incoming information into an appropriate conceptual context. The richer the existing context into which the incoming information can be incorporated, the more tightly the new data can be coupled to related ideas and the greater will be the level of comprehension. The extent to which comprehension will be precluded by an impoverished existing context will depend on the nature of the material that is being listened to or read. For example, comprehension of instructions for cooking oatmeal is probably not very demanding in this regard. In contrast, the writings of philosophical essayists such as Montaigne, Lamb, and Ruskin, are probably not fully comprehensible unless one brings to them the same breadth of knowledge as did the writers themselves.

Clearly a model that can do justice both to the complexity and the effectiveness of the processes by which we understand language is a large order. Such a model must take into account both bottom–up and top–down processes and their interaction. It must accommodate the ubiquitous effects of various types of context. It must be sufficiently sophisticated to allow for degrees of comprehension. It must be robust enough to encompass the various languages and signaling systems that people use to communicate (speech and writing being only the two most obvious means), and sensitive enough to represent the important differences among them.

No attempt is made to present such a model here. What is attempted, however, is a listing of some of the key notions that I believe should underlie the development of such a model and some of the characteristics and components that such a model might have.

1. Closed-Loop Nature of the Process.   One key notion is that of a dynamic closed-loop process, in which the conceptual model in the mind of the perceiver is continually modified and elaborated by the incoming sensory data and in which the interpretation of those data are conditioned at any given instant by the momentary status of that model. The process is assumed to be hierarchical because it makes sense to talk of levels of analysis and to think of the outputs of lower-level analyses flowing as inputs up to higher-level processes. The assumption is not made, however, that any given component process communicates with one and only one other component process, the latter being located one level up in the hierarchy. The network is assumed to be richly interconnected, with components at any given level communicating not only with (possibly) several components at the immediately higher level but also (perhaps) with high-level components more than one level removed, with other components at the same level, and with lower-level components as well.

2. Selective Processing.   The language comprehender is not indifferent or unbiased with respect to which aspects of a speech signal or text get processed. Some attention is allocated to the task of collecting data of various types and from various sources (including internal sources) for the purpose of generating hypotheses about what is being heard or read. And some is allocated to the task of testing those hypotheses. Selectivity is particularly strong in the latter case: Attention is directed toward cues that could be especially informative with respect to the hypothesis or hypotheses under consideration. I assume that, in general, the perceiver attempts to find cues that will corroborate (rather than disprove) a working hypothesis, and, only if unable to do so or forced by weight of counterevidence, will one abandon a working hypothesis and generate an alternative.

3. Maintenance of a Working Hypothesis Regarding Meaning.   It is assumed that the listener/reader always has a hypothesis (not necessarily complete) about the meaning of what is being heard/read. The status of this hypothesis changes in time both with respect to completeness and confidence. In experimental situations in which speech or printed matter is presented under adverse conditions (in noise, for brief duration, etc.), the final status of one's working hypothesis may be incomplete ("I know what the first three words are, but I missed the last few"), uncertain ("I think it said . . . but am not sure"), or both. In real-life situations, listeners/readers are likely to continue collecting data until the working hypothesis is complete and confidence in it is acceptably high, if the situation permits them to do so.

4. Maintenance of Perceptual or Cognitive Integrity and Continuity.   One purpose of the activity underlying speech understanding and reading (and particularly the former) is to maintain an accurate model of one's world. A constraint upon the language-understanding process is the need of one's model of the world to maintain its logical integrity and its spatiotemporal continuity. One cannot perceive oneself as being in Boston at one instant and in New York the next. Or, to take a less extreme and more pertinent example, a change in the substance of an utterance or a text that is so abrupt as to introduce material that is completely independent of what preceded the change is likely to make for difficulty in comprehension. The listener or reader will strive to make what is heard or seen at one instant substantively consistent with what was heard or seen a moment before.

5. The Notion of Sufficient Effort.   An utterance, or a segment of written material, is assumed to be processed only to the extent necessary to verify or disconfirm a hypothesis at some acceptable level of confidence. In particular, the more information listeners/readers have of one type by which they can generate and test hypotheses, the less they need of another. There is a tradeoff, for example, between the strength of a priori expectations and the amount of processing that is done. If the expectation for a specific linguistic unit is high because of various contextual factors, then the listener or reader will accept a hypothesis as true on the basis of relatively little confirming information. Conversely, more information will be needed to disconfirm a strong expectation. When a priori expectations are not strong, one needs relatively more information, not only to provide a basis for testing hypotheses but for generating them in the first place. In other words, one makes use of redundancy in language, of linguistic and situational constraints, and of knowledge of the world in general and of the subject in particular, to limit the amount of processing necessary to impose an acceptable meaning on an utterance or on a segment of printed text.

The general view of speech understanding and reading that prompts these observations is an eclectic one incorporating notions advanced by several investigators. The idea of a hierarchical organization of feature analyzers is at least as old as the pandemonium model of Selfridge (1959). The notion of several (top-down and bottom-up) processes or "knowledge sources," interacting in closed-loop fashion has been promoted by Rumelhart (1977). The idea of flexible multicomponent criteria for word recognition, in which lack of information of one type can be compensated for by availability of information of another type is a feature of the logogen model of Morton (1970). Flexibility is also incorporated in LaBerge and Samuels' (1974) model of reading by virtue of the assumption that the steps, or "stages," by which visual information eventuates in meaning comprehension may vary from situation to situation (sometimes a phonological recoding may be involved; sometimes it may not). Emphasis on the importance of context and the roles of knowledge and inference in language comprehension is increasingly apparent in discussions both of speech understanding and reading.

It seems fair to say that appreciation of the complexity of the processes underlying language comprehension, and of the considerable cognitive demands that they make on the listener/reader, has increased as a result of recent work in this area. Moreover, the models that are being developed are increasingly sophisticated and reflective of the growing appreciation of this complexity (e.g., Hochberg, 1970; Kolers, 1972; Marslen-Wilson, 1975; Rumelhart, 1977; Woods, 1978). However, it also seems fair to say that none of the existing models really come to grips with the basic question relating to language-processing skills. Namely, how is it that ideas get represented in, extracted from, and imposed upon arbitrary physical symbols such as sound patterns and visual shapes? A fundamental fact about speech understanding and skilled reading is that the listener/reader usually is not aware of phonemes or letters, or even of words, but of the ideas, the meanings, they convey. A satisfactory understanding of either speech perception or reading may not be forthcoming until we understand the nature of those ideas better than we do now.

Oettinger (1972) nicely sums up our current state of ignorance regarding human communication, in spite of the intensive attention the subject has received from researchers in the recent past:

> Two decades of linguistic research of unprecedented intensity have revealed only how miraculously the process of human communication performs its everyday wonders. So simple that nearly every child masters it almost unconsciously, this process is so complex that all our efforts at understanding it have yielded only fragmentary and superficial insights. . . . We are more than ever baffled by how language performs its primary function, to convey meaning. All our understanding of the mechanics of language, built up from real or fancied elementary building blocks, stops dead before the question of meaning [pp. 1; 2].

This is not to say that less is known now than before the research of which Oettinger writes was done or that nothing has been accomplished in the ensuing years. In fact much has been learned, but new knowledge has brought with it a fuller appreciation of how great our ignorance of the process of language comprehension really is. Any description—let alone explanation—of speech understanding or reading that is offered today is bound to be not only incomplete, but probably wrong in all but its grossest aspects. It does not follow that we should not theorize, only that we should not take our theorizing too seriously.

What, by way of summary, may be said of the differences and similarities between speech understanding and reading? A superficial answer to this question would focus on the difference between the physical stimuli involved and the different types of anlayses that must be performed on them. It is apparent that sound-pressure waves differ drastically from "squiggles" on paper and that the detection and analysis of structure within such disparate coding media require very different methods of signal processing. It is tempting to assume that this is the only difference between speech understanding and reading and that once one has acquired enough (phonemic or graphemic) information from the auditory or visual signal to provide a basis for accessing the lexicon of meanings, the nature of the physical signal is no longer relevant and the two processes are identical.

This view is certainly too simple. First, it assumes an open-loop serial-stage model of language comprehension that is not tenable. Second, it overlooks some differences between the types of information available to listeners and readers that have implications for aspects of their tasks other than those involving signal analysis. In particular, it overlooks the fact that speech understanding and reading typically occur in quite different situational contexts that provide different types of extralinguistic cues by which comprehension may be facilitated and also that speech and writing are typically used for different communicative purposes. Nevertheless, the differences between the two types of processes become more apparent when one focuses on the stimuli and the sensory systems that transduce them than when one considers the cognitive activity that must be involved in the determination of meaning.

What of the claim that the relationship between reading and speech is a parasitic one (Gibson, 1970; Gleitman & Rozin, 1977; Gough, 1972)? Normally reading ability is acquired only after speech skills have been fairly well developed. Methods for teaching reading typically involve the use of sight-to-sound correspondence rules and in other ways build upon previously developed skills. Moreover, it would be difficult to deny that some readers do "sound out" words subvocally even when reading silently. However, it does not follow that reading is *necessarily* parasitic on speech. And the question of whether or not it should be considered so is important for at least two reasons.

First, the question has implications for the teaching of reading to people whose speech skills have not developed in the usual fashion. An important example of people in this category are those who are born deaf or who become deaf before acquiring language. As a group, prelingually deaf people tend not to become proficient readers (Brooks, 1978; Furth, 1973). To what extent this is a consequence of the lack of oral-aural language skills on which to build, as opposed to teaching methods that are better suited to hearing children than to those who are deaf, is not known. Clearly these factors are not independent because, to the extent that the teaching methods assume competence in oral-aural language, they may not be suitable for use with prelingually deaf children.

Second, if reading is not necessarily dependent on speech, acting as if it were could have the effect of unduly constraining thought regarding how reading should be taught to children in general. Teaching it as though it must be parasitic on speech almost assures that it in fact will be thought of in those terms. Moreover, it assures that the reading process will have all of the constraints and limitations that close coupling to speech implies.

The question of whether the lexicon is accessed via a phonological code during reading has been controversial. Some investigators of reading have asserted that it is, and some have asserted that it is not. (See Coltheart, Davelaar, Jonasson, & Besner, 1977, for several quotes on both sides of this issue.) It is not always clear from the comments of those investigators who subscribe to the view that reading involves a graphemic-to-phonemic code translation whether this step is considered a necessary, or only a common, one.

On balance, the evidence seems to indicate that people often do translate print to implicit speech when reading connected text[2] but that such a translation is not essential; meaning can be accessed directly from the visual code. One piece of evidence against the necessity of going from a graphemic to a phonemic representation in order to retrieve the meaning of a word is the fact that we are able to deal with words that have different meanings associated with different pronunciations (*lead, sewer, invalid*). It cannot be the case that in reading aloud, one does not understand what is being read until one hears oneself say it. The reader's comprehension of the text must typically run ahead of the words that are being produced. If this were not so, one could not correctly pronounce words or impose correct intonation and stress patterns on utterances when reading aloud. Intonation and stress patterns are functions of larger linguistic segments than individual phonemes or words. To hold to the view that access to meaning requires passing through a phonological code, one would have to hold that oral reading involves two such coding stages: one to get the meaning of the text and another to program the speech output.

A similar point may be made with respect to the decoding of homophonous words (*sight, site, cite*), of which there are many in English. If, in the reading process, a visual stimulus got one only as far as the retrieval of a phonological code, with which one were then to enter the lexicon, it is difficult to see how the process could deal with such words.

What does all this imply with respect to the teaching of reading? The available evidence does not force one to conclude either that phonological recoding is essential to lexical access or that reading competence is necessarily dependent on oral-aural language in the sense that if one does not have good speech skills one cannot learn to read well. The evidence does indicate, however, that phonological recoding does often (perhaps typically) occur during the reading of continuous text. Whether this recoding occurs because of the way reading is taught is unclear. Whether it typically takes place before, simultaneously with, or after

---

[2]There is an interesting corollary to this observation that to my knowledge has not been studied. I have the impression that examples of just the opposite process—transformation of phonemic representations to graphemic representations as an aid to comprehension—might be found if one looked for them. The basis for this conjecture is the recollection of the experience of being for the first time in a French-speaking country, after having taken high-school French courses in which I learned to read the language passably well but acquired essentially no skill in speaking it or understanding it in the spoken form. What I found myself doing in a frantic effort to understand what was being said to me was to ask people to speak slowly so that I could visualize the words. The strategy did not work well—a major problem was the identification of word boundaries—but it got me by and reflecting on it makes me wonder whether a search for examples of sound-to-sight translation in speech understanding would produce any useful insights to the relationship between speech and reading.

lexical access is controversial; perhaps all three possibilities are realized, depending on the reader and the circumstances. It is clear that lexical access is not the only reason why phonological recoding might occur. Even if the lexicon can be accessed directly with a visual code, a phonologically coded representation of a segment of text—produced in parallel with or following lexical access—may be useful as a means of retaining surface information until the meaning of a multiword linguistic unit is obtained.

The claim that phonological recoding is not essential to lexical access is not necessarily an argument against using phonics in the teaching of reading. Using existing oral-aural language skills as a point of departure for teaching reading, and taking advantage of spelling-to-sound correspondence rules to simplify the process of learning to recognize printed words, can undoubtedly be defended on grounds other than the assumption that the only way to the lexicon is through a phonological code. Perhaps there are no better ways to teach reading, and perhaps reading will always be a speechlike activity. However, in the absence of compelling evidence for the necessity of this close coupling, one must wonder not only about the possibility of developing more effective methods of teaching reading to persons who lack speech skills, but also about whether competent speech users might not be better readers if taught in radically different ways.

ACKNOWLEDGMENTS

I am indebted to the following people for helpful discussions about the contents of this chapter or criticisms of a draft of the manuscript: Marilyn Adams, Jonathan Baron, Deborah Birkmire, Bertram Bruce, Helen Ghiradella, Paul Kolers, Richard Monty, David Perkins, and Edward Smith.

REFERENCES

Abrams, M. H., Goffard, S. J., Kryter, K. D., Miller, G. A., Sanford, J., & Sanford, F. H. *Speech in noise: A study of factors determining its intelligibility* (OSRD No. 4023). Cambridge, Mass.: Harvard University, Psychoacoustics Laboratory, 1944. (PB 19805).

Adams, M. J. Models of word recognition. *Cognitive Psychology*, 1979, *11*, 133–176.

Adams, M, J., & Collins, A. M. A schema-theoretic view of reading. In R. Freedle (Ed.), *New directions in discourse processing*. Norwood, N.J.: Ablex 1979.

Austin, J. L. How to do things with words. In J. O. Urmson (Ed.), New York: Oxford University Press, 1962.

Bassin, C. B., & Martin, C. J. Effect of three types of redundancy reduction on comprehension, reading rate, and reading time of English prose. *Journal of Educational Psychology*, 1976, *68*, 649–652.

Brooks, P. H. Some speculations concerning deafness and learning to read. In L. S. Liben (Ed.), *Deaf children: Developmental perspectives*. New York: Academic Press, 1978.

Burton, J. G., & Licklider, J. C. R. Long range constraints in the statistical structure of printed English. *American Journal of Psychology*, 1955, *68*, 650–653.

Buswell, G. T. How adults read. *Supplementary Educational Monographs*, 1937, *45*.

Cattell, J. McK. [On the time for the recognition and naming of written symbols, pictures, and colors.] In A. T. Poffenberger (Ed. and trans.), *James McKeen Cattell: Man of science*. York, Penn.: Science Press, 1947. (Originally published 1885).

Cohen, P. R., & Perrault, C. R. *Elements of a plan-based theory of speech acts* (Tech. Rep. No. 141). Urbana: University of Illinois, Center for the Study of Reading, July 1979.

Cole, R. A., & Zue, V. W. Speech as eyes see it. In R. S. Nickerson (Ed.), *Attention and performance VIII*. Hillsdale, N.J.: Lawrence Erlbaum Associates, 1980.

Coltheart, M., Davelaar, E., Jonasson, J. T., & Besner, D. Access to the internal lexicon. In S. Dornic (Ed.), *Attention and performance VI*. Hillsdale, N.J.: Lawrence Erlbaum Associates, 1977.

Conrad, R. Acoustic confusions in immediate memory. *British Journal of Psychology*, 1964, *55*, 75–84.

Conrad, R. Speech and reading. In J. F. Kavanagh & I. G. Mattingly (Eds.), *Language by ear and by eye: The relationships between speech and reading*. Cambridge, Mass.: MIT Press, 1972.

Cutting, J. E. Aspects of phonological fusion. *Journal of Experimental Psychology: Human Perception and Performance*, 1975, *104*, 105–120.

Cutting, J. E. There may be nothing peculiar to perceiving in a speech mode. In J. Requin (Ed.), *Attention and performance VII*. Hillsdale, N.J.: Lawrence Erlbaum Associates, 1978.

Day, R. S. *Fusion in dichotic listening*. Unpublished doctoral dissertation, Stanford University, 1968.

Day, R. S. Temporal-order perception of a reversible phoneme cluster. *Journal of the Acoustical Society of America*, 1970, *48*, 95.

Furth, H. G. *Deafness and leaning: A psychological approach*. Belmont, Cal.: Wadsworth, 1973.

Garner, W. R. *Uncertainty and structure as psychological concepts*. New York: John Wiley & Sons, 1962.

Gibson, E. J., Pick, A., Osser, H., & Hammond, M. The role of grapheme-phoneme correspondence in the perception of words. *American Journal of Psychology*, 1962, *75*, 554–570.

Gibson, E. W. The ontogeny of reading. *American Psychologist*, 1970, *25*, 136–143.

Gleitman, L. R., & Rozin, P. The structure and acquisition of reading I: Relations between orthographies and the structure of language. In A. Reber & D. L. Scarborough (Eds.), *Toward a psychology of reading*. Hillsdale, N.J.: Lawrence Erlbaum Associates, 1977.

Gough, P. One second of reading. In J. P. Kavanagh & I. G. Mattingly (Eds.), *Language by eye and by ear*. Cambridge, Mass.: MIT Press, 1972.

Gregory, D. S. Compressed speech—The state of the art. *IEEE Transactions on Engineering Writing, and Speech*, 1969, *EWS-12*, 12–17.

Griece, H. P. Meaning. *The Philosophical Review*, 1957, *66*, 377–388.

Hochberg, J. Components of literacy: Speculations and exploratory research. In H. Levin & J. P Williams (Eds.), *Basic studies on reading*. New York: Basic Books, 1970.

Hochberg, J. Toward a speech-plan eye-movement model of reading. In R. A. Monty & J. W. Senders (Eds.), *Eye movements and psychological processes*. Hillsdale, N.J.: Lawrence Erlbaum Associates, 1976.

Huey, E. *Psychology and pedagogy of reading*. New York: Macmillan, 1908.

Jacobson, H. The informational capacity of the human eye. *Science*, 1951, *113*, 463–471. (a)

Jacobson, H. Information and the human ear. *Journal of the Acoustical Society of America*, 1951, *23*, 463–476. (b)

Johnson, N. F. On the function of letters in word identification: Some data and a preliminary model. *Journal of Verbal Learning and Verbal Behavior*, 1975, *14*, 17–29.

Kalikow, D. N., Stevens, K. N., & Elliott, L. L. Development of a test of speech intelligibility in noise using sentence materials with controlled word predictability. *Journal of the Acoustical Society of America*, 1977, *61*, 1337–1351.

Klatt, D. H., & Stevens, K. N. On the automatic recognition of continuous speech: Implications from a spectrogram-reading experiment. *IEEE Transactions on Audio and Electroacoustics,* 1973, *AU-21,* 210–216.

Kolers, P. A. Three stages of reading. In H. Levin & J. P. Williams (Eds.), *Basic studies on reading.* New York: Basic Books, 1970.

Kolers, P. A. Experiments in reading. *Scientific American,* 1972, *227,* 84–91.

Kolers, P. A. Two kinds of recognition. *Canadian Journal of Psychology,* 1974, *28,* 51–61.

Kolers, P. A. The role of eye movements in reading. In R. A. Mont & J. W. Senders (Eds.), *Eye movements and psychological processes.* Hillsdale, N.J.: Lawrence Erlbaum Associates, 1976.

Kroll, N. E. A., Parks, T. E., Parkinson, S. R., Bieber, S. L., & Johnson, A. L. Short-term memory while shadowing: Recall of visually and of aurally presented letters. *Journal of Experimental Psychology,* 1970, *85,* 220–224.

LaBerge, D., & Samuels, S. J. Toward a theory of automatic information processing in reading. *Cognitive Psychology,* 1974, *6,* 293–323.

Lesgold, A. M. Variability in children's comprehension of syntactic structures. *Journal of Edicational Psychology,* 1974, *66,* 339–347.

Luce, R. D. The theory of selective information and some of its behavioral applications. In R. D. Luce (Ed.), *Developments in mathematical psychology.* Glencoe, Ill.: The Free Press of Glencoe, 1960.

Maclay, H., & Osgood, C. E. Hesitation in phenomena in spontaneous English speech. In L. A. Jakobovits & M. S. Miron (Eds.), *Readings in the psychology of language.* Englewood Cliffs, N.J.: Prentice-Hall, 1967.

Marslen-Wilson, W. Sentence perception as an interactive parallel process. *Science,* 1975, *189,* 226–227.

Marslen, Wilson, W. D., & Welsh, A. Processing interactions and lexical access during word recognition in continuous speech. *Cognitive Psychology,* 1978, *10,* 29–63.

Martin, C. J., & Peterson, P. W. Comprehension of auditorily presented telegraphic prose. *Journal of Applied Psychology,* 1977, *62,* 220–223.

Martin, C. J., & Sheffield, C. The effect of telegraphic prose on the reading behavior of blind and sighted students. *Journal of Applied Psychology,* 1976, *61,* 513–518.

McClelland, J. L. Preliminary letter identification in the perception of words and nonwords. *Journal of Experimental Psychology: Human Perception and Performance,* 1976, *2,* 80–91.

Miller, G. A. *Language and communication.* New York: McGraw-Hill, 1951.

Miller, G. A. Decision units in the perception of speech. *IRE Transactions on Information Theory,* 1962, *IT-8,* 81–83.

Miller, G. A., Heise, G. A., & Lichten, W. The intelligibility of speech as a function of the context of the test materials. *Journal of Experimental Psychology,* 1951, *41,* 329–335.

Morton, J. A functional model for memory. In D. A. Norman (Ed.), *Models of human memory.* New York: Academic Press, 1970.

Newman, E. B., & Gerstman, L. J. A new method of analyzing printed English. *Journal of Experimental Psychology,* 1952, *44,* 114–125.

Nickerson, R. S. Auditory codability and the short-term retention of visual information. *Journal of Experimental Psychology,* 1972, *95*(2), 429–436.

Nickerson, R. S., & Freeman, B. Discrimination of the order of the components of repeating tone sequences: Effects of frequency separation and extensive practice. *Perception & Psychophysics,* 1974, *16,* 471–477.

Oettinger, A. The semantic wall. In E. E. David, Jr., & P. B. Denes (Eds.), *Human communication: A unified view.* New York: McGraw-Hill, 1972.

Parkinson, S. R., Parks, T. E., & Kroll, N. E. A. Visual and auditory short-term memory: Effects of phonemically similar auditory shadow material during the retention interval. *Journal of Experimental Psychology,* 1971, *87,* 274–280.

Perkins, D. N. Metaphorical perception. In E. Eisner (Ed.), *Reading, the arts and the creation of meaning*. Reston, Va.: National Art Education Association, 1978.

Quastler, H., & Wulff, V. J. *Human performance in information transmission* (Rep. No. 62). Urbana: University of Illinois, Control Systems Laboratory, 1955.

Reicher, G. M. Perceptual recognition as a function of meaningfulness of stimulus material. *Journal of Experimental Psychology*, 1969, *81*, 274-280.

Rubin, A. D. *The relation between comprehension processes in oral and written language*. Urbana: Center for the Study of Reading, January 1977.

Rumelhart, D. E. Toward an interactive model of reading. In S. Dornic (Ed.), *Attention and performance VI*. Hillsdale, N.J.: Lawrence Erlbaum Associates, 1977.

Schuberth, R. E., Eimas, P. D. Effects of context on the classification of words and nonwords. *Journal of Experimental Psychology: Human Perception and Performance*, 1977, *3*, 27-36.

Searle, J. R. *Speech acts: An essay in the philosophy of language*. Cambridge: Cambridge University Press, 1969.

Selfridge, O. Pandemonium: A paradigm for learning. In *The mechanisation of thought processes*. London: Her Majesty's Stationery Office, 1959.

Shannon, C. E. Prediction and entropy of printed English. *Bell System Technical Journal*, 1951, *30*, 56-64.

Smith, E. E., & Haviland, S. E. Why words are perceived more accurately than nonwords: Inference vs. unitization. *Journal of Experimental Psychology*, 1972, *92*, 59-64.

Sperling, G., & Speelman, R. G. Acoustic similarity and auditory short-term memory: Experiments and a model. In D. A. Norman (Ed.), *Models of human memory*. New York: Academic Press, 1970.

Tulving, E., & Gold, C. Stimulus information and contextual information as determinants of tachistoscopic recognition of words. *Journal of Experimental Psychology*, 1963, *66*, 319-327.

Warren, R. M., Obusek, C. J., Farmer, R. M., & Warren, R. P. Auditory sequence: Confusion of patterns other than speech or music. *Science*, 1969, *164*, 586-687.

Wheeler, D. D. Processes in word recognition. *Cognitive Psychology*, 1970, *1*, 59-85.

Wickelgren, W. A. Short-term recognition memory for single letters and phonemic similarity of retroactive interference. *Quarterly Journal of Experimental Psychology*, 1966, *18*, 55-62.

Wood, C. C. Auditory and phonetic levels of processing in speech perception: Neurophysiological and information-processing analyses. *Journal of Experimental Psychology*, 1975, *104*, 3-20.

Woods, W. A. Theory formation and control in a speech understanding system with extrapolations toward vision. In A. R. Hanson & E. M. Riseman (Eds.), *Computer vision systems*. New York: Academic Press, 1978.

Woodworth, R. S. *Experimental psychology*. New York: Henry Holt, 1938.

13 Instruction in Reading Acquisition

Harry Singer
University of California, Riverside

Reading development consists of two overlapping phases: (1) reading acquisition or learning to read and (2) learning or gaining information from text (Singer, 1980). Instructional emphasis on the first phase decreases as students approach mastery. Concomitantly, instructional time for teaching students to learn from text increases and continues to do so as students progress through grades 1–12 (Fig. 13.1). Most commercial programs for teaching reading contain this instructional shift. In other words, elementary teachers, particularly those in the primary grades, stress reading acquisition; junior high, high school, and college teachers essentially teach their students to learn from texts in all content areas.

These two phases of reading development have a differential relationship with general intelligence. All children in the normal range of intelligence can learn to read. This continuum extends from a high intelligence level down to an IQ level of about 55 to 75 where pathology begins. The reason that all children in the normal range of intelligence can learn to read is that the objectives for this phase of reading instruction are finite. For example, students have to learn a given number of responses to print (sight words, symbol-sound correspondences, syllables, digraphs, vowels, etc.), how to blend these responses together, how to use their already fairly well-developed language abilities and knowledge of the world to anticipate identification of words, and how to select appropriate word meanings according to the syntax and semantics of a sentence or longer unit of text. If students are given adequate instruction and time to learn these responses to print and integrate them with their language abilities and knowledge of the world, they can eventually master or reach a criterion level for the acquisition phase of reading development (Bloom, 1971; Carroll, 1963). This mastery level can be attained as early as grades three to four by some children and as late as

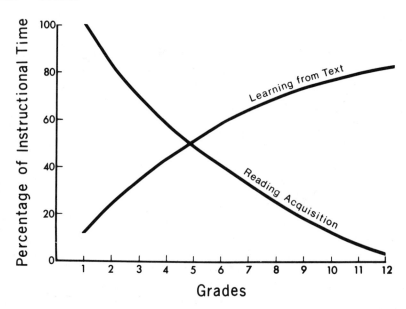

FIG. 13.1. Hypothetical curves depicting a shift in instructional time from reading acquisition to learning from text.

grades seven to nine by most students. However, about 5% of the student population is still in this stage of reading development at the high-school level.

As students learn to read, the correlation between reading-acquisition behavior and intelligence decreases, if the criterion for reading is kept constant. In other words, both students with high and low intelligence become alike in their reading-acquisition behavior, although they do so at different rates of progress and at different grade levels. Consequently, schools need to develop a reading-acquisition curriculum that is continuous, coherent, and cumulative—lasting for some students through grades one to nine and pacing students at an appropriate rate (Barr, 1973–74; Singer, 1977c) so that they can all have an equal opportunity to learn to read.

However, the second phase of reading development—the ability to gain information from text or to comprehend—consists of open-ended objectives such as knowledge of vocabulary; range, attitude, and depth of concepts; general information; and knowledge structures. These characteristics continue to grow and develop through individuals' lifetimes as a function of their experiences and cognitive development. In this phase of reading development, individuals become increasingly spread out in both their cognitive development and in their ability to learn from text. Consequently, the ability to learn from text shows an increasing relationship with IQ (Singer, 1977a). The implication for schools is to expect that the range of achievement in comprehension in the various content areas will increase as students progress through school. Hence, it is the responsibility of the school to provide the necessary instruction to cover this entire range in achievement (Singer & Donlan, 1980).

However, this chapter's primary focus is only on the first phase of reading development: teaching students how to read.

RATIONALE FOR TEACHING STUDENTS HOW TO READ

A multiplicity of methods have been devised for teaching reading (Singer, Chapter 1, this volume; Smith, 1965). These methods can be arrayed on a continuum, which is anchored at one extreme by emphasis on decoding and at the other extreme by stress on meaning (Chall, 1967). Decoding methods start by teaching symbol-sound correspondence, then blending, and finally the comprehension of words, sentences, and larger units of text. The rationale for this sequence is that it is *easier* to learn one component at a time (e.g., word recognition) and later learn the meaning of new words and ideas than it is to learn the two components simultaneously (Reed, 1965).

In contrast, meaning-emphasis methods such as the experience chart (Smith, 1965) or the language-experience approach (Van Allen & Van Allen, 1976) start out with a large unit of text (e.g., a self-constructed story) and later proceed to word-recognition tasks.[1] The rationale for this way of initiating reading instruction is that it is *easier* to start with a story because students can then use their knowledge, language abilities, and experiences as cues for anticipating and identifying words in sentence and story context (Goodman, 1970). Later, students can progress to the more difficult, more abstract aspects of printed language such as letters, digraphs, and syllables.

The proponents for decoding and those for meaning emphasis both claim that they are sequencing instruction from easy to difficult. However, the aspects of reading instruction that they sequence are different. Decoding methods give priority to teaching students responses to print, such as learning to give sounds to letters as in /c-a-t/, and then transferring these responses to identification of novel words (Samuels, 1976; Singer, Samuels, & Spiroff, 1973–74). For example, in a laboratory study to demonstrate the transfer effect of learning symbol-sound correspondences students were taught to identify novel two-letter word combinations, and were then tested for having learned the symbol-sound correspondences in these words by the ability to recognize a new word (Samuels, 1976). In contrast, meaning methods stress use of cognitive and linguistic processes as cues for expecting or guessing new words in the process of reading, such as anticipating what will be the last word in this sentence: *John hit the ball with a* _____ (Goodman, 1970, 1976). Which method of reading instruction makes

---

[1]See Chapter 1 for a historical perspective on methods of teaching reading.

reading acquisition easier to attain is not at all clear. At least there is no direct evidence to support either method's claim.

However, evidence is available to refute the claim that either method produces superior comprehension. In fact, Bond and Dykstra (1967) demonstrated that not one of the six methods that were compared, which span the entire continuum of methods for teaching reading, resulted in any statistically significant difference in comprehension at the end of grade one. These methods were:

1. A traditional basal reader method, which starts with whole word or sight word recognition and gradually introduces other word-identification techniques including phonics, structural analysis, and context clues, and has a controlled vocabulary (high-frequency words are introduced gradually and used cumulatively in the story and subsequent stories).[2]

2. An initial teaching alphabet (ita), which has a 44-character alphabet and purports to have one symbol for each sound in the language, but ita does not restrict teachers to a method of instruction, only to the use of ita as a medium of instruction (Downing, 1964; Mazurkiewicz, 1965).

3. A linguistic emphasis, which uses a sequence of word patterns that allows children to discover symbol-sound correspondences through juxtaposition of minimal contrastive pairs of words such as *pen* and *pin,* which differ in only one sound (phoneme) (Bloomfield & Barnhart, 1961; Fries, 1963).

4. A purely synthetic phonics program, which starts with one symbol-sound such as *a,* then teaches another, *n,* and combines the two to make a whole word *an,* and gradually builds up words to sentences and on to stories (McCracken and Walcutt, 1963).

5. A language-experience approach (Lee & Van Allen, 1963), in which students dictate their stories to the teacher who writes the stories (about their experiences) down, then teaches students to read their own stories, and subsequently teaches students to write and read their own stories as well as stories written by their peers.

6. A combination of a basal reader supplemented with phonics.

But methods that emphasized decoding, such as a traditional phonics program taught through a synthetic method, did have a slight edge in word-recognition achievement. In this method, for example, teachers first teach /a/, then /n/, and next have students sound out the responses to the combination of /a--n/. This finding supports the educational generalization that children, particularly those in the primary grades, tend to learn what is taught at the rate at which it is taught (Barr, 1973-74).

Actually, in either method of instruction, students eventually learn: (1) responses to printed words such as symbol-sound correspondences (i.e., sounding

---

[2]See the list of some widely used basal readers following the reference list for this chapter.

out words /c-a-t/) or first dividing a word such as *shepherd* into its two meaning-ful parts, *shep-herd,* and then sounding out each; (2) sentence constraints (use of semantics and syntactics plus world knowledge) for anticipating printed words in the text such as expecting what the final word will be in the sentence: *The car raced down the* _____; and (3) an integration of (1) and (2). This integration means that students can use both responses to words and sentences together. For example, in the sentence *The car raced down the* _____, students can anticipate the final word, say *hill,* and confirm this expectancy by sounding out /h-i-l-l/. Even as early as the end of grade one, students are learning to integrate both symbol-sound responses to print and the use of syntactic and semantic cues for anticipating words. As children continue over grades one–three to gain experi-ence in reading connected discourse such as stories, they achieve a high degree of integration in their reading skills. This integration means that if they know one word-recognition skill, such as phonics, they tend to know another one, such as use of context cues, equally well (Guthrie, 1973). Thus, the evidence indicates that methods for teaching beginning reading differ mainly in their initial se-quence of instruction, but afterwards they converge (Heilman, 1977). The impli-cation of this is clear: Use a method of instruction that teaches students how to identify printed words, and at the same time use their language ability while reading.

The language ability of most children at age 6 is already well developed. They have attained sophisticated control over their syntax, they possess a vocabulary of about 5000 words, and they have a phonological system that can adequately communicate their needs (Ruddell, 1976; Singer, 1973). If this assumption is not true, then the teacher can adapt materials of instruction to the child's level of language ability or improve the child's language ability to fit the materials. In other words, if children are to comprehend the message intended by the printed materials, they must possess a certain level of skill with the language they are going to learn to read and have some familiarity with the culture of that language (Carroll, 1976). In short, children should be taught to read in their own lan-guage.[3] For example, if a student knows only Spanish, reading instruction should start in Spanish, and the child should be taught to communicate in English simultaneously. Then the program should gradually phase out reading instruction in Spanish and phase in English.

Of course, individuals have a unique speech system called an ideolect. This ideolect enables them to recognize a person instantly from the initial sounds spoken over a telephone. Also, each person speaks a particular dialect, which is a variation in speech that is correlated with social class or regions of the country. However, some children may have a dialect that is significantly different from the teacher's dialect. If so, then when teaching dialectally different students,

---

[3]See McNeil, Donant, and Alkin (1980) for a discussion of teaching reading in a multicultural context (black-dialect speakers and Spanish-speaking children).

teachers should present meanings of new words in context, use a contextually based method for teaching word identification,[4] and accept dialectally different responses that result in appropriate meaning when evaluating reading performance (Lucas & Singer, 1976; Singer, 1973).

Another way in which reading programs differ is in their scope and sequence of instructional objectives. An instructional program that has a narrow scope may initially result in superior achievement compared to a program with a broader scope and a more extended sequence of instruction. But in the long run, the more comprehensive program has greater reading achievement. For example, Ruddell (1968) found that students learning to read through Sullivan's programmed instruction achieved higher comprehension scores at the end of grade one than students who were enrolled in a basal-reader program. Programmed reading is a method of teaching that emphasizes self-paced instruction, small increments of carefully sequenced instructional steps with gradual clue withdrawal, reinforcement of successive approximations to shape learner behavior, learner responses at each step, and immediate knowledge of results.[5] In teaching reading, programmed instruction uses mostly sentences in isolation and contrastive analysis (e.g., "I write with a *pen*" vs. "I push in a *pin*"). In contrast, basal readers usually start with a whole-word emphasis (picture-word association) and a story line. Later in the year and in subsequent grades, they include instruction in phonics, syllabication, inflected and compound words, and affixes.

Although Sullivan's programmed reading was superior to the basal-reader method of instruction at the end of grade one, Ruddell observed that the relationship between the type of program and degree of achievement was reversed at the end of grade three. Why? The explanation takes into account the interaction between the emphasis in the instructional program and the requirements of the criterion test for assessing the program. The Sullivan program emphasizes development of word-recognition skills in grade one, which pays off in the short run because the first-grade achievement test puts a premium on word-recognition ability. Students who can identify the words on the test are likely to score well. The basal-reader program also teaches word recognition plus other skills, such as word meaning, but spreads their instruction out over three grades. At the end of grade one, basal-reader students have not yet developed their word-recognition skills as well as Sullivan's students, but when the basal-reader students finally acquire and integrate their word-recognition and word-meaning skills, they can achieve a higher degree of comprehension on the third-grade achievement test because by then they have developed more of the word-recognition and word-meaning skills required by the third-grade test.

---

[4]The Houghton-Mifflin reading series (One Beacon St., Boston, Mass. 02107) emphasizes context in all of its instruction.

[5]For example, see *Programed reading,* Sullivan Associates, Webster Division, McGraw-Hill, St. Louis, Mo.

Hence, reading-instruction programs should be evaluated over the entire reading-acquisition span instead of only at the end of grade one. Furthermore, reading programs should be evaluated and adopted on the breadth of their scope and on the help they give students in achieving reading comprehension over a period of time.

Although formal initiation of reading instruction in American society does not begin for many children until the first grade, some parents start to teach their children a few aspects of reading by age 2 or 3. Also, because of the ubiquitousness of printed materials in American society, all children are at least exposed to printed words and tend to learn a few words and some letters of the alphabet before entering school. In fact, upon entrance to first grade, children on the average already know half the letters of the alphabet (Murphy & Durrell, 1964). Furthermore, under systematic instruction such as (Moore, 1963; see also Gotkin & McSweeney, 1967; Rowan, 1961) provided for his 3-year-old daughter—which consisted of an electric typewriter, a Skinnerian instructional procedure, and patient perseverance—even more progress in reading could be accomplished at the preschool level. As it is, 1% of our school population already knows how to read and comprehend materials equivalent to the second-grade level of difficulty upon entering school (Durkin, 1961, 1966).

However, our society does not deem it necessary to begin to teach 3 year olds how to read in formal programs. Nevertheless, in outlining a procedure for teaching reading, we advocate starting reading instruction with 3-year-old students, but we recommend the use of a more informal method than Moore used. We also combine in our outline two major methods of teaching reading: the natural-language method (experience chart) as a lead-in to a skill-based approach (basal reader) supplemented with recreational and enrichment (individualized or library) reading. An overview of this instructional sequence appears in Fig. 13.2.

We do not claim that this instructional sequence will produce results that are superior to other curricula because we know that children can and do learn to read equally well through many instructional procedures (Bond & Dykstra, 1967). What we do claim is that the particular procedure that we propose satisfies many instructional assumptions summarized in the following section.

SEQUENCE FOR TEACHING
READING ACQUISITION

Our instructional sequence is based upon the assumptions that: (1) the teaching of reading should capitalize on a student's language background; (2) instruction should progress from what a student knows to what a student needs to know, taught in small increments in order to maximize cumulative success in learning to read; (3) meaning should be emphasized throughout instruction; (4) systematic development of subskills is necessary and should be done in a consistent, coher-

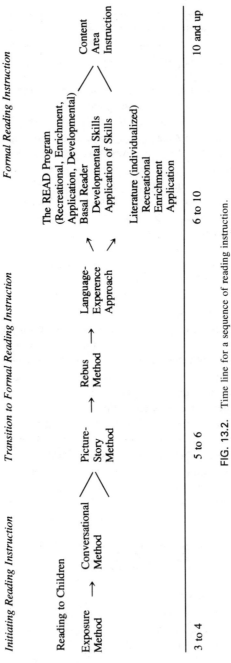

FIG. 13.2.   Time line for a sequence of reading instruction.

298

ent, and cumulative manner; (5) students should learn a variety of ways of identifying printed words, including use of context, and these ways should be practiced in connected discourse; (6) instruction should be paced in such a way that students develop toward independence in reading, greater self-confidence, and a growing feeling of mastery over printed materials; (7) students should have opportunities to engage in recreational, enrichment, and application types of reading in addition to developmental, skill-based reading instruction; (8) students and teachers, as well as parents, should get information on students' development towards mastery in learning to read and how students compare with each other on ability to learn from text; (9) emphasis in instruction should first be on reading-acquisition behavior and continue until students have mastered or reached a criterion level of performance in this phase of reading instruction, then emphasis should shift to strategies for teaching students who differ widely in intellectual capacities how to learn from text. Learning-from-text strategies are so designed that students can make progress in this phase of reading without stigmatizing any student (Singer & Donlan, 1980). However, this instructional outline focuses primarily on the acquisition phase of reading instruction.

Initiating Reading Instruction

Although formal instruction can be initiated at the preschool level, most children start their reading instruction in an informal way. One informal way is the exposure method.

Exposure Method.   The exposure method consists of reading stories to children at the preschool, nursery-school, or kindergarten level by teachers or at home by parents (Durkin, 1962). Sitting next to the reader, children can begin to learn that print communicates meaning, is read in left-to-right order, consists of words, sentences, and larger units, and that stories have a structure. Perhaps at this stage of development children only learn that a story has a beginning, middle, and end. They might also experience that a story elicits not only thoughts but also affective reactions (Guthrie, 1978).[6]

Conversational Method.   The conversational method is a little more advanced version of the exposure method (Hildreth, 1960). At the child's initiation, the teacher or parent converses with the child about any aspect of the print, story,

---

[6]Comprehension of a story is facilitated by acquiring knowledge of the grammar and the meaning of stories. Initially, the child may only acquire the broad story components, but later they acquire a more differentiated structure: that a story consists of a time, place, characters, plot, problem, and resolution (Rumelhart, 1977; Thorndyke, 1975) or that a story has a problem, goal, and one or more attempts to solve the problem and reach the goal (Adams & Collins, 1977). Although first graders already appear to have knowledge of story grammar (Mandler & Johnson, 1977), we know they definitely have achieved such knowledge prior to the sixth grade (Dreher & Singer, 1980).

or book. At this time the child may also pick up some language of instruction: that letters make up words, words (groups of printed letters with white space on each side) make up sentences (a group of words that start with a capital letter and end with a period, question mark, or exclamation point), and that sentences accumulate to tell a story (Downing, 1970). After hearing the same story read many times, some children can complete sentences by filling in the final word or phrase whenever the reader pauses toward the ends of sentences. This demonstrates not only memory at work but, perhaps, contextual identification of words.

Transition to Formal Reading Instruction

Picture-Story Method. Closer to formal instruction in reading is the picture-story method: A child draws a picture and then tells the teacher a story about the picture, frequently only a single sentence long, which the teacher prints under the story. Thus, the child begins to learn that printed stimuli are another way of communicating ideas that he or she had expressed in oral language. Although the child accumulates these picture-stories, he or she is not expected to read them at this stage of reading development. This method, useful in kindergarten classes, is a precursor to the rebus and the language-experience method.

Rebus Method. In the rebus method, the teacher reads the printed words in the sentence while the students read the pictured word (Woodcock, 1966, 1968). The method can use as few as 10–11 words, consisting of content words (I, you, me, children's names), functional words for relating the contentives to each other (to, for), two-noun determiners (a, the), action-type verbs (go, see), and a stative verb (is). With this small group of words and pictured nouns on cards, the teacher can construct an infinite number of sentences. For example, the teacher places three of the cards in sequence and reads the words on them: *I see a* _____, and then the teacher places a picture of a ball at the end of the sentence. The students then say *ball*. Eventually students may identify the small corpus of context words that have been used in this method, perhaps recognizing the words at this stage of development as though they were ideographs. The teacher can then turn over each card with a picture on it to reveal the corresponding printed words for the pictured object, which the student can learn as a sight word, and then use all their acquired words plus pictures to generate and read their own sentences (Singer & Beasley, 1970; Singer & Donlan, 1980). Thus, the teacher can build up a repertoire of sight words that can be used in the experience-chart method or the language-experience approach.

The Experience-Chart Method or the Language-Experience Approach. The experience-chart method, first devised in the 1920s (Gates, Batchelder, & Betzner, 1926; Smith, 1965; Whipple, 1920) was expanded in the 1960s to a complete reading program known as the language-experience approach or method. In this method, children have a common experience and subsequently relate it to the teacher. The teacher writes the children's story on the board, sometimes editing it, and the children then read the story. The teacher will first have the children read their own sentences, then other sentences, and finally the whole story. The teacher will then use the story in a variety of ways, such as having children pick out identical words and sounds and thus teaching them some sight words and some symbol-sound correspondences. Eventually students will be able to dictate and even write their own stories. The language-experience approach can continue into the primary grades, merging with creative writing and with instruction in grammar and spelling (Lee & Van Allen, 1963). After this method, the teacher can shift to more formal reading instruction.

Formal Reading Instruction

Basal-Reader Instruction.[7]   After students have acquired some sight words, the teacher can shift to a basal reader, to individualized instruction, or to both. The advantage of the basal reader is that the teacher can use it to provide systematic instruction in the subskills underlying reading comprehension, furnish practice for these skills in a meaningful context, and economize on teacher time.

The construction of a comprehensive scope and sequence of subskills for developing reading from grades one to six is beyond the time limitations that confront teachers daily. The subskills usually found in a basal reader (such as Ginn, Macmillan, Houghton-Mifflin, and Harper & Row) include development of symbol-sound correspondences (graphophonics), division of a word into its meaning components and then use of symbol-sound correspondences as in identification of the word shep-herd (graphomorphophonemics), instruction in syntactic relationships, and acquisition of a growing repertoire of sight words. With practice, these skills will eventually become automatic, enabling students to concentrate on attainment of comprehension (LaBerge & Samuels, 1976). If teachers did not have basal readers and had to locate materials for developing these skills or for providing practice of skills in connected discourse on their own, this search would be an uneconomical use of teacher time. Hence, it is not surprising to find that teachers are using basal readers as much now as they did prior to the explosion of methods and materials in the 1960s.

A basal reader may teach word identification through a generic process that can be used for teaching any aspect of print-to-sound correspondence such as identification of initial and final consonants, digraphs, vowels, phonograms, morpheme identifications, and word-meaning analysis (Heilman, 1977; Singer,

---

[7]Some leading basal readers, which more or less use the method described here, are listed following the reference section.

1977d). The generic process consists of grouping familiar words that have a common grapheme component, then teaching students to abstract and generalize both the grapheme component and the sound relationship to the grapheme, testing for adequacy of the print-to-sound correspondence by having students volunteer words that contain novel examples of these relationships, and finally letting students practice this word-identification process while reading connected discourse (see Chapter 1, this volume). The same procedure can be used for identifying morphemes, which are minimal units of meaning such as prefixes, suffixes, and roots.

The transfer of word-identification and word-meaning processes to the reading of connected discourse will tend to integrate these processes with the use of contextual cues (McCullough, 1945, 1972). A more direct way of teaching contextual cues is through a deletion process in which the word or word part is omitted, as in the cloze technique where every fifth or tenth word is omitted (Taylor, 1953). In this technique students have to rely upon the syntax and semantics of the sentence in order to infer the missing word or word part. Thus, the basal reader teaches students to be versatile in identifying printed words, including use of context and responses to cues in words, and to learn to mobilize their responses to printed words in various ways according to the demands of the task and their purposes in reading (Holmes & Singer, 1966; Singer, 1966, 1976b).

Students can progress through basal readers at their own pace, but presumably enough students will be in the same basal reader that they can be grouped together to get directed reading instruction and apply what they have read in group discussions or projects that include reference reading.

A method of instruction used in most basal readers is directed reading instruction. It also includes lessons in new vocabulary, development of background information assumed by the basal-reader story to be part of a student's knowledge of the world (Winograd, 1972), establishment of purposes and a perspective for reading the story (Pichert & Anderson, 1976), oral reading of the introductory part of the story, and teacher guidance through use of preposed questions. Finally, it has students silently read the remainder of the story and answer teacher-posed questions that are listed on the blackboard or provided by the teacher after the story has been read (Frase, 1967; Rothkopf, 1976).

Thus, instruction in the basal reader assumes that reading comprehension is an interactive process in which the text stimulates the reader to construct responses by drawing upon systems at the letter (literal), word (lexical), word order (syntactic), meaning (semantic), knowledge, inferential, interpretive, and evaluative levels. These systems in turn lead to expectations of each other and the text. The instructional implications from this view of reading are that the teacher should develop these systems within the reader and teach the reader to use them as an interactive process (Adams & Collins, 1977; Anderson, Spiro, & Montague, 1977; Rumelhart, 1976).

However, directed reading instruction should be modified. The teacher should initially model the kinds of questions to be asked about the type of literature being read, but the goal is to teach students to formulate their own questions and search for answers as they read. To achieve this goal, the teacher should gradually phase out teacher-posed questions and shift to student-formulated questions (Singer, 1979). For example, after the teacher has posed some questions and aroused curiosity about a particular story, the teacher can ask, "What would you like to know next about the story?" This teacher-posed question is likely to generate a student-formulated question in return. As students learn to ask their own questions, the number of teacher-posed questions can be reduced, and eventually the teacher is phased out, whereas the student is concomitantly phased in. Thus, the teacher can teach students to satisfy their own purposes in reading and acquire the process of active comprehension, a continuous process of asking and searching for answers to self-posed questions (Singer, 1979).

Knowledge of Progress. When students have mastered the initial phase of reading instruction, they can give up the basal reader. To determine whether students have learned to read, differentiated testing should be used in order to separate progress in learning to read from ability to learn from text. This separation can be achieved in the following way:

1. For assessing reading acquisition after each level of instruction (e.g., at the end of each semester in the primary grades) use the same test, such as a paragraph comprehension test standardized on a sample of children in grade one. Administer this test repeatedly at the end of each semester until children demonstrate mastery over learning to read, which can be defined as attainment of a score on the test that is equivalent to the 85th to 95th percentile.

2. For assessing ability to learn from text and for attaining a score that will provide information on how a student's performance compares with his or her peer group on a national level, use a standardized test that is norm-referenced for the student's grade level (Singer, 1974, 1977a, 1977b). The differentiated results from both types of testing are shown in Fig. 13.3.

When students have demonstrated mastery in learning to read,[8] they are ready to shift in instructional emphasis to ability to learn from text.

Students and their parents need knowledge of performance on standardized tests administered at the end of each grade. However, students need more fre-

---

[8]Learning is a relatively permanent change in performance. In assessing learning, the task must be kept constant over the successive teaching and testing trials. If so, then improvement in performance on the task can be attributed to learning. Of course, maturation has to be ruled out as a causal factor for improvement in performance to be attributable to learning. If the learning is complex and occurs over a relatively short time span, then maturation can probably be ruled out as a causal explanation.

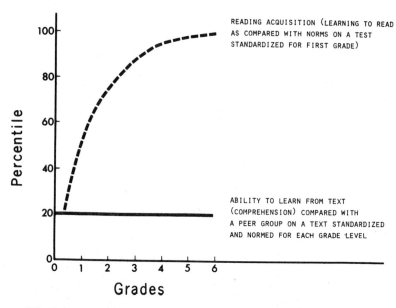

FIG. 13.3.   Hypothetical results for a particular student showing student's development in reading acquisition and ability with text. The Reading Acquisition or
learning to read curve was constructed by administering the same test standardized
and normed at the first-grade level to the same student at the end of grades one,
two, three, and four. The curve for ability to learn from text was based on *different*
test each standardized and normed for successive grade levels.

quent knowledge of progress to motivate their learning. For this purpose, we
recommend "cumulative progress charts" (Singer & Beasley, 1970). An example of a cumulative progress chart for sight-word recognition is shown in Fig.
13.4. This chart shows that a student learned 10 words in the first session, no
additional words in the second session, another 10 words in the third session, and
5 more words in the fifth session. Inasmuch as words learned are added cumulatively, the graphed line either goes up or remains at the same level; it cannot go
down.

Students can glean how rapid their cumulative progress is from visual inspection of the chart, and they can infer from the chart a cause-and-effect relationship
between their effort and their achievement. Similar charts can also be constructed
for other objectives in the instructional program, such as cumulative acquisition
of symbol-sound correspondences, knowledge of prefixes, suffixes, and roots, or
number of pages read either from a basal reader or from a book selected during
individualized reading instruction.

Individualized Reading Instruction.   A program in individualized reading
instruction is based upon an adequate classroom library of children's literature

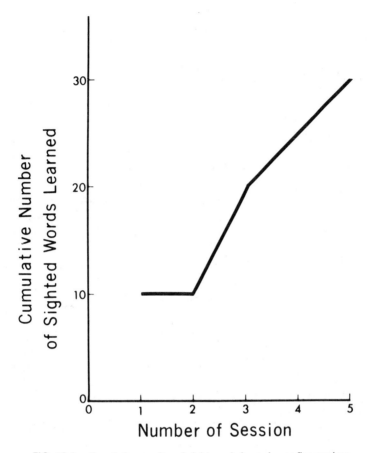

FIG. 13.4.   Cumulative number of sight words learned over five sessions.

and upon individual conference periods between teacher and students for coun-
seling students on their self-selection of books and ways of learning to read from
them (Veatch, 1954). Students can also use the classroom library for their own
recreational reading.

A disadvantage of individualized reading instruction is that when a 240-
minute teaching day is divided among 30 students, teachers can only devote 8
minutes per day to each child for instruction! Hence, teachers cannot give any
student much individual attention. To economize on their time and to maximize
instructional impact, teachers need to group students for instruction. Inasmuch as
students are not homogeneous in reading achievement nor in the subskills underlying this achievement (Balow, 1962), teachers have to group students for instruction that students specifically need on the basis of test results and observation of students' performance during instruction.

Another disadvantage of the individualized reading program is that teachers are likely to be less than systematic in developing students' subskills for attaining reading achievement. However, the weakness of individualized reading instruction for developing subskills for reading achievement is the strength of the basal-reader program. Fortunately, experienced teachers can adopt both programs, perhaps using the basal reader 3 or 4 days a week and individualized instruction the other 1 or 2.

Of course, it is also possible to teach reading for two periods each day. Then the basal reader and individualized reading instruction can be given daily. For example, an elementary school in Las Vegas, Nevada teaches a basal program in the morning and individualized reference reading in the afternoon. In this school, all the students read at grade level or above as measured by a standardized achievement test. Of course, although the lowest achiever in each grade was reading at grade level or above,, there was still a range of individual differences in reading achievement at each grade level, but it extended from the grade upwards (Singer, 1977c).

INDIVIDUAL DIFFERENCES IN
READING ACHIEVEMENT

The range of individual differences in reading achievement increases from a 4-year range in grade one to a 12-year span in grade twelve (Goodlad, 1966). Hence, teachers who are committed to the principle of providing equality of educational opportunity for all students can adopt single and multiple text strategies that will enable them to teach all students academic content without stigmatizing any student (Singer & Donlan, 1980). These strategies, combined with teachers' knowledge of their content areas, will enable students to go beyond the acquisition phase of reading development and on to the next phase, learning from text.

LEARNING FROM TEXT PHASE OF
READING INSTRUCTION

In teaching students to learn from text, teachers can use single and multiple text strategies. Single text strategies consist of: (1) the directed reading activity with active comprehension, described earlier in the discussion of the basal reader; (2) marginal glosses that contain explanatory notes; (3) reading and learning from text guides, which emphasize instruction in acquisition and levels of comprehension (informational, interpretive, generalized, evaluative, and applied levels); (4) the SQ3R study method (survey, question, read, recite, and review).

Multiple text strategies include: (1) the concept technique, which consists of texts on various levels of difficulty but all related to the same concept; (2)

inquiry, which requires that students use a library to answer a particular question arising from evaluation of texts in their content areas; (3) the project method, in which students pursue answers to their own questions about a particular content-area unit.[9]

SUMMARY

Reading development consists of two overlapping phases of instructional emphases: reading acquisition and learning from text. For emphasis on reading acquisition, teachers can adopt a comprehensive reading and writing program. The program can begin with a sequence for initiating reading instruction that includes the exposure and conversational method for 3 to 4 year olds, the picture story and rebus method for 5 year olds, and experience charts (now called the language-experience approach) for 6 year olds. The teacher then has a choice of shifting to a basal reader for systematic development of subskills underlying reading comprehension, to an individualized reading program that emphasizes the interests of children, or to both these methods while allocating instruction in creative writing (a continuation of the language-experience approach) to a separate period in which spelling, grammar and composition are taught. This combination of methods means that the teacher can have a comprehensive program for teaching students how to read. The program includes development of recreational and enrichment types of reading (individualized reading program), application of reading ability (through discussion of basal-reader stories or by means of reference reading to answer particular questions raised in discussions of literature or other content areas), and development of basic skills in a systematic way (basal-reader instruction). Differentiated testing can be used to determine when students have attained mastery of reading acquisition and are ready to shift to the second phase of reading development, instructional emphasis in learning from text.

Single and multiple text strategies are available for teaching students who vary greatly in ability to learn from text. Through these strategies, teachers can provide equality of educational opportunity by teaching all students how to learn from texts in all content areas without stigmatizing any of them. Thus, through a comprehensive instructional program for recreational, enrichment, applied, and developmental reading (under the acronym READ) and single and multiple text strategies, students can progress through both phases of instruction for reading and learning from text.

---

[9]For a more detailed explanation of these strategies for teaching students to read and learn from texts in the content areas, see the text by Singer and Donlan (1980). Some other textbooks for teaching students to learn from texts in the content areas are by Burmeister (1974), Hafner (1977), Herber (1978), and Shepherd (1978).

ACKNOWLEDGMENTS

This paper was originally prepared under a contract with the National Institute of Education for a "Basic Skills Synthesis Project" directed by Dr. Spencer Ward. It is reproduced here with permission.

REFERENCES

Adams, M. J., & Collins, A. *A schema-theoretic view of reading* (Tech. Rep. No. 32). Urbana: University of Illnois, Center for the Study of Reading, April 1977.

Anderson, A. R., & Moore, O. K. Autotelic folk-models. *Sociological Quarterly*, 1960, *1*, 204–216.

Anderson, R., Spiro, R., & Montague, W. *Schooling and the acquisition of knowledge*. Hillsdale, N.J.: Lawrence Erlbaum Associates, 1977.

Balow, I. H. Does homogeneous grouping give homogeneous groups? *Elementary School Journal*, 1962, *63*, 28–32.

Barr, R. C. Instructional pace differences and their effect on reading acquisition. *Reading Research Quarterly*, 1973–74, *9*, 526–554.

Bloom, B. S. Mastery learning and its implications for curriculum development. In E. W. Eisner (Ed.), *Confronting curriculum reform*. Boston: Little, Brown, 1971.

Bloomfield, L., & Barnhart, C. L. *Let's read, a linguistic approach*. Detroit: Wayne State University Press, 1961.

Bond, G. L., & Dykstra, R. The cooperative research program in first grade reading instruction. *Reading Research Quarterly*, 1967, *2*, 5–142.

Burmeister, L. E. *Reading strategies for secondary school teachers*. Reading, Mass.: Addison-Wesley, 1974.

Carroll, J. B. A model of school learning. *Teachers College Record*, 1963, *64*, 723–733.

Carroll, J. B. The nature of the reading process. In H. Singer & R. Ruddell (Eds.), *Theoretical models and processes of reading* (2nd ed.). Newark, Del.: International Reading Association, 1976.

Chall, J. *Learning to read: The great debate*. New York: McGraw-Hill, 1967.

Downing, J. The i/t/a reading experiment. *The Reading Teacher*, 1964, *18*, 105–110.

Downing, J. Children's concepts of language in learning to read. *Educational Research*, 1970, *12*, 106–112.

Dreher, M. J., & Singer, H. Story grammar instruction unnecessary for intermediate grade students. *The Reading Teacher*, 1980, *34*, 261–268.

Durkin, D. Children who read before grade one. *The Reading Teacher*, 1961, *14*, 163–166.

Durkin, D. Reading instruction and the five year old child. In J. A. Figurel (Ed.), *Challenge and experiment in education*. New York: Scholastic Magazines, 1962.

Durkin, D. *Children who read early*. New York: Teachers College Press, 1966.

Frase, L. Learning from prose material: Length of passage, knowledge of results, and position of questions. *Journal of Educational Psychology*, 1967, *58*, 266–272.

Fries, C. C. *Linguistics and reading*. New York: Holt, Rinehart & Winston, 1963.

Gates, A. I., Batchelder, M. I., & Betzner, J. A. Modern systematic versus an opportunistic method of teaching. *Teachers College Record*, 1926, *27*, 679–700.

Goodlad, J. I. *School, curriculum, and the individual*. Waltham, Mass.: Blaisdell, 1966.

Goodman, K. Reading: A psycholinguistic guessing game. In H. Singer & R. Ruddell (Eds.), *Theoretical models and processes of reading*. Newark, Del.: International Reading Association, 1970.

Goodman, K. A psycholinguistic view of reading comprehension. In H. Singer & R. Ruddell (Eds.), *Theoretical models and processes of reading* (2nd ed.). Newark, Del.: International Reading Association, 1976.

Gotkin, L. G., & McSweeney, J. F. Learning from teaching machine. In P. C. Lange (Ed.), *Programmed Instruction*. The Sixty-sixth Yearbook of the National Society for the Study of Education, Part II. Chicago, Ill.: University of Chicago Press, 1967.

Guthrie, J. Models of reading and reading disability. *Journal of Educational Psychology,* 1973, *65,* 9–18.

Guthrie, J. Research views: Fables. *The Reading Teacher,* 1978, *31,* 110–112.

Hafner, L. *Developmental reading in middle and secondary schools: Foundations, strategies, and skills for teaching.* New York: Macmillan, 1977.

Heilman, A. *Principles and practices of teaching reading* (4th ed.). Columbus, Oh.: Merrill, 1977.

Herber, H. *Teaching reading in content areas* (2nd ed.). Englewood Cliffs, N.J.: Prentice-Hall, 1978.

Hildreth, G. *Teaching reading.* New York: Holt, Rinehart & Winston, 1960.

Holmes, J. A., & Singer, H. *Speed and power of reading in high school* (Cooperative Research Monograph No. 14, Superintendent of Documents Catalog No. FS5.230:30016). Washington, D.C.: U.S. Government Printing Office, 1966.

LaBerge, D., & Samuels, S. J. Toward a theory of automatic information processing in reading. In H. Singer & R. Ruddell (Eds.), *Theoretical models and processes of reading* (2nd ed.). Newark, Del.: International Reading Association, 1976.

Lee, D. M., & Van Allen, R. V. *Learning to read through experience* (2nd ed.). New York: Appleton-Century-Crofts, 1963.

Lucas, M., & Singer, H. Dialect in relation to reading achievement: Recoding, encoding, or merely a code? In H. Singer & R. Ruddell (Eds.), *Theoretical models and processes of reading* (2nd ed.). Newark, Del.: International Reading Association, 1976.

Mandler, J. M., & Johnson, N. S. Remembrance of things parsed: Story structure and recall. *Cognitive Psychology,* 1977, *9,* 111–151.

Mazurkiewicz, A. J. First grade reading using modified co-basal versus the Initial Teaching Alphabet. U.S. Office of Education, Cooperative research project no. 1676, 1965.

McCracken, G., & Walcutt, C. C. *Basic reading.* New York: J. B. Lippincott, 1963.

McCullough, C. The recognition of context clues in reading. *Elementary English Review,* 1945, *22,* 1–5.

McCullough, C, What should the reading teacher know about language and thinking? In R. E. Hodges & E. H. Rudorf (Eds.), *Language and learning to read.* New York: Houghton Mifflin, 1972.

McNeil, J.D., Donant, L., & Alkin, M. C. *How to teach reading successfully.* Boston: Little, Brown, 1980.

Moore, O. K. Autotelic response environments and exceptional children. Hamden, Connecticut: Responsive Environment Foundation, 1963 (mimeographed).

Murphy, H., & Durrell, D. D. *Diagnostic reading readiness test.* New York: Harcourt, Brace, & World, 1964.

Pichert, J. W., & Anderson, R. C. *Taking different perspectives on a story* (Tech. Rep. No. 14). Urbana: University of Illinois, Center for the Study of Reading, 1976.

Reed, D. A theory of language, speech, and writing. *Elementary English,* 1965, *42,* 845–851.

Rothkopt, E. Z. Writing to teach and reading to learn. In N. L. Gage (Ed.), *The psychology of teaching methods* (Part 1). Chicago: University of Chicago Press, 1976.

Rowan, H. 'Tis time he should begin to read. *Carnegie Corporation of New York Quarterly,* 1961, *9,* 1–3.

Ruddell, R. B. *A longitudinal study of four programs of reading instruction varying in emphasis on regularity of grapheme-phoneme correspondence and language structure on reading achievement in grades two and three.* Berkeley: University of California, 1968. (Multilith)

Ruddell, R. B. Language acquisition and the reading process. In H. Singer & R. Ruddell (Eds.), *Theoretical models and processes of reading* (2nd ed.). Newark, Del.: International Reading Association, 1976.

Rumelhart, D. *Toward an interactive model of reading.* San Diego: University of California, Center for Human Information Processing, 1976.

Rumelhart, D. Understanding and summarizing brief stories. In D. LaBerge & S. J. Samuels (Eds.), *Basic processes in reading: Perception and comprehension.* Hillsdale, N.J.: Lawrence Erlbaum Associates, 1977.

Samuels, S. J. Modes of word recognition. In H. Singer & R. Ruddell (Eds.), *Theoretical models and processes of reading* (2nd ed.). Newark, Del.: International Reading Association, 1976.

Shepherd, D. L. *Comprehensive high school methods,* (2nd ed.). Columbus, Oh.: Merrill, 1978.

Singer, H. Conceptualization in learning to read. In G. B. Schick and M. M. May (Eds.), *New Frontiers in College-Adult Reading.* Fifteenth Yearbook of the National Reading Conference. Marquette, Wisconsin: The National Reading Conference, 1966.

Singer, H. Language, linguistics, and learning to read. In M. Kling (Ed.), *Language development for the classroom and remedial reading.* New Brunswick, N.J.: Rutgers University Press, 1973.

Singer, H. Measurement of early reading ability: Norm-referenced standardized tests for differential assessment of progress in learning how to read and in using reading for gaining information. In P. Nacke (Ed.), *Interaction: Research and practice for college-adult reading.* Twenty-third Yearbook of the National Reading Conference, Clemson, South Carolina: The National Reading Conference, 1974 (abstract).

Singer, H. Substrata-factor patterns accompanying development in power of reading, elementary through college levels. In H. Singer & R. Ruddell (Eds.), *Theoretical models and processes of reading,* (2nd ed.). Newark, Del.: International Reading Association, 1976. (a)

Singer, H. The substrata-factor theory of reading: Theoretical designs for teaching reading. In H. Singer & R. Ruddell (Eds.), *Theoretical models and processes of reading* (2nd ed.). Newark, Del.: International Reading Association, 1976. (b)

Singer, H. IQ is and is not related to reading. In S. Wanat (Ed.), *Issues in evaluating reading.* Arlington, Va.: Center for Applied Linguistics, 1977. (a)

Singer, H. Measurement of early reading ability. *Contemporary Education,* 1977, *48,* 145–150. (b)

Singer, H. Resolving curricular conflicts in the 1970s: Modifying the hypothesis, It's the teacher who makes the difference in reading achievement. *Language Arts,* 1977, *54,* 158–163. (c)

Singer, H. Teaching word recognition. In M. Dawson (Ed.), *Teaching word recognition skills.* Newark, Del.: International Reading Association, 1977. (d)

Singer, H. Active comprehension: From answering to asking questions. In C. McCullough (Ed.), *Inchworm, inchworm: Persistent questions in reading education.* Newark, Del.: International Reading Association, 1979.

Singer, H. *Learning to read.* Geelong, Australia: Deakin University Press, 1980.

Singer, H., & Beasley, S. Motivating a disabled reader. In M. P. Douglass (Ed.), *Claremont reading conference 34th yearbook.* Claremont, California: The Claremont Reading Conference, Claremont Graduate School, 1970.

Singer, H., & Donlan, D. *Reading and learning from text.* Little, Brown, 1980.

Singer, H., Samuels, J., & Spiroff, J. Effect of pictures and context on learning sight words. *Reading Research Quarterly,* 1973-74, *9,* 555–567.

Smith, N. B. *History of American reading instruction.* Newark, Del.: International Reading Association, 1965.

Stauffer, R. *The language experience approach to the teaching of reading.* New York: Harper & Row, 1970.

Taylor, W. L. Cloze procedure: A new tool for measuring readability. *Journalism Quarterly,* 1953, *30,* 415–433.

Thorndyke, P. *Cognitive structures in human story comprehension and memory.* Unpublished doctoral dissertation, Stanford University, 1975.

Van Allen, R., & Van Allen, C. Language experience in reading. Teacher's resource book, Levels I, II, III. Chicago: Encyclopedia Brittanica Education Corporation. Also, *Language Experience Activities in Communication.* New York: Houghton Mifflin, 1976.

Veatch, J. *Individualized reading for success in classrooms.* New York: Appleton-Century-Crofts, 1954.

Winograd, T. Understanding natural language. *Cognitive Psychology,* 1972, *3*(Whole issue).

Woodcock, R. W. A comparative study of six approaches to teaching reading to the mentally retarded. In J. A. Figurel (Ed.), *Vistas in reading.* Proceedings of the Eleventh Annual Convention of the International Reading Association, 1966, *1*, 481–485.

Woodcock, R. W. Rebus as a medium in beginning reading instruction. IMRID (Institute on Mental Retardation and Intellectual Development), George Peabody College, Papers and Reports, Vol. 5, 1968.

Zigler, E. Familial mental retardation: A continuing dilemma. *Science,* 1967, *155*, 292–298.

LIST OF SOME WIDELY USED BASAL READERS

Allyn and Bacon Reading Program 1978. 470 Atlantic Avenue, Boston, Mass. 02201

Ginn and Company Reading 720. 1976. Xerox. Education Group, 191 Spring Street, Lexington, Mass. 02173

Harper and Row. 10 East 53rd St., New York, N.Y. 10022

Holt, Rinehart, and Winston, Inc., The Holt Basic Reading System, 1977. 383 Madison Avenue, New York, N.Y. 10017

Houghton Mifflin Reading Series 1976. One Beacon St., Boston, Mass. 02107

The Macmillan Company, 866 Third Avenue, New York, N.Y. 10022

Scott, Foresman, and Company, 1900 Eastlake Avenue, Glenview, Ill. 60025

Author Index

Drewnowski, A., 176, 192, *193, 194*
Durkin, D., 10, 19, 21, *26,* 297, 299, *308*
Durrell, D. D., 297, *309*
Dustman, R. E., 39, *62*
Dyer, F. N., 251, *253*
Dykstra, R., 15, 23, *26,* 294, 297, *308*

E

Eichelman, W. H., 54, *62*
Eimas, P. D., 108, 110, *123,* 178, *194,* 275, 289
Elliott, L. L., 275, *287*
Entus, A., 177, *194*
Erdmann, B., 2, *7*
Erickson, C., 185, *194*
Erickson, D., 191, *194,* 247, *253*
Estes, W. K., 41, 42, *62,* 66, 73, *83,* 128, *136,* 146, *168,* 174, *194,* 197, 203, 208, *218*

F

Fang, S. P., 251, *253*
Farmer, R. M., 264, *289*
Fea, H., 10, 16, *28*
Fischer, F. N., 16, *27*
Fischer, F. W., 175, 176, 189, 192, *195, 196,* 199, 201, 203, 210, *219,* 246, *254*
Fischler, I., 110, 112, *122*
Fitts, P., 93, *101*
Flesch, R. P., 4, *7,* 21, *26*
Fodor, J., 178, *194*
Forgays, G. D., 247, *254*
Forster, K. I., 33, *61,* 88, *101,* 116, *122,* 140, 148, 149, *169,* 202, 217, *218, 221*
Foss, D. J., 112, *122*
Fowler, C., 16, *27,* 176, 187, 188, 189, 192, *194, 195, 196,* 199, 201, 203, 210, *219,* 246, *254*
Francis, W. N., 180, *194*
Franklin, J. D., 86, *101*
Franks, J. J., 29, *61,* 189, *195*
Frase, L., 302, *308*
Frederiksen, J. R., 115, *122,* 148, *169,* 197, *218*
Freeman, B., 264, *288*
Frick, F. C., 93, *101*
Friedman, E. A., 201, 202, *220*
Fries, C. C., 22, *26,* 294, *308*
Furth, H. G., 284, *287*

G

Garfield, L., 107, *123, 170*
Garner, W. R., 93, *101,* 275, *287*
Garrett, M., 178, *194*
Garro, L., 238, *255*
Gates, A. I., 17, 21, *26,* 300, *308*
Gelb, I. J., 182, *194,* 231, *235*
Gerstman, L. J., 203, *218,* 267, *288*
Gibson, E. J., 12, *26,* 31, 44, *62,* 70, *83,* 91, 96, *101,* 103, 114, *122,* 142, *169,* 197, 203, 204, 212, 217, *219,* 238, 244, *253,* 271, *287*
Gibson, E. W., 284, *287*
Gibson, J., 172, 173, *194*
Giordani, B., 132, *136*
Glanzer, M., 137, *169*
Gleitman, L. R., 16, *26,* 146, *170,* 182, *194,* 199, 200, 203, 210, 211, 217, *220,* 238, 241, 243, 244, *253,* 261, 268, 284, *287*
Glushko, R. J., 202, *219*
Goffard, S. J., 273, *286*
Gold, C., 90, *102,* 103, 104, 105, 109, *124,* 275, *289*
Goldman, S. R., 114, 115, *123,* 128, *136*
Goldscheider, A., 5, *7*
Goodlad, J. I., 306, *308*
Goodman, G. O., 112, *122*
Goodman, K. S., 19, 22, 24, *27,* 85, 91, 96, *101,* 125, *136, 169,* 293, *308, 309*
Gotkin, L. G., 297, *309*
Gough, P. B., 22, *27,* 30, 31, *62,* 112, *122,* 284, *287*
Gray, W. S., 17, *27*
Green, D. W., 111, *123,* 185, *194*
Greenberg, J. H., 223, 224, *235*
Gregory, D. S., 273, *287*
Gregory, M., 204, *218*
Griece, H. P., 277, *287*
Groff, P., 201, *219*
Guetzkow, H., 86, *101*
Guinet, L., 217, *219*
Guthrie, J., *27,* 295, 299, *309*

H

Haber, R. N., 85, *101,* 137, *169*
Hafner, L., 307, *309*
Hall, R., 217, *221*
Halle, M., 30, *61,* 180, *193*
Hammond, M., 103, *122,* 142, *169,* 197, 212, *219,* 271, *287*

Subject Index